RED THREAD ACADEMY

SCHOOL OF AMERICAN FOLKLORIC WITCHCRAFT

Year 1: Foundations

Course Manual

THE RED THREAD ACADEMY

SCHOOL OF AMERICAN FOLKLORIC WITCHCRAFT

Year 1: Foundations

Course Manual

Laurelei Black

ASTERIA BOOKS

Red Thread Academy Year 1: Foundations Course Manual
By Laurelei Black
Cover Design by Laurelei Black

ISBN-13: 978-1-956765-08-3 (paperback)
ISBN-13: 978-1-956765-09-0 (hardback)
ISBN-13: 978-1-956765-10-6 (digital book)

Copyright 2018, 2021

Notice of Rights: In accordance with the U.S. Copyright Act of 1976, the scanning, uploading, and electronic sharing of any part of this book without the permission of the publisher is unlawful piracy and theft of the author intellectual property. If you would like to use material from this book (other than for review purposes), prior written permission must be obtained by contacting the publisher at laurelei@asteriabooks.com. Thank you for your support of the author's rights.

Notice of Liability: The author has made every effort to check and ensure the accuracy of the information presented in this book. However, the information herein is sold without warranty, either expressed or implied. Neither the author, publisher, nor any dealer or distributor of this book will be held liable for any damages caused either directly or indirectly by the instructions and information contained in this book.

Permissions: For information on getting permission for reprints and excerpts, contact: laurelei@asteriabooks.com

Disclaimer: Information in this book is NOT intended as medical advice, or for use as diagnosis or treatment of a health problem, or as a substitute for consulting a licensed medical or mental health professional. The contents and information in this book are for informational use only and are not intended to be a substitute for professional medical advice, diagnosis, or treatment. Always seek the advice of your physician or other qualified health provider for medical conditions. Never disregard professional medical advice or delay in seeking it because of something you read in this book or any spiritual resource.

Red! Red! Are the cords we wear.

Red! Red! Is the wine we drink!

Red! Red! Is the blood of Godd!

And Red is the shade of the Housle.

Laurelei Black & Natalie Long
from "The Housle Song" © 2013

For the Family of Coven Caer Sidhe

...

and all who come to the Spiral Castle

Table of Contents

The Study Guide

How to Use This Course Guide	1
Student Progress Checklist	11
Suggested Weekly Lesson Progression	15

Unit 1: Know Yourself.

Lesson 1: Dedication Ritual	17
Lesson 2: Your Story	20
Laurelei's Story	22
Lesson 3: Your Basic Astrology	25
Lesson 4: Personal Symbols	29

Unit 2: Understand the Cosmology of the Craft.

Lesson 1: Wheel of the Year	32
Lesson 2: Sacred Space	39
Lesson 3: Elements	48
Lesson 4: Red, Black, White	51

Unit 3: Honor the Wheel of the Year through ritual and personal practice.

Lesson 1: Samhain	58
Lesson 2: Yule	64
Lesson 3: Imbolc	70
Lesson 4: Spring Equinox	76

Lesson 5: Beltaine	81
Lesson 6: Midsummer	88
Lesson 7: Lammas/Lughnasadh	93
Lesson 8: Fall Equinox	98

Unit 4: Work with Lunar Magic in all phases of the Moon's cycle.

Lesson 1: Full Moon	110
Full Moon Record Keeping Sheet	114
Lesson 2: Waning Moon	115
Lesson 3: New Moon	117
Lesson 4: Waxing Moon	119

Unit 5: Understand Sorcery, Sacrifice, and Compact and use them to perform various types of spells.

Lesson 1: Sorcery v. Magic; Ethics and Sacrifice	121
Spell Record Sheet	133
Lesson 2: Amulets and Talismans	134
Lesson 3: Candle Magic	136
Lesson 4: Witches' Ladders	138

Unit 6: Collect, cleanse, consecrate, and use some basic tools.

Lesson 1: Anvil (Oath Stone)	144
Lesson 2: Stang	150
Lesson 3: Blades	164
Lesson 4: Cauldron	166

Unit 7: Use full knowledge of ritual construction to plan, write, perform, and debrief a ritual.

Lesson 1: Basic Planning of a Ritual	168
Ritual Planning Worksheet	176
Lesson 2: Ritual Components	180
Lesson 3: Ritual Performance	186
Lesson 4: Debrief and Analysis	187

Unit 8: Prove proficiency in four forms of divination (scrying and 3 of your choosing).

Lesson 1: Scrying Mirror	188
Lesson 2: Divination Method 1	190
Lesson 3: Divination Method 2	192
Lesson 4: Divination Method 3	193

Unit 9: Practice energy work principles.

Lesson 1: Aligning the Three Souls	194
Lesson 2: Raising & Directing Energy	199
Lesson 3: Shielding & Releasing Energy	207
Lesson 4: Healing & Connecting with Others	212

Unit 10: Practice responsible and meaningful spirit contact.

Lesson 1: Triple Soul, Evocation & Banishing	216
Lesson 2: Fetch	229
Lesson 3: Familiars	235
Lesson 4: Godd-Friend	250

Unit 11: Be knowledgeable in Craft lore and history.

Lesson 1: Trad Craft Reading List 1	255
Lesson 2: Trad Craft Reading List 2	256
Lesson 3: General Witchcraft Reading List	258
Lesson 4: Other Craft Traditions Reading List	260

Unit 12: Prepare for 1st Level Self-Initiation.

Lesson 1: Planning for the Future	261
Lesson 2: Final Exam	263
Lesson 3: Self-Initiation Ritual	265

Table of Contents, pt 2

The Book of Shadows (begins on p 275 - unnumbered)

Gods, Goddesses, and Mighty Ones

Faces of the God	Cailleach	Lucifer
Faces of the Goddess	Cernunnos and Herne	Lugh
Witch Mother	Cerridwen	Maiden
Witch Father	Cuchulainn	Mother
The Ancestors	Dagda	Crone
Aradia's Gifts	Diana	Morrigan
Arianrhod	Frau Holle	Pan
Azazel	Hecate	Hymn to Pan
Bel	Ishtar	Rhiannon
Blodeuwedd	Isis	Thoth
Bran	John Barleycorn	Tubal Cain
Brigitte	Lilith	

Liber Qayin

Black Book of Lilith-Sophia
Red Book of Azazel-Qayin
White Book of Ishtar-Eve

Ritual, Liturgy, and Spells

Orkney Charm for Becoming a Witch	Cleansing Chants
Dedication Ritual	Laying the Compass
Aligning the Three Souls	Opening the Gates
Witch's LBRP	Mill Songs
Participant Roles	The Housle
Ritual Preparation	

Sabbats

Samhain
RTA Samhain Ritual
Samhain Incense Recipe
Yule
RTA Yule Ritual
Yule Incense Recipe
Here We Come A-Wassailing
Wassail Recipe
Prosperity Pomander
Imbolc
RTA Imbolc Ritual
Kolyo novena label
Imbolc Incense Recipe

Spring Equinox
RTA Spring Equinox Ritual
Beltane
RTA Beltaine Ritual
RTA Walpurgisnacht Flight
Midsummer
RTA Midsummer Ritual
Lammas
RTA Lammas Ritual
Fall Equinox
RTA Fall Equinox Ritual

Animal and Tree Spirit Allies

Spirit Allies Quick Reference
January Spirit Allies
February Spirit Allies
March Spirit Allies
April Spirit Allies
May Spirit Allies
June Spirit Allies

July Spirit Allies
August Spirit Allies
September Spirit Allies
October Spirit Allies
Samhain Spirit Allies
November Spirit Allies
December Spirit Allies

Sun, Moon, and Star Lore

The Year Wheel
Lunar Magic
Moons of the Year
Planetary Influences

Planetary Correspondences
Moon Phases
Drawing Down the Moon

Cosmology & Magical Theory

Ethics
Laws of Magic
The Three Realms
The Airts
The Humours

Earth
Air
Fire
Water
Powers of the Sphinx

Triple Soul
Black Soul
Red Soul
White Soul

Energy & Using Power

Eight Ways of Making Magic
Grounding & Centering
Seething

Energy Centers of the Body
Lame Step
Widdershins & Sunwise

Practical Craft

Spellcraft
Spell Record-Keeping
Amulets & Talismans
Witches' Symbols
Florida Water Recipe
Flying Ointment

Khernips Recipe
Sabbat Wine Recipe
Balefire
Witches' Ladders
AFW Seasonal Ladders

Divination

Numerology
Palmistry
Pendulum Divination
Rune Divination

Witches' Runic Oracle
Scrying
How to Make Dark Mirror
Witches' Runic Oracle

Tools

Saining of Tools
On Altars
Witches' Stones
Oath Stone
Stang
Three Knives

Black Knife
White Knife
Red Knife
Care and Feeding of Steel
Cauldron
Seasoning a Cast Iron Cauldron

Spirit Conjuration

Banishing Spirits
Egregore Creation
Evoking Magical Beings
Fetch
Familiar

Sphere & Pyramid
Spirit Vessels
Witches and Goetia
Spirit Magic and Communication
Affinity with Spirits

1st Degree Self-Initiation

No-Kill Fast Grocery List
No-Kill Fast Recipes
SCT Initiation Recipes

RTA First Degree Self-Initiation
SCT Raising Vows
SCT Raising Oath

Red Thread Academy
Traditional Witchcraft
Year 1: Foundations Course

How to Use The Course Guide

This course is designed to be accessible to a beginning Witch with little or no former knowledge or experience of the Craft. With that being said, some passing understanding of a few concepts (like working with energy) would greatly benefit the student, as you'll be able to "hit the ground running" in your studies. The overall aim of the Academy is to help a self-motivated student move from Dedicant to Initiate over the span of 3 year-long courses. This Year 1: Foundations course will cover a great deal of skill, lore, and wisdom in a year-and-a-day and will take the student from Dedicant to First Admission.

This is a lofty goal, though, and nobody should feel bad for falling short -- whether it takes you several more weeks or even a couple of years. Witchcraft isn't a race or a competition. You need not focus on completing in exactly one year. All I ask is that you give yourself at least one year of dedicated study and practice before taking your First Initiation. A year and a day is considered a "complete cycle" (folklorically), and you will have given yourself the basic amount of time to assimilate the knowledge and make room in your psyche for the wisdom you are hoping to gain within this Craft.

Checklist

I've included a checklist that notates all of the lessons and their corresponding assignments. You can find it at the beginning of these materials, before the actual lessons start. I offer this to you as a tool for your personal tracking and accountability of your own work.

Order of the Lessons

There is a sheet (located just behind the checklist) that provides a rough schedule for students to use, if they are so inclined. This schedule is only a suggestion, and it is open to lots of wiggle room.

Indeed, you'll have to wiggle within the schedule a little bit, by virtue of the fact that I have no idea what month and day you are starting. I had to put the Sabbats and Moon Phase lessons somewhere on the schedule, but I have no way of knowing if you dedicated on a Sabbat or precisely between them (much less which Sabbat will be the first you encounter).

And that's okay! Just jump in when you're ready and get going and feel free to switch lessons around, if the timing isn't lining up for you. Just be aware that some lessons build on each other within a progression. It'll probably be obvious to you which ones those are, but I will also make a note at the beginning of each lesson if there is a prerequisite lesson or experience.

The only lessons that should be done exactly where they are indicated in the schedule are the first two (Dedication Ritual and Your Story) and the last three (Planning for the Future, Final Exam, and Initiation). I think the reasons are obvious (or will be once you get started).

Everything else is very negotiable. If you want to do all four book analyses in the same month, do it. Want to knock out your divination proficiencies all at once? Go for it! I spread them out to make it a little easier on you, but you are the ultimate arbiter of what makes sense in your life and your practice.

I'll even say that the order was hard for me to decide, and I shifted things throughout the entire writing of this course. There is so much to cover, and some topics are so interconnected that it's hard to talk about one if the student doesn't already know about the other. The problem is: I have no idea what you know. I'm allowing for the possibility that true beginners on the Path will join this course, in which case, I've tried to make this course accessible, but I know there is still a steep learning curve. At the same time, much more experienced folks may be taking this course as well, and I am also hoping to give them something meaty as a foundation with which to build their studies for this part of their journey (as opposed to a re-hash of what they have known and done for years).

With such diversity among the people taking the course, no single approach to the lessons will suit everyone, and that's okay.

Planning Ahead

Some assignments are not conquerable in a single week. These include the 4 book analyses you will write, the 3 forms of divination in which you will prove yourself proficient, and possibly others.

In order to best address these more involved assignments, I recommend taking some time here at the beginning of your studies to familiarize yourself with the work ahead and make your own plan for addressing these projects. For instance, you might choose both your first book and the first method of divination that you wish to learn so you can start your studies well before the assignments are due in the schedule.

The Nature of THE WORK

It's only fair of me to let you know that this is a very intensive experience, and almost all of it will come from you. I know a great deal about Witchcraft and the occult, and I will be sharing some of my knowledge and experience with you. BUT! Witchcraft isn't just about knowing things. It is also (if not mostly) about doing things. I can't do them for you. I can't do the thinking for you, and I definitely can't practice this sorcerous art for you.

I'm taking the role of the "Guide on the Side" instead of the "Sage on the Stage." The lessons aren't presented as lectures, for that reason. Yes, yes, I will definitely do some explaining and extrapolating in each lesson, but the real bulk of the work will be your own reflections, meditations, critical thinking, hands-on practice, and possibly even some outside research.

At some point, you may get frustrated with me. "Why did I pay the course fee if that's all she has to say about this?" "I could have done this on my own?" "She hasn't told me anything I didn't already know!"

Trust me, I had the same thoughts, at times, about my mentor and initiator. I've had beloved students and coven mates share these thoughts out loud with me. I've had others chew on them silently -- either poisoning themselves with bitterness OR coming to the same empowering conclusion that all Witches do. The power of the Witch comes from the individual, through their own work, sacrifice, and dedication. The one who guides you is not your true teacher. You yourself are. Your Spirits are. The guide is merely one who lights the candle so you can see the Crooked Path. The one who blows the candle out so you can hear the Spirits talking … finally.

This course will only reward you in a way that is proportionate to the effort you give it. It requires that you THINK. It demands that you DO. It relies on you to REFLECT.

What is "Traditional" about the Red Thread Academy's Craft?
Honestly, the Witchcraft presented here won't be "traditional" enough for some. It'll be too traditional for others. Here is a little about the background and philosophy of this particular thread of the Craft:

I am an American Folkloric Witch. I was taught by an American Witch (Mary S.). Her teachers were American Witches (the Finnins), a "Black Gard" Gardnerian priest in 1960s Berkeley, CA, and a pair of Welsh Druids. The Finnins are the founders of the Ancient Keltic Church/Roebuck and studied with Joe Wilson, the founder of 1734, who studied with Roy Bowers (aka Robert Cochrane). The Finnins also studied with Evan John Jones.

Mary never completed her formal studies within AKC/Roebuck. She was a 3* Gardnerian HPS, an 11* (?) Druid, and a Dedicant of AKC before founding the tradition I joined and studied. This new tradition was very heavily AKC/1734 inspired. "Kissing cousins" we always said. We read and worked from the 1734 letters, and when Ann Finnin published her book *Forge of Tubal Cain* several years later, I realized we were really a bastard child of that tradition (not cousins, at all), with a little Garderian tools and hold-overs in the mix -- and a heavy dollop of Druidry.

The tradition my ex-wife Natalie and I founded, the Spiral Castle Tradition (what we blogged about as "American Folkloric Witchcraft" -- though that term is now an umbrella for a much larger group of traditions than just us), is closer to what Cochrane and Jones describe, but I will admit that there are still some notable Gardnerian influences. They lingered from Mary, and they seeped in from Natalie, who had also been a 3* Gardnerian Wiccan from her former training.

And then you must consider: we're American. This continent was colonized by people seeking homogeneity of ideology as a refuge from religious persecution and then very quickly became one of the most ethnically, philosophically, and culturally diverse places in the world. There are very few of us here who can claim any pure heritage or any unbroken lineage to any culture or tradition. I certainly can't.

Which is all to say ... a certain amount of eclecticism is perhaps authentically Traditional in the USA. Speaking only for myself, the blend of northern European (English, Welsh, Cornish, Dutch, and German) Craft/shamanism that has come to me, mixed with bits of more contemporary Craft (yes, Wicca), alongside Hermetic systems of magic (OTO, Golden Dawn, Freemasonry, etc), and the practicality of Hoodoo/rootwork just makes sense. These are not disparate systems that have never interacted. They've already touched and influenced each other. Study any two of them, and you'll see the flow between them. And they've had this flow because our ancestors (were largely very practical folks who knew a good thing when they saw it and weren't afraid to try a little of a good new thing out to see if it worked with their existing system.

"But, Laurelei," you say, "I'm not from the US." OR... ""OK, Laurelei. I'm almost entirely (insert ethnic/cultural/national group here)." My response is: That's fantastic! I honor who you are and where you come from! Let's just take a second to think about "right fit." Do you need to work in a system that is more traditional or more culturally-specific than what is offered here? Or, are you okay with a little eclecticism in your Craft -- or in your teacher? Only you can answer those questions.

THIS course is built on a strong foundation of Traditional Witchcraft, as it was taught to me, but there are other influences. RTA *is* American Folkloric Witchcraft. It is *the* teaching mechanism of the Spiral Castle Tradition. It is rooted in European folklore and shamanism. It looks to all manner of American and European folk traditions for inspiration and wisdom. It is inclusive of First Nation and African diasporic influences on American Craft practice, but treads carefully so as not to be appropriative of hereditary or lineaged traditions into which we haven't been born or initiated. We acknowledge, though, that it does have more contemporary Craft and Hermetic influence than some hardcore traditionalists present/desire. Being aware of all of our roots helps us shape an individual Craft that will serve us as we walk the Crooked Path.

Ultimately, it is my responsibility as teacher to present what I know to be a valid and workable system. It is your responsibility as a student to decide if this system works for you. I encourage you to learn this system if it resonates with you, which provides opportunity for additional study, and adapt it to meet your sense of the Arte.

Sharing Assignments

There are a couple of philosophies on the assignments that I'd like you to consider. The first is that **the work is for your benefit, not mine**. There is some meaningful objective at the heart of every task, intended to help you discover some new truth about the Craft and your relationship to it. Even if what you discover is that you don't care for astrology, or you don't resonate with scrying, or you struggle with braiding witches' ladders, that's okay. I imagine you will discover lots of resonances, skills, and things you do care for. That's the point: to dig in. To DO. So, because the work is for your benefit and not mine, it is to your benefit to embrace it. Give it a shot. A real shot. (And remember: just because something is hard, that doesn't mean you aren't making potent magic as a result.)

The second philosophy has to do with whether or not you need me to see your work. Technically, no. There are self-initiations at the end of each course, and I have come to a place of peace regarding online students self-determining their readiness for self-initiation. (Indeed, many folks purchase this manual without ever reaching out for group connection, so many students progress without any contact from me at all.) However, if you want to be initiated within the Spiral Castle Tradition, as part of my lineage -- if that's a thing that matters to you, for all the reasons that spiritual lineage can matter -- then I need to see your work and we need to build a connection.

You can also choose to share some or all of your work and participate in the RTA online community (which is hosted on the Thread App — details at the end of this chapter) just because you find that supportive for your process and your needs. I encourage everyone who takes this course, in any form, to join the free app-based online.

You'll notice a lot of written reflections and "essays" throughout the course. (I used to be an English teacher, and it shows!) Think of these as opportunities to journal deeply on your experience or your perspective. This is a way to get the thoughts out of your head (where they may be fuzzy) and into a concrete form, where you can confront them, organize them, and decide whether or not they are really your thoughts.

Scoring of Assignments

The scoring of assignments only applies to Red Thread Academy students who are sharing assignments for me to see -- with that eye toward in-person initiation at the end of the Year 3: Mastery course. But I thought it would be helpful for everyone to know the scoring rubric, for visibility.

There are only 3 scores for all assignments in this course:

Mastery (3) = The work covers a depth or breadth beyond the requirement, shows great insight, is reflective of profound talent or skill, or is in some other way remarkable. This is the rarest of scores, reserved for work that wows me.

Proficiency (2) = The work meets the requirements, shows solid progression toward lesson objectives, is complete and has no major flaws. There may still be some areas of the work that could use some polishing or deeper thought, but it is understood that this will come in time. This is the most common passing score.

Developing (1) = The work does not meet the requirements, shows some confusion or misunderstanding, isn't complete, or needs to be reapproached. This is the only non-passing score. Use the feedback provided to try again.

You will ultimately achieve Mastery (3) or Proficiency (2) in every lesson. If you get a Developing (1) score on any assignment, you will need to finish/redo it until you have reached Proficiency (2).

There is no shame in getting a low score and working to improve your skills or understanding in that area. We all have our talents, and we all have our challenges. Witchcraft is a CRAFT, which means it must be practiced for us to be skillful.

I am willing and able to give my students the time and guidance they need to gain those skills. I won't just "pass" you on an assignment because it is more convenient for me or somehow "kinder" to you. It is, in fact, not kind at all for me to let you think you are proficient in an area where you aren't.

Likewise, don't think you are somehow failing if you never see a Mastery (3) score. Those are reserved for shockingly great work. This isn't like some high schools, where if you do the assignment correctly, completely, and punctually, you'll get an A+. This is sorcery. This is spirituality. Here, the gold stars are a lot harder to come by, but they mean so much more! (Actually, I've been a high school English teacher, and A's weren't that easy to come by in my classroom, either. I'm still a believer in actual merit.)

Another educational philosophy: The worth of your work isn't based on whether or not I am impressed by it. It is based on whether or not you are finding value and meaning it. If you are asking for me to score your work, that is also a conversation I hope to have as you continue.

Supplies and Materials

You only need a few items to start this coursework. The rest, you will make or acquire as the course progresses.

- Black or white hooded robe/cloak/shawl -- This should be a natural fiber (cotton, linen, wool, or silk). Choose black if you are performing the Dedication between Fall Equinox and Spring Equinox (dark half of the year) and white for the light half of the year (the other 6 months). If you're no good at sewing, you can use a black dress or kaftan and attach a hood of a similar fabric. You can also buy a robe from an online vendor. (Check out the recommendations in the shop at www.bladeandbroom.com if you need guidance.) Just make sure the fabric is natural and that the hood is deep. Everything else (length, style, sleeve design, neck shape) is optional. You will need this for your Dedication Ritual; though, you can perform this ritual in the nude if you do not have a robe. (You will eventually need the other color as well, but it can wait for now.)
- Red, triple-braided cord -- The finished length of this cord should be about 3 yards/meters (9 feet). It is constructed by making three braids out of yarn, and then braiding them together to make a single cord. Again, the yarn should be natural fiber. You can find cotton and wool varieties easily online or in local craft stores. Alternatively, you could make strips from a natu-

ral fiber cloth and braid these. You must have the red cord at the time of your Dedication ritual. This is a labor intensive process. Trust me. I've braided so many cords in my life. But let yourself sink into the meditation of it. Consider the wisdom of the weavers of Fate as you braid.
- Binder/Notebook/Journal -- How you choose to organize your coursework is entirely up to you, but I recommend getting a large 3-ring binder and some divider tabs to keep your work organized. For most Witches, this is the beginning of their Book of Shadows. A journal or sketch pad (which can act as a mixed media journal for those who enjoy multiple modes of expression) can also be invaluable. Alternatively, you can keep a digital BoS on your computer or the cloud. Just be sure to keep a back-up and to keep it safe.

There will be other materials, tools, and supplies that you will buy as you work through the course. Each lesson provides a list of needed or suggested materials. As you plan ahead, you might take note of what you will need in the future. There are books, divination tools, altar tools, and other projects that will require that you make or buy some supplies.

Additional Resources

There are Book of Shadows pages included within this Course Guide (only in the print and PDF version — not in the app). They are taken from the growing library of pages I make available in my Etsy shop. They are here for you to print and use within your own BoS, and they are intended as supplemental reading materials for your studies; but you may not reproduce them for others. (They are all available for sale in the shop, if you would like to recommend them to friends.)

I have plans to create several videos to act as supplemental resources. As those are posted, they will be available in The Thread app. Check there for updates.

The blog entries at http://afwcraft.blogspot.com were all created by me and my ex-wife, Natalie. We are the founders of American Folkloric Witchcraft and the first (to my knowledge) to use that term. All of the work there is foundational material for this course. It is an archive now.

New content for the Spiral Castle Tradition (which is now the oldest and one of several expressions of American Folkloric Witchcraft) is being posted at http://spiralcastletrad.wordpress.com — and also in The Thread (app).

Also, I produce a YouTube channel (Blade and Broom) that features many topics that are closely related to our studies. I encourage you to subscribe for additional witchy resources.

Private coaching with me is also a resource available to you. This would involve a monthly Skype (or other VOIP) session in which we talk about your studies, your challenges, your goals, etc. Psychic readings can be part of these sessions, if you like, to help shed light on situations/questions. This is a great way to deepen your studies and to connect with me as your mentor, but you can also utilize our coaching sessions to work on goals unrelated to your Witchcraft studies. Coaching is 100% optional, of course. You can find more details at the end of the Course Guide.

The Amazon links for books and other tools on this site are made available via affiliate links. I won't have my feelings hurt if you don't use the affiliate links, but using them helps me a little and doesn't hurt you, if you're buying the book/tool/product anyway. (I do like to be up-front about it, though.)

Final Exam, Initiation, and Certificate

The final exam and self-initiation for 1st Degree are both included as part of the course materials. I've really struggled with how best to get this ritual into the hands of dedicated students at the right time while preserving some of the Mysteries around them. In the end, I believe the Old Ones have that squared away well enough on their own. (Sure, you can skip to the end and read the ritual, but knowledge is not the same as Understanding. And understanding is not the same as Wisdom.) Engage sincerely with the Work and the Rite, and it will have the impact it is meant to have. I trust that.

For 1st and (if you pursue it) 2nd Degree, we will only be able to offer Self-Initiation, for logistical reasons.

Be aware that as you approach the end of Year 3: Mastery, you can schedule a weekend-long initiation experience with me for the culmination of the entire program -- but only if I've had the opportunity to see your work and get to know you during (most of) Years 1-3. This is a different ritual than the one provided as self-initiation. It would be undertaken in a cabin in either Southern Indiana or Central Kentucky with a small but trusted team. Information about this option will be available on the Spiral Castle Blog (starting in 2021).

At the end of the course, if you're interested in receiving a certificate to commemorate your achievement, please write to me at the address below. I'll ask a small task of you (sending me a couple of specific assignments) if you haven't been my private student throughout your studies, but I would love to honor your hard work!

What Comes Next?

You are under no obligation to move onto the next course, but you will be invited to do so, if you choose.

Foundations -- akin to a Bachelor's Degree in Witchcraft. You have studied hard, sharpened your critical thinking skills, practiced and perfected the Craft basics, and you are fully qualified to practice your Craft. You have entered the Gates. You are an initiated Witch!

Practicum -- akin to a Master's Degree in a specific area of Witchcraft. You have dedicated yourself to a particular skill set and have honed your understanding and ability within that area. You have continued to deepen your practice of the Craft, and and are proficient enough to serve in the ways you have been called. You have been to the Castles. You are a Healer (or Seer, or Warden, Artisan, Conjurer, Bard, or a Votary)!

Mastery -- akin to a Doctorate Degree in Witchcraft. You have learned just about everything you can learn from another person, and you are devoted to learning directly from the Deities and Spirits after this point. You are open to the Mysteries of the Craft and have spent some time pondering those things that can't be spoken. You are ordained to initiate others into the Craft. You travel all the Realms. You are a Queen/Devil!

How far you go with your studies is entirely in your own hands. There is no "must" in this choice. There will be no pressure from me. I will fully support you in your choice, whatever you decide.

Student Discounts at Blade & Broom

Blade & Broom is a two-pronged online shop run by Laurelei. The Etsy shop houses all of our digital and physical products (like Book of Shadows pages, course guides, witchy novels, etc.). The independent shop at www.bladeandbroom.com features readings, coaching, and other ritual services. It also offers product and book recommendations through affiliate links.

As a student of mine, you can use the code RTASTUDENT25 for 25% products and services in both shops.

Blade & Broom on Etsy -- www.bladeandbroom.etsy.com -- physical & digital products

Blade & Broom website -- www.bladeandbroom.com -- psychic & spiritual services

The Thread App

You can access the app by scanning the following QR code, or by going to thethread1.goodbarber.app. Android users can choose to download from the Play Store. If you're using an iPhone or connecting from a PC, get the web app. BOTH have the same great features — videos, audios (meditations), blog content, all the lessons, pics, shared work from other students, comments, and chat.

NOTE: Once you've created a user account, contact me (through Chat or Contact in the app) so I can unlock the Year 1 sections for you! This doesn't happen automatically, since some users will be from other courses.

Questions

If you have questions related to the course-work (or the resources/discounts mentioned above) that

Year 1: Foundations
Student Progress Checklist

	Before beginning, the student should have a black or white hood/veil/cloak and a red cord (triple-braided, natural fiber).				
Unit	Objective	Lesson	Assignments/Projects	Completion Date	Score
1	Know yourself.				
		Your story	Autobiography		
		Dedication ritual	Reflection		
		Your Basic Astrology	Natal chart -- copy and reflection		
		Personal Symbols	Witch's Glove with reflection		
2	Understand the Cosmology of the Craft.				
		Wheel of the Year	Diagram		
		Sacred Space	Pictures of altars with descriptions		
		Elements	Table of Correspondences		
		Red, Black, White	Reflection		
3	Honor the Wheel of the Year through ritual and personal practice.				
		Samhain	Written debrief		
		Yule	Written debrief		
		Imbolc	Written debrief		
		Spring Equinox	Written debrief		
		Beltaine	Written debrief		
		Midsummer	Written debrief		
		Lammas	Written debrief		
		Fall Equinox	Written debrief		
4	Work with Lunar Magic in all phases of the Moon's cycle.				
		Full Moon	Full Moon spell		
			Record of Full Moon rituals throughout course		
		Waning Moon	Waning Moon spell		
		New Moon	New Moon spell		
		Waxing Moon	Waxing Moon spell		

Year 1: Foundations
Student Progress Checklist, cont.

5	Understand Sorcery, Sacrifice, and Compact and use them to perform various types of spells.				
		Sorcery v. Magic, Ethics and Sacrifice	Statement of Ethics		
		Amulets & Talismans	Make/empower amulet and talis-		
		Candle Magick	One lunar candle spell with picture		
		Witch Ladder	Seasonal protection cords (3)		
			Spell ladder		
6	Collect, cleanse, consecrate, and use some basic tools.				
		Anvil (Oath Stone)	Essay with picture		
		Stang	Essay with picture		
		Blades	Essay with picture		
		Cauldron	Essay with picture		
7	Use full knowledge of ritual construction to plan, write, perform, and debrief a ritual.				
		Basic Planning of Ritual	Ritual planning worksheet		
		Components -- liturgy, energy-raising, etc	Full copy of ritual text		
		Ritual performance	Pictures of space, altars, items, etc		
		Debrief and Analysis	Debrief essay		
8	Prove proficiency in four forms of divination (scrying and 3 of your choosing).				
		Scrying mirror	Make scrying mirror, pics, questions		
		Method 1	Short essay & full reading		
		Method 2	Short essay & full reading		
		Method 3	Short essay & full reading		
9	Practice energy work principles.				
		Aligning the Three Souls	Questions		
		Raising & Directing Energy	Energy Experiments, Seeting & Journal Entry		
		Shielding & Releasing	Questions		
		Healing & Connecting with Others	Journal Entry		

Year 1: Foundations
Student Progress Checklist, cont.

10	Practice responsible and meaningful spirit contact.				
		Triple Soul, Evocation & Banishing	Exercises		
		Fetch	Create Fetich (pic and description), Exercises		
		Familiars	Questions & pics (housing, offerings)		
		Godd-Friend	Essay & pics of altar/statue		
11	Be knowledgeable in Craft lore and history.				
		Trad Craft reading list 1	Book analysis of Trad Craft book		
		Trad Craft reading list 2	Book analysis of Trad Craft book		
		General Witchcraft reading list	Book analysis of general Craft book		
		Other Witchcraft traditions	Book analysis of other Craft tradi-		
12	Prepare for 1st Level Self-Initiation.				
		Planning for the future	Answer planning questions		
		Final Exam	Complete final exam		
		Self-Initiation Ritual	Essay following self-initiation		

Suggested Weekly Lesson Progression

Wk	Lesson Topic	Unit/Section	Lesson #
1	Dedication Ritual	Know Yourself	01-01
2	Your Story	Know Yourself	01-02
3	Aligning the Three Souls	Energy Work	09-01
4	Sabbat	Sabbats	03-0*
5	Wheel of the Year	Cosmology	02-01
6	Sacred Space	Cosmology	02-02
7	Red, Black, White	Cosmology	02-04
8	Raising & Directing Energy	Energy Work	09-02
9	Elements	Cosmology	02-03
10	Sabbat	Sabbats	03-0*
11	Shielding & Releasing Energy	Energy Work	09-03
12	Sorcery v. Magic, Ethics, Sacrifice	Magical Theory & Practice	05-01
13	Full Moon & monthly spellwork	Lunar Magic	04-01
14	Book analysis from Trad list A	History and Lore	11-01
15	New Moon	Lunar Magic	04-03
16	Sabbat	Sabbats	03-0*
17	Personal Symbols	Know Yourself	01-04
18	Waxing Moon	Lunar Magic	04-02
19	Amulets & Talismans	Magical Theory & Practice	05-02
20	Waning Moon	Lunar Magic	04-04
21	Witches' Ladders	Magical Theory & Practice	05-04
22	Sabbat	Sabbats	03-0*
23	Candle Magick	Magical Theory & Practice	05-03
24	Your Basic Astrology	Know Yourself	01-03
25	Book analysis from Trad list B	History and Lore	11-02
26	Healing Energy & Connecting with Others	Energy Work	09-04
27	Scrying Mirror	Divination	08-01
28	Oath Stone (Anvil)	Tools	06-01
29	Basics of Ritual Planning	Ritual	07-01
30	Sabbat	Sabbats	03-0*
31	Divination method 1	Divination	08-02
32	Stang	Tools	06-02
33	Ritual Components	Ritual	07-02
34	Divination method 2	Divination	08-03

35	Sabbat	Sabbats	03-0*
36	Blades	Tools	06-03
37	Book analysis from General list	History and Lore	11-03
38	Triple Soul, Evocation & Banishing	Spirit Work	10-01
39	Divination method 3	Divination	08-04
40	Cauldron	Tools	06-04
41	Sabbat	Sabbats	03-0*
42	The Fetch	Spirit Work	10-02
43	The Familiar	Spirit Work	10-03
44	Ritual Performance	Ritual	07-03
42	Ritual Debrief & Analysis	Ritual	07-04
46	Sabbat	Sabbats	03-0*
47	God-Friends	Spirit Work	10-04
48	Book analysis from Other list	History and Lore	11-04
49	Planning for the Future	Initiation Prep	12-1
50	Final Exam	Initiation Prep	12-2
51	1st Level Self-Initiation Ritual	Initiation Prep	12-3

Red Thread Academy
Traditional Witchcraft
Year 1: Foundations

Unit 1: Know Yourself
Lesson 1: Dedication Ritual

Dedication Ritual

Prerequisite Lesson None

Objective To dedicate yourself to the study and practice of Witchcraft

Materials Needed
- Black or white, hooded robe (natural fiber) -- or cloak/shawl/etc
- Triple-braided red cord
- Lancet (or sharp needle)
- Alcohol swab

Study Notes

The act of formally dedicating oneself to Witchcraft is both empowering and important. You are declaring before the Gods and your own Spirits that you will commit to a year and a day of study, to hold sacred the teachings of the Craft, and to act honorably within the Family. You are linking yourself, via a blood oath, to the Witchfather and Witchmother and to the larger Family of the Craft.

The "Red Thread" is the moniker we use to refer to the line of Witch Blood that connects the Witch to Tubal Qayin -- the Witchfather. A few of us come to this Tradition with ties to Qayin, such as bonds or possibly even Witch Marks that we reinforce through charms or the process of admission (dedication, initiation). Many create that link through specific ritual, such as the one provided here.

You can think of Dedication as Adoption into the Family of Witches, and it is at this time when the Red Thread is linked.

This ritual can happen at any time during the course of the year, as it is not linked to a specific Sabbat. Furthermore, it can happen at any age or stage of life, provided that the Adoptee has at least reached the Age of Puberty. (Most students in this course will be adults, but there is precedence for teaching the Craft to your own children, as well. My own children have been raised in the Craft. In fact, I was pregnant with my oldest child at the time of my own Dedication. She is now an adult herself and is preparing for Initiation. Just know that in-person initiation to the Spiral Castle Tradition, the parent-tradition of this Academy, is only available to students who've reached the Age of Majority -- 18 years old, in the USA.)

During the course of a coven-based Dedication ritual, the candidate is challenged and queried by the members of the coven before taking a blood oath on the Oath Stone (or Sword, or other Oath-Keeper). Within this Dedication ritual, it is understood that you will be challenging yourself, searching your own heart, and holding yourself accountable for your Oaths. (The Gods and Spirits will also hold you accountable.)

Ask yourself these three questions and consider your answers carefully:
1. Why do you choose to study and practice Witchcraft?
2. What do you most fear about walking the Crooked Path of the Witch?

Are you willing and able to hold yourself accountable for your own progress and promises?

The Red Cord, worn at the waist in all rituals, is a reminder of the Red Thread itself, the umbilical cord, and the fire of Qayin's forge.

The robe or hood is both a symbolic garment and a practical one. Robes and cloaks have been linked in the popular mind to magic and the Craft for a number of reasons. One is that they are symbolic for the body of the magician. Another is that they are a practical bit of camouflage for hiding oneself in the dark of the night. In a more mystical sense, a hood or headdress that covers the eyes is a very effective assistive piece of garb for help to achieve trance states, as it helps to block out extraneous sensory information.

Whether your robe/hood is black or white at this time will depend solely on the time of year. If your Dedication takes place in the light half of the year (from Spring Equinox to Fall Equinox), then choose white. If the opposite is true, choose black. Ultimately, you will want both by year's end.

Don't let the "thou shalts" and "thou shalt nots" get in the way of performing this dedication ritual. Don't wait until you can afford to buy or make the perfect robe or cloak. If you feel moved to perform the ritual, get the best black scarf or shawl you can now. You can always upgrade later.

The ritual below is very simple. You can elaborate on it, if you like. Just know that this simple but meaningful declaration is all that is needed to begin.

The Dedication Ritual

You will need solitude and quiet for this ritual. Come to it freshly bathed and wearing only your ritual robe, hood up (or simple, clean dark clothes, with your shawl/scarf).

Go to a place where the water meets the land (riverbank, lakeshore, beach) or a crossroads. If this isn't possible, find/make a clean and quiet place within your home and visualize standing in the center of a crossroads.

Say: "I come to this liminal place, ready to begin my study and practice of the Craft. My name is _____, and I am a Witch."

Clean your finger with the alcohol swab and draw a large drop of blood using the lancet. (This works best on the side of the fingertip, which is less calloused. Hold your hand below the level of your heart while you get the drop of blood to appear.)

Dab the blood onto your Red Cord.

Say: "I make this Oath. I vow to dedicate myself to the study and practice of Witchcraft for at least a year and day. I honor the Witch Blood that is my inheritance from the Witchfather. I vow to act with honor within the Family and to hold sacred the teachings of the Craft. I seek the starfire at topmost spire of the Spiral Castle, as well as the forge-fire at its bottommost roots. Before the Witchfather and Witchmother, I make this vow. Before my Spirits, I made this vow. Before my Holy Self, I make this vow. So mote it be!"

Spend some time in quiet meditation of the step you just took and the vows you have made. Contemplate your link to other Witches. Open yourself to messages from the Gods or Spirits.

When you are done, clap your hands three times and say, "The work is done."

Assignment

Write a brief reflection of the Dedication experience. Be sure to include the following:
- A copy of the Oath you took, if different from above
- Description of any challenges you experienced in preparing or performing the Dedication
- Insights or inspiration that came to you during or after the ritual
- Picture of robe and red cord

Additional Resources

"Tubal Cain: An Introduction" (blog post) http://afwcraft.blogspot.com/2012/04/tubal-cain-introduction.html

"Qayin Lore -- Melek Taus, Lucifer, Azazel, Shamash" (blog post) https://spiralcastletrad.wordpress.com/2012/05/20/qayin-lore-melek-taus-lucifer-azazel-shamash/

"The Line of Cain" (blog post) -- http://afwcraft.blogspot.com/2012/04/line-of-cain.html

Liber Qayin (book) a channeled work received by Laurelei and Natalie (Long) Black. The complete text is available in the BoS pages included at the back of the course materials, but there is a chapbook version available, as well. -- http://asteriabooks.com/books/liber-qayin.html

Robe, scarf, and cloak recommendations at Blade & Broom -- http://bladeandbroom.com/shop-sections/robes.html

Cotton and wool yarns at Blade & Broom -- http://bladeandbroom.com/shop-sections/poppets.html

---

BoS Pages Included

Witchfather

Witchmother

Tubal Qayin

Orkney Charm for Becoming a Witch

Liber Qayin

Red Thread Academy
Traditional Witchcraft
Year 1: Foundations

Unit 1: Know Yourself
Lesson 2: Your Story

Your Story

Prerequisite Lesson Unit 1, Lesson 1 "Dedication Ritual"

Objectives
- Tell your mundane and magical autobiography
- Gain clearer understanding of how your past influences your magical and spiritual present
- Introduce yourself to me so I have a deeper knowledge of you as a student

Materials Needed computer

Study Notes

"I am a part of all that I have met." Alfred, Lord Tennyson was onto something there. Our experiences (and the people in them) don't define us, per se, but they do help shape and color our perception, which in turn shapes and colors our choices.

You have chosen to be a Witch. Even if you were raised within the Craft, you are choosing it for yourself now. You've also chosen this course and, by extension, me as a teacher -- even if we never meet or interact personally. Those are significant choices in your spiritual and magical development. It bears asking why.

Socrates is credited with saying, "The unexamined life is not worth living." I couldn't agree more, which is why so much of the work we do as Witches relies so heavily on self-reflection. This assignment, which is entirely focused on your life, is an opportunity to look deeply into the mirror and gain a better understanding of who you are, why you have chosen Witchcraft, and what your hopes are surrounding that choice.

Assignment

You can tell your story in a couple of ways. You can either write a separate mundane autobiography as well as a magical autobiography, OR you can combine these into one autobiography. I don't care which you choose, as long as you share about yourself.

You can also choose the format that suits you best. This is your story, after all. A straightforward memoir-style essay is the standard way, but if you would rather create a YouTube video or a graphic novel or some other creative mode of expression, go for it. If you are sharing it to the group, please just make sure what you share is either a link to your work OR a .pdf or .doc file, so I can open it.

The finished product should include:

Mundane Elements --

- High points -- achievements, successes, talents
- Low points -- struggles, failures, challenges
- Family -- Who is in yours? How do you define this for yourself? Are you close?
- Hometown -- Did you grow up in one locale? Did your family move a lot? What was it like? Did you fit in?
- Education -- What was school like for you? Did you finish high school? Go to college?
- Work -- What sort of work do you do to earn a living? If you don't work at this time, what did you do in the past and how do you spend your time now? Are you fulfilled/content with this work/activities?
- Hobbies -- What do you do for fun or personal enrichment?

NOTE: Be cautious about what you share that may be personally identifying. I'm not trying to get anybody's accounts hacked or identities stolen from oversharing in a group where we thought we had trust -- so still use caution, please.

Magical Elements:
- Religious Education -- What religion (if any) were you raised in? What has your religious education looked like? What do you like about that faith/practice? What felt hollow or untrue about it?
- Initial Views of the Craft -- How were you introduced to the Craft? By whom? How did you react in those early exposures?
- Groups/Affiliations -- Have you studied, trained, or worked with a study group or coven? What were your experiences like, if so? Are you a member of any magical/religious organizations now? In what ways are you involved, if so?
- Experiences -- Have you had magical or deeply spiritual experiences? Have you had any negative experiences?
- Goals -- Why did you decide to enroll in this course? What do you hope to gain, achieve, and/or experience?
- Reservations -- Do you have any fears, concerns, or worries about this path, this course, or me as your teacher?

Be sure to provide plenty of explanation. The idea is to dig in, to really understand your motivations, hopes, and fears.

Additional Resources

Laurelei's autobiography is included in the next few pages.

BoS Pages Included

None

Laurelei Black's Autobiography

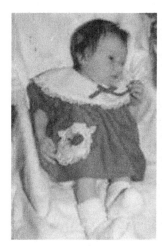  

I was born after the September Equinox 1975 a soldier and an office assistant. We were stationed at Ft. Hood in Killeen, Texas at the time of my birth.

My given name is Laura. I am named after my maternal grandmother, who was named after her paternal grandmother. Laurelei is the nickname I was given as a child in Germany, and I later took it as a stage name and then as a pen name. Black is also a family name, though not the one I was born with.

I am an only child, though I gained a stepsister when I was 20. She and I had known each other in high school, but we managed to avoid absolutely all of the challenges of step-sibling-hood since my mom and her dad married when we were both in college.

We moved a lot when I was little. Dad was stationed in Texas, then Oklahoma, Germany, Alabama, Kentucky, and Indianapolis, all by the time I turned seven. Mom and Dad divorced when I was 9, and Dad got out of the army the same year. We all stayed in Indy for about 7 years total, and then Mom and I moved to Oklahoma, which is where both of their families lived.

Dad remarried twice. Once was very brief (about 3 months). He married my stepmom Betty when I was 11. She was a school teacher, and he became a computer analyst for the Dept of Defense. They share a passion for music, art, travel, and food. They're retired in Florida now.

Mom remarried thrice. The first two were abusive jerks, but my stepdad Gary has been great. They got married in 1996, six months after I married my first husband.

As a young woman, I fell in love early and often. Had my first kiss with a boy when I was 4, and with a girl when I was 6. I met my first husband when I was 15, and I knew I would marry him and have a family. I was right. We got married in 1995, when I was 19, and we were both still in college. We separated when I was 33, though, and I've been married twice more -- to Natalie (co-founder of the Spiral Castle Tradition), and now to Joe (my partner in practically everything).

I identify as polyamorous and queer, both of which were challenges in my marriage with Scott. There were other problems in our relationship that were insurmountable. We didn't trust each other, with good reason, as we had both been unfaithful. We didn't know ourselves well enough to be honest with each other about a number of things. We wanted different things out of life. He was very conventional, and I'm a bit more avant garde. And we had very different attitudes about mental health.

We had two amazing children together -- Holly and Eric. As I revise this (Sept 2020), Holly is 20 and lives independently with her two beloveds, and Eric is 17 and making plans to study engineering after he graduates high school this year.

I met my initiating High Priestess and coven a few months before Holly was conceived. Mary Shelley and the Clan of the Laughing Dragon. I was pregnant with Holly when I dedicated and nursing her when I took my first degree. Both of the kids have grown up in the Craft. They've both had witchings as 1 year olds and other rites of passage all along the way.

I was also pregnant with Holly when I started teaching. I had gotten my BS in Secondary Education (English, theater/speech) from Indiana University. I taught for four years in Los Angeles, which is where we moved immediately following college. Both kids were born there. We moved back to Indiana when Eric was a baby. I taught for another few years, but I've been out of the classroom since 2007. I still teach, though. It's woven into the fabric of who I am.

I took 1*- 3* within the Clan of the Laughing Dragon, and I started a daughter coven to that tradition in Indiana -- Dragon's Eye Coven. CLD was based on traditional witchcraft (heavily influenced by the 1734 writings), Druidry, and a hint of Gardnerianism. That coven collapsed (with help from my HPS) when I left my first husband in 2008. The whole tradition foundered a year or two later. I'm still close with almost everyone, and I've even re-forged magical relationships with several. I learned a lot about authority and power within a coven structure, in addition to the many magical experiences I gained.

Natalie and Joe were already a couple when I met them in 2008. When I left the kids' dad, I moved in with them. Natalie and I founded the Spiral Castle Tradition in 2009 and started blogging about it in 2011 (www.afwcraft.blogspot.com). The three of us also helped found Camp Midian with some of our friends (www.campmidian.com). There are half a dozen Pagan/magical festivals that some combination of us helped found or run, including Babalon Rising, the Women's Goddess Retreat, Cunning Folk Faire, the Southern Indiana Druid and Heathen Event, and more. Joe and I still run Babalon Rising, and I still run the Women's Goddess Retreat.

I've been a speaker and ritual leader at those events and also at ConVocation, Starwood, Indy and Louisville Pagan Pride, as well as others.

I've published books about being a Priestess of Aphrodite, to whom I pledged myself in 2002 at my 2* CLD initiation. I've also published work about Witchcraft and demonology. I've published two novels, and I'm the producer of some very popular Book of Shadows pages on Etsy. Very recently, I launched a YouTube channel (Blade and Broom) and I've become a contributor for ev0ke online.

Natalie left us (and she and I divorced) in 2015, and had started her own daughter coven (Crossroads Coven in Indianapolis). I still lead and teach the founding coven, Coven Caer Sidhe.

Joe and I moved to Louisville, KY in 2016 and got married in 2017. In 2016, I started working with people with developmental and intellectual disabilities, helping them find and retain meaningful employment in the community. In 2019, I started my own agency doing that work, in collaboration with KY state agencies.

Other notable magical bits:
- I am currently a 3* Master Magician in the Ordo Templi Orientis (OTO).
- My first encounter with magic was as a child in Germany, when my mother's friend-turned-enemy told her I was possessed by a demon. I didn't know this until recently. She was an ATR practitioner of some sort, and my mother only knew that the woman buried chicken bones in our yard after a dispute with Mom. (Mom has been very anti-Craft-of-any-kind, as you can imagine.)
- I am a dedicated Priestess of Brighid, in addition to Aphrodite.
- I'm a Certified Master Herbalist, and I use these skills a lot in my magic.
- I'm a professional tarot reader and psychic medium.
- I was crowned at a Queening ritual in 2017 at the Women's Goddess Retreat with several women whom I adore.

Fun mundane bits about me:
- I was a "carnie" for a while in college.
- I used to be a professional belly dancer and instructor. I was the founder and creative director for a Pagan belly dance troupe. We danced entire rituals!
- I've studied German, French, Spanish, Japanese, and ancient Greek. I read German quite well, and I love speaking Greek in ritual.
- I study genealogy as a way to honor my ancestors. I know of English, Slavic, African, Dutch, German, French, Irish, Scottish, and Barbadian ancestors. A recent DNA test shows very heavy French, German, and Dutch roots.

Red Thread Academy
Traditional Witchcraft
Year 1: Foundations

Unit 1: Know Yourself
Lesson 3: Your Basic Astrology

Your Basic Astrology

Prerequisite Lesson

Objectives
- To begin the exploration of stellar influences on one's life and magic
- To gain a basic familiarity with the meaning of your Sun, Moon, and Rising signs
- computer

Materials Needed

Free online natal chart generator, such as https://alabe.com/freechart/default.asp

Study Notes

Celestial influences can play a significant role in both our magic and our daily lives. I do not believe that "all Pisces men do XYZ" or "all Libra women act like ABC." However, there are often commonalities within the group if we pay attention.

When most people ask what sign you are, they are only thinking of the Sun sign (the zodiacal constellation that provided the backdrop to the Sun on the day of your birth). Magicians and Witches are equally interested in your Moon and Ascendant (or Rising) signs, as these present a clearer picture. Those who study astrology in any depth will also be curious about your other planets and "houses," as well as any interesting formations that might be present (conjunctions, trines, squares, etc.)

We are only touching the tip of the mountain of information and understanding that can be gained from astrology. We can't cover all the complexities of the celestial dance that is the movement and alignment of the stars and planets. Not in this single lesson. Even a whole unit wouldn't be enough. It deserves its own year-long class, which would still only serve as an introduction.

This is enough for now.

Planets

There are two ways that the planets have an impact on your basic astrological chart. The first way has to do with the fact that every sign is "ruled" by a classical planet (Sun, Moon, Mercury, Venus, Mars, Jupiter, and Saturn). These planets are associated with traits that lend both strengths and weaknesses to each sign.

The other way that the planets influence your chart is in the fact that every planet is positioned "in a sign" at the moment of your birth. In other words, the zodiac signs provide a backdrop to the planets, depending on their placement at the moment and place of your birth. Only a person born at exactly the time and place can have the same natal chart as you. Your chart then, is like a stellar fingerprint. It is a unique blueprint of the celestial influences within your life.

Ruling Planets

Sun rules Leo
Moon rules Cancer
Mercury rules Gemini and Virgo
Venus rules Taurus and Libra
Mars rules Aries and Scorpio
Jupiter rules Sagittarius and Pisces
Saturn rules Capricorn and Aquarius

Planets in the Signs

The Sun changes signs every month and its sign reveals information about your basic personality. It is the "you" that you project, the way you hope to be seen.

The Moon changes signs every 2-3 days, and its sign speaks to your mood and emotions. This is the inner, emotional "you."

The sign on the horizon (Rising sign) changes every 2 hours. This sign represents the way others see you, the kind of impression you make on others. It also speaks to your spontaneous reactions.

Mercury changes signs every 3-4 weeks and has to do with communication and the mind. It speaks to the way you learn and how you express what you know and think.
Venus changes signs every 4-5 weeks, and it deals with love and attraction. It can reveal understandings about your romantic relationships.

Mars changes signs every 6-7 weeks, and it deals with drive and motivation.

Jupiter changes signs every 12-13 months, and it reflects luck, wisdom, and growth.

Saturn changes signs every 2-3 years, and it deals with discipline, fears, and challenges.

Uranus changes signs every 7 years, and it speaks to originality and change.

Neptune changes every 10-12 years, and has to do with dreams and healing.

Pluto changes signs every 12-14 years, and it speaks to power and transformation.

Houses

Natal charts are sky maps that are drawn on a circular chart. That chart can be divided up in a number of ways. One of the ways is to slice it into twelve sections, like the face of a clock. The first house is the section between 8 & 9 on a standard clock face, and the order moves counterclockwise from there. (So the 2nd house is between 7 & 8, and so on.)

The houses describe things of personal and interpersonal importance within each individual's life. We all have influences in each of these areas, and the configurations, planets present, and so on will reveal more information about how that area of human activity is shaped. Sadly, the free natal chart generators don't give much/any information about your houses. To learn more about what is happening in your houses, you will either want to take up the study of astrology in more depth or seek the help of a professional astrologer.

The houses are each ruled by a zodiac sign. The planets, as they are drawn on your chart, will be in various houses, lending extra significance or coloring to the way that house is impacted.

Since you may not have access to this information, I'll keep this very, very brief and let you do more research and study on your own, if you are interested.

1st House -- self, appearances, first impressions, new beginnings, your attitude. Ruled by Aries.

2nd House -- Money, values, work, daily routines, environment. Ruled by Taurus.

3rd House -- Communication, siblings, friends, neighbors, community. Rules by Gemini.

4th House -- Home, family roots, your emotional foundation. Ruled by Cancer.

5th House -- Romance, play, self-expression, creativity. Ruled by Leo.

6th House -- Health, fitness, acts of service, organization. Ruled by Virgo.

7th House -- Relationships, mutuality, sharing. Ruled by Libra.

8th House -- Intimacy, sex, bonding, shared money and property. Ruled by Scorpio

9th House -- Travel, study, higher learning, ethics, morals. Ruled by Sagittarius

10th House -- Career, goals, fame, success, achievements, public image. Ruled by Capricorn.

11th House -- Groups, friends, social causes, society. Ruled by Aquarius.

12th House -- Endings, closure, healing, spirituality. Ruled by Pisces.

Assignment

Use a free app to generate your basic natal chart. Read the report all the way through. Send me a copy of the chart and report along with a reflection that covers the following:

- How do you relate to the analysis in general?
- Do your Sun, Moon, and Ascendant (Rising) signs seem to fit you?
- What stereotypes have you heard about your Sun Sign, and do they seem to apply to you?

- How much of each element is manifested in your chart? Are you well-balanced between all four, or do you have one or two that are predominant?
- What did you find interesting or surprising about your chart?

Additional Resources

For more study about astrology, see ……

Free astrology course online -- http://www.alwaysastrology.com/learn-astrology.html

Great annotated collection of websites and books for further study -- http://unlockastrology.com/learn-astrology/recommended-books-websites/

For a glorious reading from a colleague and friend of mine, Rev. Bill Duvendack, visit http://www.418ascendant.com (He also publishes monthly horoscopes and Full Moon reports.)

Or check out his books:

Astrology in Theory and Practice (book) -- by Bill Duvendack -- https://amzn.to/2XZ6y7a

Teach Yourself Astrology (book) -- by Bill Duvendack -- https://www.lulu.com/en/us/shop/bill-duvendack-and-asenath-mason/teach-yourself-astrology/paperback/product-g928zw.html

For Fun …

"How to be a [sign]" by SailorJ -- This is a hilarious lampoon of classic make-up tutorials as demonstrated by over-the-top versions of each Sun sign. https://www.youtube.com/playlist?list=PL-ETMgN64X3MAOsxLjbYa6wDm320focRg

Lightbulb jokes -- http://www.aquarianage.org/lore/jokes/litebulb.html

BoS Pages Included

Planetary Hours

Red Thread Academy
Traditional Witchcraft
Year 1: Foundations

Unit 1: Know Yourself
Lesson 4: Personal Symbols

Personal Symbols

Prerequisite Lesson

Objectives

- To record the symbols that have been recurrent and meaningful in your life
- To understand these symbols in both universal and personal terms
- To create a Witch's Glove containing your most significant personal symbols

Materials Needed

Paper and pen
Art supplies will vary based on final product

Study Notes

Symbols are rich with meaning that is often revealed in layers and complexities that are hard to define. Symbols usually express a complex set of ideas that are cumbersome to express with words. Some symbols seem to have universal appeal or meaning, while the meanings of others are hotly debated. Many symbols also have specific and unique meanings to a certain group or individual. It is impossible to formulate any one dictionary of symbolic meanings that would be absolutely accurate, though you may find it useful to own a dictionary of symbols (or reference one online) as you help sort through the symbols that show up for you.

There may be symbols that you've carried your whole life, while others found you at turning points or significant moments. Some reveal themselves in dreams. Others might be manifesting in your daily life -- in the tv shows you watch, books you read, billboards you see on your way to work. Maybe they appear in jewelry, divination, graphics on clothing, etc. Perhaps they keep popping up through "odd coincidences."

You should begin taking notice of the symbols that are recurrent in your own life. What images, archetypes, animals, plants, colors, and shapes keep showing up?

It may take a considerable amount of time for you to identify the ones that speak most directly and deeply to you. At some point, you will need to do a series of specific meditations to narrow the field and make sure you've considered the ones you should.

Make a list of the symbols that really speak to you – that seem to indicate various aspects of your nature, your deep Self.

Keep a journal for this process, detailing the circumstance under which these symbols become apparent to you. Furthermore, be sure to keep a record of your interpretation of these symbols.

Don't forget to consider the "universal" interpretations of the symbols. You're probably aware of how your own culture has viewed many of these symbols (at least on a superficial level), and that has played a part in the layers of meaning that are conveyed to you when you interact with each of them. See if you can dig deeper, and find out how other cultures have viewed these symbols. Does it support what you know, deepen it? Or does it contradict or add paradox to the symbolic meaning? How do these cultural meanings intersect with the personal meaning YOU ascribe to the symbol?

The Witch's Glove

This obscure symbol among traditional Witches has not received a great deal of treatment or exposition. Robert Cochrane talks about it a little in his analysis of the various symbols on the menhir (an intricately carved standing stone in Brittany) in Justine Glass's book <u>Witchcraft the Sixth Sense</u> -- and again in his correspondence with Joe Wilson, who went on to found the 1734 tradition.

He doesn't give much information, though, and other Witches don't write much about this tool, either. It is one I have yet to write about in any depth, but every coven in which I have worked has explored it in a similar way, which I share with you here. (And I give you the promise of more exploration to come on this topic in the near future.)

The Glove is related to our work in the world -- our handlings. It is also a symbol of protection, directly tied to the pentagram or "star at your door." It becomes a type of Witches' heraldry to adorn a hand-shape with the symbols closest to our SELVES. A sign and a shield. An announcement and a protection.

Assignment

Once you have decided on the symbols you wish to incorporate, design a Glove that includes each of these symbols. Remember that the base materials and color of the Glove as well as the colors of the symbols will be significant. So, choose the overall design and placement with care.

The Glove doesn't have to be fabric/leather. Use any materials you like. In fact, you may want to consider what those materials represent. (A wooden plaque vs. a silk painted flag vs. a tooled- and dyed-leather crest, etc.)

Write a reflection that describes and analyzes your Glove design. This should include a complete and detailed description of all of the components of the design, including:
- The background colors/shapes (including any shape that you mounted your Glove upon, if you did -- pennant, shield, mandorla, rectangle, square, etc)
- The symbols chosen
- The colors chosen

Discuss both the universal/general understanding of these elements as well as your own thoughts/feelings about each.

Finally, put the design into practical use by making a Glove that you can display. Where you display it is your choice (altar, bedroom, living room, front door, camping festivals, coven gatherings, etc).

I hope you'll consider sharing your Glove in the group.

Additional Resources

The Penguin Dictionary of Symbols (book)-- https://amzn.to/30hKOEt

Online Symbol Dictionaries:

http://symboldictionary.net/

http://www.symbols.com/

http://www.umich.edu/~umfandsf/symbolismproject/symbolism.html/?PHPSESSID=4b115707328e8059c1572761f3acf528

BoS Pages Included

Witches' Symbols

Red Thread Academy
Traditional Witchcraft
Year 1: Foundations

Unit 2: Cosmology
Lesson 1: Wheel of the Year

Wheel of the Year

Prerequisite Lesson

None

Objectives

- To become familiar with the Spiral Castle Tradition's Year Wheel (and its components)
- To frame the cycle of Sabbats as a metaphor

Materials Needed

Paper and pencil

Study Notes

Very strictly speaking, Traditional Witches do not necessarily observe the 4 solar and 4 agricultural festivals that have been adopted by Wicca and Neo-Paganism. Historically, no culture observed all 8 of those holidays. The Celts in the British Isles observed the four agricultural festivals (Samhain, Imbolc, Beltaine, and Lammas), and the Britons who pre-dated them in England may have celebrated the solstices and equinoxes, but nobody worked with all eight.

This visualization of the year as an 8-spoked wheel was a creation of Gerald Gardner, probably because he couldn't reveal the rituals practiced by the more traditional coven that trained him.

The Sabbats celebrated by a particular group would vary from those of another group, and they would likely be tied to the agricultural cycles manifested in the region. Furthermore, the Sabbats were secondary to the Esbats (or Full Moon workings) within Traditional practice. The Clan of Tubal Cain (Robert Cochrane's coven) and the People of Goda (ostensibly his Tradition) honor 9 "knots in the ladder" -- or points in the compass … or festivals in the Wheel of the Year.

The Spiral Castle Tradition chose to work with the 8 Sabbats that are common throughout NeoPaganism and Wicca because they were what was already worked into the tidal awareness of this Tradition's founders -- me (Laurelei) and Natalie. We felt it was most important here to have a cycle of holidays that helped us (and eventually you) honor the way the tides shift both in the outer world of nature and in the inner world of the Self. The Sabbats/Year Wheel are a metaphor for the cycles of the human life -- both its span and its quality.

The Sabbats

The word "sabbat" derives from the Latin root *sabbatum* and is a cousin to words such as Sabbath (Christian), Old English *sabat*, Old French *sabbat*, Greek *sabbaton (or sa'baton)*, and Hebrew *Shabbat*, which means "to cease or rest." During the medieval witch trials, there were many attestations of the "Witches' Sabbath" -- the most notable of the holidays happening at Walpurgis or Beltaine and its opposite point in the year, Samhain.

The timing for the Sabbats varies by tradition. The solar holidays are steady across traditions that use them, happening on the solstices and equinoxes. But the agricultural holidays can be trickier to pin-point. Some groups celebrate them on the kalends (beginning) of the month in which they fall. Others calculate them astrologically (15° of the cross-quarter zodiac sign associated with the holiday). And yet others (in what is probably the most traditional method) celebrate the holidays when certain natural markers are indicated -- the flowering of a certain tree for Beltaine, the bringing in of the last harvest for Samhain, etc.

The Sabbats begin at sundown rather than at midnight, thus these festivals are often associated with the "eve" of the date listed.

Sabbat	Dates	Sun's Position
Samhain	1 Nov (also 5-10 Nov)	15° Scorpio
Yule	20-23 Dec (winter solstice)	0° Capricorn
Imbolc	2 Feb (also 2-7 Feb)	15° Aquarius
Spring	19-22 Mar (spring equinox)	0° Aries
Beltane	1 May (also 4-10 May)	15° Taurus
Midsummer	19-23 June (summer solstice)	0° Cancer
Lammas	1 Aug (also 3-10 Aug)	15° Leo
Autumn	21-24 Sept (autumn equinox)	0° Libra

As discussed earlier, no traditional peoples celebrated all eight holidays. Ronald Hutton, a professor of history at the University of Bristol, and an expert on Pagan and Neo-Pagan traditions in Great Britain, states:

"No known pre-Christian people celebrated all the eight festivals of the calendar adopted by Wicca. Around the four genuine Gaelic quarter days are now ranged the Midwinter and September feasts of the Anglo-Saxons, the Midsummer celebrations so prominent in folklore and (for symmetry) the vernal equinox, which does not seem to have been commemorated by any ancient northern Europeans." -- <u>Triumph of the Moon</u>

In groups that omit some Sabbats, the Gaelic Sabbats are considered of more importance than the Lesser Sabbats; and, of these the solstices are thought to be more important than the equinoxes. The greatest and oldest of Sabbats seem to be Beltaine and Samhain, which are both historically linked with Witchcraft.

Many Wiccan groups have ascribed an overarching storyline to the progression of Sabbats, but this is not a practice common to Traditional Witchcraft. In fact, the only story that I've ever seen ascribed with any sort of traditional merit is that of John Barleycorn, a figure from English ballads.

"John Barleycorn Must Die"
There were three men came out of the West
Their fortunes for to try
And these three men made a solemn vow
John Barleycorn must die

They've ploughed, they've sown, they've harrowed him in
Threw clods upon his head
And these three men made a solemn vow
John Barleycorn was dead

They've let him lie for a very long time
Till the rains from heaven did fall
And little Sir John sprung up his head
And so amazed them all

They've let him stand till midsummer's day
Till he looked both pale and wan
And little Sir John's grown a long, long beard
And so become a man

They've hired men with the scythes so sharp
To cut him off at the knee
They've rolled him and tied him by the waist
Serving him most barbarously

They've hired men with the sharp pitchforks
Who pricked him to the heart
And the loader he has served him worse than that
For he's bound him to the cart

They've wheeled him around and around the field
Till they came unto a barn
And there they made a solemn oath
On poor John Barleycorn

They've hired men with the crab-tree sticks
To cut him skin from bone
And the miller he has served him worse than that
For he's ground him between two stones

And little Sir John and the nut-brown bowl
And he's brandy in the glass
And little Sir John and the nut-brown bowl
Proved the strongest man at last

The huntsman, he can't hunt the fox
Nor so loudly to blow his horn
And the tinker he can't mend kettle nor pot
Without a little Barleycorn

The Year Wheel diagram above was created for use within the Spiral Castle Tradition. The original graphic was created by my ex-wife and co-founder, Natalie -- although this one is an updated version that reflects changes made to the correspondences as our development of the Trad progressed. Together, she and I created the diagram and discussed the correlations ("correspondences) of the Sabbats to other cosmological concepts that you see above. You'll refer back to this diagram (or the larger version on the BoS page) often. It is a map of our cosmos. Notice, if you will, that our Year Wheel and our Compass are one and the same. You walk in both Sacred Space and Sacred Time. (Here is shown a Mystery!)

Light and Dark

Celtic lore divides the year into two halves -- light and dark. (In the diagram above, the top half of the year is "dark" while the bottom half is "light.") These are representative of the active and passive times in our lives and in our energy. The light days are a time of plowing, planting, weeding, and beginning to harvest the projects and plans we build. They are days of busy-ness and bounty. The dark days are a time for ending, harvesting, resting, and reflecting on the work. They are days of scarcity and hibernation.

Gaelic/Agricultural Holidays

Samhain -- Life begins in darkness, and so does the year (and the day, for that matter). Samhain is both the beginning and the end of a year's cycle. It equates to the sunset, if we extend the metaphor to the day cycle. It is the final harvest, when the last of the crops have been brought in from the field. It is a time for honoring ancestors and connecting our own lives with the cycle of eternity.

Imbolc -- This is typically the coldest part of the year, the most bitter and barren. At least, this is what is happening on the surface of things. Below the surface, life is stirring, but not ready to burst forth. It equates to midnight.

Beltaine -- The freshness and fertility of spring arrive on the landscape (and the inner-scape) with renewed passions, ideas, and vigor. It is the morning, when most of the work still lies ahead of you, but some bits have already begun. It is the time when the fields are being sown and livestock are being born. The world is blossoming into productivity.

Lammas -- The noontime of the year, the sun is blazing and activity is at its height. The harvest is starting, the kids are getting ready to go back to school, craft fairs are getting underway, and the farmer's markets are loaded with goodies. This is a time of sacrifice, as the first fruits are collected.

Solar Holidays

Fall and Spring Equinox -- These holidays are times of balance, a preparatory breath and moment of calm before the shift into either the hustle and bustle of the summer or the long rest and isolation of winter.

Summer and Winter Solstice -- These holidays are times of extremes -- longest day and longest night. They are both times of great festivity, and they tend to be celebrated with bonfires. Cultures all over the world still honor these times with fires, pyrotechnics/light displays, and feasting, even though they have renamed the holidays and shifted the focus to better fit their current religions.

Animal & Tree Spirit Allies

Every month in our Year Wheel (regardless of whether there is a Sabbat) is associated with 3 Spirit Allies -- a Tree and two Animals (one of which typically flies). It can take some time to get to know these potent beings, which is why it is important to meet them in Year 1 and make a point of spending quality time with them throughout your studies. Some of them may already be familiar friends to you, while others may be mysterious strangers. The monthly spellwork assignment associated with Lesson 04-01 should give you ample opportunity to make an initial acquaintance, as should the included BoS pages.

Honoring and Working

Unit 3 of this course focuses entirely on honoring the Sabbats in a ritual setting. It isn't necessary to start at a specific point in the Year Wheel. Start with the next Sabbat that is approaching. Use the rituals provided in the text, just as a base of operation. If you're new to ritual, you may not be ready early in the course to create a new ritual. If you do choose to celebrate in a different way, be sure to notate what you did in your written debrief of the ritual.

Assignment — Create a Wheel of the Year diagram that reflects your understanding of the Sabbats. Include as much corresponding information as makes sense to you. (Options might include zodiac signs, moon names, times of day, directions, etc.) It's okay to start simple and add more later, if it suits you.

Additional Resources

BoS Pages Included — Wheel of the Year
Animal & Tree Spirit Allies

Red Thread Academy
Traditional Witchcraft
Year 1: Foundations

Unit 2: Cosmology
Lesson 2: Sacred Space

Sacred Space

Prerequisite Lesson

Unit 2, Lesson 1 "Wheel of the Year"

Objectives

- To understand the concept of sacred space within a Traditional Craft framework
- To establish shrines and/or erect altars to honor the Sacred
- To learn and practice the laying of the compass

Materials Needed

- A staff, walking stick, or cane
- Shelf or table and items for altar space

Study Notes

Traditional Craft tends to view space (particularly, natural space) as inherently sacred. It is not our words or actions that prepare or sanctify a grove, riverbank, field, or forest. These things are sacred before we arrive, and they will be sacred after we leave. When we lay the compass, we are not changing the sacred landscape in any way. We are acknowledging it. We are recognizing the Sacred within the seemingly Profane.

This is a different view of Sacred Space than you find within ceremonial systems of magic and ritual. Those systems tend to be derived from religions that view the physical world as vulgar, dirty, base, or "lesser than" the spiritual world. They do not recognize that the spiritual realm is made manifest in the physical realm, and that the physical realm is the holy and perfect container for the spiritual.

The differences in these views penetrate every aspect of belief and philosophy. I won't belabor the point beyond drawing your attention to it and acknowledging that Traditional Craft has a very different view. That view is evidenced (among other ways) in our approach to Sacred Space.

The space is sacred. The words and actions you use are clarifying and acknowledging this fact TO YOU, not imposing your views of sacredness ON IT.

This lesson is going to cover two major components of sacred space: laying the compass and establishing altars or shrines.

Laying the Compass

Most modern witches have been taught to work in a circle. The circle is an organic shape that places each of its members as equals. Energy flows smoothly when directed in a circle, and the circle serves as both container and barrier for various energies.

Cunning Folk also tend to work in a circular shape, although its "creation" and its purpose differ from the Wiccan circle. Whereas Wicca has been influenced by Ceremonial Magical traditions to cast a circle to serve as a metaphysical protection from outside energies, we view the mill-grounds (the ritual space) as a kind of cauldron. It is a container to intensify and direct energy from.

Gardnerian Wiccan circles are cast three times, once with salt and water, once with fire and incense, and once with steel (an athame or sword), and more eclectic Neo-Wiccan circles are often cast just once (usually with steel).

The compass is laid (or "the sacredness of the space is acknowledged") by marking out the space and "calling" the Directions. It can be a very simple process -- walking around the space and gesturing or saying a few words for the directions. It can also be much more elaborate, if that suits your sense Arte.

Over the three years of this course, you'll learn several ways to lay the compass. Some will build on others. Some will be alternatives to others. You can adapt some for group use versus solo practice. ALL ARE "CORRECT" because all serve the same goals -- to acknowledge the inherent sacredness of the space and to align ourselves with that Sacred Space and Time.

The compass has correspondences to the Year Wheel. The four "greater" Sabbats being linked with the cardinal directions (and times of day) in the the following ways:

North - Imbolc - Midnight - Air
South - Lammas - Noon - Earth
East - Beltaine - Sunrise - Fire
West - Samhain - Sunset - Water

It is also notable that a great many Traditional Crafters call Powers that lie opposite each other as a pair. So for example, when calling the Gates (Directions), we call North, then South -- both being called toward the center of the compass. Thus, they form a road or an energetic pathway, with the Stang (or Witch) as the center point. Then we would do the same with East and West, which creates two crossed roads -- a magical crossroads.

Ceremonial magic circles place elemental energies at different directions and call them by moving in a clockwise motion. There are valid energetic reasons for doing this. Their method moves energy very efficiently around the circle, building up to what is often called a "Cone of Power" that can be directed at a magical target at the culminating point of a spell or working.

Our method draws energy toward the center of the compass, to be directed upward, downward, inward, or outward by the Witch.

It is important to understand that the "ceremonial" methods and tools can have a place within "traditional" Craft. During and after the Crusades, Hermetic and Arabic magical concepts were more present and were adopted (to varying degrees) by some Cunning Folk. Later, the rise of magical or mystical Orders/Brotherhoods (Freemasonry, etc) further reinforced these ceremonial methods and tools and brought them to greater prominence. So many of those concepts became the basis of Wicca, but Cunning Folk in the area also adopted some of these methods. Just because we at RTA/SCT aren't teaching the Hermetic way doesn't make it invalid. It is useful to have more than one way to raise and use energy.

Back to our method:

We begin at the center of the compass and raise the stang. The stang serves as a sort of World Tree and connects the seasons and elements of the cosmology together, allowing the Witch to access them from the central focal point of the compass. If we are going to voice the calls, we acknowledge this point at the center first.

At the base of the stang is the oath stone, or anvil. It is on this stone that we make our blood oaths to the tradition and through which we call forth Tubal Cain. Near the oath stone are the cauldron and the skull. These represent the mysteries of life and death, and tie us to our ancestors. Also placed at the center of the compass are the personal fetishes of each member of our Clan.

After the raising of the Stang, we Mark the Compass.

This is done by walking the border of the working space. We use the staff as a tool for this. You can do it in a couple of ways. You can either drag the staff to mark a circle on the ground, or you can use it like a walking stick as you circumambulate the space. Either way, it is a nod to the "lame step" and walking between two worlds.

Finally, we Open the Gates.

This part of the ritual acknowledges the four directions and acknowledges the energetic relationships between them. We call them as opposite pairs, as siblings, as light and dark halves of each other.

Where you start may depend on the time of year, time of day, or type of magic you are doing. For instance, you may choose to do your Imbolc ritual at midnight and open the North gate first. If you did, you would open South next. If your working was positive in nature, you'd open West next (moving in a clockwise direction after South), and then call East.

I tend to be a minimalist in my own rituals, using only what I need for the work at hand. More often than not, that means all an onlooker would see is me wearing a set of cords, with a stick, a candle, and maybe some rocks and feathers. But other folks like tools and scenery, and we all need to assuage our own sense of Arte. So adapt the following to your own tastes.

If you have the full set of working tools and like to display them during rituals, you might see the following around your compass as you Opened the Gates:

At the north gate are placed the staves of the coven, along with the spear. Also at this gate are symbols of the Black Goddess (including a lily and a scourge). Any tools associated with air are kept at this gate, such as the censer if one is used, as well as a feather fan or other important feathers the individual or coven has acquired.

The south is the gate of the White Goddess. At her gate are placed red roses. The weapon kept here is the targe, the shield of earth. The binding cords and the bread for the red meal are placed at this gate. You might also have a noose.

In the east are the tools of fire. Here we place the blacksmith's trade (hammer and tongs) and keep a bonfire burning, if we are outdoors. The coven sword is here, as is appropriate to a weapon of steel. Also kept here are offerings for Tubal Cain, the Red God, such as dark beer.

The west is the gate of water. It is the quench tank of Tubal Cain. Representations of water are placed here. The weapon of this gate is the helm, and the masks of the Clan are kept here, as is a hood or blindfold. The wine and cups for the red meal are also kept here.

Whether you speak words, silently call, dance, etc. is up to you. If you are working alone, you have plenty of opportunity to experience different methods to see the different results you'll get. When you do work with a group, I recommend you keep experimenting.

With the Stang raised, the Compass laid, and the Gates opened, you have gone about the task of casting three magic rings. From here, the stage is set to do your magic. You may raise energy, travel into the realms of Spirit via witch flight, perform possessory or oracular work, cast spells, or do healing work ... or what have you. The choice is yours.

Practicing Laying the Compass can be done with nothing but you and your staff, which can serve double duty as both the gandriegh/Stang and as your personal pole. Never let "lack of tools" come between you and your Craft. No staff? A walking stick or a cane are both staves.

Likewise, never let "lack of words" hold you back. Gestures are very powerful. Words will come when you are ready. Get the magic in your body, in your blood.

Three Realms

Sky, land, and sea,
Three-in-one, one-in-three.
~Celtic prayer

In most traditional cultures, people have viewed both the outer world and the inner planes as corollary concepts, where the macrocosm is a reflection of the microcosm, and vice versa. A great many of these cultures, including the ones from which we draw inspiration and spiritual sustenance, see the Universe as divided into three realms.

The Three Realms can be said to incorporate an Upper Realm (heavenly, celestial sphere), a Middle Realm (earthly, terrestrial sphere), and a Lower Realm (infernal, underworldly sphere). The beneficence or maleficence associated with these realms is dependent on the culture. Each has its own dangers and its own rewards. Each is inhabitant by its own sort of people, guarded by its own warriors, and ruled by its own leaders.

American folkloric (and therefore RTA/Spiral Castle) practices draw most heavily from Celtic lore and Druidic practice, which in this case means adopted of Welsh names for these Realms. The Upper Realm is called Ceugent *(ky-gent)* and is an airy sphere of intellect, ideas,and future-sight. The Middle Realm is earthy *Gwyned*, which is the here and now, consensus reality. The Lower Realm is called *Abred*, and it is a watery realm of the subconscious, emotion, memory, and the past.

These realms are accessed spiritually through the use of shamanic trance techniques that generally incorporate the image of a World Tree or a Holy Mountain. Both of these images represent a concept called the Axis Mundi, the cross of the world. It is a nearly universally perceived spiritual and energetic construct. Carl Jung described this phenomena as the Collective Unconscious. It is also called the Consciousness Unit. However we define or describe it, shamans and witches have been going to the Tree or the Mountain since time immemorial to tap into the wisdom, insight, and healing that can be found within.

For purposes of spiritual travel (or "witch flight"), the pole is symbolized literally in our circles by the raising of the stang. By its virtue we can "ride" the stang to any place in the realms, though we may also use our own personal riding-pole, or gandreigh, to do so.

Here are some associations for each of the three realms.

First Realm
Ceugent
Upperworld, Upper Realm
Realm of Sky, Wind, Otherworld
Struggle and enlightenment
Preservation: the undying realm, absence of decay
Birth, beginnings
The mind
Breath
Expansion/expansiveness
Perspective
Movement, setting in motion (beginning)
First arm of the Triskle
Entry through flight or climbing
Metacognition
Black Knife/Athame

Second Realm
Gwyned
Earth world, Center world, Realm of Land, Middle Earth
Day-to-day struggles and concerns

Consensus reality, the here and now
Physicality
Living bones and flesh
Harsh realities
Progress, action, doing
Going through something
Middles
Limits and limitations (perceived and real)
Second arm of Triskle
No entry needed (already in this realm)
Manipulation of perception/changing one's reality/glamory
Consciousness
White Knife/Kerfane-Bolline

Third Realm
Abred
Underworld, Realm of the Sea
Barrows, cairns, caves
Deep mystery
Truth beyond substance or thought
Emotion
Healing the soul
Rest
Death and preparation
Empathy
Blood, birth fluids, menses, semen, sweat
Oceans, lakes, ponds, pools
Inner self
Subliminal, Unconscious, Subconcious
Entry through caves, wells, etc.
Springs and wells bring energy/life from the third realm to the second
Third leg of Triskle
Red Knife/Shelg

(We will explore the Realms in much greater depth as part of Year 3: Mastery studies.)

Castles - The Elemental Watchtowers

We have talked about the Gates and the Realms. The Spiral Castle Tradition also works with four Castles in our full understanding of sacred cosmology. These are places of protection and also great Mystery. They hold within them four Treasures which each seeker along the path hopes to uncover and understand. They are the Castle of Revelry (with its Golden Lantern), the Stone Castle (with its Stone Bowl), Castle Perilous (silver cup -- holy grail), and the Glass Castle (with the Glass Orb). Each is kept by a Guardian, of course. These places (as well as their keeper and treasures) have revealed themselves under the guise of numerous names in various legends.

When calling them as part of our space, we place them at the cross-quarters. You will see them on our Year Wheel associated with the Solstices and Equinoxes. (We will explore these Castles in much greater depth as part of Year 2: Practicum studies.)

Creating Physical Sacred Spaces

I love altars and shrines. Can't get enough of them. One entire wall of my bedroom is altar space, and I have two other decent sized altars in the same room. That's not counting my son's altar, which is also in my room.

Our living room has an ancestor/family altar, and my husband and daughter each maintain sacred space in their rooms as well.

Wanna hear the most outlandish part? We've all downsized our altar space recently. No kidding!

Going beyond this, my family helps maintain sacred space at a place called Camp Midian, where there are shrines and altars visited by hundreds of people throughout the festival season (summer half of the year). I personally maintain an Aphrodite Temple there, and my daughter helped establish a Freya shrine.

So, why the focus on physical sacred space?

I have several theories, but the main one is that shrines and altars connect all of our physical senses and give us a point of contact for that extrasensory awareness of the Sacred.

When we recognize a powerful place, we want to honor it. We want to preserve it and come back to it because it renewed something in us. We want to bless it, just as it blessed us. Therefore, we give it offerings and keep it clean, quiet, and/or reserved for specific use.

Likewise, we establish sacred space to honor those energies or beings who maybe aren't attached so much to a space as they are to US --- Gods, ancestors, spirits. We give them a space in our homes or on our land and say, "Come, be near me. I love you, I respect you, and I want you with me as often as you want to be with me."

The size, shape, and nature of these spaces depends on the nature of the Being or energy you are honoring, the resources available to you, and the reason you have to establish/honor the space in the first place.

Assignment

1. Establish an altar. It can be a working altar or shrine. It can be a general or specific space. It can be large or small. Include pictures and descriptions of everything in the space. Be sure to say why the items are included and in what way you use them within the context of the space. "Just because" isn't a valid reason. Dig deep and know why you chose each item. What is the connection. Also tell me about your plans to expand the space, change items in the future, or any other way you think you might change the space over time.

2.

3. Tell me about the space where you plan to (or are currently) holding your rituals. Is it indoors or outdoors? Private, semi-private, shared? How big is it? How is it equipped? What do you feel like you need (that you don't already have)? What do you love about it? What would you change? Include a pic, please

---

Additional Resources

- You tube video of Laying the Compass with words and basic tools (check RedThreadAcademy channel)
- You tube video of Laying the Compass with gestures only (check RedThreadAcademy channel)
- Fuck yeah altars on Tumblr -- http://fuckyeahaltars.tumblr.com/
- Some altar pics of my own are shown on the following page

BoS Pages Included

Wheel of the Year
Animal & Tree Spirit Allies

Laurelei's Selected Altar

Red Thread Academy
Traditional Witchcraft
Year 1: Foundations

Unit 2: Cosmology
Lesson 3: Elements

Elements

Prerequisite Lesson

None specified

Objectives

- Gain understanding of impact of Elements within Witchcraft cosmology
- Begin to develop personal Table of Correspondences

Materials Needed

- Pencil and paper, or
- Spreadsheet software

Study Notes

If you've had any prior exposure to any branch of Witchcraft or magic, you've likely already come across the idea of the four elements. Actually, if you've paid attention to video games, role playing games, fantasy novels, movies, folklore, mythology, or any other aspects of either ancient or modern popular culture, you've undoubtedly been exposed to the idea of the four elements that comprise the basis of physical reality.

Western Civilization has generally recognized them as:

EARTH

AIR

FIRE

WATER

Often there is the recognition of a fifth, non-physical element, SPIRIT.

In our discussion on Sacred Spaces, the four directions of the Compass were attributed to these four physical elements. Spirit, the vehicle that can travel between all four, lies at the center with the Stang.

These elements are simple and knowable. We come into contact with them in our daily lives. They are manifest in our body. We are in constant communication with them, although our focus is rarely on their sacred nature.

They are also complex and rich with Mystery, revealing new lessons and new understanding to those who would take the time to see, to know.

Take one of Water's lessons as an example. We are taught as school children about concepts like erosion. But take a moment to consider the infinite patience with which a trickle or drip of seemingly gentle, malleable, shapeless Water can wear down the dense solidity of rock to hollow out caves and canyons.

Each element has life-giving properties: fertile soil, oxygen-rich air, cell nourishing water, warming heat.

Each element brings death: suffocation, burial, drowning, burning.

They offer equal keys of creation and destruction within the physical world and also within the mental and emotional realms. Consider for a moment how an element like Fire might influence one's thoughts. Can you see both positive Fire-influenced thinking and negative Fire-influenced thinking? How about Fire-influenced emotional states? physical states?

Often in a course like this or in beginner Craft books, this is where you'll see a long list of associations (called Correspondences) telling you all about the magical associations of the Elements. The thing is, you already know about these Elements. You've spent your entire physical existence immersed in them. So, I want you to start making your own list, coming up with your own associations, trusting your own experience and observation.

Correspondences

In most magical practice, we are working with the idea that everything relates to something else. We have seen this idea noted in several of the Laws of Magic, in fact – most especially in the Law of Unity. (For more on the Laws of Magic, see 05-01.)

If we want to affect a given item, person, situation or whatever, we have a better chance of doing that effectively if we use objects that are related to what we want to accomplish.

Most practical magic books come with "Tables of Correspondences" for all sorts of information – colors, moon phases, astrological influences, symbols, entities, tools, days of the week, Deities, etc. These correspondences were developed based on the work of alchemists and magicians but are helpful and practical for Witches when working on spell craft.

Ultimately, what you should bear in mind is that everything in the universe is connected. As a Witch, you are weaving a web of magic. You are like a great spider, aware of the many threads that connect your needs with the outcome you seek. The more knowledge you have, the stronger your web.

While you may wish to begin your study of Correspondences by looking at the work of other practitioners, you should ultimately be guided by your own Compass. (The pun is intended. Or rather, it isn't a pun at all, in this case.)

A few Spiral Castle/RTA Correspondences to get you started:

North - Imbolc - Midnight - Air - Staff - To know
South - Lammas - Noon - Earth - Shield - To keep silent
East - Beltaine - Sunrise - Fire - Sword - To will
West - Samhain - Sunset - Water - Helmet - To dare
Center - All Seasons/Times - Access Point - Spirit - Stang

Assignment

Create your own Elemental Table of Correspondences. Your table can include more categories than the following, but it should have these as a minimum:
Direction/Gate
Deities
Colors
Tools
Weapons
Vessels/Containers
Powers/Intentions
Zodiac signs
Planets
Days of the week
Symbols
Landscape features

Other categories you might include:
Herbs
Stones
Animals
Weather phenomena
Musical instruments
Body parts/systems
Psychic gifts/challenges
Emotional gifts/challenges
Physical gifts/challenges
Intellectual gifts/challenges
Sacrificial methods
Offerings
Spirits

Additional Resources

BoS Pages Included

Earth
Air
Fire
Water
The Airts
The Humours
Powers of the Sphinx
The Three Realms

Red Thread Academy
Traditional Witchcraft
Year 1: Foundations

Unit 2: Cosmology
Lesson 4: Red, Black, White

Red, Black, White

Prerequisite Lesson   None Specified

Objectives

- To be introduced to the concept of the three sacred colors
- To start identifying the complex ways in which these colors manifest certain symbol sets within Traditional Witchcraft
- To lay the foundation for future exploration of Mysteries related to triplicity

Materials Needed

Study Notes

Black, white, and red are the three most significant colors of the Spiral Castle Tradition. This fact is peculiar to us, and it is not reflective of Traditional Witchcraft as a whole, although you will note it within a few other scattered covens or traditions. However, our practice of finding significance in the interplay between these colors -- indeed, of holding them as sacred beyond all other -- has a long history from the Celtic roots of British Craft.

In Celtic, British, and even some American lore, you can always tell when animals are sacred (or Otherworldly) because they are "marked" with the colors black, white, and red. Spectral black dogs, red dogs, or white dogs with red ears are tell-tale hounds from other planes. Kine (cattle) and swine (pigs) -- both sacred animals in their own right -- are doubly sacred when colored similarly (solid black, solid red, solid white, or white with red ears).

As you progress through your studies, you will undoubtedly notice the redundancy of these colors. Some of the most notable places will be in your study of:

- Black Goddess, White Goddess, Red God
- athame, kerfane, shelg (3 knives)
- Triple Soul

You will notice it in other instances, as well. In fact, you will soon start to see both the consistency with which these colors seem to present themselves throughout the Tradition, alongside the complexity with which they are interwoven.

Let's use this first introduction to the concept to talk about the Deities of Traditional Craft.

In truth, I use the term "Deities of Traditional Craft" cautiously, as there are not specific Gods or Goddesses that most Cunning Folk would all agree are common to all branches of the Craft. When you do your outside reading, you will likely see some disagreement about the role of a central God or central Goddess, which ones were specifically venerated by real historical Witches, etc.

The topic of the Witches' God or Witches' Goddess is both deep and broad, and I encourage you to do a lot of reading, thinking, and meditation about it. Never stop seeking the face of That Which Called You Here.

The view presented here is both useful and resonant, in my experience. In a mythopoetic sense, it rings true. In a practical sense, it works.

It is also adaptable, allowing for the idiosyncrasies of local or family influence or the specifics of personal devotion to a particular God or Goddess who has already claimed you. (More about that in lesson 10-4.) To that end, this Academy and the Spiral Castle Tradition that you are studying as part of this course is not dictating to you the names by which you call the Gods. I think you'll find that They are already here.

RED GOD

Traditional Witches often refer to the Angel or God who brought enlightenment, alchemy, and magic to mankind as the Witch Father. This being has been revered and respected by those few in each generation of humanity who were ready and open to receive gnosis — ready to understand and embrace their own divine nature. He has been despised and demonized by the masses who find terror and blasphemy in his message.

The Witch Father is usually depicted with horns between which a green fire burns. This is the Cunning Fire, the Witch Fire. It is this fire that is the symbol of enlightenment. A Red Thread of ancestry connects us to this Witch Father and reminds us that we carry the blood of the rebel, the blood of the heretic, the blood of the scapegoat, the blood of the wise within our own veins.

He is often depicted as the Sabbatic Goat, the Devil at the Crossroads. He is a transgressive God, offering us liberation and birthright. His image definitely inspires fear to those who don't know, haven't seen, aren't open, aren't ready.

He is called by many names, this Witch Father. He is Azazel. He is Qayin and Tubal Cain. He is Melek Taus. He is Lucifer. He is Shamash. It is the experience of witches in the Spiral Castle Tradition that these are not different beings. Rather, the names are different titles, different cultural depictions of the same God.

The truest name by which we know this Witch Father is Tubal Qayin (Tubal Cain, Tubelo). Often, I'll just say Qayin. These are the names we will use most often. The others, we tend to view as titles more than names.

Lucifer

Oh my Holy Goat, there is so much that needs to be said about the title of Lucifer in relation to the Witch Father. There is so much dross to sift through, so much misinformation that has been propagated about this one figure, one name, over the millenia, to reach the golden kernels of wisdom.

For now, let's keep it very simple, shall we?

Lucifer is the "light-bearer." He is Qayin in the East, the Morning Star. He is the torch-bearer of wisdom, inspiration, the Divine Spark, the Cunning Fire.

He is "Prometheus" (literally, "fore-sight"), who rebelled against God (the Gods) to give Fire (the Cunning Fire) to mankind and fell from Divine Grace.

The light he bears is the light of gnosis. It is enlightenment. It is symbolized in the burning green star between the Great Dragon's eyes in biblical texts, by the candle between the Sabbatic Goat's horns, and by the sun itself (which was said to be drawn across the sky in a chariot by Lucifer in old Italian folklore). The path of the sun is, indeed, a version of the Red Thread. It is the red line drawn by the light bearer across the sky each day.

Lucifer, the pre-Christian God, was also depicted as a blacksmith, a trade that has been intimately tied to alchemy and enlightenment since its origins. (In the Bible, Tubal Cain was credited as being the very first blacksmith.)

Lucifer has also been mythologically linked to the planet Venus, known as the Morning Star and also the Evening Star. Globally, the Deities associated with this celestial body are typically seen as originating from a heavenly realm to make an underworld journey and reemerge. Lucifer is no exception.

Azazel

Enoch reveals to us that Azazel shares with humanity "all the metals and the art of working them...and the use of antimony." As it turns out, antimony (or stibium), was critical to the alchemical process of creating the Philosopher's Stone. This same element was called kuhl (or kohl) by the ancient Arabs. (You might also recall references to women decorating their eyes with this substance, and that art also being taught by Azazel. This may, in fact, have been a veiled reference to the alchemical process and not to cosmetics at all.)

Sir Roger Bacon tells us that when antimony is processed with vitriol, it is reduced to a "noble red oil" with all of the lesser sulfur having been purified out of it in the process. Red, then, is Azazel's color.

It is doubly his color when we consider that man is made from red clay, according to Middle Eastern tradition, and that Azazel is master of the material world from which man is made, as a demiurge or creator.

The name Azazel means scapegoat of God, and there is a lot involving Azazel as a wanderer, being displaced, and walking through the world.

Melek Taus

"Melek" means "king" or "angel," and "taus" means "peacock." The peacock angel is the central figure, the benevolent and creative demiurge, of the Yezidis. He is seen as repentant after the fall from God's grace, his tears quenching the fires of hell.

Though the Yezidis would disagree, others in the Arabic world (particularly those practicing Islam), equate Melek Taus with Lucifer or Satan. Kabbalistically, Yahweh rules in the heavenly/spiritual kingdom of Kether, and Melek Taus (Lucifer/Azazel) rules in the earthly kingdom of Malkuth.

Within the sacred text of the Yezidis, the Black Book, a specific reference is made to Azazel, equating the Peacock Angel with Azazel. There are several versions of this book extent from the Middle Ages, copies transcribed online.

Utu/Shamash

The Nephilim, the "Fallen Angels" or spirits who descended into the material realm to interact with and guide mankind, were first seen as the "Shining Ones" or Gods of Sumerian lore.

Utu is the Sumerian name, while Shamash is the Babylonian name for the Sun God of justice, law, and salvation. He is linked in a triad with the Nannar-Sin (the Mood God), and Ishtar (the fertility-Earth Goddess, who incidentally is represented by the planet Venus, the Morning and Evening Star).

Robin, Puck, Holt

Moving away from the Ancient names and into the medical ones, we see Robin, Puck (or Pooka, Phuka, Bucca, or other variations), and Holt attested in the trial records, folklore, and other sources.

Robin Goodfellow, Robin Artisson, Robin in the Green, Robin of the Wood (or Robin Hood) are all makes that have been associated with the Witch Father -- the initiator and Magister.

These names end up being synonymous and almost interchangeable with Puck, which derived from a woodland satyr-type figure called a Boucca. We see this connection made for us in William Shakespeare's *A Midsummer Night's Dream* in the character of Puck, who is sometimes called Robin Goodfellow.

Holt is an English derivation of Wotan or Odin, the one-eyed, wandering God of magic and wisdom. As Holt or Hold, he leads the Wild Hunt through the winter night sky, gathering souls of the dying. (See the correlation to the biblical story of the fall of the angels or the Great Dragon who sweeps a third of the multitude of stars from the sky with his tail?)

WHITE GODDESS & BLACK GODDESS

In some parts of Europe, a central magic-teaching Goddess (or a pair of them), was honored. Archetypally, this Witch Mother was either seen as a Goddess of extremes and of balance, or she was seen as two separate Goddesses -- sisters, friends, rivals, mother/daughter (sometimes 3 of these 4) -- each taking a vital role in the instruction of a Witch. Seen as one Goddess, she is often the first Witch, the Queen of Witches, the Devil's Wife.

Within this Tradition, we will most often speak of our them as two beings. The White Goddess and the Black Goddess.

In truth, these are two faces of the SAME Goddess — the quintessential Witch's Goddess. She is both light and darkness. But just as the sun does not shine during the darkness of night, She does not fully reveal both sides of Her nature simultaneously.

Through the light half of the year, we mark the influence of the White Goddess whom we call upon as Goda. In the dark half of the year, we honor Kolyo, the Black Goddess.

However, as much as the Black and White Goddesses counterpoint each other on the Year Wheel and within the compass that we lay, we must acknowledge and understand that they work along a continuum. They are not truly separate from each other. One requires the other for full manifestation, and the dynamic balance maintained between the two is critical to the practice of the Craft as we know it.

Each holds within Herself the core of the other. Within the darkness of the night, the light of the moon and stars reaches us. During the brightness of the day, shadows lurk and provide respite.

Just as the white knife cuts in the physical realm, and the black in the astral; so, too, do the Goddesses relate respectively to the physical and astral. The two are, in fact, reflections of each other.

A rare few Goddesses are both Black and White — Hel, Hekate, Lilith. These, we know as the Witch Mother.

While the Red God has two places of honor on the Wheel of the Year and within the compass (East/Beltaine and West/Samhain), the other two stations of highest honor are seemingly divided. The White Goddess rules in the South at Lammas, and the Black Goddess dominates the North at Imbolc.

The White Goddess ~ Goda

She is known to us as Godiva (Old English: Godgifu, "god gift"), Rhiannon, Epona, Queen of Elphame, Weisse Frauen, Dames Blanches, Witte Wieven, Lady Death, Eos, Aurora, Ushas, Ausera, Ausrina, Istara, Ishtar, Astarte, Araja, Arada, Aradia, Irodiada, Erodiade, Meroudys, Herodias, Herodiana, Diana, Eostre, Ostara, Austija, Habonida, Oona, Oonagh, Una, Uonaidh, Mab, Titania, Mielikki, Andred, Benzozia.

As mistress of the Wild Hunt, she is alternatively known as frau Gode, frau Gaue, and frau Woden, demonstrating her connection to Odin. Agricultural customs of the region also preserve relics of pagan religion. When mowing rye, the villagers let some stalks stand, tie flowers among them, and when finished with their work gather around them and shout three times: "Frau Gaue, you keep some fodder, this year on the wagon." In Prignitz, they call her frau Gode and leave a bunch of grain standing in each field which they call "Fru Gode's portion." In the district of Hameln, it was custom, if a reaper while binding sheaves passed over one, to jeer and call out: "Is that for frau Gauden?!" The name Gauen connects this legendary figure directly to Odin. In Old Norse, the fourth day of the week is known as Oðinsdagr, Odin's day. In Swedish and Danish, it is Onsdag; in North Frisian, Winsdei; in Middle Dutch, Woensdach; in Anglo-Saxon, Wodenes dæg, but in Westphalia, they call it Godenstag, Gonstag, Gaunstag, Gunstag, and in documents from the Lower Rhine, Gudestag and Gudenstag. Similarly, in the History of the Lombards, the first literary appearance of Odin and his wife, Odin is known as Godan. Grimm observes that a dialect which says fauer instead of foer, foder will equally have Gaue for Gode, Guode. Thus, in Frau Gauen or Gauden, German farmers have preserved the memory of a Mrs. Odin at work beside her husband in the fields long after the coming of Christianity.

In the folklore of Lowland Scotland and Northern England, the Queen of Elphame, Elphen, Elfen or Elfan (and also Elfin Queen, Fairy Queen or Faery Queen) is the elfin ruler of Elphame (Elf-home; compare Norse Álfheimr), the usually subterranean Scottish fairyland. She appears in a number of traditional supernatural ballads, including Thomas the Rhymer and Tam Lin. She also appears in a number of accounts from witchcraft trials and confessions, including the confession of Isobel Gowdie.

The Queen of Elphame is variously depicted as attractive and demonic. A similar picture is painted by the 1591 witchcraft confession of Andro Mann of Aberdeen. Mann confessed that he saw "the Devil" his "master in the likeness and shape of a woman, whom thou callest the Queen of Elphen." Mann further confessed that the Queen of Elphen rode white horses, and that she and her companions had human shapes, "yet were as shadows", and that they were "playing and dancing whenever they pleased." Isobel Gowdie's confession also noted that the Queen of Elphame was "brawlie" clothed in white linen, and that she got more food from the Queen than she could eat.

But, in Tam Lin the Queen of Elphame is a more sinister figure. She captures mortal men, and entertains them in her subterranean home; but then uses them to pay a "teind to Hell". This ballad tells of the struggle of its heroine Janet, who must overcome the Queen's shape shifting magic to rescue a would-be victim from the Fairy Ride on Halloween. The Queen's shape-shifting magic extends to her own person. Mann's confession also noted that "she can be old or young as she pleases."

The Black Goddess ~ Kolyo

We also call the Black Goddess by the local names of Cailleach Bheur, The Morrigan, (Morrigan, Badb, Macha, Nemain), Beira, Clíodhna, Nyx, Noctiluca, Bean nighe, Cleena, Mongfind, Hel, Hecate, Kali, Fata, Nicnevin, Gyre-Carling, Beira, The Moirae (Klotho, Lachesis, & Atropos), The Norns (Urdr, Verdandi, Skuld). In the 1734 tradition, the number 1734 is a cypher for the name HIO, which adherents would chant to call upon the Black Goddess. I can attest that chanting the name Kolyo, particularly in a whispered voice, is similarly effective (and very, very swift).

Kolyo (meaning the "coverer" and "hidden") is Great Mother of All - Ubiquitous, Omnipresent, Immortal and Eternal. In Indo-European Paganism, it is She who drives the Divine Drama and gives birth to the Gods and Goddesses. The Supreme Spinning Goddess, She is the First Timeless Source who regenerates All. A Being and Power older than Time itself, Kolyo spins the threads of Fate.

The word cailleach (in modern Irish and Scottish Gaelic, 'old woman') comes from the Old Irish caillech ('veiled one'), from Old Irish caille ('veil'), most likely an early loan from Latin pallium ('cloak'). The word is found as a component in terms like the Gaelic cailleach-dhubh ('nun') and cailleach-oidhche ('owl'), as well as the Irish cailleach feasa ('wise woman', 'fortune-teller') and cailleach phiseogach ('sorceress', 'charm-worker'). Related words include the Gaelic caileag ('young woman', 'girl') and the Lowland Scots carline/carlin ('old woman', 'witch'). A more obscure word that is sometimes interpreted as 'hag' is the Irish síle, which has led some to speculate on a connection between the Cailleach and the stone carvings of Sheela na Gigs.

The name may also be related to the Hindu goddess, Kali, who shares many similar characteristics

The Morrígan ("phantom queen") or Mórrígan ("great queen") (also known as Morrígu, Morríghan, Mor-Ríoghain, sometimes given in the plural as Morrígna) is a figure from Irish mythology who appears to have once been a goddess, although she is not explicitly referred to as such in the texts.

The Morrigan is a goddess of battle, strife, and fertility. She sometimes appears in the form of a crow, flying above the warriors, and in the Ulster cycle she also takes the form of an eel, a wolf, and a cow. She is generally considered a war deity comparable with the Germanic Valkyries, although her association with cattle also suggests a role connected with fertility, wealth, and the land. She is often depicted as a triple goddess, but also as a goddess with five or nine aspects. The most common combination of three is the Badb, Macha and Nemain, but other accounts name Fea, Anann, and others.

Clíodhna (Clídna, Clíodna, Clíona, but sometimes Cleena in English) is a Queen of the Banshees of the Tuatha Dé Danann. In Irish literature, Cleena of Carrigcleena is the potent banshee that rules as queen over the sheoques (fairy women of the hills) of South Munster, or Desmond. She is the principal goddess of this country. It is said the wails of the banshee can be heard echoing the valleys and glens at night, scaring those who hear as the wail of a banshee is potent and instills fear in good people.

In Irish mythology, Nemain (or Nemhain, Nemon or Neman) is the fairy spirit of the frenzied havoc of war, and possibly an aspect of the Morrígan.

Assignment

Write a reflection on the three colors -- Red, Black, White. Meditate on their interplay. How have these colors made themselves important in your life, if at all? Do you have black cats, calicos, white dog with red ears? Do you find yourself often wearing these "family colors?" Think about and share your experience with the Red God and Black and White Goddesses. Has one or more of them come to you in dreams, visions, or meditations? Do you have a special relationship with one of them already? Is there a certain name you use for him/her?

Additional Resources

The Black Book of the Yezidis (PDF) -- http://tikaboo.com/library/Yezidi_Black_Book.pdf

Liber Qayin -- (blog post version) -- http://afwcraft.blogspot.com/2015/03/liber-qayin-complete-text.html

BoS Pages Included

Black, White, Red
Witch Father
Witch Mother
Tubal Cain
Liber Qayin

Red Thread Academy
Traditional Witchcraft
Year 1: Foundations

Unit 3: Sabbats
Lesson 1: Samhain

Samhain

Prerequisite Lesson

None specified

Objectives

- To align with the seasonal energies of the Sabbat
- To honor the Ancestors
- To honor Tubal Qayin as Lord of Death
- To practice and perform divinatory work (especially scrying)
- To practice and perform ritual

Materials Needed

Stang, candle, lighter

Cauldron, water, lancet

Anvil, hammer

Three knives (red, black, white)

Red Cord

Bread, lipped dish or bowl

Dark beer

Red wine, cup

Incense, holder, charcoal

Carved gourd/pumpkin, tealight candle

Skull (real human OR human-shaped ceramic, glass, crystal, paper-mache, wood, etc)

Lineage chant

Study Notes

Hallowmas, Halloween, All Hallow's Eve, All Saints Day, Witches' New Year, Last Harvest, Blood Harvest, Ancestor Night, Feast of the Dead, Day of the Dead

Rather than provide a solid calendar date for the Sabbats, the way the contemporary mind likes to pinpoint the exact timing of events, is more fruitful, honest, and traditional to think of these agricultural holidays in terms of the strongest point of the season. Our favorite holidays are often anticipated days and even a couple of weeks in advance, with preparatory rituals and traditions. Therefore, the traditional timing for Samhaintide is the couple of weeks surrounding the last harvest. It is the couple of weeks at the end of October and beginning of November, in the northern hemisphere. In the southern hemisphere, it's at the end of April and beginning of May. It is the time when farmers hope to get the last of the grain in from the fields before the cold and snow claim it ("taken by the Sidhe").

Samhain marks the Witches' New Year, and it is popularly known as Halloween. It is the point in the Wheel that is directly opposite to Beltane, and the intents behind the holiday and the season are, subsequently, directly opposite to those of the fertility and mirth of Beltaine.

The veil between the worlds of life and death is thin during this season because it is the time between the years. It is a portal time. It is a time when the veil between the worlds of the living and the dead is the thinnest, and communication and passage between the worlds is easiest. It is a time to commune with deceased ancestors and loved ones. Though the ancients honored and revered their ancestors throughout the year, this was the perfect time of year to set aside sacred time to honor those who had passed.

Of course, since the veil was so thin, it was also expected that some rather nasty spirits might enter through the veil at that time, which would cause folks to be wary. Guardians of various types would be placed at doors and windows and hearth (all the entry ways into the home) to keep unwanted and unwelcome spirits out. The custom of dressing in costume comes from the idea of disguising oneself so as not to be recognized by unfriendly spirits.

Furthermore, it was a time of remembrance. The ancients had a deep respect for their ancestors, and this was a time to remember the deeds of forefathers and foremothers. They would recall the names of the people in their lineage and honor them with feasts and gifts. The ancestors would have a special place in the home during this time.

Samhain once marked the time of sacrifice. In some places, this was the time when animals were slaughtered to ensure food throughout the depths of winter. Identified with the animals, the God also fell to ensure continuing existence.

Traditions
"Feeding the dead" by burying an apple or setting an extra place at the table; carving lanterns from pumpkins or turnips; placing candles in windows; necromancy; eating small, white "cakes of the dead;" lighting bonfires on hilltops; burning wicker men; scrying.

Taboos
Baking bread; eating beans or nuts; traveling after dark.

Animal and Tree Spirit Allies
The Toad is a powerful symbol of transformation, as it grows from tadpole to Toad. It has associations with fertility, magic, fairies, and Witchcraft. Toads secrete a thick white poison through their skin. This "Toad's Milk" or bufotenine is sometimes hallucinogenic, and is said to be an ingredient in some ancient flying ointments. Witches' marks are sometimes referred to as a "Toad's foot," and a birthmark shaped like a Toad is a sure sign of witch blood.

The Elder tree is associated with death and rebirth. The 13th month is a time of endings and balances, and the Elder is a tree of balance. This is a tree of the Faery. If one cuts down this tree without seeking the will of the Tree Spirits and of the Faery, a blight or curse will fall on that person. Her wood is never burned as it is considered bad luck to do so. Elder berries are a potent and delicious medicinal and are used to make wine.

Crane represents longevity and creation through focus. In Celtic lore, Cranes are often associated with the

Underworld and are thought to be heralds of war and death. They are also associated with perseverance due to the fact that they will stand for hours looking into the water and waiting for the right time to strike at fish. The Crane symbolizes "secret knowledge" which is represented by the Ogham script of the Celts, which is said to be based on the shapes of the Crane's legs as they fly.

RITUAL

Note: Adapt this ritual, if you desire. Just make sure to note what changes you made in your debrief.

I prefer to begin with all the tools and materials either on my person (like cords and knives), or placed in a basket at the Center of the Compass. From there, I move things into place, as appropriate. You may also place the items in their final locations before beginning. If your ritual is very simple, or if you work with a minimum of tools, you may choose to keep everything at the base of the Stang and not place anything at the Gates. The choice is entirely yours.

Raise the Stang

Stand with the Stang in the center of your Compass space. (If you have a full complement of tools, you might secure it in a holder, if you have one, using a personal Stang or Distaff to Lay the Compass. If not, feel free to use this one Stang as needed, placing it upright in its central holder wherever it isn't needed as a working tool in your hands.) The cauldron is placed behind the Stang, and the anvil (or Oath Stone) is placed in front of it, with the hammer on top. If you don't have these tools yet, make do. A forked stick, a bowl, and a stone will serve, if needed. Take a moment to energetically connect with the energy of the Forge-fire at the center of the Earth, far below the iron foot of the Stang; and also connect with Star-fire in the heavens, high above but still between the horns of the Stang. Breathe deeply and say, "May the three souls be straight within me." Feel yourself centered.

Lay the Compass

Using your Stang, walk the perimeter of the space, moving in a circle. Mark a circle on the ground by either dragging the Stang or dragging one of your feet. Allow the "lame step" to remind you that you walk between worlds. The Seen and the Unseen are ever present. The Living and the Dead are both here. As one of the Cunning Folk, you lay this compass as a reminder that the hedge is this, and you straddle it.

Open the Gates

Begin by calling West this time.

Stand in the Center and face the West. Hold your arms out in front of you, hands cupped. Say, "I call to the Ocean beyond the West Gate. Open the door from the West, place of Water, Azazel-Qayin's domain. By the cup, the quench tank, and the helm, I call you to open wide the Gate and send forth your road to the center of this, my compass. So mote it be!"

Turn to the East. Hold one arm up, fist raised. Say, "I call to the Sunrise beyond the East Gate. Open the door from the East, place of Fire, Lucifer-Qayin's domain. By the sword, the anvil, and the sun, I call you to open wide the Gate and send forth your road to the center of this, my compass. So mote it be!"

Turn to the South. Hold both arms down by your sides, palms flat and facing the ground. Say, "I call to the Fields beyond the South Gate. Open the door from the South, place of Earth, Goda's domain. By the plate, the soil, and the shield, I call you to open wide the Gate and send forth your road to the center of this, my compass. So mote it be!"

Turn to the North. Hold both arms up, fingers spread wide. Say, "I call to the Winds beyond the North Gate. Open the door from the North, place of Air, Kolyo's domain. By the spear, the wing, and the smoke, I call you to open wide the Gate and send forth your road to the center of this, my compass. So mote it be!"

Working

- Lighting Jack -- Hold your carved pumpkin or gourd (or turnip) in your hands and send energy into it to "wake it up." Call on a specific guardian Spirit, or ask that a guardian from your tribe of spirits comes forward to inhabit the vessel and keep watch over you and your home during Samhain-tide. Light the candle inside the jack-o'-lantern, and set it as a Ward at the edge of the Compass.

- Recitation of Lineage -- Pick up the skull. With pride and love, declare, "I am, *(name), child of (name), child of (name), child of (name), child of (name)*." Go back as many generations as you know. If you want to focus on the matrilineal or patrilineal line, you may. It is equally acceptable to recite the lineage of adoptive and foster families if that is your circumstance and preference.

- Enlivening of Skull -- Still holding the skull, send a thread of energy to the skull, feeling it come alive with the energy of your blood, your breath, your flesh. Say something like, "I invite my ancestors, those names and those unnamed, to be with me, speak with me, eat with me, dance with me, laugh with me during these dark days at the turn of the year. I offer you this vessel, now and always, as a seat in my home." Place the skull at the base of the Stang. In future rituals, always place the skull here. Outside of ritual, place the skull upon your altar or ancestor shrine.

- Dark Beer for Qayin -- At the anvil or Oath Stone, pick up the hammer. Strike the anvil and call out, "Tubal Qayin!" Strike again and call out, "Tubal Qayin!" Strike a third (final) time and call out, "Witch Father!" Pour the dark beer over the anvil/stone or into the cauldron. (If you're inside pour all of it into the cauldron. If you're outside, reserve at least part of it for the cauldron.) Acknowledge with whatever words or gestures come to you that this offering is to Tubelo. It is inappropriate to share a drink, so take a swig from the bottle to share with the Red God, if you feel so moved.

- Scrying -- Sit down in front of the cauldron. Get comfortable. Refresh the incense, if needed. Pour some water into the cauldron if more liquid is needed. Clean the top of a finger with an alcohol swab and prick with a lancet. This works best on the outside edge of a fingertip, where you are not calloused. Keeping your hand below your heart, raise a drop or two of blood. Drop them into the liquid of the cauldron. Gaze at the cauldron, relax your focus, and allow images and impressions to come to you. Don't try to force a conversation with the spirits. They will speak in their own way. You may experience images, sounds, ideas, temperature shifts, sensations, smells. Any of these may seem to generate spontaneously within your own mind, like a stray thought. Let them come. Allow the session to continue as for a little while. You'll probably have a good sense of when you're finished and nothing else is coming through. If needed, you can end the session early and begin to ground by moving into the Red Meal.

Red Meal

Moving counterclockwise, bring the sacrificial meal to the Stang or center of the Compass, while singing the House Song, below. Make at least one full circle as you tread the mill. Three is better.

The Housle Song
(To the tune of <u>Greensleeves</u>)

To Housle now we walk the wheel
We kill tonight the blood red meal
A leftward tread of magic's mill
To feed the Gods and work our Will.

Red! Red is the wine we drink!
Red! Red are the cords we wear!
Red! Red is the blood of God!
And red is the shade of the Housle

Say, "For my Ancestors, my Gods, and Myself, I do this."

Bless the bread with your right hand by saying: "Here is bread, flesh of the Earth, blessed to give us life and strength. I consecrate it in the name of the Old Ones."

Kill the bread by saying: "I take its life and give it to Them." Cut it with the red knife using your left hand.

Bless the wine with your right hand by saying: "Here is wine, blood of the Earth, blessed to give us joy and abundance. I consecrate it in the name of the Old Ones."

Kill the wine by saying: "I take its life and give it to Them." Slide the knife over the top of the cup to cut its throat, using your left hand.

Eat and drink of the Meal, making whatever personal offerings you like into the bowl.

The remainder of the wine is poured into the bread bowl. Dip your finger in and anoint yourself. This can also be used for blessing tools, etc.

The Meal is either given to the ground now (if outside) or later (if inside) with the following Declaration:

"By the Red, and Black and White,
Light in Darkness, Dark in Light --
What we take, we freely give.
We all must die. We all must live.
Above, below, and here are One.
All together -- ALL! (And none!)
Here is shown a Mystery. As I Will, so Mote it Be."

Assignment	Perform the ritual included here, or a close variation of it. Until/unless you have a lot of experience with ritual AND feel very knowledgeable and comfortable with the SCT/RTA system and symbol set, I ask that you not modify it *drastically*. The point of studying this system is to learn this system, which happens by pulling it into your mind, heart, and body. Ritual helps to accomplish that. You're going to have lots of room for experimentation in the 2* and 3* programs of study. If you do modify the rite, please include information about what you deleted, added, it changed.

Your debrief should also include:
- any impressions you had or challenges you experienced during the set-up
- a notation of the date and general time you did the ritual
- who (if anyone) was with you
- impressions, insights, and sensations you had throughout the ritual (during the opening portions, the working, or the meal)
- any challenges you experienced while executive the ritual
- ideas that this ritual sparked for you (either for other rituals or for other creative/philosophical endeavors in your world)
- anything else that you feel should be noted

Additional Resources

BoS Pages Included

Laying the Compass
Opening the Gates
The Housle
Samhain
Samhain Spirit Allies
RTA Samhain Ritual
Samhain Incense Recipe
Ancestors

Red Thread Academy
Traditional Witchcraft
Year 1: Foundations

Unit 3: Sabbats
Lesson 2: Yule

Yule

Prerequisite Lesson None specified

Objectives
- To align with the seasonal energies of the Sabbat
- To practice and perform ritual
- To keep a vigil fire through the night
- To wassail the trees and make offerings to the land spirits
- To invite prosperity into the home

Materials Needed

Stang, candle, lighter
Three knives (red, black, white)
Red Cord
Bread, lipped dish or bowl
Red wine, cup
Incense, holder, charcoal
Skull
Yule candle, log, and/or firewood
Wassail, bowl
Lemon, ribbon, orris powder, cinnamon, ginger, whole cloves, toothpick

---

Study Notes

Winter Solstice, Longest Night, Midwinter, Alban Arthan, Winter Rite

Rather than provide a solid calendar date for the Sabbats, the way the contemporary mind likes to pinpoint the exact timing of events, it is more fruitful, honest, and traditional to think of these agricultural holidays in terms of the strongest point of the season. Our favorite holidays are often anticipated days and even a couple of weeks in advance, with preparatory rituals and traditions. Therefore, the traditional timing for Yuletide is the couple of weeks leading up to the Winter Equinox. The holiday itself is celebrated on the day that is acknowledged as the Longest Night. (Astronomically speaking, three dates are within milliseconds of each other.)

Yule is the shortest day of the year and marks the change of the dark half of the year into the light. This Sabbat celebrates the return of the Sun and the life it will bring.

Solstice celebrations are universal, being celebrated in nearly every culture the world over. Groups as different as Iranians are to the Swedes, Chumash Indians to the peoples of Tibet, and Spain to Germany have very old traditions for the same solar event.

The impetus for the holiday, nearly the world over, is the fear that the failing light of the sun may not return and therefore needs some help. According to many traditions, there are evil spirits that thrive in the darkness and require light and warmth to drive them out. This accounts, in part, for the extensive use of candles and lanterns to drive away the darkness. Of course, the flame of a candle is also similar (though a much smaller representative) to the light of the Sun itself.

Structures have been built, as far back as the dim memory of mankind and beyond, that mark and honor the Winter Solstice. Stonehenge (which marks both Solstices), Newgrange in Ireland, and Maeshowe in the Orkney Islands off the coast of Scotland are some of the most well-known of these ancient pieces of architecture. However, there are also similar structures throughout Europe, Asia, the Middle East, Indonesia and the Americas. One has even been found recently in Africa. In fact, there are even many medieval Catholic churches that were built as solar observatories, capturing part of the importance of the Winter Solstice. (The Church, of course, has to keep track of the Solstices and Equinoxes in order to determine the date of Easter each year.)

The Romans celebrated Saturnalia, which was a combination of the traditions already in use by the Egyptians and Persians. These groups met in trade in Rome, and the Romans sensed both the fun and the significance of the potential for a Solstice holiday. Saturnalia was a 12-day celebration that involved decorating with greenery and burning candles to chase away evil spirits. Naturally, it became a party in the pure Roman style with the passage of time.

Yule was the Norse and Celtic celebration of the Solstice. "Yule" means "feast" or, possibly, "wheel." As with the other cultures, the Celtic and Norse traditions tend to revolve around the return of light, warmth and fertility brought by the Sun. Of course, the peoples to the North had a much rougher time in winter than their neighbors to the South, so their need for the return of light (and heat) may have helped imbue this holiday with special significance.

Boughs of holly were used in decoration because their verdant color was a strong reminder of life in the midst of the white, snow-covered world they lived in. White, interestingly, was a color of death and mourning to the Northern people, and winter was the time of the Earth's death in preparation for rebirth. (Holly was also hung in windows because of its prickly leaves and poisonous berries, which make it excellent for guardianship.)

Mistletoe (also called the golden bough) was especially sacred to the Druids, the priests of the Celts. Hundreds of customs and remedies were established around the mistletoe. However, one tradition from the past seems to influence one of our modern customs quite significantly. In older days, if two opposing armies met for battle under mistletoe, a truce would be called until the next day. This peace under the golden bough has evolved into the kissing under the mistletoe that we currently enjoy.

The Oak King and Holly King conflict is re-played at this time of year, as well. His rival, the Oak King, defeats the Holly King, who rules the waning part of the year. With the return of the Oak King, the sun is once again allowed to gain strength and power in the day. (This hearkens back to the far older concept of the Year King, who would protect the people for one year, and be given much honor and privilege for the sacrifice he is willing to make. In case of need, the Year King would be sacrificed for the good of the people.)

Traditions

Feasting; decorating evergreens; burning a special log; exchanging gifts; kissing under mistletoe; decorating with holly and mistletoe; caroling; ringing bells.

Taboos

Letting the fire go out, traveling after dark.

Animal and Tree Spirit Allies

The Goat's horns indicate an ability to perceive the future and are also associated with weapons and defense. Its thick coat enables it to survive hostile conditions. The Goat was depicted in the zodiac through Capricorn – a time of year for culminating new moves or initiating them. Originally denoting the Goat that was slaughtered, "Yule Goat" now typically refers to a goat-figure made of straw. It is also associated with the custom of wassailing, sometimes referred to as "going Yule Goat" in Scandinavia.

The Holly is the strongest protective herb, offering protection against evil spirits, poisons, short-tempered or angry elementals, thunder and lighting, and uninvited spirits. As an evergreen, it represents immortality and is said to bring luck and prosperity. Holly is also associated with dream magic, clear wisdom and courage. Its flower's petals form an equal-armed "cross" which resembles a star. The berries are poisonous to all but birds.

The Wren was said to be crowned the king of the birds, after riding an eagle to the highest point in the sky, above all other birds, and then soaring above even the eagle! The Wren is noted for its cunning for this stunt, and for the trick of building many false nests to lead away hunters. Breton Druids claimed that it was the wren who first brought down fire from heaven, forever singeing its tail feathers, causing the wren to have its distinctive blunt tail.

RITUAL

Note: Adapt this ritual, if you desire. Just make sure to note what changes you made in your debrief.

I prefer to begin with all the tools and materials either on my person (like cords and knives), or placed in a basket at the Center of the Compass. From there, I move things into place, as appropriate. You may also place the items in their final locations before beginning. If your ritual is very simple, or if you work with a minimum of tools, you may choose to keep everything at the base of the Stang and not place anything at the Gates. The choice is entirely yours.

Raise the Stang

Stand with the Stang in the center of your Compass space. (If you have a full complement of tools, you might secure it in a holder, if you have one, using a personal Stang or Distaff to Lay the Compass. If not, feel free to use this one Stang as needed, placing it upright in its central holder wherever it isn't needed as a working tool in your hands.) The cauldron is placed behind the Stang, and the anvil (or Oath Stone) is placed in front of it, with the hammer on top. If you don't have these tools yet, make do. A forked stick, a bowl, and a stone will serve, if needed. Take a moment to energetically connect with the energy of the Forge-fire at the center of the Earth, far below the iron foot of the Stang; and also connect with Star-fire in the heavens, high above but still between the horns of the Stang. Breathe deeply and say, "May the three souls be straight within me." Feel yourself centered.

Lay the Compass

Using your Stang, walk the perimeter of the space, moving in a circle. Mark a circle on the ground by either dragging the Stang or dragging one of your feet. Allow the "lame step" to remind you that you walk between worlds. The Seen and the Unseen are ever present. The Living and the Dead are both here. As one of the Cunning Folk, you lay this compass as a reminder that the hedge is this, and you straddle it.

Open the Gates

Begin by calling the West this time.

Stand in the Center and face the West. Hold your arms out in front of you, hands cupped. Say, "I call to the Ocean beyond the West Gate. Open the door from the West, place of Water, Azazel-Qayin's domain. By the cup, the quench tank, and the helm, I call you to open wide the Gate and send forth your road to the center of this, my compass. So mote it be!"

Turn to the East. Hold one arm up, fist raised. Say, "I call to the Sunrise beyond the East Gate. Open the door from the East, place of Fire, Lucifer-Qayin's domain. By the steel, the anvil, and the sun, I call you to open wide the Gate and send forth your road to the center of this, my compass. So mote it be!"

Turn to the South. Hold both arms down by your sides, palms flat and facing the ground. Say, "I call to the Fields beyond the South Gate. Open the door from the South, place of Earth, Goda's domain. By the plate, the soil, and the shield, I call you to open wide the Gate and send forth your road to the center of this, my compass. So mote it be!"

Turn to the North. Hold both arms up, fingers spread wide. Say, "I call to the Winds beyond the North Gate. Open the door from the North, place of Air, Kolyo's domain. By the spear, the wing, and the smoke, I call you to open wide the Gate and send forth your road to the center of this, my compass. So mote it be!"

Working

- Vigil Fire ~ Keep a fire burning all night. Stay with it, tending to it as needed. If you have a fire pit or place to keep a fire outside, you can build and keep it there. You can build a fire in your hearth, if you have one. Or, failing all other options, you can light a candle inside your cauldron and keep it going. This isn't always an easy task. The night is long. It invariably becomes a time for self-reflection, much as the winter itself is. But it can also be a time for mirth, family, friends, and craft.
- Wassail the Trees ~ Take the wassail bowl outside, if you aren't already outside. Salute the trees that ring your home. Wish them health and long life, and offer them a drink. Sing the song "Here We Come A-Wassailing" as you go, if you choose. As with other offerings, it is appropriate for you to share the drink, as well, if you are so moved.
- Prosperity Pomander ~ These clove-studded, dried citruses take some time to be fully made, but they are well worth it. They are a reminder of the Sun, and they help bring solar energy and blessings into the home. Prick the skin of the lemon with the toothpick, pierce the whole cloves into the hopes, and roll the whole thing in a mixture of ground orris root, ginger, and cinnamon. (Technically, the cloves will preserve the lemon and prevent rotting, so you don't have to use these spices, but they smell Divine and sunny and add a boost to the prosperity magic!) Place in a dish in your altar while it dries. Once it's dried (or close enough to dry not to drip juice on your floor), you can wrap it in ribbon and hang it in a window or from a mirror.

Red Meal

Moving counterclockwise, bring the sacrificial meal to the Stang or center of the Compass, while singing the

Housle Song, below. Make at least one full circle as you tread the mill. Three is better.

The Housle Song
(To the tune of Greensleeves)

To Housle now we walk the wheel
We kill tonight the blood red meal
A leftward tread of magic's mill
To feed the Gods and work our Will.

Red! Red is the wine we drink!
Red! Red are the cords we wear!
Red! Red is the blood of God!
And red is the shade of the Housle

Say, "For my Ancestors, my Gods, and Myself, I do this."

Bless the bread with your right hand by saying: "Here is bread, flesh of the Earth, blessed to give us life and strength. I consecrate it in the name of the Old Ones."

Kill the bread by saying: "I take its life and give it to Them." Cut it with the red knife using your left hand.

Bless the wine with your right hand by saying: "Here is wine, blood of the Earth, blessed to give us joy and abundance. I consecrate it in the name of the Old Ones."

Kill the wine by saying: "I take its life and give it to Them." Slide the knife over the top of the cup to cut its throat, using your left hand.

Eat and drink of the Meal, making whatever personal offerings you like into the bowl.

The remainder of the wine is poured into the bread bowl. Dip your finger in and anoint yourself. This can also be used for blessing tools, etc.

The Meal is either given to the ground now (if outside) or later (if inside) with the following Declaration:

"By the Red, and Black and White,
Light in Darkness, Dark in Light --
What we take, we freely give.
We all must die. We all must live.
Above, below, and here are One.
All together -- ALL! (And none!)
Here is shown a Mystery. As I Will, so Mote it Be."

Assignment

Perform the ritual included here, or a close variation of it. Until/unless you have a lot of experience with ritual AND feel very knowledgeable and comfortable with the SCT/RTA system and symbol set, I ask that you not modify it *drastically*. The point of studying this system is to learn this system, which happens by pulling it into your mind, heart, and body. Ritual helps to accomplish that. You're going to have lots of room for experimentation in the 2* and 3* programs of study. If you do modify the rite, please include information about what you deleted, added, it changed.

Your debrief should also include:
- any impressions you had or challenges you experienced during the setup
- a notation of the date and general time you did the ritual
- who (if anyone) was with you
- impressions, insights, and sensations you had throughout the ritual (during the opening portions, the working, or the meal)
- any challenges you experienced while executive the ritual
- ideas that this ritual sparked for you (either for other rituals or for other creative/philosophical endeavors in your world)
- anything else that you feel should be noted

Additional Resources

Great video depicting wassailing the apple trees -- https://www.youtube.com/watch?v=EvU2EICTNXU

"Here We Come A-Wassailing" song -- https://www.youtube.com/watch?v=OnvMQMLGSlU

"Here We Come A-Wassailing" -- some lyric variations and notes -- https://mainlynorfolk.info/watersons/songs/herewecomeawassailing.html

BoS Pages Included

Laying the Compass
Opening the Gates
The Housle
Yule
December Spirit Allies
RTA Yule Ritual
Yule Incense Recipe
Here We Come A-Wassailing
Wassail Recipe
Prosperity Pomander

Red Thread Academy
Traditional Witchcraft
Year 1: Foundations

Unit 3: Sabbats
Lesson 3: Imbolc

Imbolc

Prerequisite Lesson

None specified

Objectives

- To align with the seasonal energies of the Sabbat
- To practice and perform ritual
- To connect with Kolyo
- To enliven and bless a candle for working with Kolyo energy throughout the year
- To practice and perform seething as an energy raising technique

Materials Needed

Stang, candle, lighter

Three knives (red, black, white)

Red Cord

Bread, lipped dish or bowl

Red wine, cup

Incense, holder, charcoal

Skull

Novena candle, Kolyo label, packing tape

Florida Water or other perfume

Study Notes

Candlemas, Oiemalg, Oimelc, Bride's Day, Brigid's Day, Brigantia

Rather than provide a solid calendar date for the Sabbats, the way the contemporary mind likes to pinpoint the exact timing of events, it is more fruitful, honest, and traditional to think of these agricultural holidays in terms of the strongest point of the season. Our favorite holidays are often anticipated days and even a couple of weeks in advance, with preparatory rituals and traditions. Therefore, the traditional timing for Imbolctide is the couple of weeks at the end of January and beginning of February, in the northern hemisphere. In the southern hemisphere, it's at the end of July and beginning of August.

Imbolc traditionally marked the calving period, when the animals would begin to bear milk for their young. This is a Sabbat of purification after the long darkness of winter, and the Goddess Brighid is especially honored on this day in Celtic lands, lending her name to the holiday in many places. For us, this is the time of the Black Goddess, who may indeed come to us as one of the Brighids, or as Maman Brigitte (the appellation and image she carries into the Americas with the indentured servants who shared her worship with African slaves on the island plantations of the West Indies. This Brigitte is not just midwife to Life, but midwife to Death as well.) The Black Goddess may also show up as the Morrigan, the Cailleach, or as Kolyo herself.

Imbolc is the mid-point between Winter Solstice and Spring Equinox. It is the time of the year when one begins to notice that the sunlight is waxing once again. In colder climes, like the ones many of our European pagan forebears lived in, this would have been the coldest part of the year. They would know that Spring was on its way, but there was very little physical evidence in the land that gave obvious witness to this fact. In truth, the returning light was about the only thing that really heralded the return of warmth and growth.

Because this was the time of year that the ewes would come into their milk (for the lambs they were about to bear), the holiday was named "Oimelc" in some places. For human women, too, this could be a season of birth. (If you get pregnant at Beltane, and carry the baby to term, you'll be in labor near the beginning of February.)

Brighid is associated with this holiday due, in part, to her association with birthing and midwifery. She was one of the highly loved and honored pan-Celtic Goddesses, and this was an ideal holiday for celebrating her role as midwife and mother. Because of this, some traditions refer to this holiday as "Brighid" or "The Feast of Brighid."

Candlemas, a festival that the Christians picked up on some centuries ago, is also associated with this time of year. Many covens use this time of returning light to make and/or bless their candles.

Imbolc is one of the four Celtic fire festivals, making it one of the Greater Sabbats. Though many covens don't necessarily choose to build a bonfire for this particular Sabbat, it is most appropriate to do so.

Traditions
Candles are lit to represent the strengthening sun; dried sheave dolls are made to represent the Goddess as the young bride to be; Brighid's crosses are crafted; a crown of candles may be worn; this is a traditional day for taking an oath, or an initiation.

Taboos
Harvesting of any kind, including picking flowers.

Animal and Tree Spirit Allies
The Cat is an animal of mystery and magic, largely because she is more active and communicative at night. She is capable of observing multiple worlds (physical and non-physical) at one time without making decisions or passing judgment. She is very independent, accepting affection on her own terms and warning of caution and respect. The Cat is also a symbol of guardianship, attachment and sensuality.

The Willow has very feminine overtones. It is strongly lunar in its energy pattern. Willows are found at the edges of streams and lakes, giving them the elemental powers of both earth and water. The Willow is a water-loving tree and responds to the lunar cycle. Willow is thought to have healing properties over diseases of a damp nature. The Anglo-Saxon welig (willow) means pliancy, and willow is certainly flexible.

In the western tradition, Owl is inextricably associated with the quality of wisdom. This is due in part to its ancient associations with the Goddess Athena and also with its large forward-facing eyes. In folklore, the Owl is associated with death, night, and silence. The Owl is much noted for its unique feather and wing structure which allows it to fly silently. Owl is associated with betrayal of a spouse in the pursuit of being true to oneself, as we see in the stories of both Blodewudd and Lilith.

RITUAL
Note: Adapt this ritual, if you desire. Just make sure to note what changes you made in your debrief.

I prefer to begin with all the tools and materials either on my person (like cords and knives), or placed in a basket at the Center of the Compass. From there, I move things into place, as appropriate. You may also place the items in their final locations before beginning. If your ritual is very simple, or if you work with a minimum of tools, you may choose to keep everything at the base of the Stang and not place anything at the Gates. The choice is entirely yours.

Raise the Stang

Stand with the Stang in the center of your Compass space. (If you have a full complement of tools, you might secure it in a holder, if you have one, using a personal Stang or Distaff to Lay the Compass. If not, feel free to use this one Stang as needed, placing it upright in its central holder wherever it isn't needed as a working tool in your hands.) The cauldron is placed behind the Stang, and the anvil (or Oath Stone) is placed in front of it, with the hammer on top. If you don't have these tools yet, make do. A forked stick, a bowl, and a stone will serve, if needed. Take a moment to energetically connect with the energy of the Forge-fire at the center of the Earth, far below the iron foot of the Stang; and also connect with Star-fire in the heavens, high above but still between the horns of the Stang. Breathe deeply and say, "May the three souls be straight within me." Feel yourself centered.

Lay the Compass

Using your Stang, walk the perimeter of the space, moving in a circle. Mark a circle on the ground by either dragging the Stang or dragging one of your feet. Allow the "lame step" to remind you that you walk between worlds. The Seen and the Unseen are ever present. The Living and the Dead are both here. As one of the Cunning Folk, you lay this compass as a reminder that the hedge is this, and you straddle it.

Open the Gates
Begin by calling the North this time.

Stand in the Center and face the North. Hold both arms up, fingers spread wide. Say, "I call to the Winds beyond the North Gate. Open the door from the North, place of Air, Kolyo's domain. By the spear, the wing, and the smoke, I call you to open wide the Gate and send forth your road to the center of this, my compass. So mote it be!"

Turn to the South. Hold both arms down by your sides, palms flat and facing the ground. Say, "I call to the Fields beyond the South Gate. Open the door from the South, place of Earth, Goda's domain. By the plate, the soil, and the shield, I call you to open wide the Gate and send forth your road to the center of this, my compass. So mote it be!"

Turn to the West. Hold your arms out in front of you, hands cupped. Say, "I call to the Ocean beyond the

West Gate. Open the door from the West, place of Water, Azazel-Qayin's domain. By the cup, the quench tank, and the helm, I call you to open wide the Gate and send forth your road to the center of this, my compass. So mote it be!"

Turn to the East. Hold one arm up, fist raised. Say, "I call to the Sunrise beyond the East Gate. Open the door from the East, place of Fire, Lucifer-Qayin's domain. By the steel, the anvil, and the sun, I call you to open wide the Gate and send forth your road to the center of this, my compass. So mote it be!"

Working
- Kolyo Candle ~ Affix the Kolyo candle label onto a novena jar candle using clear packing tape or an equal mix of school glue and water. You can also design your own Kolyo label or simply write and draw on the glass jar using a sharpie marker. Hold the jar between both hands and send energy into it while you seethe (which is described next). Once ready, keep this candle on your altar all year long. If needed, you can transfer the flame and energy into a new novena.

- Seething ~ Rock back and forth, side to side, in a circle or however the energy encourages you. As discussed in lesson 09-02, the movement will likely start as something controlled and conscious; but the goal is to get out of your own way and allow the energy to move freely through you. Whisper or intone the name Kolyo while you do this. Enliven the candle with the Kolyo energy you are raising.

- Uneasy Seat ~ When you feel compelled to stop, allow yourself to sit still for a moment, sensing the energies around you. You will likely still feel wonky at this point, like you're moving. Maybe you are a little. All of that is okay. Focus on Kolyo and listen for Her voice in your mind and in your heart. Allow your spirit to sense Her and be in communication. See Her, hear Her, feel Her, smell Her, taste Her. Be in close contact with Her. Understand the messages She has for you. Let this continue until you are ready to stop, or She is. Dab Florida Water or another perfume onto your hands, feet, and the back of your neck to fully end the session and come back to yourself (and only yourself).

Red Meal
Moving counterclockwise, bring the sacrificial meal to the Stang or center of the Compass, while singing the Housle Song, below. Make at least one full circle as you tread the mill. Three is better.

<u>The Housle Song</u>
(To the tune of <u>Greensleeves</u>)

To Housle now we walk the wheel
We kill tonight the blood red meal
A leftward tread of magic's mill
To feed the Gods and work our Will.

Red! Red is the wine we drink!
Red! Red are the cords we wear!
Red! Red is the blood of God!
And red is the shade of the Housle

Say, "For my Ancestors, my Gods, and Myself, I do this."

Bless the bread with your right hand by saying: "Here is bread, flesh of the Earth, blessed to give us life and strength. I consecrate it in the name of the Old Ones."

Kill the bread by saying: "I take its life and give it to Them." Cut it with the red knife using your left hand.

Bless the wine with your right hand by saying: "Here is wine, blood of the Earth, blessed to give us joy and abundance. I consecrate it in the name of the Old Ones."

Kill the wine by saying: "I take its life and give it to Them." Slide the knife over the top of the cup to cut its throat, using your left hand.

Eat and drink of the Meal, making whatever personal offerings you like into the bowl.

The remainder of the wine is poured into the bread bowl. Dip your finger in and anoint yourself. This can also be used for blessing tools, etc.

The Meal is either given to the ground now (if outside) or later (if inside) with the following Declaration:

> "By the Red, and Black and White,
> Light in Darkness, Dark in Light --
> What we take, we freely give.
> We all must die. We all must live.
> Above, below, and here are One.
> All together -- ALL! (And none!)
> Here is shown a Mystery. As I Will, so Mote it Be."

Assignment

Perform the ritual included here, or a close variation of it. Until/unless you have a lot of experience with ritual AND feel very knowledgeable and comfortable with the SCT/RTA system and symbol set, I ask that you not modify it *drastically*. The point of studying this system is to learn this system, which happens by pulling it into your mind, heart, and body. Ritual helps to accomplish that. You're going to have lots of room for experimentation in the 2* and 3* programs of study. If you do modify the rite, please include information about what you deleted, added, it changed.

Your debrief should also include:
- any impressions you had or challenges you experienced during the set-up
- a notation of the date and general time you did the ritual
- who (if anyone) was with you
- impressions, insights, and sensations you had throughout the ritual (during the opening portions, the working, or the meal)
- any challenges you experienced while executive the ritual
- ideas that this ritual sparked for you (either for other rituals or for other creative/philosophical endeavors in your world)
- anything else that you feel should be noted

Additional Resources

BoS Pages Included
- Laying the Compass
- Opening the Gates
- The Housle
- Imbolc
- February Spirit Allies
- RTA Imbolc Ritual
- Imbolc Incense Recipe
- Florida Water Recipe
- Brighid
- Morrigan
- Cailleach
- Uneasy Seat
- Seething

Red Thread Academy | Unit 3: Sabbats
Traditional Witchcraft | Lesson 4: Spring Equinox
Year 1: Foundations

Spring Equinox

Prerequisite Lesson None specified

Objectives
- To align with the seasonal energies of the Sabbat
- To practice and perform ritual
- To bring attention to balance, both within and without
- To cleanse the Compass and the Self

Materials Needed

Stang, candle, lighter

Three knives (red, black, white)

Red Cord

Bread, lipped dish or bowl

Red wine, cup

Incense, holder, charcoal

Skull

Broom (ritual besom or practical broom)

Shell, water, salt, evergreen sprig

Candle, oil lamp, or lantern

Study Notes

Spring Equinox, Ostara, Eostre, Easter, Lady Day, Alban Eilir, Festival of Trees

Rather than provide a solid calendar date for the Sabbats, the way the contemporary mind likes to pinpoint the exact timing of events, it is more fruitful, honest, and traditional to think of these agricultural holidays in terms of the strongest point of the season. Our favorite holidays are often anticipated days and even a couple of weeks in advance, with preparatory rituals and traditions. Therefore, the traditional timing for Eastertide is the couple of weeks leading up to the Spring Equinox.

On the Equinoxes, the days and nights are equal, as the Goddess regains her strength and works her magic.

It seems that the most popular/common name for this holiday (and many of the traditions surrounding it) has sprung from the Teutonic Goddess Eostre (or Ostara). She is a fertility Goddess whose symbols are bunnies and eggs and the like. The idea of fertility has definitely stuck close to this time of the year, and even the Christians couldn't get rid of the symbols (or the name) and were forced to adopt some of the imagery into their celebration of their Messiah's resurrection (Easter).

Within Systems that focus on the cycles of the sun, this is one of the four major events in the year. The vernal equinox is the solar event that marks the point of balance between day and night, while moving into longer and longer days. It is viewed as a time of balance with the understanding that we are moving into a time of increased light, action and fertility.

Within the Greek cycle of the Eleusinian Mysteries, this is the time when Persephone returns from her stay with her husband, Hades, in the Underworld. She is welcomed home by her rejoicing mother, Demeter, who is a Goddess of the fields. During Persephone's long absence, the fields gave no food and the land was dark and cold. With her return, flowers spring to life at her feet and the land is blessed with fertility. This is the joy of the reunion between mother and daughter.

This is also one of the two times of year attributed to Aphrodite's ritual/sacred bath. Some groups use this as a time of cleansing and renewal.

Traditions
Painting and dyeing of eggs; balancing eggs on end; balancing Brooks on their brush end; chasing rabbits; playing hide-and-seek games; ringing bells; watching the sunrise.

Taboos
Wearing old garments.

Animal and Tree Spirit Allies
Rabbits are notorious breeders, and are a symbol of the fertility of spring. The expression "mad as a March hare" comes from the rabbit's habit of fighting, courting, and mating during the early spring. The tradition of the "Easter bunny", or Eostre rabbit, reflects this springtime symbolism. Rabbits have always been associated with witchcraft. They are sacred to Hecate and have the peculiar habit of gathering in a circle, the "hare's parliament". Witches are often thought to be able to transform into a rabbit.

Birch Trees represent the Otherworld. This tree is the first to bud and is considered a sign that spring is just around the corner. It is a symbol of new beginnings, the start of new plans and taking significant steps in a forward direction. The Birch is considered a protective wood for women, as it is associated with safe childbirth and protection from the Underworld. It is the wood most commonly used to kindle the magical fire.

The goose is the companion of that ancient and powerful goddess, Hulda, as Mother Goose. The goose is a fierce defender of its family and territory, and many ancient gates and warrior's graves have been adorned with the motif of the goose. We often speak of "a wild goose chase" as geese are notoriously difficult to capture or kill. The goose is a symbol of early springtime, as it denotes both snow and returning light. The goose who lays the golden egg is laying the growing sun of spring.

RITUAL
Note: Adapt this ritual, if you desire. Just make sure to note what changes you made in your debrief.

I prefer to begin with all the tools and materials either on my person (like cords and knives), or placed in a basket at the Center of the Compass. From there, I move things into place, as appropriate. You may also place the items in their final locations before beginning. If your ritual is very simple, or if you work with a minimum of tools, you may choose to keep everything at the base of the Stang and not place anything at the Gates. The choice is entirely yours.

Raise the Stang

Stand with the Stang in the center of your Compass space. (If you have a full complement of tools, you might secure it in a holder, if you have one, using a personal Stang or Distaff to Lay the Compass. If not, feel free to use this one Stang as needed, placing it upright in its central holder wherever it isn't needed as a working tool in your hands.) The cauldron is placed behind the Stang, and the anvil (or Oath Stone) is placed in front of it, with the hammer on top. If you don't have these tools yet, make do. A forked stick, a bowl, and a stone will serve, if needed. Take a moment to energetically connect with the energy of the Forge-fire at the center of the Earth, far below the iron foot of the Stang; and also connect with Star-fire in the heavens, high above but still between the horns of the Stang. Breathe deeply and say, "May the three souls be straight within me." Feel yourself centered.

Lay the Compass

Using your Stang, walk the perimeter of the space, moving in a circle. Mark a circle on the ground by either dragging the Stang or dragging one of your feet. Allow the "lame step" to remind you that you walk between worlds. The Seen and the Unseen are ever present. The Living and the Dead are both here. As one of the Cunning Folk, you lay this compass as a reminder that the hedge is this, and you straddle it.

Open the Gates

Begin by calling the North this time.

Stand in the Center and face the North. Hold both arms up, fingers spread wide. Say, "I call to the Winds beyond the North Gate. Open the door from the North, place of Air, Kolyo's domain. By the spear, the wing, and the smoke, I call you to open wide the Gate and send forth your road to the center of this, my compass. So mote it be!"

Turn to the South. Hold both arms down by your sides, palms flat and facing the ground. Say, "I call to the Fields beyond the South Gate. Open the door from the South, place of Earth, Goda's domain. By the plate, the soil, and the shield, I call you to open wide the Gate and send forth your road to the center of this, my compass. So mote it be!"

Turn to the West. Hold your arms out in front of you, hands cupped. Say, "I call to the Ocean beyond the West Gate. Open the door from the West, place of Water, Azazel-Qayin's domain. By the cup, the quench tank, and the helm, I call you to open wide the Gate and send forth your road to the center of this, my compass. So mote it be!"

Turn to the East. Hold one arm up, fist raised. Say, "I call to the Sunrise beyond the East Gate. Open the door from the East, place of Fire, Lucifer-Qayin's domain. By the steel, the anvil, and the sun, I call you to open wide the Gate and send forth your road to the center of this, my compass. So mote it be!"

Working
- Cleansing the Space ~ Using the Cleansing Chants (attached) and accompanying tools (broom, salt-water in a shell with evergreen sprig, smoking incense, and lantern or lamp) energetically clean and cleanse the sacred space in which you work. You can, of course, go a step further and cleanse the whole house and/or property. This is a great time of year for it! Visualize all the staleness of winter, all the remnants of last year's harvest, all being swept and washed away.

- Cleansing the Self ~ Using the same tools, energetically cleanse yourself. You probably already bathed before ritual, but you can use these same tools to cleanse yourself and your energy. The broom is the only one that may feel awkward, due to size and shape. Use the evergreen sprig instead.

- Standing the Broom ~ You could also use an egg for this, but since the focus of this ritual is on cleansing, the broom seemed the better choice. Center yourself in your newly cleanse space. Feel the balance within you. Work on finding that external point of balance, via the broom. Try to get it to stand on its own long enough and steady enough that you can walk away from it. Once you've found the "sweet spot," it's often easy to do again and again -- any day of the year. The size and shape of the broom affects this very little. I've done this with an angled synthetic broom in a discount department store aisle.

Red Meal
Moving counterclockwise, bring the sacrificial meal to the Stang or center of the Compass, while singing the Housle Song, below. Make at least one full circle as you tread the mill. Three is better.

<u>The Housle Song</u>
(To the tune of <u>Greensleeves</u>)

To Housle now we walk the wheel
We kill tonight the blood red meal
A leftward tread of magic's mill
To feed the Gods and work our Will.

Red! Red is the wine we drink!
Red! Red are the cords we wear!
Red! Red is the blood of God!
And red is the shade of the Housle

Say, "For my Ancestors, my Gods, and Myself, I do this."

Bless the bread with your right hand by saying: "Here is bread, flesh of the Earth, blessed to give us life and strength. I consecrate it in the name of the Old Ones."
Kill the bread by saying: "I take its life and give it to Them." Cut it with the red knife using your left hand.
Bless the wine with your right hand by saying: "Here is wine, blood of the Earth, blessed to give us joy and abundance. I consecrate it in the name of the Old Ones."

Kill the wine by saying: "I take its life and give it to Them." Slide the knife over the top of the cup to cut its throat, using your left hand.

Eat and drink of the Meal, making whatever personal offerings you like into the bowl.

The remainder of the wine is poured into the bread bowl. Dip your finger in and anoint yourself. This can also be used for blessing tools, etc.

The Meal is either given to the ground now (if outside) or later (if inside) with the following Declaration:

> "By the Red, and Black and White,
> Light in Darkness, Dark in Light --
> What we take, we freely give.
> We all must die. We all must live.
> Above, below, and here are One.
> All together -- ALL! (And none!)
> Here is shown a Mystery. As I Will, so Mote it Be."

Assignment

Perform the ritual included here, or a close variation of it. Until/unless you have a lot of experience with ritual AND feel very knowledgeable and comfortable with the SCT/RTA system and symbol set, I ask that you not modify it *drastically*. The point of studying this system is to learn this system, which happens by pulling it into your mind, heart, and body. Ritual helps to accomplish that. You're going to have lots of room for experimentation in the 2* and 3* programs of study. If you do modify the rite, please include information about what you deleted, added, it changed.

Your debrief should also include:
- any impressions you had or challenges you experienced during the set-up
- a notation of the date and general time you did the ritual
- who (if anyone) was with you
- impressions, insights, and sensations you had throughout the ritual (during the opening portions, the working, or the meal)
- any challenges you experienced while executive the ritual
- ideas that this ritual sparked for you (either for other rituals or for other creative/philosophical endeavors in your world)
- anything else that you feel should be noted

Additional Resources

BoS Pages Included

Laying the Compass
Opening the Gates
The Housle
Spring Equinox
March Spirit Allies
RTA Spring Equinox Ritual

Red Thread Academy
Traditional Witchcraft
Year 1: Foundations

Unit 3: Sabbats
Lesson 5: Beltaine

Beltaine

Prerequisite Lesson

None specified

Objectives

- To align with the seasonal energies of the Sabbat
- To practice and perform ritual
- To connect with Lucifer-Qayin
- To practice and perform guided meditation
- To be introduced to the Brocken and the Sabbat Grounds

Materials Needed

Stang, candle, lighter

Three knives (red, black, white)

Red Cord

Bread, lipped dish or bowl

Red wine, cup

Mugwort, lemongrass (½ tsp each)

Honey

Incense, holder, charcoal

Skull

Study Notes

May Day, Walpurgisnacht, Roodmas

Rather than provide a solid calendar date for the Sabbats, the way the contemporary mind likes to pinpoint the exact timing of events, it is more fruitful, honest, and traditional to think of these agricultural holidays in terms of the strongest point of the season. Our favorite holidays are often anticipated days and even a couple of weeks in advance, with preparatory rituals and traditions. Therefore, the traditional timing for Beltanetide is the couple of weeks at the end of April and beginning of May, in the northern hemisphere. In the southern hemisphere, it's at the end of October and beginning of November.

The Earth is being warmed by the Sun, bringing forth new life. Beltane is one of four Celtic fire festivals that are associated with the agricultural turns of the seasons. It is, therefore, one of the Greater Sabbats, and it marks the opposite end of the Wheel from Samhain.

Traditional Beltane activities include blowing horns (a symbol of the male reproductive power) and gathering and eating flowers, making garlands, hanging greenery (flowers being the symbols of female fertility). Hawthorn was especially sacred to this holiday. In fact, old traditions dictate that the date of Beltane is set by the flowering of the local Hawthorn trees.

Communing with fairies has frequently been associated with this holiday, and a lot of lore surrounds ways to contact and work with fairy energy during this time.

Other traditional Beltane activities include the Maypole dance and the lighting of balefires. The sacred bonfires were used in many ways. Many people would jump balefires for fertility or pass cattle and other livestock between bonfires for protection, fertility, and purification.

Beltane is linked to the Sacred Marriage (hieros gamos), and fertility is almost universally celebrated on this Sabbat. Many Wiccan traditions see this as the wedding day of the God and Goddess. Mothers and fertility are especially honored, and the contemporary secular holiday of Mother's Day may have Pagan roots associated with this festival.

Walpurgisnacht is a May Eve celebration that originated in Southern Germany (Bavaria). It started as a celebration of Catholic Saint (Walpurga), who was canonized on May 1st, but whose feast day became associated with the lingering Pagan traditions in the area and eventually became linked to an actual celebration of Witches that is celebrated even today in Germany, Sweden, Finland, Holland, and the Czech Republic.

Traditions

Dancing around the Maypole; lighting the balefire at moonrise on a hilltop; feasting; rising at dawn to gather dew and to pick flowers to decorate with; leaping the balefire for luck; romancing in the fields; playing "ding-dong-ditch" and leaving gifts behind.

Taboos

Giving away fire or food.

Animal and Tree Spirit Allies

The Bull (*Tarbh*) is associated with health, potency, beneficence, fertility, abundance, prosperity, and power. The number of cattle owned were an indicator of wealth. The Cow (Bo) represents nourishment, motherhood and the Goddess. In Celtic lands, Cows have long been considered sacred. In Britain there were sacred herds of white cattle. Ireland was gifted with cattle when three Cows emerged from the sea – one red, one white, and one black.

Hawthorns are often used in hedges (some linguistic studies show that its name may actually mean "hedge thorn"). The Hawthorn has very sharp thorns that are sometimes used for ritual tattoos. Its white flowers are often woven into garlands for doors and Maypoles at Beltane. Indeed, long ago Beltane was reckoned by the first flowering of the Hawthorn tree. Its wood is the traditional material for the Maypole itself.

No animal is a better example of the power of community than the bee. Each bee in a hive has a specific function which she will perform even if it means giving her life for the hive. Because they are the agent that carries the reproductive pollen from one plant to fertilize another, bees are strongly associated with fertility and abundance. Honey was anciently the only source for a sweetener. Thus, the bee has come to symbolize the sweetness of life.

RITUAL
Note: Adapt this ritual, if you desire. Just make sure to note what changes you made in your debrief.

I prefer to begin with all the tools and materials either on my person (like cords and knives), or placed in a basket at the Center of the Compass. From there, I move things into place, as appropriate. You may also place the items in their final locations before beginning. If your ritual is very simple, or if you work with a minimum of tools, you may choose to keep everything at the base of the Stang and not place anything at the Gates. The choice is entirely yours.

Raise the Stang

Stand with the Stang in the center of your Compass space. (If you have a full complement of tools, you might secure it in a holder, if you have one, using a personal Stang or Distaff to Lay the Compass. If not, feel free to use this one Stang as needed, placing it upright in its central holder wherever it isn't needed as a working tool in your hands.) The cauldron is placed behind the Stang, and the anvil (or Oath Stone) is placed in front of it, with the hammer on top. If you don't have these tools yet, make do. A forked stick, a bowl, and a stone will serve, if needed. Take a moment to energetically connect with the energy of the Forge-fire at the center of the Earth, far below the iron foot of the Stang; and also connect with Star-fire in the heavens, high above but still between the horns of the Stang. Breathe deeply and say, "May the three souls be straight within me." Feel yourself centered.

Lay the Compass

Using your Stang, walk the perimeter of the space, moving in a circle. Mark a circle on the ground by either dragging the Stang or dragging one of your feet. Allow the "lame step" to remind you that you walk between worlds. The Seen and the Unseen are ever present. The Living and the Dead are both here. As one of the Cunning Folk, you lay this compass as a reminder that the hedge is this, and you straddle it.

Open the Gates
Begin by calling the East this time.

Stand in the Center and face the East. Hold one arm up, fist raised. Say, "I call to the Sunrise beyond the East Gate. Open the door from the East, place of Fire, Lucifer-Qayin's domain. By the steel, the anvil, and the sun, I call you to open wide the Gate and send forth your road to the center of this, my compass. So mote it be!"

Turn to the West. Hold your arms out in front of you, hands cupped. Say, "I call to the Ocean beyond the West Gate. Open the door from the West, place of Water, Azazel-Qayin's domain. By the cup, the quench tank, and the helm, I call you to open wide the Gate and send forth your road to the center of this, my compass. So mote it be!"

Turn to the North. Hold both arms up, fingers spread wide. Say, "I call to the Winds beyond the North Gate. Open the door from the North, place of Air, Kolyo's domain. By the spear, the wing, and the smoke, I call you to open wide the Gate and send forth your road to the center of this, my compass. So mote it be!"

Turn to the South. Hold both arms down by your sides, palms flat and facing the ground. Say, "I call to the Fields beyond the South Gate. Open the door from the South, place of Earth, Goda's domain. By the plate, the soil, and the shield, I call you to open wide the Gate and send forth your road to the center of this, my compass. So mote it be!"

Working

- Sabbat Wine ~ Prepare Sabbat Wine for yourself by steeping a tablespoon of mugwort (or a blend of mugwort and lemongrass) in a cup of warm red wine for 10 minutes. Remove the herbs (easiest done when using a tea ball), and add raw honey to sweeten. I like to use a local sweet red wine and local honey, as well as local herbs (when I can get them). Drink the wine without gulping or chugging. Give it time to work with you to open your psychic senses.

- Guided Meditation ~ Journey through the attached guided meditation either by reading it aloud while recording (prior to ritual) and then playing it back for yourself during the ritual, or by reading through the meditation prior to ritual so that you are familiar enough with the steps, and then doing your best to follow those steps without guidance. You can also read through the meditation after you feel the soft focus from the wine wash over you, doing what you can to walk between the worlds of reading and meditating. (Or you can listen to the recorded version on the RTA YouTube channel.)

Red Meal

Moving counterclockwise, bring the sacrificial meal to the Stang or center of the Compass, while singing the Housle Song, below. Make at least one full circle as you tread the mill. Three is better.

<u>The Housle Song</u>
(To the tune of <u>Greensleeves</u>)

To Housle now we walk the wheel
We kill tonight the blood red meal
A leftward tread of magic's mill
To feed the Gods and work our Will.

Red! Red is the wine we drink!
Red! Red are the cords we wear!
Red! Red is the blood of God!
And red is the shade of the Housle

Say, "For my Ancestors, my Gods, and Myself, I do this."

Bless the bread with your right hand by saying: "Here is bread, flesh of the Earth, blessed to give us life and strength. I consecrate it in the name of the Old Ones."

Kill the bread by saying: "I take its life and give it to Them." Cut it with the red knife using your left hand.

Bless the wine with your right hand by saying: "Here is wine, blood of the Earth, blessed to give us joy and abundance. I consecrate it in the name of the Old Ones."

Kill the wine by saying: "I take its life and give it to Them." Slide the knife over the top of the cup to cut its throat, using your left hand.

Eat and drink of the Meal, making whatever personal offerings you like into the bowl.

The remainder of the wine is poured into the bread bowl. Dip your finger in and anoint yourself. This can also be used for blessing tools, etc.

The Meal is either given to the ground now (if outside) or later (if inside) with the following Declaration:

> "By the Red, and Black and White,
> Light in Darkness, Dark in Light --
> What we take, we freely give.
> We all must die. We all must live.
> Above, below, and here are One.
> All together -- ALL! (And none!)
> Here is shown a Mystery. As I Will, so Mote it Be."

<u>Assignment</u>

Perform the ritual included here, or a close variation of it. Until/unless you have a lot of experience with ritual AND feel very knowledgeable and comfortable with the SCT/RTA system and symbol set, I ask that you not modify it *drastically*. The point of studying this system is to learn this system, which happens by pulling it into your mind, heart, and body. Ritual helps to accomplish that. You're going to have lots of room for experimentation in the 2* and 3* programs of study. If you do modify the rite, please include information about what you deleted, added, it changed.

Your debrief should also include:
- any impressions you had or challenges you experienced during the set-up
- a notation of the date and general time you did the ritual
- who (if anyone) was with you
- impressions, insights, and sensations you had throughout the ritual (during the opening portions, the working, or the meal)
- any challenges you experienced while executive the ritual
- ideas that this ritual sparked for you (either for other rituals or for other creative/philosophical endeavors in your world)
- anything else that you feel should be noted

<u>Additional Resources</u>

Beltane guided meditation script

<u>Beltaine Guided Meditation Recording on YouTube</u> -- https://youtu.be/_cx3OYDXiXo

---

<u>BoS Pages Included</u>

Laying the Compass
Opening the Gates
The Housle
Beltane
May Spirit Allies
RTA Beltaine Ritual
RTA Walpurgisnacht Flight
Sabbat Wine Recipe

Beltaine

If you replaced the Stang at the center of the compass, retrieve it so it can be with you.

Sit in a comfortable position. You may like the Stang under, across, or between your legs, held in your hand, or across your chest throughout the duration of this mediation as your riding pole and connection to the World Tree. Swaying or rocking is often very helpful for our practice of flying out or faring forth.

Close your eyes and and follow your breath. Take long, slow inhalations, followed by long, slow exhalations. As you breathe, you notice a white mist settling around your body. It quickly becomes a thick fog obscuring sight and sound. The fog is cool and numbing, and you find yourself a little tingling and disoriented. A strange heaviness pervades your body as you continue to breathe deeply, in and out.

After a moment, the fog begins to lift, and you also feel lighter. You stand, gripping your Stang and use it as a walking stick. You move a few paces off, and the fog clings a little less, though you still can't see where you are. You take another step and are able to recognize your surroundings, though they look altered in ways that are difficult to describe fully. You notice yourself and your surroundings for a moment, seeing both this familiar place and your own self with the eyes of Spirit.

You move out of this familiar space and into unknown territory. You're surprised how rapidly the landscape shifts into unfamiliar scenery. You may have thought you knew this place well, but only a few yards from familiar ground, you find yourself confronted with a hedgerow unlike any that could have been there before. It is thick, dense, made of several kinds of hedge trees, and it is quite a lot taller than most hedges. Far on the other side of this hedge, the Dancing Place of the Witches awaits you. You can hear the distant call of the pipes and drums and bells. The sounds are so distant, you are sure it isn't your ears that hear them. You smell the wood smoke and feast meats. You can taste the promise of mead and kisses and laughter beyond this hedge.

You look down the row to the left and the right and don't see a gate. There may be one if you talk a walk, of course. A rabbit pops up from a burrow about six feet away from you. Yes, under is an option. You lean on your Stang to think and it leans back. Ah! Over it is.

You straddle the Stang and lift into air. You notice a star shining from the candle flame between the horns of the Stang and are reminded of the iron foot at the base. Be aware of the sensations you experience as you mount the Stang.

From above the hedge, you notice a wild landscape. A patchwork of ancient forests, fertile countryside, villages, hills, and a mountain range looming in the distance. It is here where the Witches dance. The peak you seek is the Brocken. The highest. Your soul knows the way.

You land at the Hexentanzenplatz (Witches' Dancing Place) to find the Sabbat in full revelry. More Witches than you'd ever dreamed are gathered here. Witches of every color, from every place, who have made covenant with the Witchfather are here to celebrate the great Beltaine Sabbat. And not just Witches are here. As you take a moment to observe the stunning spectacle, you see many Familiars, too.

This Dance is a revel for all the senses and offers any delights you care to indulge. Food, sex, music, drink, wisdom, mysticism, laughter, scent, beauty, inspiration. You stay as long as you choose, taking your fill, before eventually returning the way you came (across the sky, over the hedge, and back into the fog).

To reconnect fully with your body, move it, eat something heavy (but not too much of it at once), stomp, clap, and debrief.

Red Thread Academy — Unit 3: Sabbats
Traditional Witchcraft — Lesson 6: Midsummer
Year 1: Foundations

Midsummer

Prerequisite Lesson

None specified

Objectives

- To align with the seasonal energies of the Sabbat
- To practice and perform ritual
- To celebrate with a bonfire

Materials Needed

Stang, candle, lighter

Three knives (red, black, white)

Red Cord

Bread, lipped dish or bowl

Red wine, cup

Incense, holder, charcoal

Skull

Fire pit, fire wood, kindling OR

Cauldron, Epsom salt, rubbing alcohol

Recorded music or musical instruments, drums, etc.

Study Notes

Litha, Aerra Litha, Summer Solstice, St. John's Day, Alban Hefin, Mother Night

Rather than provide a solid calendar date for the Sabbats, the way the contemporary mind likes to pinpoint the exact timing of events, it is more fruitful, honest, and traditional to think of these agricultural holidays in terms of the strongest point of the season. Our favorite holidays are often anticipated days and even a couple of weeks in advance, with preparatory rituals and traditions. Therefore, the traditional timing for Midsummertide is the couple of weeks leading up to the Summer Solstice.

This is the longest day of the year. All around, Nature is awash in abundance and life.

This is one of the Lesser Sabbats to most Neo-Pagans, as it is one of the solar holidays. Many Wiccan groups refer to this holiday as Litha.

The Oak King/Holly King story is once again enacted, and this time the Holly King takes power and the light of the sun begins to diminish. The Holly King is the ruler of the dark half of the year, and his reign signals the beginning of the sun's wane in energy.

Midsummer is the height of agricultural work, and this Sabbat (which is usually celebrated in the cooler nighttime hours), is also the height of summer merry-making.

Traditions
Huge bonfires to encourage fertility, health and love; divination magic (especially in dreams); gathering herbs; lighting and rolling Catherine's Wheels; love magic; ringing bells at noon.

Taboos
Giving away fire; sleeping away from home; neglecting animals.

Animal and Tree Spirit Allies
The Stag is the male aspect of the deer. As such, some discussion of the qualities of deer in general is helpful to understand Stag. Deer are associated with gentleness, innocence and a luring to new adventure. Many legends exist in which deer lure hunters and/or kings into the forest for adventures. The Stag is a symbol of pride and independence. He is an example of grace, majesty, integrity, poise and dignity. The Stag is a symbol of fertility and rampant sexuality, which is also related to the Lord of the Hunt and the Horned Gods.

Ancient Celts observed the oak's massive growth and impressive expanse. They took this as a clear sign that the oak was to be honored for its endurance, and noble presence. Wearing oak leaves was a sign of special status among many ancient European peoples. There are accounts that trace the name "druid" to duir, the Celtic term for the oak. The oak is a tree of protection and strength.

Robins are very territorial, and their red breasts signal other males to leave their space. Even their bright and cheery song is used as a method of battling with other males for dominance over territory. The Robin's bright blue egg is distinctive in color. Both male and female Robins share in the feeding of the young. The Norse associated the bird with Thor and considered it to be a creature of the storm.

RITUAL
Note: Adapt this ritual, if you desire. Just make sure to note what changes you made in your debrief.

I prefer to begin with all the tools and materials either on my person (like cords and knives), or placed in a basket at the Center of the Compass. From there, I move things into place, as appropriate. You may also place the items in their final locations before beginning. If your ritual is very simple, or if you work with a minimum of tools, you may choose to keep everything at the base of the Stang and not place anything at the Gates. The choice is entirely yours.

Raise the Stang
Stand with the Stang in the center of your Compass space. (If you have a full complement of tools, you might secure it in a holder, if you have one, using a personal Stang or Distaff to Lay the Compass. If not, feel free to use this one Stang as needed, placing it upright in its central holder wherever it isn't needed as a working tool in your hands.) The cauldron is placed behind the Stang, and the anvil (or Oath Stone) is

placed in front of it, with the hammer on top. If you don't have these tools yet, make do. A forked stick, a bowl, and a stone will serve, if needed. Take a moment to energetically connect with the energy of the Forge-fire at the center of the Earth, far below the iron foot of the Stang; and also connect with Star-fire in the heavens, high above but still between the horns of the Stang. Breathe deeply and say, "May the three souls be straight within me." Feel yourself centered.

Lay the Compass

Using your Stang, walk the perimeter of the space, moving in a circle. Mark a circle on the ground by either dragging the Stang or dragging one of your feet. Allow the "lame step" to remind you that you walk between worlds. The Seen and the Unseen are ever present. The Living and the Dead are both here. As one of the Cunning Folk, you lay this compass as a reminder that the hedge is this, and you straddle it.

Open the Gates

Begin by calling the East this time.

Stand in the Center and face the East. Hold one arm up, fist raised. Say, "I call to the Sunrise beyond the East Gate. Open the door from the East, place of Fire, Lucifer-Qayin's domain. By the steel, the anvil, and the sun, I call you to open wide the Gate and send forth your road to the center of this, my compass. So mote it be!"

Turn to the West. Hold your arms out in front of you, hands cupped. Say, "I call to the Ocean beyond the West Gate. Open the door from the West, place of Water, Azazel-Qayin's domain. By the cup, the quench tank, and the helm, I call you to open wide the Gate and send forth your road to the center of this, my compass. So mote it be!"

Turn to the North. Hold both arms up, fingers spread wide. Say, "I call to the Winds beyond the North Gate. Open the door from the North, place of Air, Kolyo's domain. By the spear, the wing, and the smoke, I call you to open wide the Gate and send forth your road to the center of this, my compass. So mote it be!"

Turn to the South. Hold both arms down by your sides, palms flat and facing the ground. Say, "I call to the Fields beyond the South Gate. Open the door from the South, place of Earth, Goda's domain. By the plate, the soil, and the shield, I call you to open wide the Gate and send forth your road to the center of this, my compass. So mote it be!"

Working

- Bonfire or Cauldron Fire ~ This is best done outside, for obvious reasons, but it is possible to build a very, very small sacred fire indoors in a cauldron with Epsom salt and rubbing alcohol. Another alternative is to place a candle in your cauldron. Of course, the preference here is to build a fire outside, if at all possible. It doesn't have to be large. Midsummer fires are wonderful for revelry, music, dancing, and the high spirits that come with the joys of summer. Play music, make music. Dance. The type of music and style of dance don't matter. Get your blood up, your energy up. Have fun! Keep it going as long into the night as you like. This is a celebration of life, of the ability to DO, and of the ripeness of the world.

Red Meal

Moving counterclockwise, bring the sacrificial meal to the Stang or center of the Compass, while singing the Housle Song, below. Make at least one full circle as you tread the mill. Three is better.

The Housle Song
(To the tune of *Greensleeves*)

To Housle now we walk the wheel
We kill tonight the blood red meal
A leftward tread of magic's mill
To feed the Gods and work our Will.

Red! Red is the wine we drink!
Red! Red are the cords we wear!
Red! Red is the blood of God!
And red is the shade of the Housle

Say, "For my Ancestors, my Gods, and Myself, I do this."

Bless the bread with your right hand by saying: "Here is bread, flesh of the Earth, blessed to give us life and strength. I consecrate it in the name of the Old Ones."

Kill the bread by saying: "I take its life and give it to Them." Cut it with the red knife using your left hand.

Bless the wine with your right hand by saying: "Here is wine, blood of the Earth, blessed to give us joy and abundance. I consecrate it in the name of the Old Ones."

Kill the wine by saying: "I take its life and give it to Them." Slide the knife over the top of the cup to cut its throat, using your left hand.

Eat and drink of the Meal, making whatever personal offerings you like into the bowl.

The remainder of the wine is poured into the bread bowl. Dip your finger in and anoint yourself. This can also be used for blessing tools, etc.

The Meal is either given to the ground now (if outside) or later (if inside) with the following Declaration:

"By the Red, and Black and White,
Light in Darkness, Dark in Light --
What we take, we freely give.
We all must die. We all must live.
Above, below, and here are One.
All together -- ALL! (And none!)
Here is shown a Mystery. As I Will, so Mote it Be."

Assignment

Perform the ritual included here, or a close variation of it. Until/unless you have a lot of experience with ritual AND feel very knowledgeable and comfortable with the SCT/RTA system and symbol set, I ask that you not modify it *drastically*. The point of studying this system is to learn this system, which happens by pulling it into your mind, heart, and body. Ritual helps to accomplish that. You're going to have lots of room for experimentation in the 2* and 3* programs of study. If you do modify the rite, please include information about what you deleted, added, it changed.

Your debrief should also include:
- any impressions you had or challenges you experienced during the set-up
- a notation of the date and general time you did the ritual
- who (if anyone) was with you
- impressions, insights, and sensations you had throughout the ritual (during the opening portions, the working, or the meal)
- any challenges you experienced while executive the ritual
- ideas that this ritual sparked for you (either for other rituals or for other creative/philosophical endeavors in your world)
- anything else that you feel should be noted

Additional Resources

BoS Pages Included

Laying the Compass
Opening the Gates
The Housle
Midsummer
June Spirit Allies
RTA Midsummer Ritual
Balefire

Red Thread Academy
Traditional Witchcraft
Year 1: Foundations

Unit 3: Sabbats
Lesson 7: Lammas

Lammas

Prerequisite Lesson

None specified

Objectives

- To align with the seasonal energies of the Sabbat
- To practice and perform ritual
- To connect with Goda
- To honor the beginning of the harvest cycle
- To make personal oaths

Materials Needed

Stang, candle, lighter

Three knives (red, black, white)

Red Cord

Bread, lipped dish or bowl

Red wine, cup

Incense, holder, charcoal

Skull

Green corn husks (removed from corn), twine

Bread, corn, tomatoes, melons, local produce that's in season

Study Notes

Lughnasadh, Lugh, Harvest Home, 1st Harvest, Bread, Festival of First Fruits

Rather than provide a solid calendar date for the Sabbats, the way the contemporary mind likes to pinpoint the exact timing of events, it is more fruitful, honest, and traditional to think of these agricultural holidays in terms of the strongest point of the season. Our favorite holidays are often anticipated days and even a couple of weeks in advance, with preparatory rituals and traditions. Therefore, the traditional timing for Lammastide is the couple of weeks at the end of July and beginning of August, in the northern hemisphere. In the southern hemisphere, it's at the end of January and beginning of February.

It is a time of sacrifice and also of giving thanks for what we have, as well as making offerings of gratitude. As summer passes, we remember its warmth and bounty in the food we eat. Every meal is an act of attunement with nature, and we are reminded that nothing in the universe is constant.

This is another of the Greater Sabbats, one of the High Holy Days – a Celtic fire festival based on the agricultural wheel. One of the common names for this holiday is Lammas, which means "loaf mass." Because this is the first of the harvest festivals, grain and the first fruits were often blessed and honored at this holiday. The loaf mass was a Catholic adaptation of the blessing of the grain that clearly had Pagan roots. This holiday gave rise to country fairs that still happen at this time of year. The country craft fairs also give unknown honor to the Celtic God Lugh (since he is the master of all crafts).

This Sabbat is also often called Lughnasadh, and in this case it is named after the Pan-Celtic God Lugh whose name comes from "lugio" meaning "oath." Marriages and other contracts were made at this time. The story of Lugh/Lleu has been intimately tied with the "oath." This holiday is named after Lugh because he instituted funeral games in honor of Tailtiu, his foster-mother, who died after clearing a forest for cultivation.

Traditional activities include picking bilberries (as representative of all of Earth's bounty), playing games, having contests of wit and strength, and making a corn dolly. The corn dolly represents the harvest itself and is ploughed or burned in the spring to prepare for the next sowing and harvest cycle.

Traditions
Grain harvesting; feasting; making corn dollies; building and burning a Wicker Man; another traditional day for oaths and initiations; spear throwing and other sports challenges (in honor of Lugh).

Taboos
Not sharing food with others.

Animal and Tree Spirit Allies
The Horse is associated with the female Divine, the land, and travel both on the inner and outer planes. It is connected to the Sun and is a symbol of sexual desires. Furthermore, it is associated with power and freedom, divination, the spread of civilization, birth. Wind and sea foam often signify the power of the Horse. The Horse is often a phantom creature or provoker of nightmares, who get their name from her, as Mare is an Irish Goddess. Sovereignty is another aspect of the Horse.

Apple represents the choice between similar and equally attractive things. It is one of the "Seven Chieftain Trees" of the Celts. It's fruit and bark are used in tanning. It is related to the rose family, along with Hawthorn, and so it develops thorns from spurs on its branches. The Apple is associated with love spells, likely due to its associations with Aphrodite. Avalon, a sacred Celtic land, is named the "Isle of Apples."

The Swan is often depicted with a silver or gold chain around the neck in Celtic legends -- possibly a carry-over from the Aphrodite tradition of the golden sash. The Swan is very prominent in love stories in Celtic lands, including the tale of Oenghus and Yewberry (who is a Swan Maiden). Swan is associated with Otherworldly travel and migration of the Soul. This bird's skin and feathers were used to make the bard's ceremonial cloak. Swans are also intimately linked with shape-shifting.

RITUAL
Note: Adapt this ritual, if you desire. Just make sure to note what changes you made in your debrief.

I prefer to begin with all the tools and materials either on my person (like cords and knives), or placed in a basket at the Center of the Compass. From there, I move things into place, as appropriate. You may also place the items in their final locations before beginning. If your ritual is very simple, or if you work with a minimum of tools, you may choose to keep everything at the base of the Stang and not place anything at the Gates. The choice is entirely yours.

Raise the Stang

Stand with the Stang in the center of your Compass space. (If you have a full complement of tools, you might secure it in a holder, if you have one, using a personal Stang or Distaff to Lay the Compass. If not, feel free to use this one Stang as needed, placing it upright in its central holder wherever it isn't needed as a working tool in your hands.) The cauldron is placed behind the Stang, and the anvil (or Oath Stone) is placed in front of it, with the hammer on top. If you don't have these tools yet, make do. A forked stick, a bowl, and a stone will serve, if needed. Take a moment to energetically connect with the energy of the Forge-fire at the center of the Earth, far below the iron foot of the Stang; and also connect with Star-fire in the heavens, high above but still between the horns of the Stang. Breathe deeply and say, "May the three souls be straight within me." Feel yourself centered.

Lay the Compass

Using your Stang, walk the perimeter of the space, moving in a circle. Mark a circle on the ground by either dragging the Stang or dragging one of your feet. Allow the "lame step" to remind you that you walk between worlds. The Seen and the Unseen are ever present. The Living and the Dead are both here. As one of the Cunning Folk, you lay this compass as a reminder that the hedge is this, and you straddle it.

Open the Gates

Begin by calling the South this time.

Stand in the Center and face the South. Hold both arms down by your sides, palms flat and facing the ground. Say, "I call to the Fields beyond the South Gate. Open the door from the South, place of Earth, Goda's domain. By the plate, the soil, and the shield, I call you to open wide the Gate and send forth your road to the center of this, my compass. So mote it be!"

Turn to the North. Hold both arms up, fingers spread wide. Say, "I call to the Winds beyond the North Gate. Open the door from the North, place of Air, Kolyo's domain. By the spear, the wing, and the smoke, I call you to open wide the Gate and send forth your road to the center of this, my compass. So mote it be!"

Turn to the East. Hold one arm up, fist raised. Say, "I call to the Sunrise beyond the East Gate. Open the door from the East, place of Fire, Lucifer-Qayin's domain. By the steel, the anvil, and the sun, I call you to open wide the Gate and send forth your road to the center of this, my compass. So mote it be!"

Turn to the West. Hold your arms out in front of you, hands cupped. Say, "I call to the Ocean beyond the West Gate. Open the door from the West, place of Water, Azazel-Qayin's domain. By the cup, the quench tank, and the helm, I call you to open wide the Gate and send forth your road to the center of this, my compass. So mote it be!"

Working
- Corn Dolly ~ Fashion a human-shaped figure from the corn husks, using the string to tie the head, body, arms, and legs. Place on your altar and allow it to dry. Name your doll.
-
- First Fruits Feast ~ Offer a blessing of the seasonal fruits, vegetables, and grains. Place some of each in the sacrificial bowl before consuming them for yourself. Give thanks to Goda for the bounty. Eat and enjoy!

- Oath Taking ~ Consider an area of your life that needs a commitment from you. Make an oath to improve or address that area. Be specific. Write down the oath in your journal. Hold yourself accountable for it.

Red Meal

Moving counterclockwise, bring the sacrificial meal to the Stang or center of the Compass, while singing the Housle Song, below. Make at least one full circle as you tread the mill. Three is better.

<u>The Housle Song</u>
(To the tune of <u>Greensleeves</u>)

To Housle now we walk the wheel
We kill tonight the blood red meal
A leftward tread of magic's mill
To feed the Gods and work our Will.

Red! Red is the wine we drink!
Red! Red are the cords we wear!
Red! Red is the blood of God!
And red is the shade of the Housle

Say, "For my Ancestors, my Gods, and Myself, I do this."

Bless the bread with your right hand by saying: "Here is bread, flesh of the Earth, blessed to give us life and strength. I consecrate it in the name of the Old Ones."

Kill the bread by saying: "I take its life and give it to Them." Cut it with the red knife using your left hand.

Bless the wine with your right hand by saying: "Here is wine, blood of the Earth, blessed to give us joy and abundance. I consecrate it in the name of the Old Ones."

Kill the wine by saying: "I take its life and give it to Them." Slide the knife over the top of the cup to cut its throat, using your left hand.

Eat and drink of the Meal, making whatever personal offerings you like into the bowl.

The remainder of the wine is poured into the bread bowl. Dip your finger in and anoint yourself. This can also be used for blessing tools, etc.

The Meal is either given to the ground now (if outside) or later (if inside) with the following Declaration:

> "By the Red, and Black and White,
> Light in Darkness, Dark in Light --
> What we take, we freely give.
> We all must die. We all must live.
> Above, below, and here are One.
> All together -- ALL! (And none!)

Assignment

Perform the ritual included here, or a close variation of it. Until/unless you have a lot of experience with ritual AND feel very knowledgeable and comfortable with the SCT/RTA system and symbol set, I ask that you not modify it *drastically*. The point of studying this system is to learn this system, which happens by pulling it into your mind, heart, and body. Ritual helps to accomplish that. You're going to have lots of room for experimentation in the 2* and 3* programs of study. If you do modify the rite, please include information about what you deleted, added, it changed.

Your debrief should also include:
- any impressions you had or challenges you experienced during the set-up
- a notation of the date and general time you did the ritual
- who (if anyone) was with you
- impressions, insights, and sensations you had throughout the ritual (during the opening portions, the working, or the meal)
- any challenges you experienced while executive the ritual
- ideas that this ritual sparked for you (either for other rituals or for other creative/philosophical endeavors in your world)
- anything else that you feel should be noted

Additional Resources

BoS Pages Included

Laying the Compass
Opening the Gates
The Housle
Lammas
August Spirit Allies
RTA Lammas Ritual

Red Thread Academy
Traditional Witchcraft
Year 1: Foundations

Unit 3: Sabbats
Lesson 8: Fall Equinox

Fall Equinox

Prerequisite Lesson

None specified

Objectives

- To align with the seasonal energies of the Sabbat
- To practice and perform ritual
- To reenact a sacred drama (to the extent possible in a solitary context)
- To utilize masking as a ritual/magical technique

Materials Needed

Stang, candle, lighter

Cauldron

Anvil, hammer

Three knives (red, black, white)

Red Cord

Bread, lipped dish or bowl

Red wine, cup

Incense, holder, charcoal

Skull

"Hunter" mask of your own design and creation

Animal print-outs (placed around Compass as indicated)

Mirror (placed at base of Stang)

Colored pencils, crayons, pen (in a basket or bag that can move with you)

Study Notes

Fall Equinox, Feast of Avalon, Alban Elfed, 2nd Harvest, Fruit Harvest, Wine Harvest

Rather than provide a solid calendar date for the Sabbats, the way the contemporary mind likes to pinpoint the exact timing of events, it is more fruitful, honest, and traditional to think of these agricultural holidays in terms of the strongest point of the season. Our favorite holidays are often anticipated days and even a couple of weeks in advance, with preparatory rituals and traditions. Therefore, the traditional timing for Mabontide is the couple of weeks leading up to the Fall Equinox.

At Mabon the light begins to grow less, and once again, day and night are equal. This is the mid-cycle of the harvest begun at Lammas. Nature declines, draws back its bounty, readying for winter and its time of rest.

The Autumn Equinox is one of the four solar holidays of the year – one of the two in which the day and night are balanced, but the emphasis this time is on moving into the darkness. This is the second of the harvest festivals, and the beginning of the hunting season.

The name Mabon refers to the great hunter of the Welsh Gods, Mabon, who was taken from his mother at birth. Both Mabon and Modron, his mother, grieved for this separation. The boy was imprisoned for thirty years until a hunting party lead by Cyllwch came to find him. Mabon was the only hunter skilled and talented enough to claim the comb of a specific (and very wild) boar. The story told in the *Mabinogion relates a sacred journey in which the five sacred animals of the Celts (the Lapwing, the Stag, the Eagle, the Owl and the Salmon) are consulted in finding the hero-hunter.*

As a harvest holiday, this is traditionally the grain harvest. Thinking in Midwestern American terms (which is where Laurelei lives and how I relate to the cycles around me), this is the time of year when the farmers begin clearing the fields in earnest. The corn and wheat harvests empty the fields, and our country crafts festivals pop up in their place with candy apples, pork fritters, elephant ears, quilts, etc.

Traditions

Sharing thanksgiving for the harvest; feasting; drinking; performing the Descent of the Goddess ritual; reenacting the search for Mabon; watching the sunset.

Taboos

Passing by a burial site without paying homage; wasting food.

Animal and Tree Spirit Allies

The Boar (Torc) is as symbol of the Warrior spirit, leadership, and direction. It is wild and powerful. There are ritual boar paths in Wales, Cornwall, Ireland and Scotland. These paths exist in the Inner Realms, too. The Boar's tusks and comb are significant and are frequently mentioned in lore. The Sow (Muc) is a symbol of nourishment, as swine are a particularly potent food source. Just as the sow gives life as food, so does she take life away. Any pig farmer can attest to the practice of sows eating their own piglets after birth.

While not actually a "tree," the Vine stands firmly amongst the grove of Celtic calendrical trees, and is one of our potent Spirit Allies within the Spiral Castle Tradition. The fermented juice of the grape is wine, which appears in almost every Indo-European mythos at some point. The vine stands for the release of prophecy, predictions and omens. Grapevines are used to make baskets, wreaths and magical tools.

Fowl have been domesticated for over 8000 years as a provider of meat and eggs. Chickens are diurnal, being most active in the day. In fact, they are so associated with the coming of the day that the crowing of a rooster is seen as synonymous with daybreak. Chickens are highly social and quite polygamous. Pair bonding is unheard of. Yet despite this abundant promiscuity, there is tremendous territoriality and rivalry between two roosters as to who gets to mate with whom.

RITUAL

Note: Adapt this ritual, if you desire. Just make sure to note what changes you made in your debrief.

I prefer to begin with all the tools and materials either on my person (like cords and knives), or placed in a basket at the Center of the Compass. From there, I move things into place, as appropriate. You may also place the items in their final locations before beginning. If your ritual is very simple, or if you work with a minimum of tools, you may choose to keep everything at the base of the Stang and not place anything at the Gates. The choice is entirely yours.

Raise the Stang

Stand with the Stang in the center of your Compass space. (If you have a full complement of tools, you might secure it in a holder, if you have one, using a personal Stang or Distaff to Lay the Compass. If not, feel free to use this one Stang as needed, placing it upright in its central holder wherever it isn't needed as a working tool in your hands.) The cauldron is placed behind the Stang, and the anvil (or Oath Stone) is placed in front of it, with the hammer on top. If you don't have these tools yet, make do. A forked stick, a bowl, and a stone will serve, if needed. Take a moment to energetically connect with the energy of the Forge-fire at the center of the Earth, far below the iron foot of the Stang; and also connect with Star-fire in the heavens, high above but still between the horns of the Stang. Breathe deeply and say, "May the three souls be straight within me." Feel yourself centered.

Lay the Compass

Using your Stang, walk the perimeter of the space, moving in a circle. Mark a circle on the ground by either dragging the Stang or dragging one of your feet. Allow the "lame step" to remind you that you walk between worlds. The Seen and the Unseen are ever present. The Living and the Dead are both here. As one of the Cunning Folk, you lay this compass as a reminder that the hedge is this, and you straddle it.

Open the Gates

Begin by calling the South this time.

Stand in the Center and face the South. Hold both arms down by your sides, palms flat and facing the ground. Say, "I call to the Fields beyond the South Gate. Open the door from the South, place of Earth, Goda's domain. By the plate, the soil, and the shield, I call you to open wide the Gate and send forth your road to the center of this, my compass. So mote it be!"

Turn to the North. Hold both arms up, fingers spread wide. Say, "I call to the Winds beyond the North Gate. Open the door from the North, place of Air, Kolyo's domain. By the spear, the wing, and the smoke, I call you to open wide the Gate and send forth your road to the center of this, my compass. So mote it be!"

Turn to the East. Hold one arm up, fist raised. Say, "I call to the Sunrise beyond the East Gate. Open the door from the East, place of Fire, Lucifer-Qayin's domain. By the steel, the anvil, and the sun, I call you to open wide the Gate and send forth your road to the center of this, my compass. So mote it be!"

Turn to the West. Hold your arms out in front of you, hands cupped. Say, "I call to the Ocean beyond the West Gate. Open the door from the West, place of Water, Azazel-Qayin's domain. By the cup, the quench tank, and the helm, I call you to open the Gate and send forth your road to the center of this, my compass. So mote it be!"

Working

- Masking ~ You can either prepare your mask ahead of time, or make it as part of the ritual, depending on the complexity of your design. Your mask doesn't have to be complicated or made of expensive materials, but it should reflect the best that you are capable of making. As with all magical efforts, give and do your best, for best results. The mask should be a representation of the Hunter, which you can interpret in a number of ways. Create something that says HUNTER to you. Meditate on this before you dig into the design. Think about the best materials, the best motifs. Before you don your mask in ritual, name it and bless it. Know, as you put it on, that you become one of the hunting party in search of Mabon.

- Purpose of the Hunt ~ The Harvest is underway and the Dark Days of Winter are approaching. The tribe, the clan, the Family needs the assurance of sustenance during the lean times to come. This is a time to be grateful for the bounty of the Harvest, which is still being brought in, but it is also a time to take action to prepare for the hard times, the lean seasons. The Great Hunter acts as a guide to help you, as do the animals who point the way to him.

- Hunt for Mabon ~ In your reenacted search for the Great Hunter, you will move from one quarter to the next, spending time with each of the Sacred Animals. Begin in the East, with the Lapwing. As you move to each animal, understand that you are seeking their wisdom and guidance. Read the words on the page, then spend some time in reflection, listening for any direct message that animal may have for you. You don't have to color or journal, but the pages are designed so that you can do both, if those help. Fully tread the mill between each animal (meaning: walk all the way around the circle before stopping at the next Gate). This raises energy and is a good practice while in ritual space.

Red Meal

Moving counterclockwise, bring the sacrificial meal to the Stang or center of the Compass, while singing the Housle Song, below. Make at least one full circle as you tread the mill. Three is better.

<u>The Housle Song</u>
(To the tune of <u>Greensleeves</u>)

To Housle now we walk the wheel
We kill tonight the blood red meal
A leftward tread of magic's mill
To feed the Gods and work our Will.

Red! Red is the wine we drink!
Red! Red are the cords we wear!
Red! Red is the blood of God!
And red is the shade of the Housle

Say, "For my Ancestors, my Gods, and Myself, I do this."

Bless the bread with your right hand by saying: "Here is bread, flesh of the Earth, blessed to give us life and strength. I consecrate it in the name of the Old Ones."

Kill the bread by saying: "I take its life and give it to Them." Cut it with the red knife using your left hand.

Bless the wine with your right hand by saying: "Here is wine, blood of the Earth, blessed to give us joy and abundance. I consecrate it in the name of the Old Ones."

Kill the wine by saying: "I take its life and give it to Them." Slide the knife over the top of the cup to cut its throat, using your left hand.

Eat and drink of the Meal, making whatever personal offerings you like into the bowl.

The remainder of the wine is poured into the bread bowl. Dip your finger in and anoint yourself. This can also be used for blessing tools, etc.

The Meal is either given to the ground now (if outside) or later (if inside) with the following Declaration:

> "By the Red, and Black and White,
> Light in Darkness, Dark in Light --
> What we take, we freely give.
> We all must die. We all must live.
> Above, below, and here are One.
> All together -- ALL! (And none!)
> Here is shown a Mystery. As I Will, so Mote it Be."

Assignment

Perform the ritual included here, or a close variation of it. Until/unless you have a lot of experience with ritual AND feel very knowledgeable and comfortable with the SCT/RTA system and symbol set, I ask that you not modify it _drastically_. The point of studying this system is to learn this system, which happens by pulling it into your mind, heart, and body. Ritual helps to accomplish that. You're going to have lots of room for experimentation in the 2* and 3* programs of study. If you do modify the rite, please include information about what you deleted, added, it changed.

Your debrief should also include:
- any impressions you had or challenges you experienced during the set-up
- a notation of the date and general time you did the ritual
- who (if anyone) was with you
- impressions, insights, and sensations you had throughout the ritual (during the opening portions, the working, or the meal)
- any challenges you experienced while executive the ritual
- ideas that this ritual sparked for you (either for other rituals or for other creative/philosophical endeavors in your world)
- anything else that you feel should be noted

Additional Resources

Animal printouts for ritual are included in the next few pages of course materials

The Tale of Mabon, Son of Modron" by Skip Ellison -- http://www.dragonskeepfarm.com/Bardic/Mabon.htm

Sacred Mask, Sacred Dance by EJ Jones -- https://amzn.to/3mZAH0F

"Masks in Ritual Work" article at Therioshamanism by Lupa -- https://therioshamanism.com/2012/12/27/masks-in-ritual-work/

Paper Plate Masks -- These are super-hero themed, which isn't what we need; but it gives you an idea of what can be done. -- https://meaningfulmama.com/superhero-paper-plate-masks.html

How to Make a Paper Mache Mask -- https://www.liveabout.com/how-to-paper-mache-mask-1106527

DIY No-Sew Felt Masks -- https://www.bonbonbreak.com/diy-felt-halloween-masks/

Leather Mask Making Tutorial -- https://ranasp.deviantart.com/art/Leather-Mask-Making-Tutorial-41572623?offset=10

BoS Pages Included

Laying the Compass
Opening the Gates
The Housle
Fall Equinox
September Spirit Allie
RTA Fall Equinox Ritual
Lapwing
Owl
Eagle
Stag
Salmon

Red Thread Academy
Traditional Witchcraft
Year 1: Foundations

Unit 3: Sabbats
Lesson 8: Fall Equinox

Lapwing

Place at the East

LAPWING says:

When I first came to this forest, there was a smith's anvil. No work was done upon that anvil except for the pecking of my beak, and the anvil is now worn down to a speck. In all that time, I have never heard of the man you name. You should seek out the Stag. He has been here far longer than I.

My Reflections with Lapwing:

Next, seek the Stag at the South Gate.

Red Thread Academy
Traditional Witchcraft
Year 1: Foundations

Unit 3: Sabbats
Lesson 8: Fall Equinox

Stag

Place at the South

> STAG says:
>
> When I first came to this forest, I had only one antler on either side of my head. At that time, there was no tree but a single oak sapling. That sapling grew into an oak of 100 branches, and then fell. Now all that is left is a red stump. During that time, and since then, I have never heard of the man you seek. You should go to the Owl, who has been here much longer than I.

My Reflections with Stag:

Next, seek the Owl at the North Gate.

Owl

PLACE AT THE NORTH GATE

OWL says:

This great valley was a wooded glen when I first came here. Then men came and destroyed the forest. A second forest grew, and a second time destroyed. This is the third forest, and my wings are now nothing but stumps, but I have never heard of the one you seek. You must seek the Eagle, who is the oldest animal in the forest, and who has traveled the most.

MY REFLECTIONS WITH OWL:

NEXT, SEEK THE EAGLE AT THE SOUTH GATE.

Red Thread Academy
Traditional Witchcraft
Year 1: Foundations

Unit 3: Sabbats
Lesson 8: Fall Equinox

Eagle

PLACE AT THE SOUTH GATE

EAGLE says:

When I first came to this forest, I sat on a stone from which I pecked at the stars every evening. That stone is now worn so low that it is only a hand's breadth high. In all the time I have been here, I've heard nothing of Mabon, except when I made a trip to Llew's Lake for food. I sank my claws into a salmon, but it was stronger than me, and it pulled me under the water. We made peace. That fish is very wise, the wisest in the forest. If he doesn't know of Mabon, nobody in the forest can help you.

MY REFLECTIONS WITH EAGLE:

NEXT, SEEK THE SALMON AT THE WEST

Red Thread Academy
Traditional Witchcraft
Year 1: Foundations

Unit 3: Sabbats
Lesson 8: Fall Equinox

Salmon

PLACE AT THE WEST GATE

SALMON says:

I swim upstream on every tide until I reach Gloucester. Near that place I have found such a one as you seek. The Great Hunter for whom you search is imprisoned there. You must free the Hunter.

MY REFLECTIONS WITH SALMON:

NEXT, SEEK THE HUNTER AT THE STANG.

Mabon/Great Hunter

Place at the Stang

It is up to you to find the Hunter and entirely up to you to hear the Hunter's message for you this Autumn. Record your thoughts and impressions below. Sketch a drawing of the Hunter you found. Make note of any tools at the Stang that were most helpful to you in finding the Hunter.

My Reflections with Mabon/Great Hunter:

Red Thread Academy
Traditional Witchcraft
Year 1: Foundations

Unit 4: Lunar Workings
Lesson 1: Full Moon

Full Moon

Prerequisite Lesson

None specified

Objectives

- To establish a monthly practice in alignment with Full Moon energy
- To align with the cyclical energies of the Moon
- To practice and perform magic utilizing the Full Moon
- To meet and gain familiarity with the calendrical Animal and Tree Spirit Allies of the Spiral Castle Tradition

Materials Needed

Record-keeping/note-taking supplies

Study Notes

The word "esbat" is a derivation from the Old French term of the same spelling meaning amusement or diversion. It is not necessarily a Full Moon celebration or magical working, as Janet and Stewart Farrar and Doreen Valiente have noted in their own works. It is simply NOT a Sabbat.

Additionally, it is worth noting that People of the Old Faith (ie, Trad Crafters) usually don't use the term "esbat" at all. Many don't even use the term "sabbat." "Festival" is more common for the holidays called Sabbats, and "Full Moon" is sufficient if the specific tradition doesn't employ another term.

The Full Moons of the year are generally considered the most important and potent magickal points, and Traditional Witches tend to honor and observe the Full Moons more ardently than any other cyclical celebrations.

As a celestial body, the Moon is the nearest to us, by far, in all of the heavens. Its physical influence is evident in its enormous pull on the Earth's waters and the echoing call within each woman's body in the tidal cycle of menstruation. The Moon's etheric influence is no less significant, which is why it has been so long revered as a source of power and wonder.

Lunar Magic

The Full Moon rises at sunset and sets at sunrise. Astrologically, the sun and moon are in opposition (i.e., opposite each other in the sky and in opposite signs of the zodiac). She is visible all night long, from moonrise to moonset.

Etheric energy peaks during Full Moons, and they are considered to be most favorable for all magic.

The moon will remain full for two or three days. Etheric energy is highest during this time, and all magic is generally more potent and more focused. The full moon has a special connection to shapeshifting magic and invocation. Complete your work prior to the fading of the moon's fullness for best effect.

The 13th Moon, or "Blue" Moon can occur at any time during the year. A Moon is called Blue only when it is the second full Moon to take place that month (moon-th). The second New Moon in a month is known as a Black Moon. Blue Moons are considered to be stronger than regular Full Moons, and Black Moons are considered to be stronger than regular New Moons.

Full Moon Rituals

You are expected to honor the Full Moon each month as part of this course. You can use this opportunity to broaden your ritual and spell crafting skills, but it's main purpose is to help bring the cycles of the Moon into your life in a powerful and present way. Observing the Full Moon each month will help align your body, mind, and spirit to the event and flow of the lunar cadence.

You can keep your observances simple with practices like Moon meditations, yoga (including the Moon Salutation), divination practice, or even a simple drawing down of the Moon's energies into your body. Or you can write and perform more elaborate spells and rituals each month for your own goals.

Other Lunar Gatherings

As I mentioned earlier, Traditional Witches tend to meet and work magic during a regular lunar cycle, typically at the Full Moon. However, it is not entirely uncommon to have non-ritual gatherings in accordance with a lunar schedule.

The concept of a Full Moon gathering applies rather strictly to a group, which you are not likely to have available to you just yet. However, you may form a study group or coven of your own in the future, and these suggestions may be more relevant then.

Some ideas for non-ritual work might include:

· Socializing – A coven should enjoy some social time together. Sharing food and drink (and fun) helps people bond and form lasting relationships.

· Crafting – You can make personal tools, group tools, altar cloths, ritual robes, or even a traditional quilt with the help of your coven and it will be more frolicsome for their involvement (and much more magical).

· Business meetings – Budgeting, election of officers, and scheduling classes and rituals all need to happen, regardless of how much entertainment value these tasks hold on their own.

· Building circle or temple furniture – You can build your own altars, maypole, stang, or other large items, if you come together to work on them. Building larger pieces together gets everyone's energy in the item, and it creates a sense of group identity.

· Volunteering – Many groups volunteer their time at soup kitchens, recycling centers, homeless shelters, and other areas of need and interest in their areas.

Animal and Tree Spirit Allies

By now you have most likely had the opportunity to complete the Wheel of the Year lesson (02-01) and maybe even a Sabbat or two, so you have had some exposure to the Animals and Trees who act as guides and guardians at different points along our sacred calendar. In some ways, references to them may have seemed confusing or incomplete, and for that, I have sympathy. Ours can be a complexly interwoven system, and it is overwhelming to explain everything all at once. (And yet again, feels incomplete when pieces are reserved for later.)

I mentioned in Lesson 02-01 that our Compass reflects "both Sacred Space and Sacred Time." The Spirits -- whether we think of them as Deities, Heroic Figures, Witch Saints, Animals, Trees, etc -- that we call at different points within that Compass are aligned to energies that reflect time, place, element, power, and more. By riding/becoming the Stang in the center of the Crossroads, we can access any of those energies, as we choose.

Or, we can Tread the Mill of time and space … Walk the outer edges, follow the set pattern and come to each place of power in its turn.

It takes repeated exposure to these Spirits to know them well. There's really no way around that. You will find that you have deep affinity with some Animal Spirits, some Tree Spirits. Next year, when we meet the Kings and Queens of the Castles, one will likely resonate deeply with you. Perhaps even now, you feel a strong pull to either Tubal Qayin, Goda, or Kolyo. Then again, maybe one or more of these Spirits frightens you a little, and that's okay, too. They are all enormously powerful, and that demands a sense of caution.

With the Full Moons this year, I ask you to get to know the Animal and Tree Spirits of our Compass. Some, you'll see twice, because I will mention them again at the Sabbats, but there are five sets (those who align with January, April, July, October, and November) who are not directly linked with a Sabbat celebration. Don't give these friends short shrift. They have many lessons to teach.

HOW you get to know them can be a matter of some creativity on your part. Meditation is fantastic. Journaling -- including art journaling -- is wonderful. I've had students make scrapbook pages dedicated to each Spirit, in which they made collages, wrote passages, and added images as their understandings grew. Others have created Pinterest boards for each one (or for the month).

My own teacher assigned me and my peers the task of writing and performing spells each month that incorporated the Animal and Tree Spirits. While you can certainly work with these Spirits to meet your needs/goals, I'm not going to suggest you approach them in quite that way for a couple of reasons.

  1) I always felt that the idea of performing a spell every month "whether you needed to or not" was superfluous. There were months when I was writing spells simply as a mental exercise. Yes, it sharpened my mind, but it wasn't in alignment with my own sense of ethics or the Arte. Of course, I was required to do this exercise for YEARS -- well beyond my 1* Degree. That likely lent to my sense of overkill. If working with these Spirits to accomplish sorcerous goals speaks to you, do it.

  2) My teacher took a very "resource-based" approach to these Spirits, I think, and didn't honor them as individuals with whom we should enter into "right relationship." She did with other Spirits, but not with the Animals and Trees. It took me years to recognize that. The assignment she gave us was reflective of a very "colonizer mindset," and did not honor traditional Northern European shamanic practice nor Native American shamanic practice -- both of which influence our work. I don't want to pass that along to you. These Spirits are beings who have come to us to offer guardianship, wisdom, insight, and other gifts, but we need to be ready to give back to them in return. We need to listen.

It is for that reason that for Year 1: Foundations, it is enough that you focus simply on *meeting these 39 Spirits. If the Spiral Castle Tradition speaks to you, and you travel the Year Wheel more than once, you will talk with them, sit with them, soar with them, learn with them every year.*

Assignment

1. Write a spell which you perform at the Full Moon. Use your Spell Record sheet to document all the details, including your observations about how well it went. (See lesson 5.1 for the record sheet)

2.

3. Start honoring and working with the Full Moon each month. Your rituals don't have to be elaborate or complex. Even simple meditation under the light of the Moon can be very potent, especially as you engage in it on a recurring basis. Use the record sheet included with this lesson to notate your lunar rituals throughout your year of study.

4.

5. Find a way to incorporate the Animal and Tree Spirits into your Full Moon practice. Journal or otherwise document your impressions of each Spirit.

Additional Resources

Spell Record Sheet (05-01a)

Full Moon ritual record sheet (04-01a)

Lunar calendar (and planetary hours) apps -- Tattva for iPhone; Planetary Times for Android. Both of these are very useful for keeping track of not only the Moon phase, but also Moon age, Moon sign, planetary hours, and other astrological information.

Animal and Tree Spirit full blog entries at http://www.spiralcastletrad.wordpress.com/blog

BoS Pages Included

Lunar Magic
Moons of the Year
Drawing Down the Moon
Moon Signs
Spirit Allies Set

Red Thread Academy
Traditional Witchcraft
Year 1: Foundations

Unit 4: Lunar Workings
Lesson 1: Full Moon

Year Long Record of Full Moon Workings

In the table below, please note the dates of the Full Moons for the year, along with what you did to honor them. Try to include some detail, include a bit of reflection in terms of how effective you felt each particular activity or ritual was for you. Also, note any changes you perceive as you progress in your studies.

Date	Description of Full Moon Ritual/Activity

Red Thread Academy
Traditional Witchcraft
Year 1: Foundations

Unit 4: Lunar Workings
Lesson 2: Waning Moon

Waning Moon

Prerequisite Lesson

4.1 - Full Moon

5.1 - Sorcery v. Magic, Ethics, Sacrifice & Spell Basics

Objectives

- To align with the cyclical energies of the Moon
- To practice and perform magic utilizing the Waning Moon

Materials Needed

Record-keeping/note-taking supplies

Study Notes

The waning period of the Moon's cycle is the time after the Full Moon when the light lessens as she progresses toward her Dark phase.

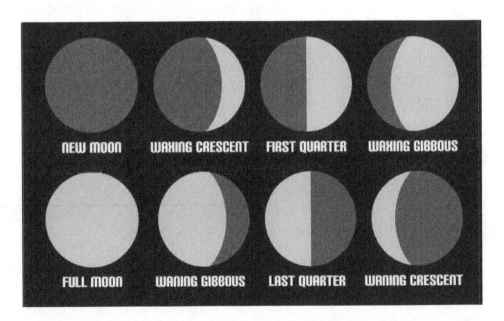

In general, as you learn to align with the energies of the Moon and work with her potent magickal influences, you notice that the time of the Waning Moon (while the Moon's light is decreasing to its ultimate darkness) is the best time to do work that likewise focuses on ideas of lessening, removing, decreasing, minimizing, etc. It is also a good time to seek answers and inner wisdom, as outside distractions are decreased.

During the waning moon, do spells to banish evil influences, lessen or remove obstacles and illness, neutralize enemies, scry, divine, and to remove harm.

These influences become stronger as the moon darkens.

The half-face of the last quarter moon is suited to work of balance and justice, but in a darker and more final sense than would be performed during the first quarter.

The days of the balsamic moon (or the waning crescent) are the most powerful time for intuition work and meditation. It is also a time to plan and prepare for the dark energy of the New Moon. The last fading crescent is the sickle of Hecate and is especially suited to the work of harvesting and the twilight sleep (a trance state).

It's worth talking here about adapting the language and intent of a spell to address a specific need. If you have a great need to pay your rent, but your bank account is lacking, and you will be under a Waning Moon between now and the due date, you don't want to focus on "bringing money to you" or "filling the bank account." Those specific intents are at odds with the lunar influences of decrease/less. Instead, you need to think about what it is that you need to remove or decrease in order to solve your problem and reach the same goal. So, shifting your thinking to "removing poverty/lack" or "decreasing the disparity in funds" will be more advantageous. "Removing the obstacles" for a given outcome is often a very effective way to use Waning Moon energy in your favor.

Assignment	Write a spell which you perform during the Waning Moon. Use your Spell Record sheet to document all the details, including your observations about how well it went. Also note which part of the Waning Moon you performed the spell (gibbous, last quarter, crescent/balsamic). (See lesson 5.2 for the spell record sheet) This spell can be combined with one of the spell assignments in Unit 5, if you desire. Just be sure to indicate clearly which assignments this work addresses.

Additional Resources	Spell Record Sheet (05-01a)

BoS Pages Included	Lunar Magic

Red Thread Academy — Unit 4: Lunar Workings
Traditional Witchcraft — Lesson 3: Dark Moon
Year 1: Foundations

Dark Moon

Prerequisite Lesson

4.1 - Full Moon

5.1 - Sorcery v. Magic, Ethics, Sacrifice & Spell Basics

Objectives

- To align with the cyclical energies of the Moon
- To practice and perform magic utilizing the Dark Moon

Materials Needed

Record-keeping/note-taking supplies

Study Notes

The Dark Moon (also called the "New Moon") is the time between the last sliver of the Balsamic Moon (or Waning Crescent) and the first sliver of the Waxing Crescent. Astronomically, it is the time when the Moon is positioned between the Earth and the Sun, making her essentially backlit and ostensibly invisible. She rises and sets at roughly the same times as the sun, as well, leaving the night sky without any lunar influence.

The Dark Moon is the most auspicious time for divination, banishing, and neutralizing spells. It is the peak of darkness, the time for blasting and battle magic.

Intensive divinations are best undertaken during the Dark Moon. This is the time to look deeply within oneself to seek wisdom and insight. This is the time to look at the Shadow self. In divination, hidden motivations can become more evident.

It is also the time to undertake workings aimed at neutralizing harmful energies being aimed your way. This is the most potent time for curse-breaking and hex-shattering magick. It is an excellent time for stopping gossip and lies.

Of course, it is also the best time to do any sort of baneful work that you need to do. This Tradition of Craft doesn't ordain for you the sorts of sorcerous workings that you can and can't do. If you feel that you MUST banish, curse, hex, or blast another person due to the wrongs they have caused you or the potential for harm they pose, then you are taught to seek counsel from your Spirits, know the sacrifice required, and proceed with your eyes wide open. Always work within your own ethical boundaries, and understand that all workings (even blessings) have a price. Sometimes, the price is the knowledge and commitment of doing the work. You will forever live with knowing that you did this spell, even if nobody else ever knows. And sometimes, the price is greater.

Banishing work is also very effective at this phase of the Moon. I don't necessarily see banishing as baneful magick, since by and large, the target is unharmed by the action. Typically, the target of this sort of work is just sent away or isolated from you in such a way that they can exist happily in their own little pocket of the world, and you no longer have to see, hear, feel, or be impacted by them. I've seen GTFO/hot foot workings where the target was offered a very lucrative job across the country and was as happy as a lark about the whole situation. Of course, you can make this work baneful, if desired.

A word about the concept of battle magick. I've seen many a young Witch (and more than a few seasoned ones) get swept up in the concept of "witch wars" and "night battles" and "psychic attacks." Be very cautious here. Check yourself and your reality filters very regularly. It is very easy to feed delusion and concepts of persecution by immersing oneself in this type of magick. You will find that you see enemies everywhere if you venture far down this path. Focus instead on good psychic hygiene, learning to banish unwanted energies/spirits, and beefing up your personal shields and protections. Seasonal protection cords (as discussed and assigned in 05-04) are an excellent practice for preventing you from ever needing to engage in the sort of battles that you hear about.

Assignment

Write a spell which you perform during the Dark Moon. Use your Spell Record sheet to document all the details, including your observations about how well it went. (See lesson 5.1 for the record sheet) This spell can be combined with one of the spell assignments in Unit 5, if you desire. Just be sure to indicate clearly which assignments this work addresses.

Additional Resources

Spell Record Sheet (05-01a)

BoS Pages Included

Lunar Magic

Waxing Moon

Prerequisite Lesson

4.1 - Full Moon

5.1 - Sorcery v. Magic, Ethics, Sacrifice & Spell Basics

Objectives

- To align with the cyclical energies of the Moon
- To practice and perform magic utilizing the Dark Moon

Materials Needed

Record-keeping/note-taking supplies

Study Notes

The waxing period of the Moon's cycle is the time after the Dark Moon when the light increases as she progresses toward her Full phase.

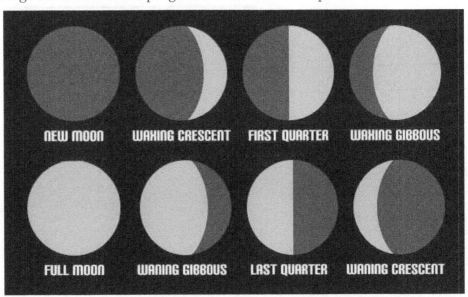

The days of and around the waxing crescent moon are the most powerful time to work spells for new growth and beginnings, which should manifest at the Full Moon. This moon is the silvery bow of Artemis and offers a fresh start to all workings.

The waxing moon, in general, is the best time to do spells for growth, beginning new projects, initiation, and enhancement. It is the time to focus on increase, gain, forward movement, and all types of abundance.

The clean half-face of the first quarter moon is also well-suited to work of balance and justice, especially with a focus on hope and positive restoration.

The days of and around the gibbous moon are the most powerful time for spells of fruition and completion. It is also a time to plan and prepare for the coming peak of energy during the full moon.

Assignment	Write a spell which you perform during the Dark Moon. Use your Spell Record sheet to document all the details, including your observations about how well it went. (See lesson 5.1 for the record sheet) This spell can be combined with one of the spell assignments in Unit 5, if you desire. Just be sure to indicate clearly which assignments this work addresses.
Additional Resources	Spell Record Sheet (05-01a)
BoS Pages Included	Lunar Magic

Red Thread Academy
Traditional Witchcraft
Year 1: Foundations

Unit 5: Lunar Workings
Lesson 1: Sorcery v. Magic, Ethics, Sacrifice & Spell Basics

Sorcery v. Magic, Ethics, Sacrifice & Spell Basics

Prerequisite Lesson   Unit 2

Objectives
- To distinguish between magic and sorcery
- To acquaint the student with the basic Laws of Magic
- To provide a background for the Models of Magic
- To begin a discussion of personal Ethics
- To develop an understanding of the role of sacrifice in magic
- To get an overview of the types of spells available
- To institute a system of a magical record-keeping for spells

Materials Needed   Record-keeping/note-taking supplies

Study Notes

This lesson is dense with information that you will undoubtedly need to come back to again and again throughout your studies. Truthfully, the study and application of the Artes (or even a branch of them, such as these Workings) can't be distilled down to a single lesson, unit, or even a single course. It is a lifetime of practice and discovery that may have begun some time ago for you -- or may have started when you began this course.

We will begin this lesson by first discussing the difference between magic and sorcery, both of which are available to us.

MAGIC VS. SORCERY

Magic (sometimes spelled "magick" within the Craft and occult community, in order to differentiate it from stage magic) is not inherently the same thing as sorcery. The terms get used almost interchangeably by contemporary Witches and other practitioners (including myself, at times), but they have very different implications and roots.

I credit Robin Artisson (the contemporary Craft writer, not the tutelary Spirit of Dame Alice Kyteler) with bringing this distinction to my awareness. He's written about it across several books and articles, all of which are well worth the read -- and very much in alignment with this Tradition. His work describes and encompasses an ecology of the spiritual landscape and is founded on European, pre-modern, Spirit-based traditionalism.

His writing reminds the reader, as I do with you now, that MAGIC draws from a personal reservoir of energy and power (or from creating a channel of that energy to siphon it from the area around oneself), whereas SORCERY relies on relationship and compacts with Spirits. Looking back as far as Sumerian, Chaldean, Egyptian, and Greek practices, you find that the words for these types of workings reflect the differences in these ways of working with the Unseen.

One is not inherently better or worse than the other -- not in our Witchy view, at least. Witches tend to be very practical and use whatever tools and methods are available. I'll use magic OR sorcery. I can raise energy OR ask a Spirit to help.

Historically, sorcery and witchcraft have been eschewed as the lesser or lower practice by systems that are heavily influenced by Western Hermeticism and Ceremonial Magic. Psh. I'm not going to dive into all of why this is, but it comes from Neo-Platonism, which holds celestial, etheric energies in higher esteem and demeans earthly, material energies. Every conceivable idea or energy can be put on the spectrum. Spirits are one step above the material plane, and therefore, they are "kakos." In Greek, "kakos" means everything from low to ugly, dirty, bad, and even evil. Guess what, though? So are the earth, the body, and all that is feminine, according to this philosophy.

COMPACT & RELATIONSHIP

Magic is a little more straightforward in the sense that you are 100% in charge of mustering up (and directing) the energy needed for your working, as we'll explore in Unit 9 ("Practice Energy Work Principles"). There are factors to account for, but it is much more within your control. I think perhaps that is part of its appeal for many people. There's a sense of science to it. (Aleister Crowley even has a famous quote that calls magic "The method of science, the aim of religion.")

Sorcery, on the other hand, involves another being with a will of their own acting in partnership with you to achieve a goal. Where many of the medieval grimoire writers go astray (in my not-at-all-humble opinion) is in trying to exert control over the Spirits with whom they should be working as partners. In order to dictate an outcome, those writers dominated the Spirits, and they suggest you do the same. I do not.

Much to the contrary, I suggest you only ever engage in sorcery with a Spirit with whom you are able to establish a reasonable, mutually beneficial relationship. To reiterate: a partnership. That might look different from one Spirit relationship to the next. You might be BFF's with Elligos. You may have an Alruna who sings, dances, and drinks with you in the kitchen while you cook. Another might act like a physical trainer -- always a little distant, but pushing you to reach the goal you set. Another may be an intense lover -- revealing insights and Mysteries to you during passionate, private moments. (Not kidding.)

These Spirit-relationships can really take just about any tenor or temperature that a human one could. Employee/contractor, friend, lover, family member, adviser, specialist. They can be short or long-term. Some last a life-time. Some may even end with unfulfilled promises -- most likely on your end, if you don't meet your side of the bargain.

Spirits want and need different things from us. They'll let you know what they want. Each compact will be unique. If in doubt, offer something like a traditional offertory incense, coins, a vessel, or liquor -- all of which have long traditional association with spirit offerings.

We'll talk about Spirits even more in Lesson 10-03 ("Familiars").

Not sure yet about working with a Spirit? Don't feel like one is presenting themselves? No worries. You may not be hearing them, even though they are there. Two groups of Spirits that are almost certainly close at hand: Ancestors and Spirits of Place (landwights, genus locii, lares, etc). Start by establishing relationships with these. No need to jump into workings and compacts yet. Get to know them first. (Gotta say hello before you can make a deal. It takes time to build trust.)

In the meantime, let's look at some of the principles that govern the practice of magic.

LAWS OF MAGIC

The Laws of Magic are not rules that your Maid/Queen, Magister/Devil, or another Witch will hold you accountable for. In simple truth, they are more like scientific principles that apply to the practice of magic. Different authors have suggested some different groupings of "laws" based on the way they noticed magic working. We will be exploring just a few here. The more you study and actually DO MAGIC, however, the more these ideas will make sense to you.

… Or possibly NOT. Some of them are founded on bad scientific principles and now have expressions that contemporary practitioners might even find offensive, in addition to being obsolete. For this reason, I encourage you to think deeply about these precepts to figure out which ones you accept and which ones you reject.

(Honestly, these concepts apply to sorcery, ie Spirit-work, as well. But they are universally referred to under the heading of "Laws of Magic" so I will leave it at that for now.)

Adapted from Real Magic by Isaac Bonewits:

Law of Knowledge – The more you know about a given person, object, or situation the more effective and complete your magic will be concerning that object, person, or situation. Research and study are very important skills within the Craft. Shun ignorance.

Law of Self-Knowledge – Knowledge of yourself and your own strengths and weaknesses is the most important knowledge you can have when working magic. If you are blind to who and what you are, you will fail at both your magical and mundane endeavors. Don't shy away from introspection.

Law of Cause and Effect – If exactly the same actions are done under exactly the same conditions, the same effects will be produced, usually. Similar strings of events usually produce similar outcomes. We say "usually" because you can't completely control the conditions. Chaos will find her way in.

Law of Synchronicity – Two or more events that happen at the same time are likely to be associated. Very few events are isolated from nearby events.

Law of Association – When two or more subjects, items, etc. have elements in common and are thereby similar or alike, control of one facilitates control of the other.

Law of Similarity – Having an accurate image/sound/smell of an object or being facilitates control over it or them.

Law of Contagion – Objects or beings that are in physical or psychic contact with each other continue to react after separation.

Law of Positive Attraction – Like attracts like. To create a particular reality you must put out energy of a similar sort.

Law of Negative Attraction – Like attracts unlike. Energies and actions often attract opposites.

Law of Names – If you know the complete and true name of a person, object or process you can have control over it.

Law of Words of Power – Certain words can alter the internal and external realities of those uttering them. Their power may rest in either the sounds themselves or in their meanings.

Law of Personification – Any energy can be considered to be alive and to have a personality and be dealt with accordingly.

Laws of Invocation and Evocation – You can communicate with entities from either inside or outside yourself.

Law of Identification – It is possible, through extreme association between oneself and another being, to be able to share power and knowledge. This often begins with a process of imitation, then identification, and ultimately possession until the knowledge and power is shared.

Law of Infinite Data – You will never run out of things to learn.

Law of Finite Senses – Both the range and the type of data available limit every sense of every being.

Law of Personal Universes – Every sentient being is the center of his or her own universe. This is a powerful concept. You are the center of your world. On some level, you've always known this. You experience your own reality, and it may or may not be exactly the same as the reality anyone else has. In fact, it can't be. The view out their eyes isn't the same as yours, and it hasn't been from your first day. We've all agreed to certain terms and arrangements, which we call "consensus reality." On some level, though, your universe is different than mine, and you are the one ultimately in control of your world.

Law of Infinite Universes – The total number of universes into which all possible combinations of existing phenomena could be organized is infinite.

Law of Pragmatism – If you believe it, if it works for you, no matter on what level of reality it works, then it is true and real.

Law of True Falsehoods (Law of Paradox) – A given concept, idea or act can violate the truth patterns of a given reality, yet still be true as long as it works in a specific context. In other words, it is possible to be wrong and still be correct.

Law of Synthesis – The synthesis of two or more opposing patterns of data will produce a new pattern that will be "truer" than either of the first ones were.

Law of Polarity – Any pattern of data can be split into (at least) two patterns with "opposing" characteristics, and each will contain the essence of the other within itself.

Law of Dynamic Balance – To survive and grow in power and wisdom, one must keep all aspects in balance.

Law of Perversity – If anything can go wrong, it will. Most of us know this as Murphy's Law. It certainly has its place in magic.

Law of Unity – Everything is connected. Ultimately, each object that you think of as solid is nothing more than a collection of atoms – energy. Trees, buildings, gasses, people, tectonic plates, and paper plates – we're all energy, and we're all connected to each other. Given all the other laws, this means that we have an effect, both magical and mundane, on absolutely everything.

The 7 Laws of Hermes Trismegistos

These rules of magic come to us from ancient Greece and Egypt. They are the basis of what is called Hermeticism.

1. **Law of Mentalism** – The Classical Greeks referred to the Supreme Being as the All. Sometimes the All was also called the "logos," which is the word in ancient Greek with the longest dictionary entry. It means "word," but it also means everything having to do with a person's words or speech, including their thoughts and reasoning. It is the word from which "logic" is derived. The Law of Mentalism reminds us that the All is mind itself, and the All encompasses everything in the universe. Magic is an act of thinking.

2. **Law of Correspondence** – All things are related. The physical, spiritual, and mental realms are connected, with one flowing out the other. The separations that we perceive between them are illusions.

3. **Law of Vibration** – Everything vibrates. Nothing rests. Modern science has confirmed that everything vibrates, just at different frequencies. Our eyes perceive light frequencies at different wavelengths as various colors in the spectrum. The same principle applies to auditory perception. New breakthroughs and understandings are happening all the time in the realm of quantum physics to confirm what magicians and Witches have practiced for millennia.

4. **Law of Polarity** – Everything has its opposite. According to Hermetics, opposites are actually the same in their core nature, but they differ in their degree or rank. As examples, you can think about heat and cold, peace and war, love and hate.

5. **Law of Rhythm** – There is a constant flow of energy. The tide always turns. The cycle always continues. When the pendulum swings to the right, it will eventually swing equally to the left. This is true in politics, business, weather and magic. This is the reason why there is always some price to be paid for magic. You must account for this law.

6. **Law of Cause and Effect** – Every action has a reaction. Remember that spiritual, mental and physical causes can all create effects in any of those realms. So thoughts can produce physical effects, good or ill.

7. **Law of Gender** – Creation requires both masculine and feminine principles. This is evident in nature, even down to electrons and protons in atoms. Interestingly, within all that is feminine, lies the core of the masculine, and vice versa. We are, therefore, complete as individuals.

* Spiral Castle Tradition absolutely does NOT operate on the Law of Gender. This isn't the right spot to explain why or how, but we'll let it be sufficient to say that SCT/RTA is comfortable with expressing polarities and elemental expression without bringing gender/sex into the equation. (Look to the Spiral Castle Trad blog for discussion on this.)

MODELS OF MAGIC

One of the most difficult aspects of working or talking with other Witches or Magicians is often finding the common ground in the common language we share. We are all doing magic, but we aren't all approaching it the same way. A German Magician called Frater U∴D∴ broke down the distinctions in the ways different magic-users approach and talk about magic into a system of models, which I will briefly share here.

Spirit Model -- This is the most traditional model of magic, and it is one that most Traditional Witches operate from, at least in part. In this model, the Witch/Magician/Shaman, recognizes spirits as entities separate from themselves and enlists their aid in magical endeavors via bargaining, prayer, contract, partnership, etc. The Spirits can range from nature spirits to Ancestors to daemons to Gods, etc. Many practitioners of this model operate within a set of strictly prescribed parameters and must meet obligations as instructed by their Spirits and their religious tradition.

Energy Model -- Those who operate within this model view the world and everything in it as a set of interconnecting vibrational energies. By tapping into the correct vibrational pattern or energy level, change can be affected. Light, color, sound, emotion, and intention are all part of the energy spectrum, as are thoughts, diseases, etc. By aligning with the desired energy, the outcome can be reached. This model was in evidence as early as the start of Hermetic practice and has its roots in Gnostic and early Platonic thought.

Psychological Model -- This relatively modern model is heavily influenced by the work of Jungian psychology and is the basis for a great deal of modern ceremonial magick. It posits that one's entire reality is a project of their thought and that by changing their thoughts, they can change the world. Spirits of every sort, then, are archetypal expressions of the magician, and magic is the process of conforming the reality to the Will by virtue of shifting the thought processes of the magician.

Information Model -- This model is very modern and says that energy on its own is "dumb" and required information for direction. Conversely, information on its own lacks intent and energy. Within this model, however, it is possible to transmit vast quantities of information across time and space to "program" objects and energies to accomplish a magical objective.

Meta Model -- I've also heard this one described as "Chaos Model" and it is my experience that a great number of Traditional Witches use this model. Meta Model practitioners are aware of the models and see their strengths. They are able to choose between and blend models to best suit the working at hand. Some traditionalists would argue that only methods and practices that were authentic to a given area/era are truly "traditional." However, I have read enough of historical accounts to see that Witches have always been very adaptable and were willing to use whatever worked to get the job done. That "whatever works" philosophy is the hallmark of Meta Model.

ETHICS

Webster's New World Dictionary defines *ethics* as "the system of morals of a particular person, religion, group, etc." The same reference defines morals as "principles of standards with respect to right and wrong in conduct."

I was trained in a variation of Cochranite Craft, and we had no Ardanes (Witch Laws). Nor did we give oath to the Wiccan Rede. We did, however, expect each member of our Clan to spend time developing a personal statement of ethics that reflected his/her own moral convictions. The statement was not so much a codified set of rules, but an understanding that one has with oneself regarding what is right and wrong. Having looked deeply into that well, woe be unto the Witch who does not hold to her own moral standards!

The Craft (in its truest sense) does not offer a moral guidepost. It is a system of magic, a way of reaching out to the Unseen World and being more closely a part of it. The Black Goddess, White Goddess, Tubal Qayin -- do not look to them for your moral compass, for they are Nature's Compass, Magic's Compass. They are Powers, neither "male-" nor "bene-" (bad, good).

You are responsible and accountable to yourself, your family, your cuveen/clan, your community, your country, and your world. How you keep yourself on your path is up to you.

That being said, as a piece of Craft Lore (and even as a starting place in thinking about your own ethics), it is interesting to look at the Ardanes and the Rede. Bear in mind that these pieces are modern constructs with occasional bits of arcana thrown into the mix. Some of the advice here -- for we can only truly consider it advice and not Law -- is worth a look. Other pieces seem very out of keeping with the Craft as we know it.

The Ardanes

The Ardanes or Ordains first appeared in Craft documentation in 1957, when Gerald Gardner presented them to his coven after a disagreement about his own interactions with the media while insisting on secrecy within the coven. No known record of them in any older documentation exists prior to that date. While it is possible that he received them from his own initiator and teacher (as he claimed), the mix of archaic and modern phrasing in the Ardanes would suggest that they were created at that time.

Doreen Valiente, among others, was suspicious of these Laws which (unsurprisingly) eventually led to her ousting from the coven by Gardner.

These Laws have had several iterations, and they vary amongst covens/Traditions who hold to them. Some are anachronistic, misogynistic, or oddly Christo-centric. A fairly close copy of the original Gardnerian Ardanes exists in the additional resources for this lesson.

The Rede

Many, if not most, Wiccan traditions use the Wiccan Rede as the foundation of their code of ethics. The first published form of the Wiccan Rede is a couplet that appeared in 1964 by Doreen Valiente: "Eight words the Wiccan Rede fulfill, An it harm none, Do what ye will." Rede is a Middle English word meaning "advice or council," while, in this case, "*an*" is an archaic conjunction meaning "if." Other versions, including much longer poems, have been written since then, but this is the basic tenant of Wiccan ethics. (We aren't Wiccan, I know; but we need to start our discussion of ethics somewhere.)

Much exegesis has been written on this topic, and debates are continually waged within the Wiccan and Witchcraft communities over the exact meaning and execution of these few words. On the one hand, the Rede seems simple enough. It is a mandate to do no harm, much like the Golden Rule or the Hippocratic Oath. On the other hand, words like "harm" and "will" can be seen as vague or amorphous to members of disparate traditions. Is "harm" the same or different than "hurt?" What about "will" and "want?" Or is "will" closer to True Will?

Then there's the question of self-defense. Is it ever okay to harm someone if they're attacking you? A common psychic shielding technique involves mirroring negative energy back to its sender. If this causes harm, have you violated the Rede? The logic for any of these questions can get rather circular as you ponder them, and if you follow a debate of this sort online, it will often do just that.

Some traditions use other similar creeds (but with different implications) as the basis of their moral and ethical codes. One prominent standard, though not Craft in origin, is the Law of Thelema which says, "Do what thou Will shall be the whole of the law. Love is the law; love under will." Aleister Crowley wrote these words in 1904, inspired in part by the writings of Francois Rabelais in 1543. Rabelais had said, "DO AS THOU WILT," because men who are free are inclined to virtue and disinclined to vice. Here, we are absolutely talking about doing one's True Will and not simply doing the whim of the moment.

Ultimately, I encourage you to pursue a line of *independent* thought regarding ethics and a Code. In other words: know what YOU believe to be ethical behavior and hold to it. Remember that ethics and morals are not really about being held accountable to a power higher than yourself. If you believe an action is wrong, and you proceed in doing it, you will pay a very high price for doing it.

Yes, this does in fact mean that baleful and baneful magicks are open to you. "All is permitted. Nothing is forbidden." You may do that which you find necessary to do. Just understand that all actions have reactions. Your magick may have consequences. Natural consequences always include living with the knowledge of what you have done. If you know that what you did was necessary, then you can be at peace.

SACRIFICE

Not all magical texts will teach you this secret, and not all Witchcraft traditions know this truth. However, I was taught in Craft traditions that understood that all magic required some level of sacrifice from the Witch or magician. All magic has its price.

Think back about the Hermetic Law of Rhythm. The pendulum of energetic flow is always in motion. When you push it in a direction for your own needs and means, it will eventually swing back in an equal and opposite direction. This happens whether you're using magical or mundane means.

We see the Law of Rhythm very clearly in the world around us through phenomena like the rise and fall of the world's great empires, the swell and recession of the tides and the economy, and even the cycle of our thoughts from positive to negative. The Law of Rhythm is also in effect when we perform magic, but because we live and function primarily in a world of consensus reality, we don't always perceive the backwards swing of the pendulum for what it is. The give and take of energy, when magic is involved, doesn't always appear connected even though we know there must be one.

As informed Witches, we should enter into our magical practice with an eye on the price to be paid. Part of your divination before doing spell work should be determining the type, intensity, and timeline of the price to be paid.

Types of Magical Price

The types of magical price are numerous, and you can really get very creative. However some general categories might include:

- Money – Actual spendable cash and coin is a time-honored energy exchange for magic. Bending a coin and leaving it on the ground, throwing coins in a well, and donating money to a charity are all viable methods of paying a monetary price.
- Discomfort – Sacrificing physical comfort is often the price required for a Witch. Wearing something uncomfortable, sleeping somewhere uncomfortable, or otherwise inducing some level of pain may be needed.
- Blood – A blood price may be required for more powerful spells. Since blood is infused with the life force of the Witch, it is the ultimate price. We'll cover blood magic and blood oaths in more depth in Year 2 (Practicum).
- Goods/Gifts – Sometimes you will need to sacrifice a physical object. The sacrifice can happen either by placing it on an altar or shrine so that it is no longer available for your use or by destroying it elementally (throwing it, burying it, burning it, or drowning it).
- Abstinence -- You may need to give up something you enjoy for a period of time (or possibly forever) to achieve your goal. A type of food, a sexual act, caffeine, cigarettes, speaking, etc. Any activity or indul-

gence that is a habit, routine, or pleasure is up for the offering here.

Intensity of the Price

Not all spells carry the same magical punch, and not all prices extract the same energetic debt. Some are very intense and some are very small exchanges. The fact is, though, that if you don't account for any price at all, the universe will take it from you unprepared.

When you perform your divinations and find that the price is of a type and intensity that you are unwilling or unable to pay, you can make the choice to abandon the spell altogether or pursue the magical need through entirely mundane means. Perhaps the physical exertion will extract a smaller toll than the magical one.

Timeline of the Price

The energetic debt may not be due at the exact moment of the spell. Your divination and meditation should inform you of the timeline of your sacrifice. Perhaps you will need to pay the price before performing the spell, or perhaps after. In some instances, or when your divinations are unclear on the matter, pay the magical price in close proximity to the spell.

You'll also want to know if the payment needs to be made on an on-going or recurring basis. Some magicks don't let you go so easily. You'll want to ask up front.

SPELL-CRAFTING BASICS

One way to open the discussion of spell-crafting is to walk through the process step by step. Here is a suggested recipe for writing an effective spell.

Define the NEED. What do you need to happen? Will it happen through the natural course of events? Is this need in everyone's best interest? Will someone/something be harmed if you get what you need through magic? Are you okay with that harm?

Determine the INTENT. This is the final outcome or purpose of the spell. What do you plan to accomplish by doing this spell? What do you want to change? What result do you want? Make sure you understand and describe for yourself how you feel, what you will see/hear/etc when the outcome has been obtained. You want to be able to feel it as a reality when the spell is concluded -- and feel gratitude for it.

Plan the BODY of the spell. What tools do you need? What sacred space do you require? What Deities, Elements, trees, animals, herbs, energies, mythical creatures, etc. do you plan to use to empower the work? What oils, candles, incenses, symbols or other objects can you use? Will you chant? How will you raise and focus energy? Will you make an amulet or a talisman? When should your spell be done for maximum effect? Is the time of day, lunar phase or astrological sign important? All of these things will have some effect on your spell. Is your need strong enough to overcome possible astrological conflicts? Where should you do your spell for greatest effect?

DOCUMENT your spell craft. Write down everything you have decided to do. Write down the words of the spell, since variations in wording can change the outcome of the spell.

REFLECT again on what you have decided to do. Look at the whole thing. Are there any troublesome areas? Are your intentions clear? Is this spell in keeping with your personal ethics? Will it achieve the desired outcome? What are all the possible ramifications of this magic? Have you done divinations? What have they told you? What is the price of the magic?

PERFORM the spell. Document any last-minute changes as well as the impressions that you got while performing it. Make note of the outcome in your records and reflect on the overall effectiveness as well as the minutia.

Types of Magic

We've spent a lot of time covering the rules and ethical considerations governing magic, and a great deal more time could be spent on these. However, with the basic information in hand, it is time we turn our attention to the real treat where magic is concerned – doing it.

There are seven kinds of magic, generally speaking. Though each of these can be further subdivided and combined to make new categories, these seven are fairly all-encompassing of the types of magic you will encounter in spell books and grimoires.

Natural Magic

Natural magic involves using the natural elements and the laws of the natural world to achieve a magical goal. Totemic work, herbalism, stones, and elemental magic are all examples of natural magic.

Talismanic Magic

A talisman is a protective device made by a Witch or magician. An amulet is similar in construction, but it varies in purpose. Whereas a talisman repels negativity, an amulet draws desired qualities or outcomes to it. Talismanic magic involves the creation of these magical devices.

Ceremonial Magic

Ceremonial magic is loosely defined as a type of magic that is reliant on ritual. Ritual itself is an act of magic, so a Sabbat or Esbat falls under the category of Ceremonial magic.

Invocative Magic

Invocation and evocation are the arts of inviting Spirits (or astral or etheric energies, if you prefer) into the magic circle or into the Witch's body. These are often done for the purpose of requesting or making them do the magical task at hand.

Sympathetic Magic

Sympathetic magic functions on the principle that "like attracts like." This is probably the most commonly used magical construct within the Craft. The use of poppets, candles, color, and even many forms of natural magic relate to sympathetic magic.

Contagious Magic

Contagious magic relies on using a sample of target in order to affect (or draw power from) the larger host. By incorporating nail clippings, hairs, or bodily fluids of a target, we are able to directly impact that target. Similarly, we harness the energy of an appropriately aligned animal, plant, or even a place by including some piece of it within the fetish.

Illusionary Magic

Illusionary magic is described as the magician's stand-by. It involves training yourself to see what isn't there until you can actually see it. We also refer to this as visualization. For a Witch, this isn't just about visual sensation, it refers to all sensation. You should be able to fully imagine the sight, sound, taste, touch, and smell of the new reality you are trying to create through your magic.

Divinatory Magic

Acts of divination are magic. This includes Tarot, runes, pendulums, water witching, bibliomancy, augury, necromancy, scrying, and any other method of predicting the future or gaining spiritual insight into the etheric realms.

Assignment	Compose your own Statement of Ethics. Be thoughtful and precise. Provide some level of explanation. Dig deep. (Around 500 words -- can be as long as you need it to be.)

05-01a Spell Record Sheet

Additional Resources	*Psychic Witch* by Mat Auryn -- Sure to be a modern classic for students of witchcraft who are interested in traditional (as opposed to ceremonial) means of sorcery and power. -- https://amzn.to/2HH4E5E

Why Witches Need to Study Metaphysics (video) by Blade and Broom --

https://youtu.be/xJA4FEXkZvY

Why and How to Work with Ancestors (video) by Blade and Broom --

https://youtu.be/dZYpev6DEJU

Personal Ethics in Traditional Witchcraft (video) by Blade and Broom --

https://youtu.be/Qvsr2dlYQno

Real Magic by Isaac Bonewits -- More in depth discussion on the Laws of Magic -- https://amzn.to/3l1cDbQ

High Magic by Frater U:.D:. -- More about magic in general, and also a much more detailed look at the Models of Magic -- https://amzn.to/2ScoCHf

Modern Magick by Donald Michael Kraig -- A classic of magical education and a personal friend of mine. If you feel like you need a primer in magical principles, and you don't mind the ceremonial approach, this is a good place to look -- https://amzn.to/3cLQr2D

Encyclopedia of 5,000 Spells by Judika Illes -- This is an invaluable resource when researching spell ideas and components. I rather think every Witch ought to have a copy of this on the shelf -- https://amzn.to/3cPfv9a

Gardnerian Book of Shadows, which includes the Ardanes -- http://www.sacred-texts.com/pag/gbos/gbos38.htm

"The Witches' Creed" by Doreen Valiente -- http://www.sacred-texts.com/bos/bos083.htm

BoS Pages Included

Ethics
Laws of Magic
Spellcraft
Spell Record-Keeping

Red Thread Academy
Traditional Witchcraft
Year 1: Foundations

Unit 5: Lunar Workings
Lesson 1: Sorcery v. Magic, Ethics, Sacrifice &
Spell Basics

Spell Record Sheet

Specific Purpose:		
Moon Phase & Sign:	Sun Sign:	Planetary Hour:
Animal/Plant/Tree Allies:	Deities:	Other Spirits:
Type of Sacrifice:	Intensity of Sacrifice:	Timeline of Sacrifice:
Materials:		
Pre-Spell Set-up:		Location:

Steps:

1.

2.

3.

4.

5.

Results Did the spell work? How long did it take to manifest? Is there a time limit on the spell? Does it need to be repeated? Describe the specific results and how they manifested/ Notate other observations, including anything unusual that happened during performance for the spell.

Red Thread Academy
Traditional Witchcraft
Year 1: Foundations

Unit 5: Lunar Workings
Lesson 2: Amulets & Talismans

Amulets & Talismans

<u>Prerequisite Lesson</u>

5.1 Sorcery v Magic, Ethics, Models of Magic, Basic Spellcrafting

<u>Objectives</u>

- To distinguish between a talisman and an amulet
- To gain an understanding of talismanic magic
- To design and empower a talisman for a specific magical goal
- To find and utilize an amulet for a specific magical goal
- To design a personal sigil or bindrune

<u>Materials Needed</u>

Varies

<u>Study Notes</u>

Designing and creating talismans (and recognizing and using amulets) are critical skills for a Witch. You will find them to be potent pieces of your magick and spellcrafting, and they may even be focal points of your rituals.

Amulets and talismans are often used as interchangeable words by those who don't practice magick. Even those within the Craft can sometimes confuse the meanings of the two terms. However, careful study and consideration of historical talismans and amulets will reveal their differences. While both are magical objects purported to bestow protection or certain forms of good fortune upon their bearer.

More specifically:

An **amulet** is a naturally occurring object whose physical properties give it inherently protective or magical energies. For example, a stone with a natural hole (a "hag stone"), the fur or feathers of your spirit animal, and the parts of a sacred tree are all amulets. An amulet doesn't necessarily need to be embellished or empowered – just claimed, recognized and honored (and used). It can be cleansed and empowered, if desired, of course.

A **talisman** is a man-made object designed and produced for a specific magical purpose. It may incorporate natural materials or it may not. It can be inscribed or drawn on a piece of paper or other surface or be an object that includes braiding and knotting, color associations, beads, magical alphabets, sigils, numbers, sacred geometry, metal- or woodworking, textiles, etc. The possibilities are almost endless in terms of both construction and application. It must be prepared and charged by a Witch to have power.

Amulets and talismans are usually (but not always) small enough objects to be portable, and they are very frequently worn or carried in a pocket or pouch to convey their properties to their target.

Assignment

- Find an amulet (or identify one you already have). Take a picture of it and write a description of its magical properties. How do you use this amulet? How effective has it been for you? How did you first start using it? Did you prepare it in any way? Why/how?

- Make a talisman for a specific purpose. Take a picture of it and write a description of its magical properties. What design elements were incorporated into this talisman and why? How do you use this talisman? How effective has it been for you? How did you prepare it?

Please note that the preparation/creation of these pieces can coincide with your spell assignments or other ritual work, if you choose. Just be sure to label assignments clearly so it is obvious that they are meeting more than one requirement.

Additional Resources

The Complete Book of Amulets & Talismans by Migene Gonzalez-Wippler -- https://amzn.to/3cFUz4a

The Black Pullet: The Science of Magical Talisman --a medieval talisman grimoire -- https://amzn.to/2Gmgzoy

BoS Pages Included

Amulets & Talismans

Candle Magic

Prerequisite Lesson 5.1 Sorcery v Magic, Ethics, Models of Magic, Basic Spellcrafting

Objectives
- To become more familiar with basic candle magic
- To practice some candle magic
- To experiment with a new form of candle magic (candle garden)

Materials Needed
Several candles of varying sizes/types
Holders for tealights and votives (since they will melt and spread)
Tray or mirror to define working space

Study Notes

We have probably all used candles in magic at some point already. We have blown out candles on birthday cakes all our lives while making a wish, which is the simplest form of candle magic. Most of us have probably lit novena candles (the tall, cylindrical prayer candles) or taper or chime candles in response to a prayer request from friends online or in our everyday lives.

In fact, the prayer candle is a worldwide magical phenomena (along with lighting incense while praying) as it is a custom in so many of the world's religions. Praying with a focus and a tool is nothing if not an act of magic in the eyes of a Witch.

For candle magic, we are likely to take color associations and scents into account. Furthermore, we might have dressed the candle in some fashion – inscribing it with words or symbols, anointing it with oil, sticking tokens in the wax, etc. These are all helpful additions to using candles in spells and rituals. If you haven't done this already, start working with some very basic candle magic using colors, inscriptions, and dressing oils. The color associations should be drawn from the Table of Correspondences you are building (from Lesson 2.2).

The simplest way to inscribe a candle is to use either the point of your knife or a wooden bamboo skewer to carve into the wax. You can write things like the name of the target, desired outcome, or draw symbols.

The oils used can vary depending on intention. This part can get complicated, so let's keep in simple for now. Olive oil makes a fairly neutral base as a dressing oil. Mix in a few drops of an essential oil that is aligned to your purpose. Not sure what that might be? Just visualize your desire infusing the bit of olive oil that you rub onto the length of the candle.

Working with a novena and finding it tricky to inscribe? You can scratch symbols into the wax on the top, burrow holes into the wax and bury herbs or charms related to your intent, and/or draw symbols on the glass with a Sharpie.

Another way to add to the power of the basic candle is to create a candle garden – an arrangement of candles on a tray or platter (something that visually groups them together) -- I like a mirrored tray or tile. The garden may have candles grouped based on recipients, type of magic being done, or some other connecting force. So for example, if you are doing a number of different candle spells for members of your family, they might all be part of the same garden. Or you could have a healing candle garden burning for several people who are otherwise unconnected except that they all need that type of magic right now.

Assignment   Create your own candle garden for a specific purpose. Take a picture of it and describe the "why" and "how" of the arrangement in your Spell Record Sheet.

Additional Resources   05-01 Spell Record Sheet

BoS Pages Included   Candle Magic

Red Thread Academy
Traditional Witchcraft
Year 1: Foundations

Unit 5: Lunar Workings
Lesson 4: Witches' Ladders

Witches' Ladders

Prerequisite Lesson 5.1 Sorcery v Magic, Ethics, Models of Magic, Basic Spellcrafting

Objectives
- To further explore different types of magical practices
- To gain experience with cord and knot magic
- To learn about witch ladders used for both spells and meditations
- To practice making witch ladders for protection on an on-going basis
- To design and make a witch ladder for a specific magical goal

Materials Needed

3 nine-foot lengths of colored perle cotton, yarn, or cord (for seasonal cords)

Beading cord, yarn, string, etc

Beads, charms, stones, feathers, etc

Study Notes

The simplest sort of witch ladder is a single string, thread, or cord into which the Witch ties a series of knots. The magic of the Witch -- her power and intent -- is stored in each knot and can be unleashed at a later time.

The exact same type of ladder can be used as a devotional tool, a sort of Witch's rosary, in which she plans the steps on the ladder to lead to a devotional goal.

Of course, witchcraft isn't at all about doing things in the simplest manner, and we ARE a crafty lot. We enjoy weaving together numeric and color symbolism, and so our ladders tend to have more than one strand -- and often more than one color -- braided and knotted together. We include charms, beads, bone, feathers, and more to add oomph to our magic.

Below is a picture of a drawing that was included in the "1734 Letters" that I printed from Joe Wilson's website in early 2000. While all of the writing is still available, I am a little dismayed that most of the pictures have entirely disappeared from the Internet. (The text at the bottom of each page clearly said, "Not to be sold under any circumstances for any purpose. Must be freely distributed.")

At any rate, this picture (labeled "THE KNOTS") shows three possible place-

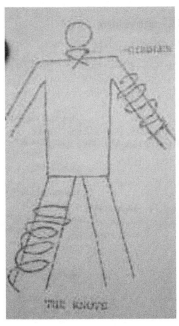

ments for "GIRDLES" -- or ladders. In Robert Cochrane's writing "On Cords," he describes the use of both devotional and magical cords:

"When worked up properly they should contain many different parts--herbs, feathers and impedimenta of the particular charm. They are generally referred to in the trade as "ladders," or in some cases as "garlands," and have much the same meaning as the three crosses. That is they can contain three blessings, three curses, or three wishes. A witch also possesses a devotional ladder, by which she may climb to meditational heights, knotted to similar pattern as the Catholic rosary."

This rhyme is often seen accompanying Witches' Ladder spells:

By knot of one, the spell's begun.
By knot of two, the magic comes true.
By knot of three, so it shall be.
By knot of four, this power is stored.
By knot of five, my will shall drive.
By knot of six, the spell I fix.
By knot of seven, the future I leaven.
By knot of eight, my will be fate.
By knot of nine, what is done is mine.

When making a ladder, you will typically work from the outsides toward the middle. So, your first knot is on one end of the cord, your second knot is on the other end, and your third knot is in the middle. If you have more than three knots (as in the rhyme above), you place new knots between established ones, still alternating sides. So, for instance, the fourth knot would be between knots 1 and 3. In this way, the placement of knots becomes an act of weaving, as well.

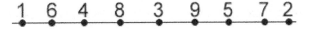

Cords as Markers of Admission

One of the Robert Cochrane (Roy Bowers) "writings" that you'll want to read is titled "On Cords." It first appeared in issue 3 of *The Pentagram* in March 1965. In it, he discusses two aspects or uses of the traditional Witch's Ladder.

The first is the piece of magical craft that we'll be covering soon. It involves using the cord for spellwork. (We'll be practicing that specifically as a seasonal protection spell covered within this lesson in a moment.)

The second use of cords is that of the devotional ladder. While many of us will make and use multiple devotional ladders for trance and meditation work related to a variety of focal objects, a great many Witches receive their first ladder as a cord (or set of braided cords) that marks their admission to a coven. If you have already performed your Dedication Ritual, then you already have this devotional ladder, though you may not have used it in this manner.

The cords are usually a length of silk or wool rope, braided yarn, or upholstery cord, whose thickness, length and color vary by tradition. They are versatile, as they are used for cinching ritual robes, indicating rank or degree, measuring the circle, and sometimes for binding blood flow in certain circumstances. When used to control blood flow, they may also be called the cingulum.

Cords used as a cingulum help alter consciousness and they are often employed in initiation rites. There are a few different ways to tie the cords to act in this capacity, but the most common is shown below. However they are used, a cingulum should be administered with care to avoid causing damage or harm.

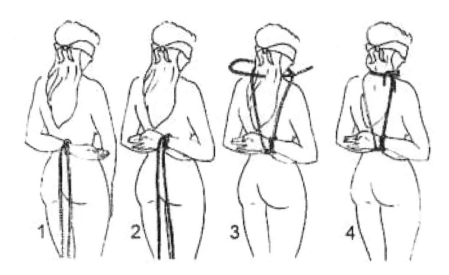

Cords can also be used as a meditational or trance tool in much the same way as a Catholic rosary. Because they are usually braided and knotted, often with multi-colored fibers, they bind together symbols and imagery that is important to the Witch who wears them. Meditating on a particular knot, strand, or other element of the cord will produce a focused experience on the symbol set contained therein, while working through all the knots (climbing the ladder) produces a transcendent state.

The Spiral Castle Tradition uses a specific progression of cords as markers of admission to the Mysteries. Each strand of cording that we use is made of 3 hand-braided strands of wool or cotton yarn.

Adoption Cord -- single red cord -- This cord represents the umbilical cord, the blood of birth, and the fire of Tubal Cain. It is a manifestation of the Red Thread. The purpose of the Adoption Rite is to forge a formal magical link between the student and the Tradition and to establish a formal training period of at least a year and a day. It also reminds her of her link to all Children of Qayin. You (probably) took this cord when you began your studies. You may have made it for yourself, or you may have requested that I make it for you.

Raising Cords -- single black and single white cord braided together with existing red cord -- This set of cords is the foundational set that a Witch within the Red Thread Tradition will use. It is the same set that every Witch who has completed the first year of training and passed the trials will make/receive. The cords are fashioned so that there is a loop on one end, and a long set of tails on the other where the cords remain unbraided. The knot that holds the loop fast is the White Goddess knot. The knot closest to the tails (which somewhat resemble three flails of a scourge) is the Black Goddess knot. A knot is tied in the middle of the braided section -- the Tubal Cain knot. A Raised Witch is a full member of the Trad, and she wears the most potent symbols of our Craft when she dons her cords.

When the 2nd and 3rd (Self-)Initiations are reached, new cords are made which are separate from the triple-

cords.

Service Cords -- single colored cord -- This one is braided and knotted to represent the specific focus area that you have studied throughout your Practicum year. It can be worn on the arm or hung from the triple cords at the waist during ritual.

Queen/Devil Cords -- 1 strand each grey-green-red cords -- The symbolism of this cord is intended to remind members at this level of the sacrifice, liminality, and continued deep connection required for those who would not only walk the Crooked Path, but light the way for others. These cords are worn as a garland at the neck.

(There is so much braiding that goes into making these cords. When you make them for yourself, you will know something of the Mysteries of Kolyo. Something of weaving Fate. Of magic. We have often laughed and lamented together about the cord-braiding club to which we have been recruited -- but it is a "joke" that hides something very potent. These cords hold so much memory and so much hope.)

Protection Cords

At each solstice and equinox, we make new personal protection cords. These cords are intended to empower protection in the areas of magical intent, emotional wellness, and physical safety. We change them with the season in order to best utilize the energy and magical currents of these changing periods of time. Because this is a magic we call upon daily for personal protection on all planes, we want it to stay fresh and re-charged, as well. Re-working the spell at each seasonal change gives it the boost needed to stay potent and ever-present.

Almost everyone comes under psychic attack at some point or another. Very often, those draining or targeting our energy are unaware of their negative impact. Sometimes, however, they are very aware and specifically intend us harm. In either case, I have found these seasonal protective witch ladders to be more than sufficient to the task.

These cords are also effective protection against the accidental harms from energies that would be attracted to our magic -- to feed off of us or our energy simply because we are Witches with power. This is Psychic Self Defense 101.

We make these cords not in sure expectation of problems, nor do we desire to create the very problems we wish to avoid. Protection is just that: a spell to protect us from both random and deliberate events that could cause us harm.

Supplies

- Perle cotton floss in these shades. (These align with the Castles and their Treasures, which we will study in more depth in Year 2: Practicum). You will need 3 colors for each season. (You can always choose to weave in a red thread, if you choose.)

Spring Equinox– golds and yellows

Summer Solstice – greens

Autumn Equinox – silver and reds

Winter Solstice – blue and white

- Any charm or amulet that you wish to add to the cords
- Protection Oil and Incense

Instructions

A. Assemble all materials in your workspace.
B. Cast the Compass.
C. Focus your energy on the work to be done. Think of all the areas in which protection may be needed. Decide on which Gods, Goddesses, energies, etc. that you wish to call on to empower your work. You may wish to take time to write some of this down. Or even design empowering chants, songs, etc.
D. It also helps if protection candles and incense are burned during the making of this spell.
E. Making the cord:
F. After your energy is focused, cut three pieces of each color cord. All of the pieces should be at least 5 to 6 times the diameter of your wrist or ankle or that many times as long as you wish the finished cord to be. You can tie and/or braid charms, amulets, stones, feathers, etc. into the cord as you construct the magic, if you wish.
G. Bundle all of the threads up evenly and fold them in half.
H. Hold the cord in both hands and begin to focus all of your magical energies into the cords. Use words, chants, songs, evocations, or whatever works for you. Begin to empower the cord to provide you with protection.
I. First, focus this energy on the Gods whom you wish to evoke for protection. When you feel that They are responding, tie a simple knot into the folded end of the threads, while sending the God energy into the knot. (Be sure to leave a small loop of threads on the end so that you can trim it when you are done. This makes the fringe on each end.) This knot seals the protection of the Gods into the cords.
J. While thinking of all the areas and things that protection is needed for and thinking of the safety that this spell provides, braid the entire hank of threads together. When the braided cord is at the desired length (remember that you will be tying several more knots into the cord, so make it longer than your finished size needs to be) begin to think of the Goddesses whom you wish to empower this protection spell. Tie a simple knot at the end of the braided cord while evoking the Goddesses' protection into the cord. (Be sure to leave some threads on the other side of the knot. These will be trimmed to make the fringe on the end of the cord.) This will seal the Goddess energy into the cord.
K. Think of each of the Spirits or Totem Beings that you chose to ask for protection and Aid. Focus on them individually, and when you feel like each has granted their protection and energy, tie a knot into the braid.
L. Seal your working by lightly anointing the cord with protective oil.
M. After removing the old cord, trim the ends of the new cord to make a fringe and tie the cord around your ankle or wrist. If you do not choose to wear your cord all the time, place it in your mojo bag and carry it with you as much as possible.
N. Release the Sacred Space.

Assignment

1. Design a meditational ladder for a specific goal. Be very intentional about your choice of number, color, and composition of materials. Take pictures and write a thorough description of your design process and also of your results when using this tool. How effective was this ladder for you?
2. Make seasonal protection cords for yourself throughout the year. As you make a new set, you can bury or burn your last set (in an intentional, ritualistic manner). Take pics of each set of cords. At the end of the course/year, include all of the pictures and a brief reflection on this process/tool. (It is expected that you will have a chance to make at least 3 sets of seasonal cords throughout the remainder of the course.)

Additional Resources

"On Cords" by Robert Cochrane -- http://www.1734-witchcraft.org/cords.html

BoS Pages Included

Witches' Ladders
SCT Seasonal Ladders

Red Thread Academy
Traditional Witchcraft
Year 1: Foundations

Unit 6: Tools
Lesson 1: Anvil (Oath Stone)

Anvil (Oath Stone)

Prerequisite Lesson None specified

Objectives
- To gain an understanding of the place and importance of working tools for a Witch
- To learn and develop techniques for cleansing and charging tools for Craft use
- To learn about the role of the Anvil as an Oath Stone within some branches of Traditional Craft

Materials Needed

Anvil (of any size)

Ball peen hammer

Thumb-pricking tool (lancet, red-handled knife, etc)

Study Notes

On Tools

While many Witches of most traditions make a big fuss about all of the lovely tools available to a Witch, and there are a few that you are going to be required to make/buy and use as a part of this course, I want to make one fact pristinely clear:

You don't have to have ANY of them to practice magic.

That's a shocking statement, I know, and perhaps not the most popular one among shopkeepers and booksellers. I am both a shopkeeper and bookseller, and so I know how threatening to business it can be to say to a young Cunning Person: "Everything you need for your Craft, you already possess." (You'll notice that my shop focuses more on giving people information than on giving them goods, though -- and there's a reason for that.)

I know it to be the absolute truth (that you don't need the props or costumes or magic purple feathers), and I would hate to think of a single aspirant to the Craft hesitating to do magic or celebrate a Sabbat for lack of a tool.

I was taught by a standard that I'd like to pass on to you:

"If you can't do your Craft naked and alone in a concrete room with nothing in it but yourself, you can't really do it at all."

So much of our practice comes from the practitioner – the need, intent, power, focus, visualization, ability to release the power. The rest comes from the Spirits with whom we work -- and the strength of the relationship we have developed with Them. The tools and regalia, even the words themselves, are simply a means of helping the Witch or magician in the task.

I'm rarely going to quote Gardner, but I will in this case. In 1953, he explicitly says that because magical supply shops don't exist, a Witch must extemporize. This is not the case for us. Most towns of moderate size have a Pagan or New Age store, and online retailers are in abundance.

However, a "poor Witch," as Gardner puts it, can still extemporize if need be. After all, we have all of the tools we need for ritual in our bodies, if not our cupboards. Earth, Air, Fire, Water and Spirit combine in you. That is magical enough not to be thwarted by lack of nifty props.

Now, don't misunderstand. I love the props and costuming as much as the next Witch. I was a theatre teacher and director of many student productions. I love a ritual that LOOKS as symbolically rich as it sounds and feels. But if the energy is missing, the witchiest _looking_ tools and most dramatic-_sounding_ reading of lines will not endear it to me. I want **power** in my ritual, not just theatre.

The tools that we use and the garments and jewelry that we wear all speak to parts of our subconscious mind. They are visual, auditory, tactile and even olfactory triggers that we are in liminal space – that space between worlds, between times. The moment you slip on your ritual robe or smell the temple incense, your consciousness begins to alter. It's not just scene-setting, it's mind-bending. The more often you work with a set of tools, the more power they have. Walking naked into the empty concrete room, if you were to repeatedly do this for ritual, would start to signal to your subconscious that it is time to shift. You would feel a change when you began disrobing or when you first walked through the door.

Witches may use tools for a variety of reasons, but the most important reason of these is that tools act as conduits for directing power or as vessels for holding power. Because of this ability to receive and hold power, the tools we use the most/closest have a knack for becoming "ensouled." They form or attract a presence. They become a partner, separate from the Witch, but closely allied.

This doesn't happen with every tool, though. You'll have to feel your way through it. And even when/if your tools have that life, that spirit, that being of their own, that doesn't mean that the Witch is unable to do the Work without the tool at hand. Tools in this state, after all, will sometimes decide for themselves that their life with you is done or that they are worn out — and they'll disappear or break.

Though an adept Witch may not need a tool in all circumstances, most adepts still work with them, for a variety of reasons. Most novice Witches require tools at all times while they're learning to direct their personal power.

Tools of Traditional Witchcraft

Which tools are common to Traditional Witchcraft?

This is actually a little tricky. Wicca is fairly codified and takes its associations and correspondences (including the list of tools that a Witch must have) from Ceremonial Magick and Western Hermeticism.

While I've been part of two Traditionalist-flavored systems that have been heavily influenced by the Hermetics and have incorporated a cup-paten-blade-wand system for the basic working tools, it is entirely inaccurate to say that these tools are in standard use among Traditional Witches.

Truthfully, the tools vary from Trad to Trad. Cords, such as witches' ladders, are very common, as are a variety of stones and bones (used for a variety of purposes). Blades are both useful and symbolic, and the various types of magical sticks are in evidence (including the Stang). Different types of pouches or bags are used, as are certain bowls or cups. Some of these are adopted out of necessity, and many have layers of rich symbolic meaning that become more evident after years of use.

It is perhaps more appropriate to denote which tools are of greatest focus within THIS Tradition.

In this year of study, you have already made/acquired (or will make/ acquire) the following:
- Cords (initiation cords, seasonal witch's ladder protection cords, spell ladder)
- Anvil/Oath Stone
- Cauldron
- Three Blades (red-, white-, and black-handled)
- Stang
- Keek Stone (Scrying Mirror)
- Soul Fetch/Fetish
- Spirit Vessel (Bottle/Doll)
- 4 divination tools

If you progress to the 2nd (Practicum) and 3rd (Mastery) Degrees of Study, you will also have made/acquired these tools:
- Alraun (optional)
- Gandreid
- Mazey Stone
- Crane Bag
- Focus Area Tool (for your Craft specialty)
- Stone Bowl
- Skull & Bones
- Lamp
- Glass Orb
- Silver Bowl/Cup
- Ring
- Necklace
- Garter
- Bracelet

This isn't including any other tools that you may feel personally drawn to use, or any of the jewelry or garments that you may want to use as part of your magical practice (something we'll cover at the Mastery level, as well).

Acquiring Tools

With all the amazing tools to be had, how does a Witch come by them?

There are no hard and fast rules about acquiring tools, for the most part. You can make the tool you need, buy it new, buy it from a secondhand shop, or receive it as a gift. If it is necessary for some reason for you to make the tool because the meat of the Mystery is in its crafting (or because this is the best way to empower it), I'll note that in the lesson and/or assignment.

One good rule of thumb is that you should buy or make the very best tool that you can, in terms of craftsmanship. The tool is an extension of yourself. You can do without it, but since you're choosing to work with it, you are imbuing it with your energy. Each time you work with it, it becomes more and more a part of you. A poorly-made blade, a plastic piece of jewelry, or a fraying robe can hinder your energy. It is better to have a plain, but clean and sturdy, tool rather than a highly embellished, but weak or soiled one.

Preparation of Working Tools

When you have a tool that is new to you – regardless of whether it is newly made, newly found, newly purchased, or newly gifted – you need to make it your own on an energetic level.

The best way to do this is to cleanse them using salt, smoke, water, fire, or light (or a combination of all five, if you can manage it) and then mark the tool with either your blood, sexual fluids, or the contents of the bowl in the Housle/Red Meal (see 7.2 Ritual Components).

After this, use your instincts about whether this is a tool that should be used only in ritual and shielded from the touch/sight of the uninitiated, or if this is a tool that you might use frequently and build a close kinship through daily contact.

Storage and Disposal of Tools

Most of the Witch's tools don't require any special handling in terms of storage when they're being used on a regular basis. Common sense should be your guide in regards to maintaining their physical cleanliness and integrity, of course. Learn something about caring for steel and cast iron, in particular, as many tools are left to rust by lazy Witches who don't respect the steel.

If you are storing an item for a longer period of time, however, you may want to take special precautions. Obviously, you'll ensure that it isn't harmed physically by packing it away carefully, but you'll probably also want to pack it with a sachet of protective herbs, stones, or even a talisman.

Witches tend to be collectors of tools, and it is rare to dispose of one altogether. However, there are times when necessity dictates that a tool be destroyed or abandoned. You are likely to be the best judge of this situation, as the tool will feel foreign or "wrong" in some way to you.

When this happens, you will need to dispose of your tool using as many of the Elements as you can. Throw it, drown it, burn it, and bury it, if possible. Do this all in sacred space, of course.

The Anvil/Oath Stone

There are several types of stones that are important to Cunning Folk. With Tubal Cain being such a central figure within the lines of the Craft that have influenced this Tradition, however, it is no surprise that the Oath Stone upon which we take our vows and form our sacred blood bonds is his anvil.

I feel that it is most honest here to point out that this point of symbolism comes less from specific lore or myth as handed down from others, and more from mythopoesis -- that poetic sense of symbolic elements fitting together and clicking into place.

This is a piece of American Folkloric Witchcraft that came first from the Clan of the Laughing Dragon, the coven I was trained in as a young Witch. There, the anvil wasn't the Oath Stone. We had no such stone. Our oaths were taken upon a Sword (and all vows, including coven bonds, were still made in blood). But the anvil was used in every single ritual that we performed as a way to call upon Tubal Cain, the Forge Master. We struck the hammer to the anvil three times, each time pausing to call his name. It was powerful. It still gives me chills when I call to him this way.

When my son was about 5-years-old, I was away from home and the anvil was sitting at its place (when not in ritual use) at our family's hearth. He picked up the hammer and started striking, which brought his father running from the other room. He stopped the boy and asked him what he thought he was doing, intending to scold him for disrespecting this sacred tool. My son, not missing a beat, looked his father in the eyes and said in a voice filled with reverence, "Daddy, this is how we talk to God."

This IS how we talk to God. Through our blood. Through Tubal Cain's blood. Through the heartbeat that is pounded out in the rhythm of the hammer strokes.

The symbolism of the forge is powerful, alchemical, mystical. The anvil is the foundation of Stone. The forge is the transformational Flame. The bellows are the Breath. The quench is the Sea (both womb and tomb).

Ours is a path of the Mysteries of Life and Death and all that lies Between. It is Creation and Destruction. Destroying in order to Create. Mixing Fire and Water to temper the steel and make it stronger. Knowing how and when to do that in the right proportion.

And the anvil is the rock, the hard place on which this great work happens. It is the altar on which we are pounded and shaped (at our own request!) into something useful, something beautiful, something dangerous.

The earliest anvils were actual stones, of course, and a great many cultures have had ceremonies involving oathing and coronation stones. The Lia Fail (Stone of Destiny) and Jacob's Pillow are two well-known coronation stones upon which dynasties of monarchs took vows to serve God and country. Furthermore, the custom has long-existed in Celtic countries for couples to make their wedding vows upon an oathing stone.

Within this Tradition, the Anvil as the Oath Stone sits at the base of the Stang when the Compass is drawn, along with the Cauldron.

Assignment

Further research Anvil/Oath Stone in regards to:
1) its relation to similar tools within "Western Magic" (Neo-Paganism, Ceremonial Magic, Wicca, etc.),
2) its uses within a Celtic context (if any),
3) generally accepted construction methods/materials, and
4) your personal preferences in regards to construction and use.

Additionally, you will need to purchase an Anvil. It can be a small jeweler's Anvil or a larger 55lb (or bigger) one. You'll also need an appropriately-sized hammer for striking the Anvil you have chosen.

Write an essay, exploring the concepts above, and also including:
- information about the tool's purpose
- rationale for the choices you made in selecting this one
- the cleansing and consecrating process you used
- your feelings/impressions while using this tool

Include a picture of the final product.

Additional Resources

BoS Pages Included

On Tools
Witches' Stones
Oath Stone

Red Thread Academy
Traditional Witchcraft
Year 1: Foundations

Unit 6: Tools
Lesson 2: Stang

Stang

Prerequisite Lesson

None specified

Objectives

- To become familiar with the function of the gandreigh in its many forms
- To understand the purpose of the Stang in relation to the Axis Mundi
- To craft a personal Stang for use in ritual and shamanic work

Materials Needed

Forked branch, hayfork, distaff
Woodworking tools

Study Notes

The stang is the central tool and main "altar" of our tradition. When we lay our Compass, our other tools are arranged around it. Even when we have a working surface like a table upon which other types of magical work might be done, we often place a small Stang (like a distaff) as a focal point.

A Stang, in its most basic form is simply a forked stick set with its long end into the ground. It acts as an axis on which magic can turn, and as a pole that can be "ridden" by the shaman or witch into different realms. Its forks represent the horns of the Witch Lord.

Robert Cochrane called it as *"sacred to the People as the Crucifix is to the Christians."*

The stang is sometimes represented by an iron-tined pitchfork or a pole with the skull of a horned beast on it. Often in these configurations there will be a candle or torch lit between the two horns or tines, in the style of the icon of Baphomet, or as is shown in this woodcut from 1594 of a sabbat at Treves.

Any wood is suitable for use as a Stang, although ash, with its connections to Yggdrasill, the tree on which Odin was hung shaman-like for nine days, is a popular choice.

There are many examples of witches using the Stang to fly in early woodcuts, and we'll talk later in this lesson about the connections between the Stang and the Broom.

The stang has antecedents in the Yggdrasill of Norse lore, the Poteau Mitan (Middle Pole) of Haitian Voudon, and the ascending-pole birch tree of the Yakut shamans. It is both a world-pillar on which the cosmos (represented by the witches compass) turns and a gandreigh.

A gandreigh is a riding pole used to fly out astrally to access different realms. The gandreigh can be a broom, a staff, a stang, or even a wand that the rider uses to send forth a fetch for the astral body to inhabit.

Nigel Jackson writes:

"The stick is the Gandra which is both the magic wand and stick that straddle the Witch of the North. It is a variant of the classic broom or forked stick of witches in Europe. The armies of the night-flying creatures on sticks are called "the gandreigh" in Old Norse. This applies to the flight of witches and the dead ghost hunting Wild."

The gandreigh is not used for physical flight through consensus reality, rather it acts as a world tree by which we can access levels of being through "flying" (or climbing) up and down the pole.

The Stang (or staff, or broom) is a personal tool which acts as an expression of the energy that is the World Tree. It is the witch's most personal tool and is usually destroyed upon a witch's death or given as a kuthun (a witch's inheritance).

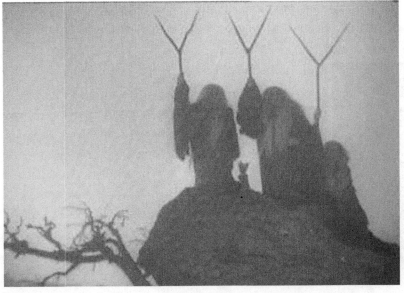

The Stang on the Hill (or, The World Tree, or the Spiral Castle)

Background and Purpose of the World Tree

The mythology and function of the World Tree seems to be a universal theme in cultures all over the world. References to a World Tree (or Cosmic Tree, Tree of Life, etc.) can be found in the Scandinavian, Finnish, Baltic, Hindu, Shinto, Native American, Mayan, Siberian, Hebrew, Christian, Egyptian, Mediterranean, Byzantine and Celtic spiritual beliefs and practices (to name only a few – the most easily discovered).

The World Tree takes many forms, extends into many realms, is associated with many animals, but essentially has the same function in each culture. It always, no matter which version of the world tree is being described, connects the realms of existence in a sort of pathway that is (or is a symbol of) the act of creation. Through it, communication and the gaining of knowledge is possible. It is a symbol of both the macrocosm (the universe) and the microcosm (the person). It is infinitely complex and surprisingly simple.

Connecting the Realms

The World Tree connects the realms of existence as they are seen and numbered according to a particular culture. The most common representation of this seems to be the idea of three realms (sometimes being divided into three sections). The Upper, Middle and Lower Realms – usually described as the heavens, Earth and the Underworld; or the Land of the Gods, the Land of Men and the Land of the Dead.

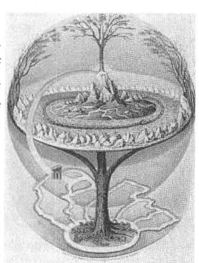

Communication/Messages

Many of the Gods receive messages from animal or spirit beings who travel up and down the tree. Likewise, shamans and priest/esses the world over are said to have the ability to climb the tree to gain the knowledge/wisdom of the other realms and to communicate with both Deity and the dead. This allows them, then, to bring back the advice or wishes of the spirits that guard and protect human life. Indeed, one of the shaman's or priest's responsibilities has always been to know the wishes of Deity (in whatever form it takes) and to communicate those wishes and wisdoms to the people.

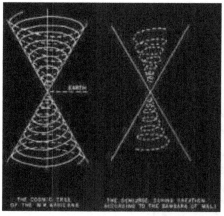

Consciousness Unit

There is a body of evidence that suggests that the World Tree is a depiction of the "Consciousness Unit" (or CU) – sometimes also called the Collective Unconscious (though I think that is a misnomer since so many spiritual seekers are, in fact, conscious of it). Those who have been trained in out-of-body, meditative and astral techniques have all witnessed a similar structure that can be described as a tree. However, in some cultures, it was described as a mountain (hill, mound, Tor) or a tent (or in the case of the Celts, a Spiral Castle or Silver Wheel).

It is generally seen as nested spheres of energy or consciousness – one structure that houses several others, which house yet more. Although the people who saw it were all likely to have seen exactly the same structure, they used different words to describe it when they were once again in the physical world. This, of course, would all be based on cultural and linguistic limitations and understandings. The most universal description is that of a tree.

Priestly Training

In many cultures, there is the pervasive use of the World Tree as a tool for the training and initiation of priests/shamans. Though the ceremonies differ somewhat, many of them involve a time of sacrifice upon the tree. Others require that the initiate climb the tree (either physically, spiritually or both) to seek information or to trace the steps of creation/wisdom. It is, of course, not surprising, then, to think of Odin's 9 nights on Ygdrassil as a sort of initiatory model – leading to the use of vision quests, the witches' cradle, and the actual climbing of a tree as part of the priest's initiatory process. (The Hanged Man in the Tarot could be said to be suspended from the World Tree to seek a new perspective or initiation into greater mysteries.)

Stars and the World Tree

There is a great association between the World Tree and two specific celestial bodies. The first is the North Star (Pole Star). In many cultures, this star is said to be the pin or tack at the top of the World Tree. (It reminds me of the star atop a Christmas tree, though the association would have been much older than Christianity. It was probably a part of the Cabalistic mysteries, and therefore absorbed unwittingly into the Christian mythos. Or, which is more likely, since I have seen no reference to the Pole Star in the Cabalistic World Tree information I found, it was probably assimilated from the older Indo-European practices and beliefs. Perhaps the Yule tree used in so many Germanic tribes was, in fact, an echo to Ygdrassil.)

The other celestial body associated with the World Tree, specifically in Mayan culture, is the Milky Way. Of course, I take some liberty in referring to an entire galaxy as one celestial body, but the idea is understood. In some descriptions, the Milky Way is called the World Tree. In others, it is seen as perpendicular to the World Tree.

In fact, the Mayan calendar is said to spring from the World Tree. It is this same calendar which, with the Mayans' uncanny mathematical understanding of the "wobble (or precession) of the Earth's axis, dates the Winter Solstice of 2012 as the point when the next cycle of that same wobble will begin. It is on this date that the North Star, from the Earth's point of view, will point directly into the center of the Milky Way.

The starry connections to the World Tree are significant for the Tradition at hand, as well. In Robert Cochrane's writings, pay attention to his references to "Caer Ochren." They are in close concert and connection to the statement "I am a Hill," which he follows up with a description of a castle of seven gates, upon a gloomy hill, turning to the elements.

Crosses and Mountains

I am grouping crosses and mountains together because I see them as two similar, perpendicular derivations of the World Tree concept. Mountains, specifically, have been mentioned in several works as other ways of seeing the CU (the thing that the World Tree represents – that is to say "everything.")

I only go into this idea of perpendicularity because its recurrence seems significant to me. In fact, the World Tree itself is sometimes described as vertical, sometimes as horizontal. Perhaps it is both, in a sense.

Or, it could be, as the Cabalists have described it, that there are two different trees that are essentially one World Tree. The Tree of Life, in this line of thought, is vertical, and the Tree of Knowledge is horizontal. (They are depicted as columns running between certain spheres.)

This perpendicular meeting between two poles/columns/pillars is the symbol of a cross. It is balance. It is life hinged on wisdom, and wisdom hinged on life. It is the cross of sacrifice as seen in the Christian mythologies. It is the equilateral cross of the elements in the Celtic cosmology. It is the tree on which Odin hung. Moreover, it is the crossroads at which magic and initiation happen.

Then there is the mountain, whose base is the horizontal axis. The line from the base to the peak is the vertical axis. In some cultures, a specific mountain has been their World Mount. And mountains the world over have been deemed as sacred. In fact, many cultures have created mountains as representations of the concepts embodied within the World Mount/World Tree concept. The Great Pyramid of Egypt is a prime example of this, while the Celtic Tors are examples known to many others. The sacred mountain connects the realms just as the World Tree does. The Tor provides access to the three realms. Medieval witches, too, were said to fly to Bald Mountain at Samhain for their great revel.

The Animals of the World Tree

Typically, eagles are said to dwell in the uppermost branches of the World Tree, with other birds living in some of the lower ones. Deer and horses are associated with the trunk of the tree, while snakes are seen twisting around the roots.

Although these images are fairly consistent throughout the various cultures, the Norse Ygdrassil houses all of them, and a few others. Specifically, there is an eagle at the top (which associates the eagle in my mind, then, with the Pole Star). Between the eagle's eyes perches a hawk. There is a dragon that is twisted among the roots, as well as other snakes and serpents who help him gnaw at those roots. A certain squirrel delivers messages between the Dragon and the Eagle, who are feuding. Other bringers of messages associated with Ygdrassil are the ravens who bring messages to Odin of Midgard and Niflheim (the middle and lower realms). There are also stags, a goat, and a hart who roam the branches and trunk and eat the leaves of the tree.

Interestingly, the name of the tree means "Odin's Horse" (because he rode it to attain enlightenment). This is interesting because so many of the other World Tree mythologies have sacred kings or gods tethering their horses to the trunk of the World Tree. Furthermore, the word Cabala is derived from the same Latin word as the word for horse (equus). (I know it seems like a stretch, but the Spanish word for horse is caballo, and the Italian is cavallo, which certainly show the progression of the word into derivations.) Therefore, horses are largely associated with the World Tree. So much so that at least one version of the World Tree is named as a sort of horse -- a means in itself of "traveling."

Stang-Rider

Just as a priest or shaman is trained to ride the tree, so is a witch or any of us of sorcerous ilk trained to ride the Stang, walk through the Spiral Castle, fly on the broom. The broom, after all, is fashioned from a forked staff -- a stang at its heart! These tools are aids in achieving soul flight, in fully experiencing the world around and within us, before and behind us, below and above us. In a great many ways, they are all the same tool, just fashioned in a different package.

The Stang, The Broom and the Spiral Castle

I have worked exclusively in covens that have used the Stang as a central point of focus in ritual. Because of this, I have a couple of nifty pics of Stangs that were once near and dear to my heart.

The picture above depicts the Stang adorned for a wedding -- hung with an arrow, which is draped with a white linen shirt. This adornment is used in other situations, as well, which we'll describe in detail later in the lesson. (In the covens of my former Tradition, the Stang was located behind the main altar, which was oriented to one side of the ritual space. You'll note how that differs from the Spiral Castle Trad's placement of the Stang in a moment.)

This particular Stang was made by one of my coven brothers. It had an Ash handle, iron horns (or prongs), iron foot, and an iron hook between the horns for hanging the ram's skull, arrow and candle. It was a tremendous piece!

Fore-running Configuration of the Spiral Castle Trad

The Stang in the picture above was the tool of the coven for which I served as HPS in that same Tradition. It was a converted pitchfork, which meant that it had a Hickory handle and iron (cast-iron) horns. One of my coven brothers cut and ground down the middle prongs to provide us with the piece you see. At the time of this photo, it still needed its branding sanded off and its foot shod with iron. (This is sometimes done by simply driving an iron nail into the butt-end of the pole. Coffin nails work very well for this.)

In the Spiral Castle Tradition, the World Tree sits at the middle of our cosmological system. When we lay the compass, we signify this central focus by placing the Stang at the epicenter of the circle. At its base we place the anvil (and hammer), which is our Oath Stone; the skulls and crossed bones (representations and keys to the Ancestors); and our personal fetishes.

We envision the Tree as sitting atop a Tor, a ritual mound with a sacred chamber inside.

The Tree, the Stang and the Broom share a certain transvective power with each other. (In truth, the Broom's base staff is a small Stang, as you will see soon.) What the Spiral Castle does for the entire Tradition (accesses ALL wisdom, ALL experience, ALL the realms, gates and airts), the Stang does for the Coven, and the personal gandried does for the individual Witch.

In his letters (have you started reading those yet?), Cochrane says that the Mystery of the Broom is "spinning without motion between three elements." He also relates this Mystery to the Qabbalistic Middle Pillar and the "path to the 7 gates of perception." He is, of course, talking about the practice of trance-work and meditation -- and using these tools (the Broom, is the metaphor for the tool) in order to access ALL THAT IS.

The Broom (according to copies of Cochrane's letters which I have that actually include illustrations) is constructed from a small, forked Ash staff. Between the prongs of the fork, a sacred stone is bound. The strips used for binding (willow), the broom twigs (birch), and the handle(ash), are each different sacred woods. The stone is one he calls "balanite," which turns out to be basalt -- a lava or volcanic stone with a slight magnetic charge that was once also called "touchstone" and used to determine the purity of precious metals like silver and gold. Adding it to the core of the broom, connects it in amazingly energetic ways to the forge of Tubal Cain!

Stang and Distaff Mysteries

Evan John Jones claimed that Robert Cochrane informed him that there were three branches of witchcraft. These were said to be memorialized on a megalith detailed in Justine Glass's much-maligned book *Witchcraft: The Sixth Sense* for which Cochrane was a source of information. Though he intentionally provided Ms. Glass with misinformation throughout the book, he claimed until his death that the analysis he provided regarding the menhir and the Mysteries of Witchcraft were true. The meat of his analysis, available in full in Justine Glass's the book, is repeated as Craft teaching in Evan John Jones's work *The Roebuck in the Thicket*. (And later in *The Taper That Lights the Way*)

Traditional Mysteries

The first branch of mysteries is the masculine mysteries, centering on the legends of the Horn Child and the Sacrificial King (the Oak & Holly King stories). The second branch is the feminine mysteries, centering on the mysteries outlined in Robert Graves' The White Goddess and the weaving of Fate. The third branch, which Cochrane claimed was lost to time, were the Necromantic mysteries. These have been reconstructed somewhat by modern practitioners like ourselves in rituals such as ancestral worship and the Tapping of the Bone.

The stang, revealed by PIE etymology to be a "stick" or "pole," is perhaps the most complex tool of Traditional Craft. In it are contained each of the three paths of Craft.

The Stang and Male Mysteries

The most common interpretation of the stang concerns the masculine mysteries. The stang is often thought of as a simple representation of the Horned Lord or Witchfather, with its forked tines standing in for the horns of the God. Sometimes the skull of a horned animal is bound to the stang to reinforce this idea. This practice may have old ties to the use of horned animals as a substitute sacrifice for the King.

Many, if not most, versions of Cochranite Craft use the same elemental quarter associations that we have described here before. Furthermore, EJ Jones actually writes about a very similar deity association, as taught to him by Cochrane, to what we use here at Spiral Castle Trad.

East = Fire, the birth of the sun, the seat of the Horned Child

West = Water, the place of the dead, the seat of the Master of the Wild Hunt, the Sacrificial King

North = Air, winter, the Dark Goddess

South = Earth, summer, the Light Goddess

In both the East and West, though not always specifically identified with the name Tubal Qayin, we can recognize him in his guises as the light-bringer and the lord of the dead.

East and West, Fire and Water, are opposed in the Traditional Witch's compass, as are North/Air and South/Earth. Elemental opposites are called into the center along roads of power. We very literally have a crossroads at the center of the compass. What's more, we have a Devil who stands there. He is the Witchfather, the Horned One. The stang, with its horns, is symbolic of Qayin himself and of all the masculine mysteries.

The stang is often dressed by hanging two arrows (sometimes with points up, sometimes with them down) on the shaft. These arrows are symbolic of the male mysteries, as well.

The Stang and the Mysteries of the Dead

The stang is also the world-tree upon which we travel through the three realms, which we have now discussed and reiterated several times. It allows us to move from this realm to the land of the dead, among other places. It is a gandreid that we use to ride to the Sabbat, to cast the caim, and to center the compass. These attributes make it a prime tool of magic, and one without which we would struggle to contact the dead. An animal skull upon the stang speaks of the masculine mysteries, but it also speaks of the Mighty Dead.

Often, a stang is outfitted so that it can hold a candle between its horns. The flame is said to be the Cunning Fire, the light shared by all Witches. When there is no candle, there is often a middle tine. This middle path, neither masculine nor feminine, is attributed to the Dead.

Our coven places skulls and bones (either crossed or uncrossed, depending on whether we intend to access the Dead or not) near the base of the stang, as well.

The Stang and Feminine Mysteries

The third branch of witchcraft, and the third use of the stang, is as a traditional woman's tool -- that of the distaff. The older versions of a spinner's distaff was either a two or three pronged "stang" ("stick"). The distaff and spindle were once the main daily working tools of all women, and Cochrane is very specific in his writings about the distaff being the main working tool of women of the Craft. The distaff is a traditional

handspinner's tool used for holding raw fibers as they are spun into thread on a spindle. Robert Cochrane in his article "On Cords" states:

"The so-called 'sacred object' held in such reverence by some witches was in fact a weaver's distaff–and could easily be mistaken for a phallic symbol. The weaver's distaff, bound with reeds or straw, appears frequently in rural carvings and elsewhere. It again has reference to the Craft and supreme Deity. It would appear that the witches were not in the least influenced by Freudian concepts."

Sarah Lawless, in her excellent post about magical sticks ("on Staves," which is temporarily unavailable, but I've linked it in the Additional Resources anyway, in the hope she'll re-launch her site someday), suggests from her studies that the distaff/stang wrapped in flax for spinning was mistaken for a broom in folklore and art. Quite possibly. The stang is certainly a tool for travel.

My first coven/Trad, which was also Cochranite in origin, didn't always hang two arrows on the stang. Often, it was a single arrow, with a linen shirt hung from it. The shirt was either white or black, depending on the ritual or time of year. We cannot deny that the stang is the hayfork that represents the Horned God, but it is also the spinner's distaff (a symbol of the Black and White Goddesses). The linen shirt on a single arrow is an allusion to the flax wrapped around the distaff.

When we view the stang as a feminine tool in the center of the magical space, the compass can be viewed as the spinning wheel of the Fates, our own Black and White Goddesses.

Stang Lore -- Construction, Magic, Dressing

We've covered already what a Stang IS. Perhaps it's time we cover what one DOES with it.

Over the years, I've tried to collect as much lore and writing on Stangs as I could find. I'm sad to say there isn't much available. That isn't to say that people aren't using Stangs, just that they aren't writing much about them.

Still, I'm happy to share the little hodge-podge I've cobbled together in the hopes that it's of use to us all. Our coven adores the Stang as a working tool -- for group and individual work. I think I can safely speak for all of us in saying that we would LOVE to hear what you all are doing with Stangs, particularly if it varies from the bit of lore accumulated here.

Also, I am starting to see more being posted online from other practitioners, particularly from blacksmiths who are also Cunning Folk.

The information shared here comes from a variety of sources, including:

- class notes from Clan of the Laughing Dragon (my former Trad)
- Robert Cochrane/Roy Bowers writings (including the copies of the "1734 Foundations" that I printed in 1999/200 that had so many illustrations and are no longer available online in their original form)
- The books listed in the Additional Resources below

Construction Basics

A Stang is usually made of Ash, relating it to the World Tree, but Ash is getting hard to come by in the Americas due to the work of the emerald ash borer. At this point. I think most American Traditionalists would suggest using any sacred wood, and I would add, any American sacred wood. I like Oak, and I really like Hickory. (Hickory is the hardwood of choice in these parts for tool handles, and it has a long association with the forge, which makes it a good wood for the Stang in my book.)

You want a nice dry piece of wood that is forked into a Y shape. Otherwise, you'll need a simple pole that you can attach horns or metal prongs in order to create a hayfork. Of course, you could also *begin* with a hayfork, and that wouldn't be wrong, either. The Museum of Witchcraft sells Stang tops (and shoes) that you can fit to the pole of your choice if you like, as well.

If you're using a piece of wood, you'll probably want to remove the bark and give the whole piece plenty of time to dry. You can also treat the wood, once dry, with linseed oil to help preserve it.

"Shoe" the Stang with iron, either by adding a metal cap to the base or by driving an iron nail into it. I prefer to drive an old-fashioned "coffin nail" into the base. This connects it energetically to the iron of the forge. The horns connect it to the Pole Star.

The size of the Stang is really up to you. It can be taller than you by just a bit, about Staff-height, or roughly distaff-length.

You may want to fashion a hook or a flat space between the "horns" of your Stang for placing a candle or hanging a skull, arrows, etc.

Placement of the Stang

According to Lady Sabrina, "when the Stang is accompanied by the cauldron, it represents the totality of life-giving properties of the masculine and feminine powers of the universe." The covens in which I've worked have always located the Stang with the cauldron, along with the anvil. In the case of the Spiral Castle Tradition, we envision this all on the Sacred Hill, the Tor. The Stang is the World Tree, as we have discussed before. The Cauldron is the Well, and the Anvil is the Stone (our Oath Stone). This Mound, Tree, Well, and Stone combination is a powerful one for us and it works very well as the central point, the Axis Mundi, of our Mill.

The Stang is also the tool we use to mark the Moat, the outer edge of the compass. So it is both center point and circumference, in a manner of speaking. It doesn't stay standing on those outer edges, but it is used to circumscribe them.

Stang Magic

Riding the Stang is a ritual that is used to manhandle one's superiors or to run a person out of the village. It is alternatively known as skimmington, skimmity, or rough musicking. The basic idea is that a gathering of folks join in the making of loud, obnoxious noises -- often at night -- from the various locations in the village to the doorstep of the offender.

You can make a "sprite trap" or "spirit trap" with a stang by embedding a charged stone between the forks and weaving a pattern of red thread. These are usually made of Rowan or Ash wood and incorporate specific symbols into the woven pattern.

As discussed elsewhere, the Stang is used for flight and trance magic, the specific nature and logistics of which will be discussed when we talk in more depth about Flight in Year 3 (Mastery) -- though they are touched upon and briefly experienced elsewhere, including in our Beltaine ritual this year.

Also, the Stang will be used in every Sabbat festival and every Full Moon to cast and center the caim. You will learn this magic best through practice and repetition, and in this way, you will come to know this most personal tool of the Witch on an intimate and careful level.

Dressing the Stang

A horned skull hangs on the Stang most of the time. It can be ram, stag, bull, or goat. You can choose a single skull that you work with exclusively, or you can choose different ones for different types of workings/seasons. This skull represents the Witchfather and the center of intellect.

Atop or behind the skull, between the horns, is a candle. This is Cunning Fire, and it is also a symbol of balance.

On the shaft of the Stang, hang 2 arrows -- one black, one white. For us, these are all the dualities in our Trad -- the Black & White Goddesses, the light & dark halves of the year, etc. From Spring to Fall, the arrows point up, and the white arrow is on front, representing the dominance of the White Goddess. From Fall to Spring, the opposite is true -- the arrows point down, and the black arrow is in front.

We hang linen shifts (robes/shirts) -- one black, one white -- at different times from the Stang, as well. We hang the black shift from a single black arrow during blasting magic or any time when we need an added level of invisibility or protection. We hang the white robe from a single white arrow for weddings, initiations, etc.

A bloodied white shirt can be hung on the Stang for several types of magic. It can be used in healing and vengeance magics, as well as in maternity and Women's Mysteries.

Seasonal wreaths and garlands can also go on the Stang.

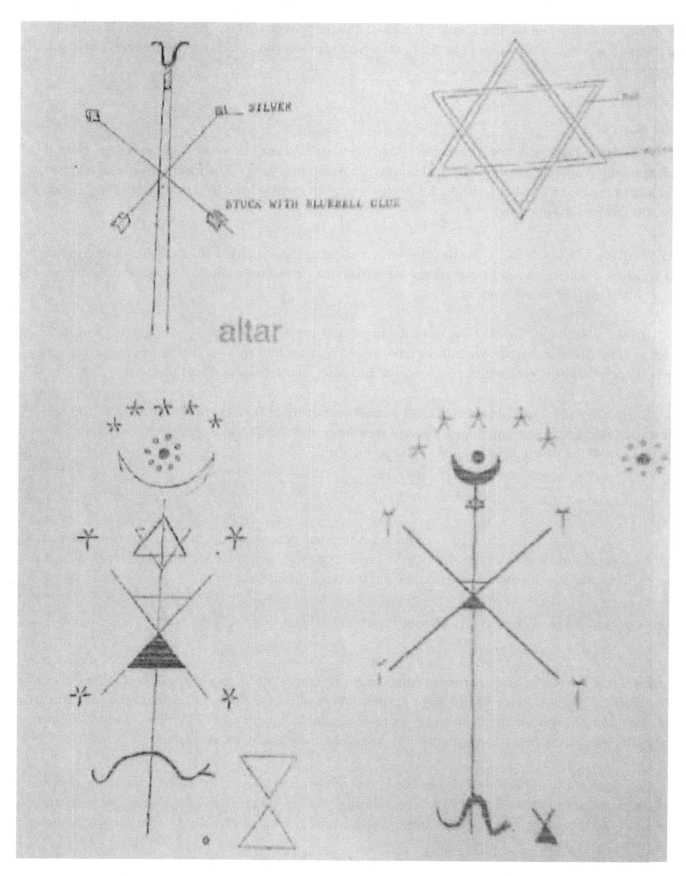

Page from my 1734 notes regarding Stang dressing

Assignment

Further research Stang in regards to:
1) its relation to similar tools within "Western Magic" (Neo-Paganism, Ceremonial Magic, Wicca, etc.),
2) its uses within a Celtic context (if any),
3) generally accepted construction methods/materials, and
4) your personal preferences in regards to construction and use.

Additionally, you will need to make (or modify) a Stang, by your own hand.

Write an essay, exploring the concepts above, and also including:
- information about the tool's purpose
- rationale for the choices you made in selecting this one
- the cleansing and consecrating process you used
- your feelings/impressions while using this tool

Include a picture of the final product.

Additional Resources

Call of the Horned Piper by Nigel Jackson -- Out of print, which makes it outrageously expensive, but very well worth the read -- https://amzn.to/3jsGVnT

Sacred Mask, Sacred Dance by EJ Jones -- https://amzn.to/30lITi9

The Taper that LIghts the Way: Robert Cochrane's Letters Revealed by Shani Oates -- https://amzn.to/2twc40M

The Stang (blog post on Patheos) -- http://www.patheos.com/blogs/byathameandstang/2016/08/the-stang/

"How to Use a Stang" blog post by Sarah Anne Lawless -- http://sarahannelawless.com/2011/02/27/how-to-use-a-stang/

"On Staves" blog post by Sarah Anne Lawless -- http://sarahannelawless.com/2010/03/10/on-staves/

Artes and Craft — blacksmith, cunning folk, and friends of mine who run arguably the coolest Witch Shop I know. My Stang came from here. You have to ask about them, though. They often aren't listed. (Secret stash!) — http://www.artesandcraft.com

Troll Cunning Forge on Etsy -- blacksmith and cunning man who makes amazing Stangs and blades! -- www.etsy.com/trollcunningforgeus

BoS Pages Included

The Stang

Red Thread Academy
Traditional Witchcraft
Year 1: Foundations

Unit 6: Tools
Lesson 3: Blades

Blades

Prerequisite Lesson

6.1 - Anvil (Oath Stone)

Objectives

- To develop a framework for understanding the roles of the three knives of the Craft
- To begin collecting the three knives
- To begin working with the three knives

Materials Needed

Black-, white-, or red-handled knife

Study Notes

There are three knives associated with our tradition. These knives each represent the three realms, and the White Goddess, the Black Goddess, and the Red God. Each knife is used in a very specific and exclusive way.

The first of the knives is the black-handled blade, traditionally called the Athame. It is usually a double-edged blade. It is the tool of the first realm and relates to the Black Goddess. The Athame is used for cutting and inscribing energy. It is used primarily to cut energy links. It is the Witch's primary weapon when in liminal space.

The second knife is the white-handled blade, the Kerfane. It is the tool of the second realm and relates to the White Goddess. The Kerfane is used for cutting and carving in the physical realm. It may be used to fashion a wand, carve into a candle, cut cords, or harvest herbs. If the Kerfane is sickle-shaped and used for harvesting plant materials it is usually referred to as a boline. The white-handled knife is often a single-edge blade. As a Kerfane, it is a straight blade.

The third knife is the red blade, the Shelg. It is the tool of the third realm and relates to the Red God of the Forge, Tubal Qayin. The Shelg is used for blood magic and sacrifice. It may be used to open a small wound in the flesh in order to produce blood for oath-taking or binding links. It is also used during the Housle to activate the Red Meal as a true sacrifice. Although sterile lancets are often used in place of the Shelg for safe bloodletting in small amounts, the Shelg is still symbolically passed over the wound to seal the link to Qayin. It can either be a traditional blade, it is may be a pin-shaped "thumb-pricker."

The three blades are personal tools that are very rarely, if ever, shared with others. While some among the People will use their blades for all manner of work, both mundane and magical, many reserve their blades for magical tasks alone.

Assignment

Further research one of the blades in regards to:
1) its relation to similar tools within "Western Magic" (Neo-Paganism, Ceremonial Magic, Wicca, etc.),
2) its uses within a Celtic context (if any),
3) generally accepted construction methods/materials, and
4) your personal preferences in regards to construction and use.

Additionally, you will need to acquire an athame (or one of the others).

Write an essay, exploring the concepts above, and also including:
- information about the tool's purpose
- rationale for the choices you made in selecting this one
- the cleansing and consecrating process you used
- your feelings/impressions while using this tool

Include a picture of the final product.

Additional Resources

Artes and Craft — blacksmith, cunning folk, and friends of mine who run arguably the coolest Witch Shop I know. Paul makes very thoughtful and lovely authames, kerfanes, and bolines. — www.artesandcraft.com

Troll Cunning Forge on Etsy -- blacksmith and cunning man who makes amazing Stangs and blades (including the RED knife, which is hard to find!) -- www.etsy.com/trollcunningforgeus

BoS Pages Included

Three Knives
Black Knife
White Knife
Red Knife

Red Thread Academy
Traditional Witchcraft
Year 1: Foundations

Unit 6: Tools
Lesson 4: Cauldron

Cauldron

<u>Prerequisite Lesson</u> 6.1 -- Anvil (Oath Stone)

<u>Objectives</u>
- To better understand the symbolism of the cauldron
- To acquire a cauldron for personal ritual use
- To begin working with the cauldron in a meaningful way

<u>Materials Needed</u> Cast iron bean crock or Dutch oven (these make much better, less expensive, and more practical cauldrons than the ones cast with pentacles)

<u>Study Notes</u> The cauldron is an ancient vessel of cooking and brewing that is associated in myth and legend with deep wisdom and transformation. This association stems, in part, to the story of Cerridwen and Gwion Bach, in which Cerridwen sets her young farmhand the task of stirring a brew that is meant to bestow vast wisdom upon the one who drinks it. When three drops bubble onto Gwion's thumb, and he sucks the scalding burn, he is granted all the wisdom in the brew, and a perilous and transformative chase ensues. Eventually, Cerridwen consumes Gwion, when she is a hen and he is a grain, later giving birth to him as the renowned bard, Taliesin.

Another famous Celtic cauldron was that of the Dagda. His was called the Un-Dry Cauldron, for it was said to be bottomless. No man ever walked away from it unsatisfied. The cauldron had a ladle so large that two grown men could fit inside it.

Bran the Blessed had a cauldron called the Pair Dadeni ("Cauldron of Rebirth"), as recounted in the Mabinogian, a Welsh cycle of stories, that could restore the dead to life.

Robert Cochrane writes about the "two words that do not fit in the cauldron" as a mystery of the Craft. The answer to this riddle (which he provides in one of his letters) is "Be Still," for within the cauldron lies all motion, all potential, and all things. It cannot hold stillness, but this too is a mystery. The cauldron is used not just for the brewing of potions, but also as a vessel for scrying in liquid or flame. To accomplish this we must find stillness within the cauldron, by quieting our own minds.

The cauldron is also very similar to the Holy Grail of legend. We must ever seek it and its mysteries, for in it lies true communion with the Gods, and deep healing of our souls. "Who does the Grail serve?" is the riddle traditionally associated with this quest. The Grail serves all who seek it with honest intent, for it is only in not questing for the mystery that it serves no one.

"In fate and the overcoming of fate, lies the true Grail." ~ Robert Cochrane

In addition to being an important symbolic part of the Tradition, the cauldron is also a wonderful scrying tool (as are all water-bearing vessels). For more on this, see Lesson 8.1.

Assignment

Further research Cauldron in regards to:
1) its relation to similar tools within "Western Magic" (Neo-Paganism, Ceremonial Magic, Wicca, etc.),
2) its uses within a Celtic context (if any),
3) generally accepted construction methods/materials, and
4) your personal preferences in regards to construction and use.

Additionally, you will need to acquire a Cauldron.

Write an essay, exploring the concepts above, and also including:
- information about the tool's purpose
- rationale for the choices you made in selecting this one
- the cleansing and consecrating process you used
- your feelings/impressions while using this tool

Include a picture of the final product.

Additional Resources

3-footed cast-iron Dutch Oven -- https://amzn.to/2XIDGjI

Cast-iron 1-pint Kettle -- https://amzn.to/2Y4Vp3G

BoS Pages Included

The Cauldron

Red Thread Academy
Traditional Witchcraft
Year 1: Foundations

Unit 7: Student Ritual
Lesson 1: Ritual Planning Basics

Ritual Planning Basics

Prerequisite Lesson None specified

Objectives

- To gain an understanding of all the considerations of ritual planning
- To formulate an idea and begin drafting a plan for a student ritual (which can be either public or private, group or solo)

Materials Needed

Study Notes

You will be doing lots of magic this year at the Moons (and have probably already gotten started on that), but you are only required to write and perform ONE full ritual. Trust me, though, I remember the challenge of writing and performing my ritual. It can be a big deal.

I'm here to help you eat this elephant. Well, … I'm here to help you plan the meal. I've already eaten my elephant. But we're going to get you started on yours just like I did mine (like everyone does theirs). One bite at a time.

First, please let me take some pressure off. You do NOT have to plan a public ritual. You don't even have to plan a *group ritual. You can plan a ritual that only you will experience, if that is more appropriate to your needs, circumstance, or personality. Then again, you MAY plan a group ritual, if you prefer.*

Elements of Ritual

There are several basic steps to creating and leading a good group or solitary ritual. You will need to carefully consider and make provisions for each of these steps.

In the sections that follow, we will fully address each of the following elements of a successful ritual:

- Discussion of Purpose & Goals
- Preparation of Space
- Attunement & Self-Purification
- Cleansing the Space

- Laying the Compass, Raising the Stang, & Opening the Roads
- Calling the Powers
- Statement of Purpose
- Ritual Observance/Magical Working
- Grounding of the Power
- Red Meal
- Clean-up
- Debrief

Discussion of Purpose & Goals

In order for a ritual to be successful, every person involved in it needs to "be of one mind." This means that everyone in the ritual is working toward the same goal, sending energy toward the same purpose, and not working toward opposing objectives.

"Are we of a mind?" is often a query that is posed by a coven/ritual member before moving into the work, in fact, after having stated the goal aloud. However, in order for everyone to answer honestly in the affirmative, a frank discussion about the purposes and goals of the ritual at hand needs to happen before the ritual ever begins.

This doesn't have to be a complicated or lengthy conversation, but it must be an honest one. Furthermore, the ritual leaders needn't divulge all the details of the ritual, particularly if it is an initiation or some other rite that requires an air of mystery. Being "of a mind" doesn't mean that everyone has the script (if there even IS a script). It just means that everyone knows what we're trying to accomplish.

Preparation of Space

You'll need to physically prepare the space according to your needs. You need to take every aspect of your ritual into consideration. One way to approach this is to think about the five senses.

SIGHT – candles, altar dressings, statuary, others' garments
SOUND – music, drumming, chants, liturgy, vibration of names, singing, evocations
TOUCH – personal tools, robes, jewelry (things that touch you); binding & scourging; movement (dance, mudras, casting the circle)
TASTE – bread & wine for the Red Meal
SMELL – incense, anointing oils

This list is rudimentary, but it is a place to start. Make sure that you also include items like lighters, containers, etc.

Attunement & Self-Purification

After the space is prepared, you'll need to get yourself energetically ready for the work you are going to do. In order to do this, you'll want to attune and purify yourself.

Attuning yourself involves bringing your energies into alignment with the work at hand and with the other members of the circle, if present. You can do this through any one of a number of visualization exercises.

A simple attunement involves picturing your personal energy core resting at the center of your body. This energy, then, extends down like the roots of a tree and up like its branches. You are able to draw energy up from the roots and down from the branches and leaves, allowing the energy to flow through the breath. You are connected to the other members of your circle through these interconnected roots and branches, with your individual trunk standing strong and separate. (You can do this as a solo or group visualization.) Another attunement we will/have learn(ed) this year is called the Triple Soul Alignment (Lesson 9-1), which is both simple and elegant, and will work very well for both solo and group work here.

Following the attunement, you can self-purify with salt-water and incense. Salt-water represents a blending of earth and water, while incense is a combination of air and fire. With these two tools, you are purified by all four elements, cleansing you fully for ritual.

Purification of Space

It is now time to cleanse the ritual area with the elements. You can use any representations of the elements that appeal to you, however, it is helpful to use representations that are evocative of cleansing activities, such as smoke (fumigation), broom (sweeping), salt water (washing) and fire (burning). It is appropriate that the person who is calling each element will be cleansing the circle with that element.

One way to cleanse with an element is walk around the space in a clockwise circle while using the appropriate tool. Sprinkle the water, swirl the smoke, sweep with the broom, and shine the light of the fire. Walk the circle at least one full time, preferably three full times, starting and finishing at the place where you keep the cleansing tool being used.

Some spaces need cleansing more often than others. If you have a dedicated space that you use all the time for magic, you may not need to cleanse it every single time you do ritual. If you're using a public space, or a space you share with others, cleanse it. Not sure? Cleanse.

Laying the Compass, Raising the Stang, and Opening the Roads

You should always acknowledge the sacred space by laying the compass, as discussed in Lesson 2.2. Other Witchcraft and Pagan traditions might call this "casting the circle and calling the quarters." Whatever name you prefer, you should establish your sacred space and understand the geography of your sacred landscape before beginning.

Calling the Powers

For us, calling upon our Deities (the Black and White Goddesses and the Red God), is usually inherent in calling forth our sacred space. In this sense, we recognize them as ever-present with us. However, there may be times when we want them more actively with us for ritual. For instance, we may be calling upon Tubal Qayin to be among us as we do a ritual based around concepts of smithing, or perhaps we call on Kolyo for a weaving ritual. We have called all of them directly for possessory oracles.

Statement of Purpose

While this piece happens just about in the middle of the this list, this had to have been the first thing you planned and decided upon, and every other choice within the ritual is intimately linked to it. Everything you have done is here to fulfill this purpose, and everything you do from this point forward is to enact this purpose. Be very clear with yourself and with the participants regarding the purpose of this ritual. By stating your intention aloud in the magical space – after everything is consecrated and all of the wards and entities are in place – you make this purpose clear to all of the magical and astral energies and beings present. At this point, everything human and energetic is "of a mind."

Ritual Observance/Magical Working

You've finally come to the point in the ritual where you get to do the work or the celebration you came to do. In your previous/outside reading and work in regard to the Craft, you may have come across certain "rules" or mandates about when magic should or shouldn't be performed. Some groups feel that Moons are for magic and Sabbats are for celebrations, or vice versa.

The traditional group (Clan of the Laughing Dragon) that I was raised-up in taught me that any time we got together and raised power, we should put it to use. We did magic every time.

When my ex-wife and I founded Spiral Castle Trad, we rarely met as a group for Full Moons because our coven was so distant from each other. When we met for Sabbats, we generally stuck to one of two types of ritual workings -- flight to the Sabbat grounds (Hexentanzenplatz) or possessory oracle. Both were very powerful and revealing, but after so many years of the same two rituals, my sisters and I decided to start experimenting again!

I will not be dictating for you the types of rituals you can and cannot do. It is my strongly held belief that even TRADITIONAL Cunning Folk experimented and adopted new ritual forms and magical technologies. If you are a creature of habit and prefer to do the same Full Moon ritual each month, the same Yule drama, the same Samhain oracle, etc, you are at liberty to do so. My strong suggestion is that you do so with intention. Make choices in your Craft.

Since you do have options between pure celebration, pure magic, and a blend of the two, let's talk a bit about the mechanics of how to work these out within the ritual.

If you are conducting a ritual for celebratory purposes, you will generally raise power as an offertory or celebratory act for the occasion. In this case, it makes sense to raise the energy during or after the action of the celebration.

If, however, the purpose of your ritual is to work magic for a personal or group goal, there may not be any celebratory liturgy (like a drama or speech about the role of the Gods) in your rite at all. If you are raising power for magical work, you will likely raise that energy as an act unto itself, or you will blend it with the spellcrafting.

Of course, it is entirely possible to celebrate a holiday AND work magic in the same ritual. Creativity and conscience are the limiters of possibility where ritual is concerned.

You'll need to decide how you intend to raise the power before the ritual ever begins. If you are working alone your options are slightly different than those available to a group of even meager size. Options available even to a solitary include walking the circle, chanting, drumming, dancing, and erotic stimulation. Always consider which is the best option for the task at hand.

If you are doing a spell or magical working, you have the opportunity to be very creative. Choices of materials and the specific form your working will take are limitless.

However, in terms of planning your rituals, I would caution you to do a great deal of divination and meditation about the work to be done BEFORE you gather the participants, if any, in the circle. (It is in meditation and divination that you may receive guidance about the need or direction of a spell or that a particular Deity may give you the purpose and entire layout of the ritual, if you listen.)

Grounding the Power

After you have sent the power to its intended target, you may be left with some residual energy. Whether you are or not, actually, you should be prepared for the eventuality that you or someone else in the circle may need to be led through a grounding exercise. Choose one that you feel comfortable leading.

I think I've noted elsewhere, but I will state it here for the record: This tradition does not "close the circle." The compass remains. We simply acknowledge it. So, there is no need to release Deities, close roads, or lift the compass. If you have called upon an entity that isn't normally with you, you may find it advantageous to ask them to depart. It is always appropriate during the Red Meal to give thanks and to share a portion of the meal with the Deities, Ancestors, and Spirits with whom you work.

Red Meal

The Sacrificial Meal, called "Housle" or "The Red Meal" in this Tradition, will be discussed in greater detail in Lesson 7.2 -- although you've already experienced it at several Sabbats.

For now, you need to consider what type of food and drink you will use for this sacrificial meal. Consider its appropriateness for the work of the ritual, the Deities, and the space in which you are performing the ritual. (For example, if it is a ritual in a public park, alcoholic beverages will generally be prohibited.)

Clean-Up

Be sure to get everyone's help in cleaning up, if it is a group ritual. I've seen the covenstead left a shambles because everyone left before cleaning up after a great ritual. Whoever's home the covenstead happens to be in doesn't have any greater responsibility regarding the ritual gear than any other person.

If you're doing this ritual solo, obviously all the brunt of set-up and tear down will be on you. Does this change how elaborate or simple you want the rite to be? How many materials you want to include? You should still try to give yourself a rich sensory experience, I'd suggest, as that is part of the magic of ritual.

Debrief

Take a little bit of time to sit with each other, if this was a group ritual, and talk about the experience. Pass a talking stick or take some other step to ensure that each person gets to have the floor to voice their thoughts, insights, sensations, etc. This is a very revealing experience, and you'd be surprised at how many folks have never had the chance to talk with others about the rituals they've been in together. (NOTE: This is one last opportunity for everyone to ground any excess energy before they drive home.)

If you're working solitary, take the time to journal about the ritual.

Also, eat some more bread, salt, and other grounding foods.

Participant Roles for Group Ritual

I offer this list in the event that you are planning a group ritual. While you may not be leading or planning one at this point in your studies, it is likely that you will do so at least once (and maybe more, if you're so inclined) if you progress and continue, at some point.

Priest/Robin (Magister, Devil), Priestess/Maid (Dame, Queen) – Most groups refer to the man or woman who "centers" the ritual by one of these titles. "Centering" a ritual refers to the weaving together of the group's energy and keeping the ritual cohesive and on-track. Traditionalists don't always bestow these titles on someone in a permanent sort of way (though some groups do, as a way to recognize clergy or other leadership positions within a coven).

For our Tradition, a Maid and/or Robin can center the ritual either together or on their own. This is a title used only within the confines of a given Sabbat or Moon. "Jillian was Maid of the May," would be a way to say that Jillian led the Beltaine ritual.

Dame/Magister refers to the leaders of the coven for us, while Queen/Devil are titles for coven leaders who have raised-up daughter covens. (All of these titles -- Robin, Devil, Maid, Queen, etc -- are used in different ways by different traditional Witches. This is just how they have come to be used by Spiral Castle Trad.)

Quarter Callers – Very often a different individual will be assigned to each Quarter. Sometimes, only one or two individuals will call all the Quarters, moving around the Compass (or pivoting) to do so.

Herald/Summoner – Sometimes a ritual will benefit from someone calling the celebrants to the door of the Compass. Sometimes the Summoner will go to a separate space to retrieve a person who has been isolated from the ritual and bring them to the ritual grounds. The Herald/Summoner serves that role, welcomes them, and will often also issue a challenge before allowing admission.

Thurifer – This person will pass the smoke of incense over each participant as they enter. This is almost always accompanied by someone asperging (sprinkling) participants with saltwater.

Guardian/(Wo)Man in Black – The nature of some rituals requires an extra level of protection. You may want an Outer Guardian if you are in an exposed public area, or you may need an Inner Guardian if you anticipate difficult psychic work. Choose this person very carefully. They should be very experienced in such work.

Before Leading a Group Ritual

Before leading a group ritual, it is wise for a person to demonstrate an ability to do ALL of the following:

1. Align the Three Souls

This major skill is the mainstay of meditation and a cornerstone of staying healthy. At its most basic level, this alignment means clearing out all the little distractions of your mind and body and concentrating on what you're doing and how you're feeling. You must be able to do this easily for yourself, as you will have to lead the entire group through this process before the ritual begins.

2. Lay the Compass

This is the sacred space, and you need to feel confident about its strength and security. The person centering the ritual is usually expected to lay the compass. It is imperative that you feel confident in your ability before you lead group magic.

3. Open the Roads

"Hey, you!" might work to call an entity, but may not always create a friendly relationship. Quarters are places that house a combination of smaller and LARGER astral beings that will help protect your compass after it has been cast. These entities (and the tools associated with them) have energies aligned in association with the specific associations of each Quarter.

Poetic language triggers the minds of the participants, but be cautious about your word choice. Astral beings tend to be very literal.

The person leading the ritual doesn't generally call Quarters, but you will want to have shown the ability to call and maintain each Quarter several times before you ever lead an entire ritual. Since the person centering the rite is pulling all of the energy through himself in order to weave the web of energy and magic, he must be intimately familiar with each Quarter.

4. Evoke, Invoke, Release, Banish

Evocation and invocation mean invitation. Evocation is calling entities to a place outside of your body. Invocation is calling them into yourself or another body. Be very aware of what you are doing. You don't have to be able to invoke before leading ritual, but you need to know the difference between the two types of calls.

The flipside to this coin is knowing how to thank and release evoked and invoked energies. You should be polite but firm. Furthermore, you should have a "bag of tricks" available should your polite request not be enough.

5. Raise Energy

We've mentioned several already: clapping, dancing, stomping, chanting, drumming. We could add yelling, laughing and praying very easily. Common trance-inducing activities are all means of raising energy, and anything that captures your attention and gives you a sense of fun works well for energy raising.

6. Direct Energy

It's not enough to raise energy. You also have to send it somewhere. You may be able to raise a whopping amount of energy, but keeping it trapped inside your body can actually be quite destructive. Directing the energy the group has raised takes discipline in visualization and skill in describing what task precisely you wish that energy to perform.

7. Visualize

This skill isn't just about your mind's eye. It's also about your mind's ear, nose, skin, and tongue. When you completely visualize something, you need to make it so completely real that it exists to all of your inner senses.

8. Meditate

There are several schools of thought on meditation. Zen Buddhist meditation may be the ability to think of nothing (or to let go of your thoughts), but meditation within the Craft is more about the increased ability to think of *something*. It is about focusing your concentration on an area of interest and letting your mind explore the possibilities surrounding it. You need to be comfortable with both guided and unguided meditation.

9. Psychic Self-Defense

Psychic self-defense refers to the ability to shield or protect your aura. This is a basic skill for any magical practitioner, and it generally includes a visualization that can be aided by spell components to turn off your psychic vulnerability.

10. Ground Excess Energy

After ritual, always take a time out so you can readapt to ordinary reality. One of the ways that we do this is with our de-briefing process. As the leader of the rite, you will also lead this portion, so be prepared to help others ground their energy through discussion, food, and any other means that may be necessary. Be aware that other means may be required.

Assignment

Your ultimate goal is to write a ritual that you will then perform. The first step, and the focus of this particular assignment, is simply to complete the Ritual Planning Worksheet for your student ritual.

Your ritual can be for a Sabbat festival or for a complete Full Moon ritual. The Sabbats, Full Moon observations, and spell lessons I have provided in this year of study have been designed to give you a pretty well-rounded view of several different types of rituals available to you, but they are not exhaustive of the types of magick and ritual available to you. Hopefully these and your independent reading have inspired you to design a ritual of which you can be proud.

This is usually one of the last projects that students complete, though that doesn't have to be the case.

Additional Resources

Ritual Planning Worksheet 07.01a

BoS Pages Included

Participant Roles
Ritual Preparation

Red Thread Academy
Traditional Witchcraft
Year 1: Foundations

Unit 7: Student Ritual
Lesson 1: Ritual Planning Basics

Ritual Planning Basics

<u>Purpose & Goals</u>	*What are you trying to accomplish with this ritual? What outcome or vision do you have? What do you hope to change or achieve or celebrate/honor by enacting this rite?* Answer:
<u>Timing & Location</u>	*When and where will you perform this ritual? Why was this date/time and location chosen? How does this setting impact the purpose of the ritual?* Answer:
<u>Preparation of Space</u>	*What physical items will you need to prepare the space for ritual? Consider all of the components that will contribute to the sensory experience of the ritual -- Sight, Sound, Touch, Taste, Smell. This will include all of your tools, garb, candles, music, etc.* Answer:

<u>Attunement & Self-Purification</u>	*What sort of grounding and centering and/or cleansing exercises are needed or preferred for this ritual? Why have you chosen these methods? If you have forgone any such methods, why do you feel they are unnecessary?* Answer:
<u>Purification of Space</u>	*Do you plan to cleanse the space using cleansing chants and tools? Why/not?* Answer:
<u>Laying the Compass</u>	*This portion of the ritual should be somewhat similar for all students in the RTA Year 1: Foundations course. The process of Laying the Compass is more or less the same for us all, though your sense of Arte may guide you toward some distinct personal touches. If you are aware of some differences in the way you Lay the Compass, please describe them here. Furthermore, if you are lucky enough to be working with a group to whom you are assigning specific roles for Laying the Compass, you may elaborate here, as well. This is also a good place to ask questions, if something about this section is evading your understanding.* Answer:

<u>Calling the Powers</u>	*Are you calling on any Spirit, Deity, Ancestor or other being who isn't normally called as part of the Compass calls? To what end? In what way will you be working with this Power? Do you know them well? Do you need to take any extra precautions? How will you be calling upon them? How will they be leaving at the end of the rite?* Answer:
<u>Ritual Observance/ Magical Working</u>	*Without providing the full script or outline, give an overview of what you intend to do for the ritual. What type of celebration or magical operation is this? Are making a talisman, and if so, what type? Are you performing a ritual drama? If this is a group ritual, what tasks are others performing in the ritual? What skills do they need to have, and are you sure that they have them?* Answer:

Grounding the Energy	*If you raised energy, what do you plan to do to ground any excess?* Answer:
Red Meal	*What do you plan to use for the Housle? Why these? Do they have special significance? Will you be using the contents of the Housle bowl for any special blessings?* Answer:
Clean-Up	*Think ahead to the clean-up. Will this ritual produce a lot of mess? Is there anyway to avoid that? If others will be participating in the ritual with you, note how you can enlist their help in this process.* Answer:
De-brief	*What questions will you ask yourself to test the success of this ritual? How will you know you've done a good job? How will you know that you have accomplished your goals, carried out the ritual successfully, etc? Formulate a list of criteria to consider. Also, be sure to give yourself time to consider the unexpected and to process your thoughts and feelings. If this will be a group ritual, give others the opportunity to provide you with feedback, as well.* Answer:

Red Thread Academy
Traditional Witchcraft
Year 1: Foundations

Unit 7: Student Ritual
Lesson 2: Components of a Ritual

Components of a Ritual

Prerequisite Lesson 7.1 - Ritual Planning Basics

Objectives
- To learn more about the specific components of ritual
- To develop a library of liturgical pieces to draw inspiration from
- To further expand a student ritual for performance

Materials Needed Completed Ritual Planning Worksheet (with feedback from Laurelei for 1-on-1 students)

Study Notes

What is Liturgy

Liturgy is a form or formulary according to which religious worship is conducted. It is particularly used in public, ritualized religious worship, but it can be used in private ritualized worship, as well.

More simply, it is the ritualistic elements of ritual. The chants, the repeated, rote, scripted parts that we say again and again. These are the parts that feel both comfortable and sacred because they are so familiar.

However much an individual or group may like to experiment, the fact that they are performing "ritual" means that some aspect of the work has been ritualized. Something is being repeated.

Some of the liturgical pieces that I have found most useful and meaningful from my own practice have been the following. I'm including a description of them here and the actual Book of Shadows pages in the section titled "Spell, Ritual, and Liturgy" with the BoS content at the back of these materials.

Cleansing Chants

In my home covenstead (Coven Caer Sidhe), we do not cleanse the caim for every rite. However, there are times when we feel it is necessary, and we are often guided by instinct in these situations. We also usually cleanse the space with representatives of the Airts when we perform rites outside of our normal surrounds or anytime we are performing BIG magic.

The cleansing chants found in the attached BoS pages are patterned on rhymes taught to me in my first coven, although they have been altered a bit (in some cases, quite a bit).

I have been using these (or similar) chants for over twenty years, and they feel very good to me.

Opening the Gates

I am a fan of heart-felt, spontaneous words, so I have to admit that these are NOT the words I use to open the gates each time I cast the caim. I say whatever I feel. Sometimes I say nothing at all. But I provide the Calls on the BoS page provided as a starting place.

Witch's LBRP

This IS one I say and do as written. I have done it as a stand-alone ritual in the mornings/evenings (as a sort of energetic yoga), and I have done it prior to other rituals as an act of preparation.

In the late winter and early spring of 2013, my ex-wife and I began adapting the Lesser "Banishing" Ritual of the Pentagram for use within the American Folkloric Witchcraft model. the help of our coven sister, "the Pythia," we wrote the ritual on the included BoS sheet and published it on our blog.

Our variation of the LBRP was influenced by Aleister Crowley's Star Ruby ritual (itself an adaptation of the LBRP). It uses forms of the Red God (the Witchfather) and the Black and White Goddess (the Witchmother) in place of the traditional Hebrew names of God. It also replaces the Archangel guardians with the four Watchtowers or Arthurian Castles that are incorporated into that Tradition.

The purpose of the LBRP is to banish all undesired or unwanted forces from oneself and the local area and to create Sacred Space. Many ceremonial magicians practice the LBRP as a daily magical exercise to discipline the mind and create internal and external peace.

Mill Songs

These are great all-purpose chants for energy-raising. I thought about including them in Lesson 9.2 which deals more specifically with raising and directing energy, but since this lesson has to do with parts of ritual, and Mill Songs are used almost exclusively when Treading the Mill, I thought it best to include them here. "Treading the Mill," of course, means to raise energy by means of moving in a circle. There are various ways to actually move about the circle, including using the Lame Step (which I describe below).

Housle

It is a common part of many religious traditions to partake in a small, sacrificial meal at the end of the rite or ceremony. We, too, participate in a Eucharistic tradition of imbibing en-spirited wine and consuming en-spirited grain as representations of sacrifice needed for the magic we have performed.

In many witchcraft traditions, this meal is called "Cakes and Ale" or "Cakes and Wine." We call it the Housle, or Red Meal, and base it in part on a ritual created by fellow walker of the crooked path, Robin Artisson.

The full ritual is outlined on the BoS page, and indeed, it can act as its own entire ritual. It is important to remember to give a portion of this meal to any Powers that we invited to contribute their might to the working that was done in the ritual. Pour out or leave out a portion of the bread and wine for Them in some discreet place outside when you are finished.

Guided Meditations

I haven't included a number of guided meditations here, although one of the Sabbats for this year's lessons does include a guided meditation. Some traditions rely heavily on these pieces of liturgy for their Sabbat workings, and you might find yourself particularly drawn to writing and incorporating them into your own work. They are an example of liturgy that you might consider including in your student ritual.

Our tradition does use guided meditations as part of our overall teaching and learning process, and you will eventually find several at our YouTube channel. If you choose to take Year 2: Practicum, these will be referenced more heavily in the curriculum.

Possessory Oracles

This is another type of liturgy that I haven't included in your BoS pages. We will not cover possessory work until Year 3 (Mastery). It is important work for a Witch to know how to do, but it is very tricky to explain and teach via distance education. Since we have to build up to that, and build rapport, it needs to wait until we have a solid base with each other.

Sacred Drama

This is another example of liturgy that I can't easily include as a BoS page, but I have worked into the Sabbats. The Hunt for Mabon in your Sabbats is a type of Sacred Drama (which was really tricky to work out for a solitary ritual, by the way -- but I think I proved that it can be done!).

Working with Energy in Ritual

There are so many ways to work with energy in ritual. The two things that I mention here are just additional bits that didn't fit neatly into other categories that I have covered elsewhere. Some of the energetic methods (like Treading the Mill) are covered in the list above. Some are covered in Lesson 9.2. Others are more aptly called "healing" or "divination," but are still forms of magic and energy-work (are they not?).

When it comes to what you need to know or might want to know for ritual construction and creation, the sky is really the limit. Undoubtedly, some students working through this material are more adept ritualists than I am and will blow my mind with what they do for their student ritual. Others have never once attended a ritual with another living person and are terrified of this project -- and are still apt to do amazing and thought-provoking things!

So, two more ritual-based energetic concepts to consider …

The Lame Step

The "lame step" is one of the old and identifying markers of Witches and of their God. And their Goddess. Nursery rhymes show us the evidence of the lame step in magic, the Forge God (the first and mightiest God of the CRAFT) is more often "lamed" than not, and the Witches' Goddess hobbled on a goose's foot.

Let's look at these examples, and then, let's look at what the lamed step signifies.

The Forge God and the Lame Step

The lame step could be said to originate, as it relates to magic, with the God of the Forge. The first being worshiped as a Forge God has been linked to magic. (In his book *Masks of Misrule*, Nigel Jackson notes his assertion that T'Qayin and Azazel are the same being.) Nearly all Forge Gods were depicted with a lame step or a misshapen leg in antiquity. The mundane reason for this was very likely due to the residual heavy metal poisoning suffered by actual smiths -- or the fact that otherwise strong men who had suffered some crippling childhood disease or injury could still be trained to blacksmith work. Whatever the case, the image of the smith is intimately linked with that of hobbled or ham-strung, yet powerful, man. A man who understands something (and potentially EVERYTHING) related to the alchemical process, and therefore magic. In the case of T'Qayin and Azazel, this image is that of a goat-footed God.

The goat-foot is one variation of lame step, and it is very intimately linked to the forge. That heavy metal poisoning we discussed bunched the muscles of the leg in a way that it pulled the smith's legs and foot up into a position like he was walking on a stiletto heel. Goat-footed God.

The Goose-Footed Goddess

The lame step appears again in the Witches' Goddess in at least one instance. In France, there is a notable story of La Reine Pedauque, the goose-footed queen. Though there is some casual optimism that her story is based a historical queen (named Berthe, who loved spinning fanciful tales for children), the goose-foot is never satisfactorily explained. What is absolutely clear is that La Reine Pedauque becomes (or always was) Mother Goose. Clearer still, with even a little digging and reflecting, is that Mother Goose, is so closely related to the Teutonic Hulda that they are reflections of one another.

Frau Hulda, Mother Hulda, Holda, Holle, Hel. She rides a goose through the night sky and is a spinner. She is the Dark Grandmother and the White Lady.

With her goose-foot, she shows us another aspect of the lame step.

The Lame Step in Nursery Rhymes

<u>Cock-a-doodle-do!</u>
Cock-a-doodle-do!
My dame has lost her shoe,
My master's lost his fiddle stick
And knows not what to do.

Cock-a-doodle-do!
What is my dame to do?
Till master finds his fiddle stick,
she'll dance without her shoe.

I love (and I mean LOVE) picking apart nursery rhymes for folkloric Craft clues. This one caught my interest on a number of levels. I'll stay away from the bits about how the magister needs his blackthorn staff (the master's fiddle stick) and just point out that the dame is inviting the lame step here. Lots of nursery rhymes feature characters with just one shoe. This forces them to hobble a bit -- like their God, like their Goddess.

Here, the dame MUST, but then she goes into it gladly, dancing within the compass.

I can think of three others where characters lose a shoe. In one, the boy goes to bed in his stockings, but missing a shoe. In the second, a girl has lost one of her holiday shoes. In the third, the princess dances out of one of her shoes (and again the fiddler is mentioned). All of these not only point to the lame step, but also to the Witches' Sabbat.

What is the Significance of the Lame Step?

The lame step, I've come to realize, is a marker for those who walk between the worlds. Symbolically, it represents having one foot in consensus reality and one foot in the realms beyond the veil. The lame step is a way of showing that you are between the worlds.

The Compass is Laid by treading the Mill using the lame step. And generally, the most potent form of treading the mill to raise energy is done with the lame step as well.

I'll throw this into the mix as well. From many culture, you see walkers between world and visionaries with limps, canes, staffs, and single eyes, different-lensed glasses, etc. There is a liminality expressed in the way these figures move. In the way they see. There are lessons and Mysteries there.

Widdershins & Deosil

The terms deosil and widdershins come to common Craft usage from older German and Gaelic terms that refer generally to clockwise and counter-clockwise movements, respectively.

Deosil is a more modern spelling of the Irish and Scots Gaelic terms meaning "right" or "sunwise" -- as in "turning in the direction of the sun." It was considered propitious to turn to the right and to favor right-handed movements, a propensity that carried over into ritual practice and was handed down into superstition to the point that some people even believed that drinking or performing other actions with the left hand could prove to be fatal.

Widdershins, on the other hand, comes from an old Germ word *widersinnig* ("against" + "sense"). *This form of "sense" is actually most closely related to words like "practicality" and "aptness." So, to move widdershins is to move against the norm.*

This bears out when we look at the way the word was cited in the Oxford English Dictionary's entry. In an early attestation from 1513, where it was found in the phrase "widdersyns start my hair", i.e. my hair stood on end.

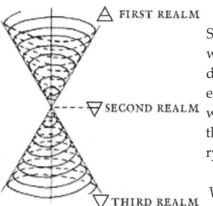

Some traditions have strict rules about only moving deosil or only moving widdershins within the caim. This Tradition uses both types of movement during ritual, though we use them very deliberately. We acknowledge that every step within the compass is an act of treading the mill. Be cognizant with each step you take of whether or not you are building on the magick of the work you are aiming to do, or if you are unwinding it by moving contrary-wise.

We choose to tread the mill in both directions, depending on the nature of the rite. We use the mill to lead us either up and out or down and within. When treading sunwise, the energy rises upward spiraling us into the first realm. Treading widdershins brings the energy down into the land where we can access the third realm. Neither of these movements is more desirable than the other, they are both as necessary and as benign as the positive and negative poles of a magnet.

When casting the caim we call inward towards the Stang. We call the gates and two-by-two to create the old straight track that joins each gate to the center like the spokes of a wheel -- or the crossroads.

The circle is thrice cast, as of old, but by the power of the gates and guardians, not by the power of ourselves as casters. The circle is cast not to hold energy out or even in, but to sain (cleanse/bless) the space.

First we Raise the Stang. This is the first "circle." The navel.

Then we Lay the Compass by marking the border with the lame step. This is the second circle.

Finally, we Open the Gates, two and two, opposites facing each other. This is the third circle. The crossroads.

Assignment

Continue fleshing out your ritual. The next step is to write the full script or the fully detailed outline. Leave nothing out. A reader should be able to know *exactly* what is going to happen at every point in the ritual.

Additional Resources

BoS Pages Included

Lame Step
Widdershins & Sunwise
Opening the Gates
Cleansing Chants
Witch's LBRP
Housle
Mill Songs

Red Thread Academy
Traditional Witchcraft
Year 1: Foundations

Unit 7: Student Ritual
Lesson 3: Ritual Performance

Ritual Performance

Prerequisite Lesson

7.2 - Components of Ritual

Objectives

- To perform a ritual that the student has designed
- To be responsible for the successful completion of the ritual
- To document all aspects of the ritual's execution, within reason

Materials Needed

Full Ritual Script/Outline

All necessary Materials, as dictated by script

Camera/phone for documentation (optional)

Study Notes

It's time to perform your Student Ritual. There really isn't much to say here in the Study Notes. The bulk of this lesson comes from *doing. The proof is really in the pudding, for this one.*

Take your time and relax. You have the time and space to revise and edit to get the details in place for your ritual beforehand. Don't feel rushed.

Assignment

Before and after the ritual, take pictures of the altar(s), the Compass, yourself, the materials, any products, etc. If you feel comfortable taking video during the ritual and then sharing part or all of the video as part of your essay (in the Lesson 7.4), that would be acceptable, too. (It is NOT required.) Be sure to spend a good amount of time after the ritual is complete answering the questions you identified in your Planning Worksheet in Lesson 7.1 regarding the De-Brief.

Additional Resources

BoS Pages Included

Red Thread Academy
Traditional Witchcraft
Year 1: Foundations

Unit 7: Student Ritual
Lesson 4: Debrief & Analysis

Debrief & Analysis

Prerequisite Lesson

7.3 - Ritual Performance

Objectives

- To analyze and evaluate the performance of a ritual
- To identify areas of success within a ritual
- To identify areas of needed improvement within a ritual

Materials Needed

Full Ritual Script/Outline
Ritual Pictures/Videos
Ritual Planning Worksheet

Study Notes

We spent some time talking in Lesson 7.1 about the reasons for the Debrief session at the end of a ritual. It gives you and any ritual participants the opportunity to make some sense of the rich symbolic landscape you just exited, provides you with additional time to ground, allows you to transition back into consensus reality, gives you the opportunity to reflect on what worked for you as a magical operator (as well as what did not), let's you take stock of any fumbled stage directions or other poorly handled "business" that might need to be practiced for smoother experience, etc.

In short, taking the time to talk through (or write about) what happened in the ritual, let's you make sense of each part of the ritual on multiple levels. You can break it down in terms of how it impacted your thinking, how it stimulated your physical senses, what emotions were triggered, or what spiritual insights you gained.

At the same time, you can also look at how the ritual can be improved in all of these ways.

Assignment

After having done a thorough debrief of the ritual, write a detailed analysis. Walk through each part of the ritual step-by-step (including any preliminary steps, such as ritual baths or cleansing the space) and offer insight into how and why each part worked (or didn't). Share the impressions you received during the ritual, as well as what you might do differently if you were to do a similar rite in the future. Include your pictures (with captions for context, please).

Additional Resources

BoS Pages Included

Red Thread Academy
Traditional Witchcraft
Year 1: Foundations

Unit 8: Divination
Lesson 1: Scrying

Scrying

Prerequisite Lesson None specified

Objectives
- Learn the basic techniques related to water scrying
- Craft a scrying mirror
- Attempt scrying in a dark mirror, glass of water, and cauldron

Materials Needed

Cauldron
Water glass
Picture frame with glass (or clock glass)
Black enamel
Paint brush
Black velvet

Study Notes

Though you can scry with any of the elements, water scrying might be the oldest version of divination known to humans. It reveals much in connection with our emotions, psyches, past-lives, ancestors – all of the things we associate with the 3rd Realm (the Underworld). We use this Realm a good deal for trying to find connections in the bases of our beings. Learning to navigate these waters will help you understand the underpinning issues and patterns involved in your most complex situations.

The technique for scrying in any element is going to be more or less the same. In short, you will enter a meditative state, relax your gaze while looking in the direction of your scrying tool or element, and then simply allow the messages or images to come to you. If you are using a cauldron, water goblet, or dark mirror (as you will in your assignment for this lesson), it is helpful to do this work in a darkened room with a single candle flame whose light is shining on the surface of the water or glass, but isn't directly in your line of vision. This is a similarly good effect for crystal spheres, by the way. (Actually, limiting other visual stimuli while scrying is often helpful, though the more you practice this technique, the more you will develop your own tricks.

Some people like to add oils or herbs to the water. Some add a silver coin or gemstone to a bowl, cauldron or cup. These are all acceptable, though they may change the nature of your messages/images. Experiment, but be sure to note any additions you have made to the pure water.

To Make a Dark Mirror ("Keek Stone")

Essentially, this tool is made by painting the backside of a piece of glass with black enamel (probably 2-3 coats to account for streaks). You can get fancy with frames, wooden boxes, clock glass (painting the outside of the bowl, as it were, so that you gaze into a deep well of black), magical embellishments, etc. Try to make it of a size in which you'll be able to see your whole face at no further than arm's length away.

Assignment

Make several scrying attempts using the cauldron, your keek stone, and a water glass. Record your results as journal impressions. The hope is that you will have at least one successful attempt with each tool. Include pictures of your dark mirror with your scrying results.

Additional Resources

Crystal Balls and Crystal Balls: Tools for Ancient Scrying & Modern Seership by Scott Cunningham -- https://amzn.to/30jeH7m

BoS Pages Included

Scrying
How to Make a Dark Mirror

Red Thread Academy
Traditional Witchcraft
Year 1: Foundations

Unit 8: Divination
Lesson 2: Divination Choice #1

Your Choice of Divination Tool #1

<u>Prerequisite Lesson</u>   None Specified

<u>Objectives</u>
- To prove at least a minimum level of competency in 3 forms of divination, as chosen by the student
- Of these three, to prove proficiency or even fluency with one of the forms
- To be able to use both hard (objective) and soft (subjective) forms for divination
- To perform readings in a variety of settings for a variety of querents

<u>Materials Needed</u>   the tool and accoutrements related to the divinatory form

<u>Study Notes</u>

You must prove competency in three different forms of divination. It will be best for your studies if these are three distinctly different types of divination. Smoke scrying and scrying with a keek stone are different, but similar enough that I would advise against it. Yes, you will get different results and have different experiences. And if you are very drawn to scrying, I highly recommend that you explore different methods and tools as you enter Year 2: Practicum. But for now, give yourself more breadth and variety in your experience to get a feel for what is available to you. Test out some wildly different things if you can before you decide which three you will study in greater depth.

With one of the three divinatory forms, you must be able to demonstrate a higher level of proficiency, as well. I want you to have some competency with all three, of course. Your readings should follow some sort of form, be understandable, have interpretations that resonate (if they are strictly intuitive) or adhere to conventions (if they employ traditional forms). But you are not necessarily expected to have memorized the meanings or placements at this stage of your studies if Tarot or Norse Rune or Celtic Ogham are part of your systems. In other words, you are allowed to use a reference book during your readings, if you must. I'd prefer that you aren't relying on it throughout the whole reading, though. Some of the reading should absolutely be an interpretation that comes from you, and that isn't sitting in the book.

At least one of these forms must be a "hard" form. By this, I mean that it must be objective or have a largely standardized meaning. Divination forms in this category include Runes, I-Ching, Tarot, Ogham, etc. Almost anything that comes with a book for you to learn what the symbols mean. Yes, there is wiggle room. There is still lots of room for personal interpretation. But there are only so many things that the Tower card can mean in the Tarot. To be truly proficient, you'll want to prove to yourself that you are learning and using a system that has a more fixed set of meanings.

Likewise, one of the forms must be "soft" or subjective. Scrying in smoke or water or event acrylic paint swirls is one example. Throwing bones is another. These are systems that might have books on the market with authors explaining their process or offering a guidepost, but there is no single way to do it. No set of symbols that works for everyone. It relies on your personal symbol set. This will help you with trusting your intuition and working within this sort of loose structure, as well.

The third choice is entirely free will. Forms that don't fit easily into one of the categories above could be considered here -- Ouija, pendulum, etc -- or you could double-down on a category above.

Assignment	For each of your 3 divination forms, you will need to write a brief essay (500-1000 words) discussing its history, folklore, and your own experience using the tool. You will also need to include the following logs/records of divination practice with this tool: • Daily Divinations (performed everyday for a week) • One Divination performed at the Full Moon • One Divination performed for another person
Additional Resources	Thoth Tarot -- Aleister Crowley and Lady Frieda Harris -- My absolutely favorite Tarot deck. It has layers of rich symbolism, including art, color, numerology, astrology, Qabalah, and more -- https://amzn.to/36iS8mY Understanding the Thoth Tarot -- Lon Milo Duquette -- The best book I have found for learning the Tarot, especially the Thoth Tarot -- https://amzn.to/2S7ejEq Ogham: The Celtic Oracle of the Trees -- Paul Rhys Mountfort -- https://amzn.to/36gUxyA Taking Up the Runes -- Diana Paxson -- https://amzn.to/36d5XDA
BoS Pages Included	Numerology Palmistry Pendulum Divination Runic Divination Scrying How to Make a Dark Mirror Witches' Runic Oracle

Red Thread Academy
Traditional Witchcraft
Year 1: Foundations

Unit 8: Divination
Lesson 3: Divination Choice 2

Your Choice of Divination Tool #2

Prerequisite Lesson
08-02 Your Choice of Divination Tool #1

Objectives
- To prove at least a minimum level of competency in 3 forms of divination, as chosen by the student
- Of these three, to prove proficiency or even fluency with one of the forms
- To be able to use both hard (objective) and soft (subjective) forms for divination
- To perform readings in a variety of settings for a variety of querents

Materials Needed
the tool and accoutrements related to the divinatory form

Study Notes
Continue researching and practicing with your divination tools. I suspect that you are working with these tools and techniques concurrently, though it is possible to focus on one, complete that area of study, and then move onto the next.

Be sure to research books on the market that might support your studies, aside from the guidebooks that you may have purchased with your cards/tool.

Assignment
For each of your 3 divination forms, you will need to write a brief essay (500-1000 words) discussing its history, folklore, and your own experience using the tool.

You will also need to include the following logs/records of divination practice with this tool:
- Daily Divinations (performed everyday for a week)
- One Divination performed at the Full Moon
- One Divination performed for another person

Additional Resources

BoS Pages Included

Red Thread Academy
Traditional Witchcraft
Year 1: Foundations

Unit 8: Divination
Lesson 4: Divination Choice 3

Your Choice of Divination Tool #3

Prerequisite Lesson — 08-02 Your Choice of Divination Tool #1

Objectives
- To prove at least a minimum level of competency in 3 forms of divination, as chosen by the student
- Of these three, to prove proficiency or even fluency with one of the forms
- To be able to use both hard (objective) and soft (subjective) forms for divination
- To perform readings in a variety of settings for a variety of querents

Materials Needed — the tool and accoutrements related to the divinatory form

Study Notes

Continue researching and practicing with your divination tools. I suspect that you are working with these tools and techniques concurrently, though it is possible to focus on one, complete that area of study, and then move onto the next.

Be sure to research books on the market that might support your studies, aside from the guidebooks that you may have purchased with your cards/tool.

Assignment

For each of your 3 divination forms, you will need to write a brief essay (500-1000 words) discussing its history, folklore, and your own experience using the tool.

You will also need to include the following logs/records of divination practice with this tool:
- Daily Divinations (performed everyday for a week)
- One Divination performed at the Full Moon
- One Divination performed for another person

Additional Resources

BoS Pages Included

Red Thread Academy — Unit 9: Energy Work
Traditional Witchcraft
Year 1: Foundations — Lesson 1: Aligning the Three Souls

Aligning the Three Souls

Prerequisite Lesson None specified

Objectives
- Learn the difference between grounding and centering
- Develop a grounding and centering practice
- Practice grounding and centering in preparation for future energetic work
- Learn and use the Three Soul Alignment

Materials Needed

Study Notes

Grounding and Centering are two separate but related energetic practices, but the terms get used very frequently in conjunction with each other. They should not be mistaken as synonymous terms, though. They are not the same thing.

These are very basic techniques, and while I would love to assume that everyone coming to this course is already using some type of grounding and centering practice, experience says that won't be the case. Moreover, experience also says that we won't all be using those terms the same way. So, even if you think you know and do these well, take a quick read and check in. And hey, if you're new to all this, don't feel bad. We all started right where you are at some point. Once upon a time, I, too, was a baby Witch who was only ever grounded and centered by accident, and I had to learn.

Why Do I Need Grounding & Centering?

Most of the time, you go about your day without particularly noticing the state of your energy. Is it balanced? Is it scattered? Is it this mystically grounded and centered business we keep yammering on about? Truthfully, I couldn't say. I don't know you, and I don't know what it feels like to live inside your skin or even to exist near you while you handle your life.

Generally speaking, if you find that you are handling life's ebbs and flows, ups and downs, dramas and joys with some grace and foresight, your energy is probably fairly balanced, grounded, and working from your center. You are proactive, not reactive. You are very zen and cool. You might be my hero.

I have to work to achieve that level of calm and collectedness. I used exercises like the ones mentioned below when I was first learning, plus I've also benefited from other mindfulness and meditation practices all throughout my journey along the Crooked Path. Even as an experienced Witch, I still need to take a moment to ground and center myself when I feel my energy "run amok" or "go wonky" (technical terms).

Your energy can be "off" in lots of ways that would benefit from grounding and centering techniques. Your energy is probably "wonky" if you are feeling spacy, disoriented, clumsy, confused, overwhelmed, anxious, agitated, hyper, drained, etc. You might have too much energy coursing through your system, not enough energy, *someone else's energy,* or just too many conflicting energetic desires of your own.

Actually, when you're in the middle of feeling this way, the WHY is less important to figure out right at that moment. Analyze how you got there later so you can work on avoiding repeat scenarios. In the moment, what you need is a technique to ground.

Grounding

"To ground one's energy" means to root oneself, to draw energy from the earth, and to allow one's excess energy to flow into the earth. If you are familiar at all with the electrical trade, it is much like grounding an electrical current. This allows for better flow and steadier, more focused control of the energy current running through your system (your physical, spiritual, emotional, and energetic bodies).

There are many ways to accomplish energetic grounding. The simplest is to make yourself aware of your energetic connection to the earth and allow your energy to balance out with it. You're standing right on it, all the time. Even if you're inside a building, only thin layers of concrete (rock) separate you from (and yet connect you to) the Earth. Visualize that connection and tap in. Or, if you need to get hands on, go outside and get your hands and feet in some dirt, on some stones. Stomp, dance, walk. Move your energy in rhythm with the ground, and this alone will ground you.

Actually, movement and (certain) food can both be very grounding. (Sugar and alcohol and highly processed foods will NOT help. Do not grab a twinkie and a beer and think you are grounding. You are not.) Do you remember being told when you were young to go play or to run off your extra energy? That still applies (though I find dancing to be a lot more fun than running these days). Likewise, if you find yourself trembling after a vigorous and moving ritual or a difficult interaction with someone, for the love of sweet Aunt Sally, eat something. Bread and salted butter are especially helpful.

Grounding jewelry can also help keep your energy on an even keel day to day. I wear a balanite (basalt/black lava) bracelet almost every day. It has been so effective that I often take it off and put it on the wrist of my daughter or my best friend if they are having a panic attack and don't have something of their own that is grounding. I have put it on the friend often enough that I left my original bracelet on her and have made myself a new one.

I used to wear a hematite necklace or ring, and they were also effective. Other grounding stones include black tourmaline, black obsidian, red jasper, gold tiger's eye, shungite, and smokey quartz. Most black stones are actually quite effective for this, but I have found that balanite (basalt/lava) works best. It is also called touchstone, and it has a long history of use in Trad Craft.

Several essential oils can also be very grounding. A few that are relatively easy and inexpensive to buy include sandalwood, cedarwood, vetiver, patchouli, and frankincense. Put several drops in a diffuser, in a carrier oil to wear on your skin, or even drop onto the basalt bracelet. (It is actually a new trend to use the black lava bracelet as an anti-anxiety oil diffuser. Hello?!?! Yes! That's exactly what I've been saying for years. Me and Robert Cochrane.) ;)

A meditative modality for grounding is to visualize your energy flowing through your body. Do this by closing your eyes and connecting to your breath. You can be standing, sitting, or lying down. Notice the light and color of your own energy. Check in with yourself and see what you notice about the way the energy moves and feels. Return your focus to your breath. Notice your inhales and exhales. As you exhale, push tendrils of your energy out and down like roots toward the ground. As you inhale, relax. Exhale and gently stretch and push those tendril roots down some more, sinking into the ground. Inhale, relax. Exhale, push and stretch deeper into the earth. Inhale, pull the earth energy up through the connection you have made, feeling the rich soil and solid stone. Exhale, stretch down deeper, feeling the layers, feeling your roots gaining purchase and strength. Inhale, pulling solidity and security up into your trunk. Pull into your heart and mind, if needed. Continue breathing, in and out. Breathe easily, feeling your connection and the natural flow of power between you and the earth.

Centering

"To center one's energy" refers to the practice of bringing one's energetic awareness into a core energy center (or chakra) in the body. Centering is about focus and clearing the mind of distractions. It helps us to be present in the moment.

Most Witches, in my experience, use a location in their belly for this -- either the sacral chakra or the solar plexus chakra. Some use the heart chakra, which is the center-point of the 7-chakra system. (I feel like I have to note here, though, that the 7-chakra system is a very Eastern concept and is not a part of Traditional Craft. I'm referencing it because the chakras have become such a useful tool for talking about where energy sits in the body, and they are part of our larger culture at this point.) I was taught to bring the energy into my body and "set it swirling in the cauldron in [my] belly."

Again, one can center using a number of techniques and tools. Linking back to the meditative practice described above for grounding, if you have just grounded, you now have an open channel to the ground below you. Do the same for the sky above. It is exactly the same, except you are reaching up and drawing on celestial energy (starfire), which you gently draw into your energetic body. As I mentioned, your "cauldron" (belly) is the receptacle of those energies, which swirl and mingle. Let them expand and fill you with the energy you need, and then let them recede back to a comfortable space where you can move about your day. Know that you can always reach up or reach down and touch into those primal and eternal energies to draw on them. And you can always rebalance, if needed.

If you want to make jewelry to aid in centering, consider using blue lace agate, Herkimer diamonds, celestite, lapis lazuli, citrine, quartz crystal, kyanite, sodalite, and amethyst. I have worn a quartz crystal pendant that my grandfather made since the year I started practicing the Craft. I don't wear it every day, and it has been strung on several different necklaces over the last twenty-two years; but it has always been an important piece of magical jewelry for me. These days, it hangs on a string of quartz chips so that the pendant just about reaches my belly.

Aligning the Three Souls

We'll be talking about the tripartite nature of the soul in more depth in Lesson 10-1, so for now, let's just keep it simple.

Many traditional religions have a belief in a 3-part human soul. Furthermore, there is a sense that each of the three soul-parts are seated at certain energy centers in the human body -- the belly, the heart, and the crown.

The Spiral Castle Tradition talks about these three soul parts as:

The White Soul -- at the crown -- the Higher Self, the HGA, the Dove

The Red Soul -- at the heart -- the Ancestral Soul, the Hamingja, or Bone Soul

The Black Soul -- at the belly -- the Fetch, the Fylgja, the Ego

Aligning them is an act that both grounds and centers us, and it is something we can do quickly, easily, and simply every day over the span of just a few short breaths. It doesn't necessarily require any tools or extra ritual, although it can be made more elaborate, if you like.

I highly recommend that Spiral Castle Trad Dedicates and Initiates take the time to do this Triple Soul Alignment as a daily practice, in addition to using it as a practice prior to ritual or as means of finding balance in times of upheaval.

Start by getting your feet planted or otherwise feeling your connection to the earth below you. Then state, "May the Three Souls be straight within me."

Continue by taking a deep breath out, sending your energy like a taproot into the earth. On the inhale, pull the earth's energy (and with it, the Forge Fire at the center of the earth) into your belly — the seat of the Black Soul (the fetch, the personal identity, the Soul most connected with this life and your sense of Self).

On the next breath, pull the energy higher, to your chest — the seat of the Red Soul (the Bone Soul, the ancestor connection through blood and fire).

On the third breath, pull the energy higher yet, to the skull, the crown of the head — the seat of White Soul (the higher self, the Holy Guardian Angel, the God-Self).

On the final breath, pull/push the energy all the way through yourself, connecting to the Star Fire above, releasing the breath with a sigh. You are connected to the Witch-Fire above and below, within and without. All three soul-parts are connected and in harmony.

Assignment

Answer the following questions and send me your replies. Please share as much detail as you feel comfortable. This is an opportunity for you to do some self-exploration.

1. How would you describe your energy on an average day? On a really good day? On a bad day?
2. How do you handle stress? Surprises? Being startled? Embarrassment?
3. Do you get angry easily? Tearful?

4.Do you practice yoga, take fitness classes, go to a gym, lift weights, run, or otherwise workout? Tell me about how you show love to your body and ground your physical energy.

5.Do the grounding meditation a few times and tell me how it works out for you. OR, tell me about a grounding practice that you have been using effectively for a while. Is this something you can use prior to ritual or spellwork?

6.Do the centering meditation a few times and tell me how it works out for you. OR, tell me about a centering practice that you have been using effectively for a while. Is this something you can use prior to ritual or spellwork?

7.Did you make or do you already own any grounding and/or centering jewelry? Describe it or include a picture. How long have you had it? Does it work well for you?

Additional Resources

The Four Agreements by Don Miguel Ruiz -- This book isn't specifically about grounding and centering your energy, but it is about mindfulness, which is very connected. I have found it very helpful in my on-going efforts with being present, which is an important Craft skill. -- https://amzn.to/3iicQpi

8mm Black Lava (Balanite/Basalt) Beads -- if you want to make your own Black Soul/grounding bracelet -- https://amzn.to/3jcArsZ

8mm Clear Quartz Beads -- if you'd like to make your own White Soul/empowering bracelet -- https://amzn.to/2HzYBQ7

8mm Red Coral Beads -- if you'd like to make your own Red Soul/centering bracelet -- https://amzn.to/3n7p8EX

(Or combine all three for a fantastic Triple Soul Alignment bracelet!)

BoS Pages Included

Aligning the Three Souls

Energy Centers of the Body

Red Thread Academy
Traditional Witchcraft
Year 1: Foundations

Unit 9: Energy Work
Lesson 2: Raising & Directing Energy

Raising & Directing Energy

Prerequisite Lesson 9.1 Grounding & Centering

Objectives
- Identify sensations associated with energy work in the physical body
- Introduce and practice several ways to raise energy
- Discuss and practice shaping, building, coloring, texurizing, and otherwise manipulating energy

Materials Needed

Study Notes

In this lesson, we are going to be talking about the energy or Power of the Witch from the perspective of not just making it stable or centered within the body, but gathering it, generating it, building it, expanding it, and moving it in a controlled and directed manner.

The techniques in this lesson go hand-in-hand with those in lesson 9.1. You need to be working from a grounded and centered place in order to control the energy (and not have it controlling you instead). Continue to work on grounding and centering techniques throughout your studies. They are not a "one and done" sort of assignment.

We're going to kick off our discussion by looking at eight rather specific ways of raising energy for magical purposes that are taught to contemporary Witches, then look at a traditional folk way (seething) in more depth, before moving onto some rather New Age-y but very useful energy training exercises that you can use to practice these skills.

Eight Ways of Making Magic

Gerald Gardner, the founder of Wicca, wrote about the Eight Paths of Power in his Book of Shadows. While we are distinctly neither Gardnerian nor Wiccan, we can certainly start our conversation here as a jumping off point for looking into the ways that Witches raise energy.

According to Gardner, the "eight ways of making magic" are:
1. Meditation or concentration
2. Chants, Spells, Invocations, Charms, Rites, Runes, Etc.
3. Projection of the Astral Body, or Trance

4. Incense, Drugs, Wine, and whatever is used to release the Spirit.
5. The Dance and kindred practices
6. Blood Control, Breath Control, and kindred practices
7. The Scourge
8. The Great Rite

You can combine many of these ways to produce more power.

1. Meditation or concentration

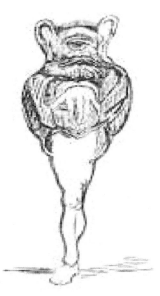

Meditation by Witchcraft standards didn't always have the connotations of Eastern zen philosophy that it now has. In western thought, it just meant "focused thought" or concentration. This sort of focused concentration on a subject is the most basic form of raising and sending energy. The evil eye is nothing more than negative thoughts clarified through intent and projected through the sense of sight. Meditation is a deeper form of concentration, and can be enhanced through specific postures and gestures. These postures can be compared to eastern yogic traditions although they have roots in Celtic forms of magic, such as the one-legged one-eyed stance which emulates the posture of the crane and the fachan for battle magic. Fergus Kelly in *The Guide To Early Irish Law* makes a statement that helps define it as a magic that kills. Kelly writes:

> "...some of their sorcery was effected through *córrguinech*, a term which seems to mean 'heron (or crane) killing', and apparently involved the recitation of a satire standing on one leg with one arm raised and one eye shut."

2. Chants, Spells, Invocations

This way of raising energy encompasses many different techniques, all of which have to do with the spoken word. Chanting is the original idea behind "enchantment." The words of a chant can reinforce the intent of the magic, or they can be seemingly nonsensical words with traditional meaning. An example of this kind of chant is the popular so-called "Basque Witches Chant."

Eko, eko, Azarak

Eko, eko, Zomelak

Bazabi lacha bachabe

Lamac cahi achababe

Karrellyos

Lamac lamac Bachalyas

Cabahagy sabalyos

Baryolos

Lagoz atha cabyolas

Samahac atha famolas

Hurrahya!

Spells, just as they sound, were once written or "spelled" documents detailing the results desired. This form of magic was especially popular in ancient Rome, when "spells" would be written on lead tablets and given to one of the elements (burning, tossing into water, burying, etc.) The Celts and Norse had similar practices, stitching their sacred alphabets into clothing for protection or carving it into objects for blessing or blasting work, as needed. Nowadays a spell is any set of actions that brings about change through an act of magic.

Invocations and evocations are actions of magic which use the voice to call upon Spirits or Deities to aid in the magical working, either by possessing the Witch (invocation) or simply by being present (evocation). In either case, the Spirit or Deity is lending power to the work to assure success.

3. Projection of the Astral Body, or Trance

In truth, all of the ways of making magic seek to bring the magician into a form of trance, even if it is very light. Through trance we perceive other realms and can manipulate the energy links that connect all things as one. Almost all of the "ways" listed here will produce at least a light trance state in a practitioner, and some will produce a profound one in almost everyone.

What contemporary society has come to call "astral projection" is something that Cunning Folk have generally always called "flight." We're going to cover "flying out" in more depth in lesson 10.2 (Fetch). Also, our Beltaine ritual this year (lesson 3.5) features a guided meditation that is a flight to the Brocken. The Year 3/Mastery level of the Red Thread Academy includes a unit-long intensive study of witch flight, and there are additional opportunities in Year 2/Practicum for exploration of this useful and delightful modality.

Guided meditation, drumming, and seething are all very effective ways to seek a trance state. (We're going to cover seething in much more depth later in this lesson.)

4. Incense, Drugs, Wine, etc.

Entheogens (substances which, by definition, enable us to embody the Gods) have a long and storied history in the Craft, particularly the Solanaceae family. They have been used in flying ointments, transformation elixirs, herbal incenses, smokes, anointing oils, washes, and any mixture you can think of. Also popular in certain circles are amanita muscaria, wormwood, damiana, hashish, syrian rue, and countless others. Wine, of course, is central to the Red Meal, and also serves as a gentle way to let slip our egos and find ourselves outside of consensus reality when used in moderation. All of these substances are dangerous, and several of them are also illegal. Several of them can be lethal, even in small amounts. This is one of the ways of magic that should not be attempted by the untrained Witch.

As you continue your studies, if you decide to experiment with entheogens, I would offer you these cautions:

    1. Don't use entheogens as a substitute or replacement for actual energetic practices. Do get lazy and let the drugs or alcohol do the spiritual work for you.

    2. Don't use entheogens without a "safety" in place. Be knowledgeable about possible side effects of whatever you are using, and have someone in the area who is not using it who can make sure you are physically okay. This person needs to have an iron will and be unfailing in their resolve to call upon emergency services if you are showing signs of overdose or poisoning.

    3. Remember that less is more. You don't need much. Start very, very small in your dosing and see what opens up. Give it lots of time

4. If you think you can fly, you have to start from the ground. (I have a festival friend who hands out LSD tabs like they're mints, but she always gives them with that same advice. "You have to take off from the ground.")

It might sound like I'm a big advocate for drug and alcohol use within the Craft. Truthfully, I'm not. I'm an herbalist and a pragmatist, so I value their role, in moderation; but I've also seen the havoc people wreak in their lives when they abuse these substances.

My favorite entheogens are two that are quite safe in all but outlandish doses. They are my recipes for Sabbat Wine (a mulled sweet red wine with lemongrass and mugwort, with honey) and Non-Toxic Flying Ointment. I also make several incenses that are highly effective for shifting my consciousness almost instantaneously.

5. Dancing

Dancing may be the oldest form of celebration and communication. It is central to the raising of power through the treading of the mill. The mill is tread by moving in a circle (often with a "lame step" that is representative of the Red God or the Goose-Footed Goddess) over ground where the compass has been laid. More vigorous mill-treading can happen in large groups where the spiral is danced inward and outward in a kind of follow-the-leader procession. Dancing in circles around a bonfire is an ancient and pan-cultural tradition. This form of raising power can be witnessed at many sabbats and festivals around the world. Another fairly well-known and very effective energetic pattern for dancing in groups involves leading the group around the circle clockwise for three full rotations, the counterclockwise for a quarter rotation, and repeating this for as long as the group is able. Instead of raising a "cone" of power, as generally happens, the group raiser a "tower" of power which is taller, thicker, and more forcefully aimed at its target. Typically, the group is able to dance longer periods of time, as well. Some large crowds have been able to maintain this dance upwards of three hours.

6. Use of the Cords

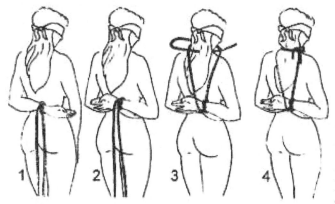

These, also known as warricking and stropping, are often used in combination to produce the desired trance state within Gardnerian Wicca and its derivatives. The cords are used to slightly restrict blood flow to certain areas of the body while the person being bound is made to stand or sit in uncomfortable positions also used to restrict circulation. This practice is not as commonplace among traditionalists in the sense that it isn't used at Full Moons or as a routine part of magical practices. That isn't to say that it might not be used for certain extraordinary experiences or magical needs, but it isn't "common."

The use of cords within Traditional Witchcraft is more commonly tied (pardon the pun) to initiatory cords and knot magic. Through the contemplation of certain knots, plaits, and other features of the cord a trance state can be achieved much like in the use of a rosary or prayer beads. (See lesson 5.4)

7. The Scourge

This is another tool and method that I find more common to Gardnerian Wicca and may have been part of their Mysteries, but is limited in its use within truly Traditional Craft. Where it has found its way into what I'll call revival Traditionalist Craft (like RTA), are places where teachers like me are drawn to the symbolism or symmetry of a particular tool or method that has gained a foothold from either early/formative or prolonged exposure to ceremonial practices or other influences.

The Gardnerians use the scourge regularly to induce trance by flicking it in a light stroking motion to encourage blood flow into certain areas (usually the base of the spine while they kneel in child's pose). Light, rhythmic application of the scourge can produce trance just as would a steady drumbeat, or the use of the lamed step.

Some covens use a scourge as part of initiatory or other gateway rituals, where the strike of the flails can either be mild, moderate, or even more severe. In these cases, the symbolism of the scourge varies widely from coven to coven, but the effect is almost always to alter consciousness in some way. Whether the trance state created from light flicking or the "sub space" (to borrow the terminology from the BDSM community) of moderate to intense "flogging," a distinct shift happens.

What the scourge shouldn't be used for in any coven is punishment. Witches are grown-ups who are accountable to themselves and their Gods (and that, within reason). We take oaths within our covens to act honorably and to follow certain rules in order to protect each others' privacy, but we are not children to be "spanked" because we have misbehaved. (And, yes, I have heard of the scourge being used as punishment in recent years. It was a heinous abuse of power, enacted in a semi-public setting in which none of the other coveners said or did anything to intervene. They were probably all too shocked by the insanity of it. This happened in the early 2000's.)

8. The Great Rite

The Great Rite "in truth" is the act of sexual congress between two individuals who have each invoked a God or Goddess. Another term for this act is the *hieros gamos* or *Sacred Marriage. What Gardner was actually getting at by including this as one of the ways of making magic was the idea of sexual energy being used as a conduit for magic. Anyone can do this, partnered or not, invoked or not. It is quite popular in modern chaos magic circles, particularly those influenced by the work of A.O. Spare.*

The Great Rite "in symbol" is routinely performed in the Wiccan version of the eucharistic sacrament, in which a cup and a blade represent the dualistic creative forces of the universe that bless the cakes and wine at the end of the ritual. This happens at the end of every ritual, much the same as our Housle or Red Meal concludes stands as an offertory conclusion to all of our rituals and can also be an independent ritual You'll note that our sacramental meal has less of a sexual theme and more of a sacrificial theme, though.

Sex magic within Traditional Witchcraft is fairly commonly practiced but not quite as openly written about. Actually, that's perhaps an inaccurate statement. It's difficult to write about. Gardnerain and Alexandrian sex magic often happened within the circle in a semi-public setting. It was ceremonial by nature. Traditional Witches tend to practice sex magic of a more private and personal type, and we are generally more secretive about sharing any of our experiences with people who aren't our People.

Some groups use sex magic as part of group work, and some don't. I have feelings and experiences about this that color my own philosophies. I have watched too many groups fall apart because of very complicated sexual relationship boundary overlaps. Lots of polyamorous people who thought they were communicating well (but weren't), thought they were respecting their partners' needs (but weren't), and thought they wouldn't feel neglected or jealous by the shifting dynamics (but did). You add in things like differences in degrees and hierarchies or roles and duties and now you have folks who think preferential treatment is happening because so-and-so is sleeping with the Magister (or is getting treated badly because they decided not go out with the Dame again). It gets complicated and ugly really fast.

I adore working with sexual energy, though. And group sexual energy is extra potent! There are workarounds. I won't go into all of that here since this is a Year 1 lesson and most everyone taking it is likely to be in a solitary situation. But I do lead a class at festivals called "Look Ma: No Hands! (Sex Magic Without Touching)." I'd be happy to adapt that to an online format, if folks are interested, when you're ready.

I'll state for the record that nobody should ever require of you that you engage in any sort of sexual activity in order to participate with them magically. That's manipulate and predatory. Get as far away as you can from any "teacher" or "guru" who tries to tell you that the Great Rite in Truth is required for initiation. If they don't have the chops to test your adeptness without sex, then they don't have the chops to test it during sex either.

That wraps up the eight ways identified by Gardner. The list is fairly inclusive, if you look at some of the items (like dancing, trancing, and meditation) with a fairly broad view, which we did. Our lessons throughout this year, including the rituals and spells, are designed to give you the chance to experience and experiment with a almost all of these "ways," and I can speak truthfully in saying that I will not be offended or shocked if your spellwork or personal magic seeks to explore things like sex magic or Sabbat Wine, as long as you have given yourself some safety nets. Some of these ways will resonate with you. Others will not. Don't give up on something just because it feels strange or awkward at first. Keep going and see if you can develop your own groove.

Okay, let's take a closer look at seething.

Seething

Seething is a linguistic derivative of *Seiðr (Seithr)*, which is a type of sorcery that was practiced in Norse society during the Late Scandinavian Iron Age. Modern witches use seething as a way to shamanically get outside of themselves, into an altered state, and to raise the Power for charging a spell, tool, or talisman or to come into contact with Spirits. Whether the seething practice that has come down to us is a well-distilled form of the sorcery practiced by Norse women (for it was primarily a women's magic) or a corruption of it, that is hard to say. Based on the resources we have (the Eddas, etc), it seems that what we practice now is very much linked to what they did then. This is a spiritual heritage that has been passed through our ancestors -- the Witches they couldn't burn, as the popular saying goes.

"To seethe" has also come to mean "to be turbulent, to boil." The word had this definition by the Middle Ages, as well, and you will probably able to guess as your read the description below that the trance state achieved by this technique is not one of zen and peace. Much like the name suggests, you will be "working yourself up" when you seethe.

There are two modern interpretations of the practice of seething based on accounts in old Nordic sagas and other ancient literature. The first method is very much like the practice of Treading the Mill. The witch bears a gandreigh, or riding pole, such as a staff, broom, stang, hobby-horse, or wand. He then treads a wide circle while focusing power on a central point, such as a stang, altar, or lead witch. Alternately, the witch may choose to use their own gandreigh as the focal point and circle around it while holding it as the axis point.

The second method of seething is much more adaptable to any situation, although it may not be as historically accurate. It entails the raising of great emotion and force of Will through the act of rocking back and forth (or side to side, or in a circle), or clenching and unclenching the muscles of the body in rapid succession. It is from this method that we gain the modern usage of the word "seething," as in: "I was seething with anger."

Anyone who has "zoned out" while relaxing in a rocking chair can understand how this method works. By simple rhythmic control of the animal body, the mind becomes free to wander as it will. By adding a strong emotional component to the movement the mind keeps its focus on the magical work being done and the Power is raised. This technique of seething is very similar to the Gardnerian Wiccan practice of ritual scourging to raise the power, as it both controls the blood flow and heightens the emotional state.

It is also very useful for altering consciousness when seeking to interact with Spirit realms, which we discuss in lesson 10.1 Evocation and Banishing.

I recommend trying both methods. By the end of this course, you will have created your own Stang, so you will have the tool to attempt the mill-treading version of seething, and the rocking/swaying version can be done anytime you have a few minutes to allow yourself to get into and out of the energetic state. You can generally control how far you go into the trance state by controlling the speed, rhythm, direction, and intensity of your rocking or swaying, your muscle control, and your breathing. To start with, don't worry so much about contracting and releasing the muscles, just focus on the movement and your breath.

Energy Exercises

These are exercises you can do on your own, but some can also be modified and expanded if you are able to get one or two partners to join you. A spouse, roommate, or offspring are the likeliest candidates, and they will probably be amazed and entertained by the metaphysics of what you are studying.

1.
Rub your hands together a little and then move them apart about an inch. Concentrate on the space between your palms and fingers. Visualize an energy cushion there. You may even be able to feel it already. Test the springy sensation of the energy fields of your two hands touching each other. Take some time to experiment and test just what you can sense through your palms and fingertips. Run one hand over the back of the other without touching the skin. Stay an inch or more away. Test how far your hand can be and still have the energy body feel the sensation. Play around with this.

2. Bring your hands back together. This time, visualize sending more energy into your palms to create a small ball. (Note: At the level of energy work in these exercises, drawing from your own energy reserves probably won't deplete you, but it's a good idea to get in the habit of grounding and centering so you are drawing on universal energy stores and not your personal ones.) Manipulate the ball by adding energy to it. You can also expand the ball without adding energy to it and see how that feels different. Try doing things like adding more Water (or other elemental) energy to the ball. You can even get very specific and add ice energy or rain energy by calling on your memories and experiences of those things (or by having a sample, symbol, or other representation of them nearby to focus on). You can also do things like alter the texture and consistency of the energy ball. Start, by noting what it "feels" like now. Is it smooth? Staticky? Fluffy? Change it to something different. Then to something else. Can you make it spiky? Squirmy? Mushy? Can you make it very hard and impenetrable? How about flexible like rubber? If you had a partner, you could practice trading the ball back and forth with each other, with or without

telling each other how you have changed it. As a partnered activity, this is a great exercise for working on psychic development, as well as energy perception and visualization.

3. Focusing again on the energy ball in your hands, allow it to return to an energetically neutral color for you -- whatever it was when you first built the ball. For most people, that is clear/white or maybe a bluish-white light. Sit with the ball for a moment, and make sure you are grounded and centered. Note the color, texture, size, and density of this ball. Since we don't have a specific target for magic today, it doesn't make sense to direct that energy at some unknown or random target that we are making up on the spot for the purpose of this exercise. (If you have some goal in mind that you would like to give a little boost, feel free. I just don't choose to make one up before we've gotten into ethics and our discussion of spellcraft.) So, my recommendation for practicing a controlled direction of this energy is this: direct the energy back into your own system. Pull the energy ball toward your belly and let it sink back into your energetic cauldron. Pay attention to the sensations as it remains a ball for a moment before swirling back out into the energy flow that creates a circuit through you.

4. One last super cool activity I highly recommend trying is making divining rods from 2 metal (or plastic-coated metal) clothes hangers and 2 straws. Cut the hangers and bend them so they form L-shapes. Slide the straws on the short arms of the L's. Hold onto the straw-encased arms loosely enough that the long arms can swing. At first, they will swing all over the place. But as you start to focus, they too will focus and come into alignment with your thoughts. You can think "left" and they will point to the left. You can think "Fido" and they will point at the place in the room where the dog is lying curled on the floor. This experiment is described in detail in the book E-Squared (in the resource list below) and is such a great way to prove to yourself that "energy flows where your thoughts go." More than that, you can show yourself what unfocused thought does to your energy by trying to hold onto confusion or doubt. Do it with the rods and tell me the results.

Assignment	Do the energy experiments described above and journal about them. Record your experiences, making note of sensations, questions, or other things that come up for you.
	Do at least one seething session to raise energy and write about your experience, recording your experiences as above. Be sure to note which method you used.
Additional Resources	"Sex Magic in Traditional Witchcraft" (blog post) by Sarah Anne Lawless -- Fantastic Article on the subject of sex magic -- http://sarahannelawless.com/2010/07/30/sex-magic-in-traditional-witchcraft/ — NOTE: This article isn't available in its original location (Sarah's blog) anymore, because she disabled her blog and website in 2019. It is still findable via Google search, though, along with other writings of hers.
	"Seidr & Norse Shamanism" (blog post) by Sunnyway.com -- http://www.sunnyway.com/runes/seithr.html
	E-Squared: Nine Do-It-Yourself Energy Experiments That Prove Your Thoughts Create Reality (book) by Pam Grout -- https://amzn.to/3ielhSF
BoS Pages Included	Eight Ways of Making Magic Seething

Shielding & Releasing Energy

Prerequisite Lesson

09-02 Raising & Directing Energy
02-03 Elements

Objectives

- To use personal and universal energy to create personal Shields for psychic protection
- To create a variety of energetic barriers for use in different settings
- To practice releasing and cutting off energetic flow, as necessary

Materials Needed

Saltwater, Florida Water, or perfume

Study Notes

Now that you've got some practice with raising and directing energy and we've started working on your elemental correspondences within a traditional system, it'll be a bit easier to start putting this energy work into practical application. The most logical place to start is shielding. You may already have a method for shielding in place, in which case this lesson may only serve as a refresher for you (or give you some alternative tools). But I can't assume all students come with the same background, so we have to introduce the basics, just in case.

To create an energetic shield, you will start by grounding and centering. You don't want to create your shield from your personal energy stores, per se. While that could be fine for your basic needs most of the time, it can also be very draining. In fact, if you are a Highly Sensitive Person (HSP -- as described by Elaine Aron), as I find that a good number of Witches are, you may find yourself very often drained by everyday interactions with others. Learning how to manage your boundaries, interpersonal as well as energetic, will go a very long way in helping to give you balance and peace so you can accomplish those things that you have set as priorities without losing your mind.

So, yes, ground and center and gather in energy from Above and Below. You are always at the center of your own compass, whether you are intentionally laying a compass or not. So you can draw on the energies around you at any time if you are grounded and centered.

When we did the energy ball exercises, you focused on bringing energy to your palms. For shielding, you bring the energy outward through your whole body.

Your energetic body naturally extends for several inches past your physical body. Some people are able to see this energetic body. There are cameras that can photograph it. Certain cultures have names for the different layers of the energetic/spiritual body (bodies). We will talk more about the Triple Soul in lesson 10-01, but for now it is enough to agree that the concept of the energetic self is well-documented and actually visible by some people/instruments.

When we create an energetic shield, we are often extending that energetic body a little further and always reinforcing its outer perimeter. In its natural state, it allows other energy to flow through it -- ours goes out, others' comes in. The more empathic you are, the more you pick up on other people's emotions, moods, and physical illnesses, etc through this sort of energy exchange. You can also be extremely sensitive to physical energies like those from gemstones or woods or other objects with their own inherent power.

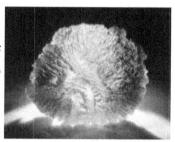

I was at a psychic fair a few years ago and had just purchased a moldavite ring. Fantastic stone! I bought it because I consider it a powerful representation of Witch Fire -- specifically of Tubelo's Green Fire (the cunning fire, the green fire between the eyes of the Dragon at the Fall of the Angels). It's a star-stone (tektite). Specifically, it's a type of glass created when a meteorite struck a particular area in what is now the Czech Republic. I had to build up a sort of tolerance to this stone when I first came into contact with it. I could look, but I couldn't touch it for long. It made the top of my head tingle and vibrate so forcefully that it could trigger a migraine for me. So the day I bought it, I put it in my pocket at the store where I was working as a Tarot reader and returned to the psychic fair around the corner where I later joined a conversation with a group of people I had just met. About five minutes into the chat, a young man started to swoon, and said, "I'm sorry, I don't know what's wrong. I was doing fine, but I feel really dizzy all of a sudden." We got him in a chair and asked the usual questions about whether he was hydrated and fed. I stepped away for a moment and when I came back, he rather shockingly said it was me that made him dizzy. He was fine when I left, and tilt-a-whirl when I returned. It was only then that I remembered the moldavite and the reaction I normally had to it. I was starting to build my tolerance to it, but this guy was even more sensitive than me. To test me theory, I took it out of my pocket and sent it away with a friend (not showing or telling him what it was). He was immediately fine. He later came over to my booth to have a look at the ring and almost passed out when I unwrapped it from the bag! Needless to say, that young man was not likely to ever buy moldavite for himself. It was practically kryptonite, in his case. I, on the other hand, wear my ring every time I do ritual work (and often just when I want a boost).

The point of the story is that as Witches, we need to be aware that we need good shields in our daily lives for more than just "negative energies." Social media these days is very fond of reminding us to sage our homes and put quartz in our windows and "clear the negativity away." I'd rather RTA Witches remember that we need balance. We need to take care of ourselves, and sometimes that means understanding that what is absolutely fabulous for someone else can make us sick or weak or off-kilter. It is our responsibility to know where our boundaries are and to reinforce them. Our shields are one of the ways we can do that.

Two Basic Types of Shields

You might think it's a little simplistic to say that shields come in two basic flavors, and you're right. We're going to talk in a minute about how you can make them as complex and unique as your specific energy signature. But in terms of basic function, your shields are going to do one of two things (more or less). They will

either be:
- Receptive, or
- Reflective

Like it says on the tin, a receptive shield (essentially) takes in the energy and a reflective shield sends it back.

Now, HOW they do that is where all the cool, fun, and creative bits happen. This is where your imagination and force of Will come into play.

Shield Construction & Composition

Your intention for the shield and how you visualize the energy forming around you determine what the shield looks, feels, and functions like.

You can decide if you want the shield to be permeable in one or both directions so you can send and/or receive energy (to/from loved ones, perhaps; or even sensations from co-workers or others with whom you would normally maintain some sort of link).

You can also decide how thick, tough/hard, etc the outer walls of the shield will be. Some shields might work best for you if they are thick and gelatinous like placenta or a hard-boiled egg-white. Others might need to be 10-foot thick concrete walls. Some might only need to be a thin bubble-layer membrane.

Like our energy balls, shields can be composed of raw (and also specific) elemental energy as well as the energy of specific stones, trees, animals, and natural forces. As you practice and work with this type of magic, you can create thunderstorm shields, oak leaf shields, raven shields, amethyst shields, etc.

Finally, you can layer multiple shields, so that you have inner and outer walls of protection. Maybe you always keep your innermost shield up, have a mid-range shield that you lower at home with your partner or closest friends (unless they're on edge), and have an outer shield that is in place any time you leave your home or have company over.

Infinite Applications

So, even though I said above that there are two basic types of shields (receptive and projective), you can see that there are really an infinite number of specific shields available to the inventive Witch. Let's take a look at a few examples, just for kicks and giggles.
- Receptive thick stone wall shield like the "castillo" forts intended to catch and hold incoming energy, where it will be neutralized & absorbed
- Receptive lava flow shield intended to melt incoming negativity (erected only during suspected/known confrontation)
- Receptive cotton batting shield intended to filter and cushion off-hand negativity and harshness (as an inner shield)
- Reflective clear quartz mirror shield with high shine and faceted cuts intended to send amplified energy back to originating source
- Reflective hurricane shield intended to send negative energy back to its source along with powerful destruction

I think you get the picture. The possibilities are endless. My advice, if this is new for you, is to start simple with something you can visualize and maintain for an extended period of time. You can build on the skill from there.

Releasing (& Cutting Off) Energy

We've talked a lot about get the energy flow started and rolling, but there may be times where you need to detach from it. There are a couple of ways you can do this. The simplest is using visualization.

We've used the tree visualization for grounding and centering, and so using the same visualization in reverse should be an effective way to disengage from an overstimulating energetic experience, if needed. Simply draw your "roots and limbs" back in toward yourself and strengthen your shields. (Actually, I'll add here that some people find disconnecting from the energy but connecting to the physical earth is very helpful to diffuse the excess energy in their systems.)

Another method that can be helpful is running your hands under cold tap water for a few moments/minutes. Similarly, saltwater is very helpful, as is Florida Water (which I talk about more in 10-1 Triple Soul, Evocation & Banishing). To use these, you can either dip your hands and feet into a small amount or sprinkle them onto your hands, feet, crown of the head, chest, and back of the heart. (These are the energy centers I find most effective. You may find that you need to focus somewhere other than the heart and head. The belly, perhaps. Maybe only the hands.)

You might also consider keeping a large stone that you pour excess energy into, like a battery that you can draw from at a later time when you are feeling low. Quartz is always a good choice for this, but there may be another that would work equally well for you. I have one for personal use that is labradorite.

A Word About Psychic Attacks & Battle Magic

Since we've talked so much in this lesson about shielding and sending energies back to their originating sources, it is natural for the question to arise about people intentionally sending negative energy to you.

Most people aren't intentionally sending any negative magic in your direction. They might be giving you the "evil eye" by looking enviously upon you or thinking unkind things about you. They might be saying unkind things about you, and therefore "cursing" you in that way. And those actions can carry energetic oomph that needs to be dealt with. But the truth is that most folks aren't collecting thunderstorm rain and pissing in bottles of rusty cut nails to throw on your doorstep.

Most.

If you are a newbie, you are almost certainly just trying to avoid the normal, everyday slings and arrows. The evil eyes and forked tongues of your peers can be dealt with by good psychic hygiene (grounding and centering, shielding, cleansing, and occasionally a little hex-breaking).

It is not entirely uncommon, though, to develop a "frenemy" or even an adversary or two within the Craft community after several years of experience. I don't want to dwell on this point because I feel that it makes newer Witches paranoid. If I only give you a hammer, you'll think every problem you encounter is a nail.

I've watched folks get eaten up with the idea that they were being attacked by psychic energies all the time.

If this is a worry for you, skip ahead to lesson 5.4, Witches' Ladders, and learn how to make this wonderful protection talisman. As a Witch, you should be able to put a key protection spell or two in place and NOT have to watch your back all the time.

If you find that you feel constantly "under attack," it is time to check your shields and revisit your grounding and centering routines. Unless you are aware that you are fighting for something that is meaningful and worthy of your defense/offense, you might just be drawing the lightning of anxiety or anger.

Assignment

1. Try making several different types of shields. Tell me about your results. Do at least one reflective and one receptive shield. Try one from each element in your mix. Which ones felt the best to you? Explain.
2. Brainstorm a list of 5 or 6 shields you might try in the future.
3. Which method of releasing or stopping your energy flow works best for you?
4. What are your thoughts or experiences with psychic attack?
5. Share any thoughts or other experiences you'd like to mention that have come up for you in this lesson.

Additional Resources

The Highly Sensitive Person: How to Thrive When the World Overwhelms You (book) by Elaine N. Aron -- a practical look at boundaries and understanding how to navigate the world as an HSP -- https://amzn.to/3cIhA6N

"Toxic Positivity Culture: Why Pagans, Polytheists, & Occultists Should Guard Against It" (blog post) by Scarlet Magdalene -- more about Law of Attraction bullies, but worth the read; lots to extrapolate toward our end of the magickal garden, where the roses have thorns and the snakes can bite -- http://www.patheos.com/blogs/teaaddictedwitch/2018/08/toxic-positivity-culture/

"Common and Not-So-Common Shields" (blog post) by State of Mind -- interesting article on different types of psionic shields (if a little "battle magic" oriented for my taste) -- http://astateofmind.eu/2013/03/04/common-and-not-so-common-shields/

BoS Pages Included

The Witch's Shield

Red Thread Academy
Traditional Witchcraft
Year 1: Foundations

Unit 9: Energy Work
Lesson 4: Energy Healing & Connecting w/ Others

Energy Healing & Connecting with Others

Prerequisite Lesson   09-03 Shielding & Releasing

Objectives
- To gain a theoretical understanding of connecting with other people energetically (even if you work in a solitary setting)
- To explore ways to connect across distances
- To apply principles of energy work to healing modalities

Materials Needed

Study Notes

I grouped this week's concepts together because connection and healing go hand in hand. (Pun not intended, but it certainly works.) You can do energetic healing just for yourself, and there will certainly be times when you will; but most of the time you will be doing it for someone else. After all, the energetic healings we do for ourselves are usually minor adjustments and course corrections that we think of as balancing, alignment, centering, and simple resting (or other self-care terms) more than actual healing. But when we do the work for someone else, we give ourselves proper credit for having done a bit of work. (And we more properly acknowledge their need, whereas we are likely to downplay our own needs and not call this magic what it is when we do it for ourselves.)

Healing Yourself With Energy

Once upon a time, I thought that only *some people* had talent with healing. I believed that, like divination, all Witches could and should learn a bit about some sort of healing. I was taught that healing is a skill we can all develop to at least a rudimentary standard -- like sewing. (Anybody can sew a button on a shirt. It takes more aptitude, patience, and skill to become a dressmaker.)

I now suspect that all people have more than a little talent with healing, if they are only able to find the mode of healing where their talent lies. We all have bodies, after all; and we all need to maintain their health. We are all gifted with some level of intuition regarding what is good and right for this body, this mind, this emotional and spiritual being that is each of us. We are the subject matter experts, in fact, although some of us may be struggling to remember that after years of dealing with parents, spouses, or others who have undermined that authority. Still, we are the ones living in these bodies. We are the ones who can hear the pulse increase, taste the heartburn rise, smell the headache coming. We know what soothes and what savages.

We might not be experts in what works for everyone (or even for most people), but if we pay attention to ourselves and listen to our bodies and the feedback they give us, we can know what works for us. We can be healers for ourselves.

Journaling and meditation (or at least grounding and centering) are central to this. If you don't take time to be mindful of your body and your emotions on a regular basis, you can't know what sort of response you are having to the foods you eat, the company you keep, the activities you pursue, or the changes you make in your life. Without taking some sort of time to observe yourself, you will most likely just launch yourself willy-nilly from one set of circumstances to the next, hoping the next change feels better than the last.

In terms of healing yourself, start with the physical sources of the problem, and address the energetic gaps alongside them. So, if you have the flu, you know it's a virus you will be "riding out" with rest and fluids, per doctor's orders. Maybe you'll also be having some herbal tea that is a blend of echinacea, licorice, ginger, mint, and yarrow -- which you've put together to help support your immune and respiratory systems. And since you're a Witch, every step of making and drinking that tea becomes infused with energy and magic -- from a blessing you say while setting the water to boil, to thanking the herbs for their power, to threading magic into the cup while the tea-ball steeps, to visualizing the potent vapors reaching your lungs as you enjoy the aroma of the cup, to absorbing the combined energies as you sip the brew. And that's just the tea! You may still take a bath and a nap this afternoon, both "self-care tasks" that you can load with energetic healing for yourself.

If you are doing an energetic self-healing that doesn't have any physical components (which is rare), you will start with grounding and centering. From there, do a quick "scan" of your energetic body. What feels out of place or icky? Direct clean, healing Universal energy to those areas to fill in the gaps or clean up the gunk.

Some people visualize healing energy as a certain color. Blue seems to be a favorite. Bluish-white light is another favorite. It may just look like white light to you, and that's okay, too. Or, it may have a scent or a texture. We don't all perceive energy visually. I think the most important thing is for you to develop a rapport with the energy so you know what is healthy for you and what is dis-ease or mal-aise in your system. If something looks/feels/sounds/smells/tastes off, start working on both the physical and energetic ways to get back to good. You have to know what health is like in your system and also what un-health is like in order to bring your body and mind back to health.

Connecting With Others

Let's talk a little about energetically connecting with others before we talk about doing healing work with/for other people.

First off, it's important to know that you don't have to be in close physical proximity with another person in order to send or receive energy from them. A very quick look into quantum physics' concepts like entanglement will let you know that distance and even time are non-factors with regard to energy. If two objects are entangled, then an action on one can cause a reaction in the other, regardless of location. This is why sympathetic (like attracts like) and contagious (the part affects the whole) magic have always been so profoundly effective and have been used by witches and shamans the world over.

You have to be able to connect into the energy of the target for the magic to be effective, though. So, having a snippet of hair or nails, dirt from their footprint, a clothing item you know they've worn (better yet, one that is still dirty -- gross, but connected) is fantastic. And failing that, be able to tap into their energy in other ways -- either through close connection or deep personal knowledge.

If you are physically in the same room with someone, (and you have their permission) then yes, you can put your hands on or near them and get a physical feeling of their energy. The same way that you have done this for your own energy, you can do with them. You can do very similar energy exercises (energy ball, shields, etc) to get a sense of each other. You can "hold hands" and develop a sense of trust on this deeper, invisible level. Perhaps you have a Craft friend who would be interested in trying out some of these techniques with you. If not, perhaps you have a partner, roommate, sibling, child, or even pet with whom you can practice. (That's right. Don't discount Fido or Fluffy. Pets can give consent to be energetic partners. If they don't want your energy on them, they will walk away.)

You can also practice energy work with another student in the Red Thread Academy. Since energy isn't bound by time or distance, you can do energy experiments with each other.

Healing Others With Energy

There are countless ways to use energy to heal yourself and others. Most involve using some sort of physical tool as a focal point, though some (like Reiki) rely strictly on the mind of the healer.

In all cases, you must be able to do the following:
1. Connect with your target (the person in need of healing)
2. Be clear regarding the goal of the work
3. Be grounded and centered
4. Raise energy
5. Direct it toward your target

When it comes to directing the healing energy to the target, most healers will either use visualization, a tool, a hands-on manipulation, or a combination of these in order to focus the energy into the body system or area most affected. For instance, if a person is suffering from a debilitating migraine, the Witch might place an amethyst on the migraine-sufferer's forehead while placing their own hands on the person's temples and visualizing soothing energy flowing into their head and neck.

It is often best to address the whole body and not just one area, as pain or illness in one part can indicate an imbalance that impacts the whole. So while the first response may be to give immediate relief to the migraine that is happening right now, in the example above, it is always ways to look at the triggers of the migraine. Are there food allergies the person is unaware of? Stressors they are ignoring? Are the headaches caused by barometric or hormonal cycles that may be unavoidable and demand periodic rest from an otherwise over-busy person? Listen to the messages of the body.

Some of the most common tools of energy healing include:
- Crystals, crystal elixirs, crystal grids, etc.
- Herbs and herbal preparations (teas, tincture, ointments, salves, mojo hands, incenses/smudges, etc)
- Flower essences, Essential oils & aromatherapy

- Singing bowls, tuning forks, voice
- Pendulums
- Rattles, drums
- Wells, baths, springs, sacred waters
- Witch's staff, knife, cauldron, skull, cloak, cords & other personal tools
- Witch ladders, talismans, amulets

Almost all of the personal tools of the Witch can be used in healing applications (as well as hexing applications, really). It is beyond the scope of this lesson to explore why and how that is so, but if you are called to healing work, this probably already makes sense.

Furthermore, if you are called to the healing arts in your professional work, you can absolutely add the power of the Witch to that work. If you are a massage therapist, for example, grounding and centering at the start of your day, and connecting energetically with your clients will keep your energy reserves fresh and help you better understand how best to help and heal them. Indeed, many professional healers admit that they are intuitively using their gifts in the workplace already. Most of the best ones have that "magic touch" that has been developed through years of listening with the inner senses.

Assignment	Write a journal entry about your thoughts and experiences regarding healing work and connecting with others on an energetic level. Have you had the opportunity to connect with others yet? What has that been like? What concerns do you have? What are your thoughts/hopes/concerns about healing work? What would you like to explore regarding these areas?
Additional Resources	Witchcraft Medicine: Healing Arts, Shamanic Practices, and Forbidden Plants (book) by Claudia Muller-Ebeling -- fantastic book that covers a variety of healing modalities in traditional Craft -- https://amzn.to/2Sjfgtf Energy Healing: the Essentials of Self-Care (book) by Ann Marie Chiasson MD and Andrew Weil MD -- looks at traditional healing practices from around the world for use in promoting personal wellness -- https://amzn.to/3cKQTOF Hands of Light: A Guide to Healing through the Human Energy Field (book) by Barbara Brennan and Jos. A Smith -- a scientific approach to energetic healing -- https://amzn.to/3l1I5qB
BoS Pages Included	

Red Thread Academy
Traditional Witchcraft
Year 1: Foundations

Unit 10: Spirit Work
Lesson 1: Triple Soul, Evocation & Banishing

Triple Soul, Evocation & Banishing

Prerequisite Lesson   None specified

Objectives
- To map the three parts of the soul and understand their interconnection
- To begin a dialogue about Spirit work, Spirit Tribe, the Mighty Dead, etc.
- To introduce basic evocation and banishing techniques for safety in calling forth and releasing of Spirits
- To introduce basic tools of Spirit communication

Materials Needed

Study Notes

Buckle up. This is a long lesson. We've got a lot to pack into this one, and there wasn't an easy place to put a lot of this stuff in some other lesson. But since Traditional Witchcraft, according to some definitions, is synonymous with spirit work, it's imperative that we get this started on the right foot.

First, I'm going to share a piece that I am adapting for you from something I wrote for *Witch Way Magazine in* December 2016. This article deals with the concept of the Triple Soul -- and the Black Soul most specifically. (You're getting more detail on the souls than what I gave in that article.)

I feel like it's important for me to preface this first part of the lesson with a bit of a disclaimer. We're exploring something here that I call "soul mechanics" or "soul mapping." Much of magic and witchcraft is theoretical or fringe territory, meaning that it isn't scientific and quantifiable by modern standards. But I feel like when we are talking about the anatomy of the soul, the Afterlife, and the terrain of the Spirit World, we are threatening to topple several sacred cows.

I'm not asking you (in this lesson, unit, course, or tradition) to believe in anything that you think is hogwash or to renounce any beliefs that you already hold sacred. However demonstratively I state a philosophy in this course, I'm not asking you to sign the Devil's Book in your blood that you now hold this new truth to be self-evident. What I AM asking is that you consider it -- that you hold it, taste it, feel its weight, judge its merit, walk up and down the aisle in it to see if it fits or if it rubs. In some cases, I may be asking you to use a common vocabulary within the parameters of this trad/course (because "spiritual shorthand" makes it easier for us to communicate with each other about big, complex concepts).

So, let's consider together ...

The Triple Soul

So many of the Spirits available to a Witch as helpmates can be classified as the Dead. The spirits of our Ancestors, of Heroes and Heroines, and of our spiritual forebears are just a few of the Mighty Dead who might make themselves available to you in your work. Many of the spirits listed in the Ars Goetia (the Lesser Key of Solomon), for instance, were once mortals who now serve as Familiars to Witches and Magi. (We will cover the Legion in more depth in future articles, as I am passionate about working with these Spirits and have dedicated a lot of energy to their research.)

The Dead have an inherent advantage to working with us, versus other types of spirits. Namely, they are capable of understanding humans and the concerns of mortal existence in a way that, for instance, Angels cannot. Even spirits who lived millennia ago are more likely to sympathize with our ordeals than those beings who have never "walked a mile in our shoes," as the adage goes. Furthermore, since they tend to exhibit human-esque emotions, we tend to relate better to the spirits of the Dead than to many other types of spirits.

In the Red Thread Tradition, as in many world shamanic traditions, we recognize that all living beings are born into this world with three souls (or three parts to the soul). These three souls correspond to the triple colors of witchcraft – namely, red, black, and white -- the sacred triplicities and the otherworldly colors of the Celts.

(I've only recently learned that another American Traditional Witchcraft group -- the Feri Tradition -- teaches about the three souls, as well. They use different terms and they describe them a little differently than we do, but if you're interested in learning more on this topic, check out what they have to say, as well. Just remember, if you go looking at other traditions -- like Feri, Huna, Hebrew, etc -- that those are different models that have different symbol sets. Their three souls don't match up in easy alignment with ours.)

The first soul is the Black Soul, or "spirit." This is our astral body, and it is capable of traveling beyond this world into other realms while we live. The spirit is what we identify as our Self, our ego. It is our identity in this lifetime, and it is an exact copy of "us" in the astral realms, although it can take any form you wish for it (the fetch). Upon death, the spirit (Black Soul) may wander as a ghost or revenant, it may stay to act as a guide or guardian to others, or it may travel back to the cosmic cauldron where its energy will dissolve to create new spirits.

The second soul is the Red Soul, or "eternal soul." We often call this the Bone Soul, as it lives in the bones of each of us and cannot be destroyed. It is the divine spark of the Witchfather's blood within every true witch's heart. The Bone Soul, after death, is awarded a period of rest in Ynys Avalon (or Elphame, Helheim, or the Summerlands – whichever name you prefer), after which it is reborn. The eternal soul holds our past life memories and our connection to our ancestors.

The third soul is the White Soul, or "higher self." It is also known as the Holy Guardian Angel. The higher self exists just above our bodies, like a crown or halo. Inspiration, enlightenment, and divine wisdom all come to us through the higher self. It is one of the main goals of a witch to gain knowledge of this higher self and to commune with it regularly. The eternal soul (Red/Bone Soul) is alchemically married to the higher self

(White Soul), and so true lasting communion is revealed to us upon death – and possibly even within our lifetimes.

THE BLACK SOUL SELF AND PAST LIVES

So, the Black Soul is that part of our spirit that retains memories and the personality connected to a particular life. It is very individual, and it is separate from the Higher Self (White Soul) and the Bone Soul (Red Soul). It is the part of the energy structure that may become a ghost, haunting a particular location; but more often, it is the Black Soul who acts as a guiding Ancestor. If you've talked to the Mighty Dead via a medium or a talking board, this is the Black Soul of that Ancestor. The White and Red Souls have remained together and gone on to do other work, probably as another incarnate being. An interesting dramatic twist, then, is that a Black Soul that was once your own can act as a Familiar to your current self. That Black Soul Self can be a powerful Protector, Teacher, Healer, etc – whether or not you're ever aware of its personal connection to you. (We'll talk more about Familiars and members of your Spirit Tribe in Lesson 10-02 Familiars.)

If you do become aware that one of your guiding spirits is your Black Soul from a previous life – or if you start to learn more information about a past life – it is important to stay objective. Remember that this spirit is NOT YOU. You are gifted with a new Black Soul, unique to this life. And while your Red Soul and White Soul may recognize this Black Soul from your past, they recognize it as part of the eternal family of your Being. As such, you should be neither proud nor ashamed of the personality or actions of this part of your distant past. Rather, allow your current Self to learn what lessons it can under the guidance of this mentor. You can learn a great deal about the progress of your Soul through the ages by communicating with a previous Black Soul. You can see patterns and recurring symbols. You can even gain an understanding of prior traumas that may be impacting your current incarnation. Try writing a story about this person that you were, asking your own previous Black Soul Self to lay the story out for you.

ANCESTORS

The more common expression of the Black Soul is that of an Ancestor – a spirit from within your biological (or even adopted) family line. Of all the spirits you might work with as a Witch, none are as vested in your survival and success as your very own ancestors. Christian Day, in his book Witch's Book of the Dead, says it best when he says, "Nobody loves you like your grandma."

It has been my experience that almost every family has a matriarch or patriarch who is keeping a watchful eye on each of their descendants. (For those of you like me, who come from families where adoption has touched you or your family line, I find that both biological and adopted ancestors tend to watch over us.) This progenitor has usually been doing so for several generations, and she may or may not come forward right away to announce her presence. You'll be one of many children that she watches, in this case. You may also have parents, grandparents, aunts, and uncles that have crossed the veil but are still looking in on you. That close relationship continues after death, or it can. At any rate, it usually continues for the Dead, whether the Living are aware of it or not. Contemporary Western society is not taught to honor the Dead or to revere our Ancestors, and in this we are a minority. Most of our own Ancestors had a greater reverence for prior generations, and ancestor worship is a hallmark of eastern culture.

Even within most Craft traditions, the Dead are only given homage on one day or at one season of the year. The veil may be thinnest at Samhain, but the world of spirit and the world of flesh are never far separated. The wise Witch knows this and honors the Mighty Dead all year long.

The Ancestor Altar is the most common way to maintain the connection with our Ancestors throughout the year. Dedicate a shelf, table, or bookcase to your Mighty Dead. Place pictures and names of the Dead there, along with beans (the food of the Dead), ghost water, anisette, graveyard dirt, and a ghost light (candle) there for them. Or dress your Ancestor Altar as instructed by the Spirits.

"Blood calls to blood." The very life force of the human being is carried in the blood. Lives and spirits are links together by blood bonds, like those shared by family. Some memory of Ancestors you've never met lingers in your blood, in your DNA. You can draw on the blueprint that is there, in your own flesh and blood, to reach these Spirits.

It is also possible to share more than just a genetic tie to your Ancestors. In some cases, we have chosen to reincarnate as our own descendants, making us Ancestors to ourselves. This is another variation on the way we might end up interacting with our own previous Black Souls. So, why would we come back within our own bloodlines? Because blood ties are deep and eternal, whether we acknowledge them or not. Through this tie, our spirits have connected themselves to others in an extended family. Our clan or tribe often chooses to be together, learning new lessons and sharing important experiences with our kindred.

This large family of spirits often extends to people with whom we do not share a genetic tie in this life – close friends whom we seem to know and recognize from some bygone era. These are our souls' mates, and we feel most at home when we are together. Within the Craft, our covenmates tend to be "kin" to us in this deep soul sense. Many Craft traditions formalize this bond by making new blood bonds with each Initiate, thereby acknowledging and strengthening the Red Threads that knits us together.

Okay ... having looked at some of the basic philosophy of how the Souls operate and interact, we can talk a little more about Summoning (or Evoking) Spirits ... and then about Releasing (or Banishing) them.

Spirit Evocation

First off, let's differentiate between evocation and invocation.

Evocation is the act of calling a Spirit to you -- as in near you. You might also hear this called summoning, stirring, contacting, or simply calling. This is a skill we will practice to a level of proficiency this year.

Invocation is the act of calling a Spirit into you. You might also hear this called channeling, possession, being ridden, or aspecting. This is not a skill we will specifically study this year. However, if you continue through Year 3 (Mastery), you will study and prove proficiency in the art of invocation by the time you have completed that course.

The Spirits whom you evoke may be Ancestors or Human Guides (Black Souls of a deceased person), Goetic spirits, Djinn, elemental spirits, wights, or any number of different spirit types from land spirits to mythical creatures to interdimensional beings. The more you work with Spirits, the stranger it gets (and somehow, the less strange it all gets).

If you've never called a Spirit before, it may sound insane for me to imply that within a few months you may have a very rational conversation with a dragon in your head. I understand that. Magic does sound nutty when we try to explain it to people who haven't experienced it. (Sometimes even sharing an experience with other Witches can be difficult, if it is very personal, unusual, or on the edges of typical experience. We aren't always able to understand the magic someone else has.)

There are a few types of Spirits that are commonly experienced by Witches, though. These are ones that we are going to go in search of during your Foundation Year. Three, to be specific.

- Ancestors
- Familiars (which is more of a category than a type)
- Godds

I won't be surprised if you've already had some experience with one or more of these.

Actually, there's a fourth, but it's tricky. It's a version of yourself that you send out of the body as a Spirit. The Fetch. We're going to work with the Fetch this year, as well, in Lesson 10-02.

So, let's talk about how to call a Spirit.

Evocation 101

(*The following is an article I wrote for* New Witch Magazine *in 2006. It deals with the topic of evocation for beginners in a way that I think is very effective. In it, I use the example of evoking a Quarter, but the principle is the same for evoking a Spirit.*)

"Calling" is an integral part of many Pagan rituals. First thing: the type of call we're going to be discussing in this article is the most common. It is called evocation.

An evocation is used for calling whatever astral entities or spaces you want to have present in your ritual – Realms, Quarters, Dragons, Totems, Guardians, and Deities (usually). This can also be thought of as "inviting" these beings into your circle.

The concept is not to "compel" beings as in cheap horror movies; (no sane person ever tries to compel transpersonal beings against their will) but instead to offer a polite, and hopefully enticing invitation for the gods (etc.) to commune with you.

Okay, what do I have to say?

Nothing. I mean that. You don't have to speak any words at all. You can evoke any energy you wish while being absolutely silent. There's comfort in that; if words fail you on the night of the ritual, you can still call your Quarter quite effectively.

So, what is it that I am supposed to do? You bring the energy of the Quarter, the physical characteristics of that Quarter, the guardians of that Quarter into your circle. It's a very personal, unique feeling, I think, when it happens. I can't tell you what to do — or even what it will feel like. In my experience, here is what works.

1. Invite the being/energy you wish to contact with your mind. See it coming from the place where it dwells to the place where you are.

2. Re-create the sensations you association with that energy within your own body. The more you have worked with that energy or played "energy ball" the easier this process might be. If you've never played it, and you don't know the sensations, put your hands on objects that are like that elemental thing. (If Earth, use soil, rocks, etc. If Air, feel the wind. You get the idea.) At any rate, feel that energy in your bones, muscles,

and skin as you call.

3. Pull that energy to you with your spirit. For me, this frequently feels like pleading (or something like it). This feeling often centers in the heart or solar plexus.

But I WANT to say words!

Of course you do. We usually use words when we are working with other people. We want them to know we are doing it and we want them to know when it is done. We like to engage our voices and speak the poetry of our spirits. Words are fine, if you don't place all your focus on them.

But what do I say?

Ok, I can see I need to get to that. I'm going to model for you what you could say, with the understanding that it is more important that you find words that are meaningful to you. Basically, all you need to do is name the thing (with as many names as you like), describe it, say what you want of it, and seal the deal.

Okay, okay. I will give you an example, but don't just take and use it wholesale. Find the images, the names, the colors, the associations,

and the other specifics that make the most sense to you.

"I call to the West, to the Guardians of Water. Water, where life begins — the planet's life began in the oceans; my body's life began in the waters of birth. And in the West, where the cycle ends — we travel to the land of the setting sun, to the islands of the dead. I call you, Guardians of Water and West to be here with us and offer us your protection and your intuition. Be here now. So mote it be."

Now what?

Practice. You can practice your evocations outside of specific ritual circumstances, so you aren't so terrified when you find yourself in the limelight of a group ritual.

Cast the circle (or other protective space) and evoke the elements, beings, and spaces you are trying to know better. You can even call them just one at a time to get a better "feel" for calling and maintaining a connection with each on an individual basis.

The point is: do it. This is your Craft. Don't wait for someone else to craft it for you.

Other Thoughts on Evocation

I have done a lot of work with Goetic Spirits (so-called "demonic" Spirits listed in the Solomonic texts), and I am including some pages from my BoS project that deal directly with that body of work. The word *goetia* is a Greek word that deals directly with Witchcraft, and Spirit Work is very much tied to the Craft in every age and place on the planet.

The medieval goetic texts advocate a very strict and ceremonial approach to Spirit conjuration and summoning that is tantamount to slavery and torture. Some magicians will tell you that this is the traditional model for working with these Spirits, and the Witch or Mage who flinches from these practices is risking their own safety while flouting culture and tradition. Others, like myself, will point out that most of these Spirits were co-opted from older cultures where they were once honored as Deities (and not demons), and any Witch, Mage, or Shaman who needs to bind and torture a Spirit to gain their cooperation needs to rethink working with that particular Spirit. Perhaps they would be better off finding one whose personal Will was in alignment with that of the Witch -- or whose favor could be bought. I'd rather work with a mercenary than a slave, after all.

In brief, you should know a little something about the Spirits you call. You are bringing their attention to you, after all. And while you can create a construct like a triangle/pyramid/black mirror to house them, this isn't the friendliest way to greet a guest you have invited (and not very traditional). "Hey, Jane! Thanks for coming for tea. You'll just need to sit in this cage I made for you while I ask a few questions." Nope. Not friendly.

Much better to feel confident that you are safe with Jane before inviting her. You know she's not likely to pull a knife on you, pluck the stuffing out of the sofa, or kick your cat. And if she gets rowdy, you know you can show her the door. Which brings me to banishing ...

Basic Banishing and Psychic Hygiene

Maintaining your psychic and energetic health is one of the most important aspects of spiritual work and spirit keeping. Without a basic knowledge of how to get rid of "psychic sludge" you will find yourself dealing with physical, mental, and emotional trouble.

The mental, physical, emotional, and energetic "bodies" of a person are all connected to each other. Furthermore, they all need regular maintenance, activity, and care to stay healthy. Most people know this is true of the mind, the body, and the emotions; but many people don't know they even HAVE an energetic body -- and have no idea how to care for it.

Banishing is a basic technique of psychic hygiene. To BANISH something is to make it leave. I feel it is important to know how to banish before you ever call a spirit or energy to you. You wouldn't let someone in your house without knowing you can get them to leave. Some guests, like some spirits, will leave on their own at the end of a visit. Others need to be told politely that the time is up. And some folks have to be told (forcibly) to GO.

There are a few different ways to handle this. I would highly recommend performing a banishing. It could be something as complicated as the Star Ruby or Lesser Banishing Ritual of the Pentagram. Or you could banish the entity by proclaiming "Get out" while focusing on the intruder. I like something a little in between. You can say/chant the following Greek words:

Hekas, o hekas, este bebeloi.

It translates to "Afar, afar, o ye Profane." So, really, it is saying "Get out, bad spirit." But in Greek. I like it because it links into that energy-connected part of the brain, and it makes a very nice chant.

Whatever you say, say it with meaning and conviction. And picture the spirit/energy being forced away.

You can also use physical items to banish. Florida Water or some other very floral perfumed water can be sprinkled around you and your home. You can cleanse yourself with salt-water -- including swishing some in your mouth. You can cleanse and banish with herb bundles -- or burn an incense stick that has a clearing effect.

All of these techniques should work wonders. You may have to "banish, rinse, repeat", as I like to say. Banishing is like sweeping the floors. Dust and schmutz can come back, and you have to sweep again.

Small Laurelei Sidebar on "Smudging"

Quick thoughts on "smudging" and cultural appropriation: The word smudge is English with Germanic roots and the action of cleansing objects, spaces, and people with smoke is almost universal. However, doing so with bundles of dried white sage, palo santo, braided sweetgrass, and certain other herbs are very specific practices that are customary to First Nations. Be honest with yourself about where you are using a cultural practice, and then ask yourself truthfully whether it has been passed to you in some meaningful way. Are you honoring a part of heritage by practicing this folk-way? Are you honoring a local/regional cultural tradition by learning and preserving this traditional practice? Or is this something you have taken (maybe inadvertently) because it was trendy, convenient, or you didn't know you had alternatives?

As Folkloric Witches -- particularly as American Folkloric Witches, for those of us who are in the Western Hemisphere -- we have space and ability within ourselves and our practice to enfold our Indigenous roots into our Craft. I find those very compatible, in fact. But we should do so intentionally and with respect.

LBRP for Witches

In the late winter and early spring of 2013, my ex-wife and I began adapting the Lesser Banishing Ritual of the Pentagram for use within the Spiral Castle Trad model. With the help of our coven sister, the Pythia, we wrote the ritual below and published it on our blog on 3/25/2013.

Our variation of the LBRP is influenced by Aleister Crowley's Star Ruby ritual (itself an adaptation of the LBRP). It uses forms of the Red God (the Witchfather) and the Black and White Goddess (the Witchmother) in place of the traditional Hebrew names of God. It also replaces the Archangel guardians with the four Watchtowers or Arthurian Castles (which we will be studying in more depth next year).

The purpose of the LBRP is to banish all undesired or unwanted forces from oneself and the local area and to create Sacred Space. Many magicians practice the LBRP as a daily magical exercise to discipline the mind and create internal and external peace.

This is not a strictly traditional practice. It is, if anything, an attempt to blend some traditional concept with ceremonial practices. If you find it useful, use it. Otherwise, lose it.

The Qabbalistic Cross

Imagine a ball of light above your head. Reach up with your right hand and grab the light. When you touch yourself with that hand, part of the light will go into you.

Touch your forehead as you say *"**Corona**" (Crown). Let it fill with the light.*

Touch your pelvis at the pubic bone and say *"**Serpens**" (Serpent). Let it fill with light.*

Touch your right shoulder and say *"**Clementia**" (Mercy). Let it fill with light.*

Touch your left shoulder and say *"**Severitas**" (Severity). Let it fill with light.*

Hold your hands in prayer over your heart and say *"**Benedictiones**" (Blessings). Let it fill with light.*

Feel your whole body fill with the cross of light.

The Pentagrams

Face East. Before you in the air, draw a giant pentagram using your right index finger (or if you prefer use the whole hand) in the direction shown in the illustration. Imagine that pentagram shining in front of you. Take a step forward with your left foot. Just the left. Leave your right one where it is. The size of the step will be determined by your space. At the same time that you step forward, thrust your open hands, side by side, palms downwards, into the pentagram, as if you are diving in. This is called the "Sign of the Enterer." As you enter the pentagram you will say one of the names of the Witch God or Goddess.

Here, at the first pentagram you will shout *"Lucifer."* Lucifer is the Light-Bringer, the Lord of Illumination of the World and the Mind. He is called in the East as the bright aspect of Tubal Cain, and the lord of elemental Fire. Lucifer is called with a jubilant shout to celebrate the rising of the sun in the East.

Step back with your left foot so it is once again beside your right foot. Touch your right index finger to your lips like you are making the "Shhh, no talking" gesture. Point your right index finger to the center of the pentagram and make a quarter turn to your right. As you do so, draw an imaginary arc of white light around to the next direction.

Draw a pentagram in South. Enter the pentagram while singing *"Goda."* Goda is the White Goddess, the Queen of the Seelie Court and Lady of Death-in-Life. She rules the Southern quadrant, the place of elemental Earth. Her name is sung for she is the Lady who shall "have music wherever She goes."

Make the "shhh" gesture and turn to the right, drawing an arc.

Draw a pentagram in West. Enter the pentagram intoning *"Azazel"* in a low voice. Azazel is the Lord of the West, the place of elemental Water. He is Tubal Cain in his aspect as the Lord of the Dead, and is both the angel who taught magic to the daughters of man and the angel who collects our souls for their great rest. The West is the place where the sun goes to die, and it is to the West that we all must travel upon death. Azazel's name is intoned in a low voice of mourning and respect.

Make the "shhh" gesture and turn to the right, drawing an arc.

Draw a pentagram in North. Enter the pentagram whispering *"Kolyo"*. Kolyo is the Black Goddess, the Weaver of Fate and the Lady of Life-in-Death. She rules the North, which is the home of elemental Air. Her name is whispered for she is an ancient mystery.

Make the "shhh" gesture and turn to the right, drawing an arc. This final arc connects all four pentagrams into a single circle.

The Watchtowers

You are now standing in the center of a circle of white light. At each quarter there is a giant, glowing pentagram. Now we post a watchtower between each pentagram. Face the southeast and open up your arms. Stretch out like you are a cross: feet together, arms out at shoulder height. Call the watchtowers to their posts. Stand in the cross position and say:

"Before me stands the Castle of Stone. Behind me stands the Castle of Glass. On my right stands the Castle Perilous. On my left stands the Castle of Revelry."

These are four of the great castles of myth and legend. The Castle of Stone is Caer Bannog, the Castle of Glass is Glastonbury, the Castle Perilous is the silvery Grail Castle, and the Castle of Revelry is the Golden Castle of the Beacon of Awen.

Spread your feet and lift your arms to stand in pentagram-position and say: *"Around me flame the pentagrams. Above me shines a six-rayed star, and below me spins a three-armed triskle. I stand within the Spiral Castle. I am the World Tree."* This declaration places you in all three realms, and allows you to traverse shamanic space. It states that you are the World Tree, and that you ride the stang to other realms.

The Qabbalistic Cross (Closing)

Now repeat the Qabbalistic Cross as you began.

Imagine a ball of light above your head. Reach up with your right hand and grab the light. When you touch yourself with that hand, part of the light will go into you.

Touch your forehead as you say *"**Corona**" (Crown)*. Let it fill with the light.

Touch your pelvis at the pubic bone and say *"**Serpens**"* (Serpent). Let it fill with light.

Touch your right shoulder and say *"**Clementia**" (Mercy)*. Let it fill with light.

Touch your left shoulder and say *"**Severitas**" (Severity)*. Let it fill with light.

Hold your hands in prayer over your heart and say *"**Benedictiones**" (Blessings)*.

Let it fill with light.

Feel your whole body fill with the cross of light.

Basic Spirit Communication

Whew! We've covered a lot of ground already!

Now that we've discussed some really basic ideas about what Spirits are, how to call them, and how to ask them to leave, I want to talk about how to communicate with Spirits.

I actually find this to be a very simple thing to do. As a Spirit worker, I've had many clients come to me with questions and doubts about their abilities to communicate directly with the Spirits in their lives, but in 99% of cases, I have found that the person is just heavily bogged down with self-doubt. They are usually hearing very clearly, and my job (as a Tarot reader or psychic medium or coach) has been to confirm the thing they already knew. I can't count how many times I've had a client jokingly ask, "Why am I paying you to tell you what I already know?" With all seriousness, I usually answer, "You don't believe your own truth yet. But you will."

You have to learn to trust your intuition. The voice that you hear in your head that sounds like you and yet DOESN'T sound like you -- might be a Spirit. The strong urge to do something unusual, the precognition of events, the recurring phrase or symbol or pattern -- these can all be messages or flags from a Spirit trying to get our attention. The biggest hurdle is often recognizing the Spirit who wants to make contact.

Of course, it could be you initiating contact with the Spirit world, and not the other way around. (Or it could seem this way, at least.) In fact, one of the exercises in this lesson asks you to reach out to an Ancestor to establish contact with someone in your family line to act as a Guide. But then what? How do you communicate after the connection has been made?

There are many ways to interact with Spirits -- and many, many terms for these interactions and ways of knowing. I like the term "ken" for how I most often "know" -- a sense of deep and broad understanding as if passed from mind to mind. A sense of knowing that is difficult to put into words. "Clairsentience" is another way to put it. (It means "clear-knowing" in French.) You can also hear (clairaudience) and see (clairvoyance).

I like to use tools/techniques to aid me in communicating with my Spirits sometimes, and you might also find that useful. A few that I have found particularly helpful include:

- Automatic/Spirit-writing -- For me, this is best done by using a regular notebook and pen/pencil. I start by writing a question to the Spirit and then immediately writing the first response I "hear" in my head, without censure. As I write, more words come, and I write those as well. Typically, what happens is that my hand and active self (Black Soul) get so preoccupied with the act of writing that my Red Soul is open to the messages of other Spirits. The words flow, and the dialogue comes easily. If anything, it is hard to keep up with the writing, and an actual conversation starts to take place.

- Pendulum -- You can use a stone pendulum that was crafted for the purpose of being a divinatory tool, or you can use a necklace with a pendant or heavy charm. If you use a necklace, it should be one that you wear regularly. Always ask the pendulum to show you what a "yes" and "no" look like for that session. Also, be sure to stick to yes/no questions, and only ask one question at a time. You can get more elaborate, if you like, by creating a pendulum board -- or using a pendulum with a talking board.

- Talking Board -- I love a talking board. They take a lot of energy to operate on your own (or even with a partner), and you have to be very clear with Spirits that you will not be tolerant of shenanigans. Be confident in your ability to banish before attempting to use one, but don't be afraid of this tool. It is no more dangerous than a cell phone. Just like a cell phone, you would not dial at random and invite the stranger on the other end to engage in whatever conversation they desired. (Or a chat room in the "old days" of the Internet. Those were risky days, eh? You never really knew who was lurking in there or what sort of "chat" was waiting for you. But you didn't burn AOL in a garbage barrel because it was an evil tool. Neither is the talking board. Like our use of the Internet, we need to have grown up a bit since the 90's so we can use it without freaking ourselves out.)

- Scrying Mirror -- We make one of these in Lesson 08-01. This is the black mirror (aka: dark mirror or keek stone).

- Other divination tools -- tarot, runes, ogham, stones, bones, shells, smoke, etc. Don't discount your traditional divination tools.

Assignment

Exercise #1 -- Aligning the 3 Souls

I was taught the basis of this alignment exercise by Ivy Mulligan, author of *The 21rst Century Seidr: A Workbook for the Modern Heathen and Asatru*. She actually presented a variation of this exercise in her book, though I was a Seidr/Volva student of hers. In Lesson 9-2, when we discussed "Grounding and Centering," I offered a different variation of the same Alignment exercise. Hopefully, you have been practicing that exercise for some time now. I offer you this slight variation now. Try it out and see which suits you best.

Say: "May all Three Souls be straight within me."
Begin what is called 4-cycle breathing (4-counts to inhale, 4-count hold, 4-counts to exhale, 4-count hold). Do this while visualizing the souls and gathering in energy.

The White (Dove) Soul is connected to the Black Soul (Fetch) by the Red (Bone) Soul. When you have the energetic charge built up, look up, and blow your breath upward, asking the Red Soul to link all three souls together and divide the energy between them for the healthiest you. Know that it is done.

Do this exercise daily for a week and journal your results.

Exercise #2 -- Banishing

Use one of the banishing techniques described above to do a space/personal clearing -- "Hekas," censing with herbs, asperging with waters, LBRP, Star Ruby, or the Witches' LBRP. Describe your results. Do you have a banishing technique that you have used that differs from these? If so, describe it in detail. How confident do you feel in your ability to banish?

Exercise #3 -- Ancestor Work

Set an ancestor altar somewhere in your home. It doesn't have to be elaborate, but it should be somewhere that you can routinely make offerings to your ancestors. Take a picture to include with this lesson and describe the things you've included, along with the rationale for each. On the day/evening when you dedicate and make your first offering at this altar, spend some time meditating there and invite an ancestor to make him-/herself known to you as a guide and guardian. Be sure to ask if there is any special offering s/he would like, and also ask if there is anything you should know or do now to begin your relationship with them.

Additional Resources

Check the RTA YouTube channel for the Witches' LBRP video -- I'll be getting that uploaded soon

Star Ruby (website) -- http://hermetic.com/sabazius/starruby_rit.htm

Lesser Banishing Ritual of the Pentagram (website) -- http://www.kheper.net/topics/Hermeticism/LBR.htm

The 21rst Century Seidr: A Workbook for the Modern Heathen and Asatru (book) by Ivy Mulligan -- https://amzn.to/36iExfp

BoS Pages Included

Triple Soul
Black Soul
Red Soul
White Soul
Ancestors
Florida Water
Khernips
Witches' LBRP
Banishing Spirits
Egregore Creation
Evoking Magical Beings
Fetch
Familiar
Sphere & Pyramid
Spirit Vessels
Witches and Goetia
Spirit Magic and Communication
Affinity with Spirits

Red Thread Academy
Traditional Witchcraft
Year 1: Foundations

Unit 10: Spirit Work
Lesson 2: The Fetch

The Fetch

Prerequisite Lesson — 10-01 -- The Triple Soul, Evocation & Release, Spirit Communication

Objectives
- To better understand the Fetch as an aspect of the Soul
- To experience the Fetch as the Animal Self
- To experience Witch Flight
- To create a Fetch as representation and vessel

Materials Needed

Stang

Crafting supplies (relative to your Fetch)

Study Notes

Witches fly. It's part of what we do. We have a relationship with the Witchfather, we are familiar with Spirits, we do magic, and we fly. We may do other things. We may debate how we do these things, but generally, we do them.

In this lesson, we are going to talk about HOW Witches fly. Witch flight, of course, is not an act of levitation. Rather, it is what we would call in modern terms "astral projection." It is a sending of the astral body (the Black Soul or the Fetch) on a journey in the Invisible Realms.

Thinking back to the "8 Ways of Making Magick," you'll be able to guess that there are many ways to induce flight. The goal is to achieve an altered state of consciousness, so techniques like drumming or rattling, dancing, and chanting can all be very helpful. Some Witches have good results with warricking (binding with cords) and stropping (using the scourge) in order to "get out" of themselves. Seething is an excellent way to shift oneself into a trance state for flight.

Three tools seem to be the most traditionally linked to flight, regardless of the method used to induce the trance. Those tools are Sabbat Wine, the gandreid, and the fetch.

Sabbat Wine is a loose term that can be applied to both herbals drinks and also ointments that are applied to the skin. These entheogens are used to aid the Witch is shifting consciousness. Traditional formularies included highly toxic herbs like belladonna, wolfsbane, datura, fly agaric, and other strongly mind-altering plants that not only induced the sensation of rushing flight, but could also cause death if not administered by someone knowledgeable in the Poison Path. Subtler herbs like mugwort, calamus root, lemongrass, cinquefoil, clary sage, and balm of gilead can be employed in your infusions or ointments with delicious and highly effective results. One doesn't need to be catapulted from their body to fly, after all. Furthermore, wine, cannabis, and herbal incenses are also part of the panoply of herbal resources available in aiding the Witch in flight. Heed this warning, though: Do not depend too heavily on any Ally for your flight. If you can't do it without them, you can't really do it. Use the Ally as a learning aide, a Guide, a friend, but never as a crutch.

I won't spend too much time talking about the gandreid here, or the riding pole. We've talked a lot about the Stang already, and your Stang is a gandreid (or gandr, gandra, or gander). There are others, and we will talk more about them (and more about Flight, in general) in Year 3: Mastery.

Nigel Jackson writes:

"The stick is the Gandra which is both the magic wand and stick that straddle the Witch of the North. It is a variant of the classic broom or forked stick of witches in Europe. The armies of the night-flying creatures on sticks are called "the gandreigh" in Old Norse. This applies to the flight of witches and the dead ghost hunting Wild."

I'd also have you consider this lovely little nursery rhyme. You're probably familiar with Mother Goose. Do you remember in Lesson 07-02 Ritual Components when we talked about the Lame Step and the Goose-Footed Goddess? (If not, flip over to that section and do a quick read of just that part.) Okay, here she is a children's rhyme! Nursery rhymes actually hold a lot of the secrets of the Old Religion, if you take the time to look and listen.

She's on a GANDER -- a GANDR! Not a goose, but a gandr, and in her hand is that true gandr -- her magical stick. So when Mother Goose (a byname for Frau Holle) wanted to fly, she would ride a gandr. Of course she did. We do, too!

The Fetch is an energetic form that the Witch creates and projects her Black Soul (astral body) into during flight. Some Witches do this so seamlessly and naturally that they are unaware of the projection and believe this is the natural form of their Black Soul. In truth, this Fetch is an energetic shell that acts as a protective barrier and can even be sent independently of the Black Soul by an adept Witch.

The Fetch can be built to look like an exact copy of the Witch's physical body, or it might be constructed to look like a natural or mythological Animal Form. It can also be a combination of these forms. Whatever the nature of the Fetch, it should be one that the Witch resonates with on a deep level. Indeed, the Fetch should suggest its shape to the Witch (in a manner of speaking), more than the Witch defining the shape consciously.

Interestingly, this Fetch is not sentient in its own right. It is a shell that awaits the Black Soul to inhabit and enliven it. When it is en-souled (or programmed with enough directed energy) it can move among the Realms and even be seen in physical, consensus reality by some.

It is a good idea to create a physical vessel or "home" for the Fetch to inhabit when you aren't using it. The vessel (called a Fetich) can be practically anything, and since the Fetch is not a being of Will the way a Familiar is, it won't have its own opinion about what sort of vessel it prefers. You can make something that strikes your fancy and fits your needs. You might consider a large stone, a wood carving, a leather engraving, a painting, a sculpture, a statue, a spirit bottle, a doll, a talisman. In the picture to the right, mine is the wooden hare sculpture.

The more you work with a particular Fetch, the more powerful it becomes. You are feeding it energy each time you enter it and send it forth. You can also feed it energy when it is in residence in its house. Furthermore, you can create more than one Fetch and Fetich (house), though this is admittedly a division of your energetic resources. You may, however, find that you have reasons for doing this. You may also discover that you wish to deconstruct or destroy a Fetch, which you can do by destroying the Fetich and reabsorbing the energy. This should be avoided, if possible, though. In fact, you'll probably find that you have psychological or emotional resistance to such destruction. This is because the Fetch is a sort of egregore or Spirit. And while it may not have Will or sentience of its own, it does have a sort of Life. Still, that Life is an extension of yourself -- of your Black Soul, specifically. If the vessel is no longer able to serve, it must be cleared and rebuilt.

The Scottish witch Isobel Gowdie (according to the record of her trial in 1662) used the following charm to activate her Fetch:

I shall go into a hare,
With sorrow and sych (such) and meickle (great) care;
And I shall go in the Devil's name,
Ay while I come home again.

To change back, she would say:

Hare, hare, God send thee care.
I am in a hare's likeness now,
But I shall be in a woman's likeness even now.

Here are two more poems that link the Hare to Witchcraft and the Fetch. I could literally talk about this particular connection all day, but I won't. The connection between rabbits and Witches may be older than black cats and Witches, though. In fact, as Judika Illes points out in her massive volume Encyclopedia of Witchcraft, cats weren't even the most likely animals to be a Witch's corporeal familiar in the Middle Ages, as the cat wasn't a common household critter at that time. The term "pussycat" most likely referred to the rabbit (Latin "lepus"), an animal that was much more associated with witchcraft, lunar magic, necromancy, and shapeshifting. And shapeshifting is very similar (if not identical) work as going into the Fetch. (Old George Pickingill's coven was said to fare forth as a warren of hares from the graveyard, as were other groups of cunningfolk.)

"The Graveyard Rabbit"
by Frank Lebby Stanton

In the white moonlight, where the willow waves,
He halfway gallops among the graves—
A tiny ghost in the gloom and gleam,
Content to dwell where the dead men dream,

But wary still!
For they plot him ill;
For the graveyard rabbit hath a charm
(May God defend us!) to shield from harm.

Over the shimmering slabs he goes—
Every grave in the dark he knows;
But his nest is hidden from human eye
Where headstones broken on old graves lie.

Wary still!
For they plot him ill;
For the graveyard rabbit, though sceptics scoff,
Charmeth the witch and the wizard off!

The black man creeps, when the night is dim,
Fearful, still, on the track of him;
Or fleetly follows the way he runs,
For he heals the hurts of the conjured ones.

Wary still!
For they plot him ill;
The soul's bewitched that would find release,—
To the graveyard rabbit go for peace!

He holds their secret—he brings a boon
Where winds moan wild in the dark o' the moon;
And gold shall glitter and love smile sweet
To whoever shall sever his furry feet!

Wary still!
For they plot him ill;
For the graveyard rabbit hath a charm
(May God defend us!) to shield from harm.

"The Hare"
by Walter de la Mare

In the black furrow of a field
I saw an old witch-hare this night;
And she cocked a lissome ear,
And she eyed the moon so bright,
And she nibbled of the green;
And I whispered "Wh-s-st! witch-hare,"
Away like a ghostie o'er the field
She fled, and left the moonlight there.

Don't let my preference sway you! I'm very fond of the hare. The toad, the goat, and the owl are all very linked to Witch Flight, as well, and there are many animals world wide that have a long association with faring forth, shapeshifting, second sight, otherworldly messages, etc. The point is for YOU to find your shape, be comfortable, and do the work. The right shape might be you-shaped.

When your Fetch fares forth from your physical body, you will normally find that it has a better sense of where to go than you would have consciously thought. Remember that this is your Black Soul. It is not your conscious mind. When it leaves your body and looks around, the surroundings may be familiar-seeming, but you are not in the realm of physical consensus reality. The place where you start shares some attributes with the physical realm, and as we mentioned earlier, a talented psychic may be able to perceive your Fetch as a near-physical presence; but it is a *shade off (pun intended).*

As your Fetch moves through this other-world, choices open up. You are almost always given the opportunity to go up, go down, or go through. Up stairs, up ladders, up in elevators or escalators even (since we are modern beings and brains use whatever symbols are ready at hand). Down holes, down stairs, down cave mouths, down wells. Through doorways, through gates, through veils, through openings in hedges, through mist or fog. All of these transitions signify the shift from THIS familiar world to the other realms of Spirit.

Most of the time, your Fetch is able to navigate these other realms using something very similar to what I would call dream logic. If you start the journey with the intention of going to the Brocken (the primordial Dancing Place of German Witches), and you lay your compass, drink your Sabbat Wine, seethe, and allow a mist to surround you in your mind until you are able to leave your body comfortable lying on the ground while your Fetch runs like a rabbit -- you can trust that the rabbit will run through the Spirit realms to the Brocken. (Or if you prefer to jump on your Stang and fly, you don't need the star charts to plot a course. Your Black Soul is the star that knows the way already!)

You can also trust that your Fetch knows how to find its way back to your body. Sometimes, though, it needs a little more encouragement to settle all the way back in once you're back. Remember to ground and center. Food and the soul alignment should be very helpful after flight.

Assignment

1. **Meet Your Fetch** -- There are several ways you can do this, of course; but I recommend the following exercise. You will need your Scrying Mirror, a candle, and a lighter. You will also want to have journaling materials handy. Do this exercise outside at night or in a darkened room. Align the three souls within yourself and Lay the Compass. Light the candle and place it where you can see the flickering of the light without it being directly reflected in the mirror. You want to be able to see the suggestion of your face, but not the stark details. Gaze with a softened focus into the mirror. Allow a fog to fill the surface of the mirror. As the fog clears, notice the features you see. Notice as many features as you can. Is the face looking back similar or the same to the physical visage your body bears? If not, is it a human(oid) face that looks different? Is it animal or mythozoological? Is it a combination? Use the mirror or your mind's eye to see the remainder of your Fetch's body, as well. Allow the fog to fill the mirror and clear again, revealing the face you normally see before you leave the compass. Journal this experience in detail. Describe your Fetch fully.

2. **Create a Fetich (vessel)**. It doesn't matter what sort of Fetich you make (or buy), as long as it makes sense to you. Take a picture of it. If you buy one, as opposed to making it, be sure to cleanse and dedicate it to use. Whether purchased or hand-crafted, include a description of your vessel along with the picture. Write a journal entry explaining why this is the right vessel for your Fetch.

3. **Use Your Fetch to Fly** -- From within the Compass, use your Stang to seethe and fly to the Hallowed Wood. I'm not writing out explicit directions for this process here because we have covered different methods for seething in Lesson 09-02, and there is a trip to the Brocken (which is a different place, but a similar method) covered in Lesson 03-05. The Hallowed Wood is not a well-known meeting place of Witches. Instead, it is an Otherworld place that I have hallmarked for us. You'll know it by these signs: ancient stands of trees that you wouldn't normally find together and Stang/Cauldron/Anvil combo with a thick woolen red cord hanging from the Stang. When you make this journey, be sure to write the details of the experience.

Additional Resources

BoS Pages Included

The Fetch
Flying Ointment
Sabbat Wine

Red Thread Academy
Traditional Witchcraft
Year 1: Foundations

Unit 10: Spirit Work
Lesson 3: Familiars

Familiars

<u>Prerequisite Lesson</u>   10-02 Fetch

<u>Objectives</u>
- To begin identifying Spirits Known to the Witch (or Familiars)
- To distinguish between Corporeal and Incorporeal Familiars
- To develop an understanding of the Spirit Tribe
- To build a Spirit House for your primary Familiar

<u>Materials Needed</u>

Journaling materials

Crafting materials specific to your Spirit House (bottle, bird-/dollhouse, box, doll, paints, etc) -- will vary based on your needs

<u>Study Notes</u>

Witches have a long and storied relationship with the Unseen World and with spirits of many types, abilities, and personalities. Those spirits with whom we are most familiar have a special place in our lives and our magic.

I'm not necessarily talking about your favorite kitty, Miss Witch.

Okay, in one respect, I *could* be talking about your favorite kitty, but let's be really up-front that when a Witch talks about a "spirit known to her" -- a familiar spirit -- that isn't a historical implication of the household cat. (When we talked about the Fetch in Lesson 10-02, we talked a little about how the historical familiar was more likely a rabbit than a cat, but I'll own up to the iconic stereotype of the Witch with her black cat. I've had 6 pure black cats in my life, 4 of whom always involved themselves in my magic. My ex-wife had two, Hex and Jinx.)

Of course, that isn't to say that your physical (corporeal) Familiar can't be a cat -- or a dog, or a turtle, a snake, or any other creature with whom you have a working magical relationship. My point is that your being a Witch and having Puff or Ruff in the house doesn't automatically make Puff or Ruff your Familiar. Your kitty or pup may just a pet. Like anyone else, they have to have both an interest and a talent in the magic to be a magic-user.

Corporeal Familiar

A *corporeal* Familiar is a living animal with whom you have a working, magical relationship. This animal shows an interest and adeptness for the type -- at least, for some types -- of magic you perform. Some Familiars love ritual, and they present themselves promptly at the start of every circle and spell. Some are magnificent energy workers, and they'll help you direct healing energy. My ex-wife's cat, Jinx, did both of these. Hex (his sister), on the other hand, prefers to observe and comment upon the making of potions and mixing of herbs. (See, I told you I'm perfectly willing to accept cats as Familiars.)

My rabbit George also loved ritual and energy movement, and he took a very active role in ritual work, when he was part of the circle. On a harness and lead, he would go from one quarter to the next -- at exactly the right time -- and then to the main altar. Fred, my other bun-bun, paid special attention when I was working with the spirits of the dead. (Both of my rabbits have passed now, and Fred seems to have crossed over completely. Nobody in my family reports seeing him since he died. George, however, has continued to stay with me as an *incorporeal* Familiar, which we'll talk about in a moment. George is the little black Netherlands Dwarf on my shoulder in the picture here.)

You also need to give them time to grow into their abilities. Very young animals, like very young children, often haven't reached an age yet where they notice magic at first. They don't know what to expect as "usual" versus "unusual" so magic is sort of routine to them. My cat Dash is now 3 years old, and it wasn't until he was about 9 or 10 months old that he noticed magic was a thing. But when he noticed, he noticed in a big way. We're still figuring out where his talents are, but he is Johnny-on-the-Spot any time I start working with any of my tools. You can see in the picture that he loves the talking board I made. (He seems to be a Guardian. Just ... an easily spooked one.)

Most animals like energy, and many animals are willing to help with the healing process in some capacity. As for willingness or talent to be a Familiar in magic, you really need to pay attention to the proclivities of the specific animal. They aren't all interested or able, no matter how much you love each other.

Incorporeal Familiar

Witches didn't just have animals who helped them manifest their magic. Lore and witch trial records (not ALL of which can be complete fabrications) are filled with accounts of Witches calling upon Familiar spirits to do their bidding.

Nature spirits, angels, demons, magistelli, Deities, the Mighty Dead, the Good People (fairies). There are a host of unseen forces with myriad names. Witches have certainly worked with all of these.

Don't shake your head. Witches most certainly HAVE worked with both Angels and Demons. Let's not forget that the word "angel" comes from the Greek ἄγγελος pronounced "angelos," which means messenger. "Demon" also comes from the Greek -- δαίμων pronounced daímōn, meaning nothing more or less than "spirit." Neither was inherently benevolent, nor was the other malevolent. Can they be goodies and/or baddies? Sure. I bet you can be nasty when provoked, too. I bet you also know some folks who are nasty even when not provoked, but it isn't based on genetics, race, class, gender, or any other broadly defining characteristic. Their nastiness is a personally-defining attribute. It's the same with these Spirits. You find sweetie Demons and jackass Angels, too. Approach all UN-familiar Spirits with caution. You don't know them, and they don't know you.

Like most beings, angels and demons are primarily looking out for themselves, but they're willing to make a deal with you. Actually, I think that can be said of ALL non-corporeal spirits. Some are naturally more amiable and inclined to work with you. Some, not so much. A few can be down-right nasty, but don't let their category be the deciding factor. There are more fey that I would recommend avoiding than there are Goetic demons, frankly.

In fact, Paul Huson, in his book Mastering Witchcraft (a classic that I HIGHLY recommend in our reading lists) suggests getting in touch with a particular Goetic demon pretty early in your Craft practice. I have long maintained that conjuring demons is a historical part of the craft. Having a good working relationship with a couple of these spirits is a good thing for a Witch, and the work we have done in this unit is ample to prepare you for conjuring and communicating with those Spirits with whom you feel an affinity.

Maybe it's because I'm a necromancer, as well, but I also advocate reaching out to the Mighty Dead in search of a familiar spirit willing to guide you. As I said in Lesson 10-01, quoting (now paraphrasing) Christian Day, nobody loves you quite like grandma. It may not be a grandma you ever met in life. It may be an ancestor from you back in your heritage, but our ancestors have a vested interest in our survival. We do them honor by reaching out to them and learning from them.

The Unseen World enfolds us, and we Witches walk within it, while maintaining a connection to consensus reality. Our Familiar Spirits help us navigate and understand the Unseen, for they are a part of that world.

The Familiar Relationship

The most important spirit in a witch's life is her Familiar Spirit. The term "familiar spirit" is actually shorthand for "a Spirit known unto a Witch." In the medieval witchcraft trial records as well as the lore of that time, witches' familiars were reputed to take the form of an animal, an imp, or a person – if and when they took physical form at all. Your Familiar may show up as a real-world, physical animal; but you may also perceive it as a spirit-being in animal, human, or other form. Mine, for example, very regularly manifests as a black cat and also as a girl who looks like a "dark Alice in Wonderland." Every roommate I've ever had has seen the black cat, and a few very perceptive folks have seen her in girl-form.

The Familiar can do a number of jobs for the Witch, but the key feature of the Familiar is that she is the Witch's primary working companion in the realm of the Unseen. You may have lots of spirits with whom you work, but your Familiar is the one you know and trust the most.

Your Familiar is also like a best friend in the spirit world. You will come to know this Spirit better than any other. You may even know him better than you know your siblings or physical-plane best friend. You'll hear her voice, offering guidance instruction, encouragement, and perspective. Furthermore, he will get to know you better than most people will ever know you. Because you can communicate without words, your Familiar will have insights into your experience that you may have never voiced to a living soul. Because your Familiar is almost always with you (or nearby), she will see patterns in your life that you may have missed. He acts as a guardian, a guide, and a friend – even when you feel abandoned by the rest of the world.

Familiars often fulfill particular roles within our "Spirit Tribe" (a concept we'll explore in more depth in a moment). Because of this, they are usually quite gifted in a particular area of spirit work. Mine is very much a teacher, for example. My ex-wife's familiar was a healer. Perhaps yours is your protector or joy guide. A Familiar can be a Spirit who works with you in any capacity.

Theirs will be the voice you hear first and most clearly in your head – other than your own, of course. You may already know precisely who your Familiar is because you have worked together for so long already. Of course, the opposite can also be true. Your familiar spirit can be so much a part of your inner process that you've not yet taken the time to sort out the difference between his voice and your own. You just know that when you listen to your instincts, things work out.

In addition to whatever roles this spirit may play within your Spirit Tribe, she can also serve another important function. She is your gatekeeper into the larger world of Spirit. This is an especially important job as you learn to hear, see, and otherwise interact with the Mighty Dead, your Spirit Tribe, and other people's spirits. Your Familiar, acting as a gatekeeper, will help you sort through the energies of the well-inhabited worlds of Spirit.

Many Familiars, because they work so intimately with us, will want a little bit of special treatment. Almost all familiars want some sort of "house" that can act as a center of rest and recuperation for them. They also like having a vessel because it gives them a physical place to exist, and it feels good to take physical form, at least for a little while. Jars, lidded baskets and bowls, and capped bottles all work well for this. Jewelry, crystals, and dolls are also traditional vessels for familiars. Your Familiar will often be very specific about what she wants. Just listen.

They all usually like and benefit from offerings, as well. Mine wants crystals and keys. She also asks me to smile just for her sometimes. Yours may prefer a saucer of milk once a week and an occasional cut of your steak. I know of a friend's familiar who wants her to burn something from time to time. The Spirit doesn't care what is burned. She just wants the ash – or the transformation created by the burning. Talk to your Familiar to find out what gifts they prefer.

These offerings are not bribes or payments. They are gifts – tokens of friendship. Through them, you are offering energy (love, gratitude, respect) to your friend and partner. You are showing appreciation for their place in your life and showing concern for their well-being.

The Spirit Tribe

Most Witches are going to find that they don't have just a single Spirit present in their life. Most Witches have a group – a circle of friends, a Spirit Tribe or Court. These Spirits usually work together to help you live your best life, and they will usually get along with each other. Usually. Like your flesh-and-blood friends, though, they can sometimes have personality conflicts, differences of opinion, and poor working relationships within the group. As you get to know your Spirits, you will know how they work with each other.

Let me offer this caveat before we really start cataloging and identifying your Spirit Tribe:

These categories and labels are at least somewhat fluid. You may have more, less, or different Spirits in your tribe. I'm offering these identifiers as a starting place for you to explore your spirit community. Please don't feel that you are lacking in some way if you discover that your tribe is different than what I describe.

The Spirit Tribe (what some spiritual communities call the Inner Band) is made up of those Spirits and Guides who interact with you daily. You may not always be aware of them, but they are with you. The most common ones (healer, teacher, protector, joy guide, runner) that we all tend to have in common are the ones who help us with living in our day-to-day lives. The Spirit Tribe members that are unique to us give us our quirky or original outlook and often have individualized help to give.

Teacher – brings you new information and helps your process it
Healer – aids you in keeping your body and mind healthy
Protector – erects shields for mental, physical, emotional, and psychic defense
Joy Guide – brings you comfort and merriments to keep your mood bright
Runner – secures the resources you want and need in the local, physical world

If you find that YOU have a talent or gift in one of these areas, you are probably working very closely with the Spirit in your tribe who acts as a guide to you in that area. For instance, if you are naturally talented at energy healing, or you're a compassionate and caring nurse, your Healer has a big role in your life. Are you especially good at divination and helping people understand the symbolism linked to Tarot, runes, etc? You have a special bond with your Teacher.

These, of course, are only the most common ROLES that spirits can fill. Think of these as general job functions. There are other job functions, too, that might be more specialized or unique to your life, your talents, and your needs. This is to say nothing of the TYPES of spirits (demons, angels, Djinn, etc). As we continue our exploration of the Spirit World, we will look more deeply at both the roles and the types of spirits that you may encounter.

Through all of this, one of the greatest tools I can recommend for any Spirit-Keeper is a journal. I know you've heard this advice before – for all of your magical studies – but I think it has special bearing in spirit communication. Keep track of your experiences and observations. Allow yourself to write TO your Spirits, as if they are pen-pals of yours. Be the scribe while they write back to you. Over time, you will be amazed at the results. (I referred to this as "automatic writing" in Lesson 10-01. It's one of my favorite ways to communicate with Spirits. It doesn't require special tools, doesn't freak out muggle passersby, you can do it in a coffee shop. It's practically perfect in every way.)

Spirit Teacher

No matter how you felt (or feel) about school, you probably had at least one teacher who made a positive impact on your life. Maybe he took the extra time to help you through a challenging concept, believed you could achieve a goal even when you had doubts, or simply offered a daily smile for you in an otherwise unfriendly world. Whether this person was a professional educator at school or a mentor in a less formal setting (a coach, a babysitter, a favorite aunt, or an inspiring employer) doesn't matter. All of these are examples of "teachers" – folks who bring new information into our lives and help us process that information.

Your Teacher Familiar acts in very much the same capacity. She knows things that you don't, and she brings them into your realm of experience. The Teacher is part of your system of intuition – she helps you "know" something when you have no logical, rational way of knowing it. She also brings new information and educational opportunities to you by helping you "stumble upon" just the right book, website, class, or person who has the information you need. Think about those times when you were wondering about a topic or idea, and a friend randomly mentioned the same idea at lunch the next day or you found a link to an article via social media. That is your Teacher Familiar at work!

The Teacher doesn't just bring in new information, though. Oh, no! He also helps you assimilate this new learning, this new insight. He helps you make sense of it, to bring it fully into your world. He also helps you process dilemmas or life situations between the current problem and the information or experience you already have.

When you have an "a-ha!" moment while trying to resolve a question or learning something new, you can be sure your Teacher was helping you – whispering in your ear or showing you the patterns. They also tend to work with our dreams and daydreams to help us sort through our puzzles. In these times, when our conscious mind has finally quieted, we are more open to the guidance of the Spirits.

Writers, teachers, and psychic readers (just to name a few) usually have good working partnerships with their Teacher Familiars.

Exercise to Connect with Teacher Familiar:

Teachers like to communicate, in general, and they'll talk in whatever way you are most likely (and able) to "hear." That might mean clairaudient ("clear-hearing") expression in which you hear the voice of your familiar (either as a voice speaking in your inner, spiritual ear, or as a voice completely separate and outside of you). It can also mean writing (such as automatic writing), a talking board, or showing up in your dreams to converse with you.

Automatic writing is a method you can use without much preparation or particularly special tools. You just need paper and a writing utensil. As with most spirit work, though, I do recommend taking a brief moment to ground, center, and create sacred space. This can be done in the span of a few deep breaths with visualization or a simple prayer to the Divine to guard and guide you as you walk between Realms.

At the top of the paper, write a greeting to your Teacher. "I welcome my Teacher spirit to come and talk with me." (Use your own words, if they feel more comfortable.) After that, write down anything and everything that comes to you. Write down your first thoughts, and don't silence the Teacher by saying to yourself, "No, this is just my imagination." Remember that spirits need a vehicle for communication, and our visionary, imaginative faculties are a great tool.

One of the truly useful aspects of this exercise is that when we sit down with pen and paper to write, there is a lag between the thought in our minds and the time it takes to write the words on the page. While our conscious minds are busy telling our hands to write those particular words, there is an easy gap in conscious thought that allows a Spirit to send us more words. Those are THEIR words, not ours. This is communication.

As you write, ask for your Teacher's name and physical characteristics to come through. You may see (or hear, smell, taste, feel) information that will later clue you in to your Teacher's presence. Perhaps you'll be given a whole and complete picture of this spirit. Maybe you'll smell the aromas and odors associated with a particular learning experience from your past – a favorite teacher's perfume, formaldehyde or chemicals from a science lab, or the scent of chalk dust. However you experience this information, it is correct and good, and it will be useful for you in identifying your Teacher from among a number of spirits.

You can use this exercise for connecting with other types of spirits, as well, but I recommend it here because Teachers tend to be the most verbal. I use this technique all the time with my familiar, S. It is a useful communication tool far beyond the "getting to know you" stage of spirit work.

Healing Familiar

Even if you don't see yourself as a "healer," the chances are quite good that you have a Healer Spirit in your tribe. It is your Healer who reminds you of those foods you should or shouldn't eat, and the activities that most benefit or harm your mental and physical health. Your Healer's chief concern is your well-being, whether mental or physical.

Some Healers are very verbal but it's just as likely that you'll have a sort of "physical knowing" about your Healer's presence or advice. After all, one of their chief concerns is your body. Instead of "talking" to you or showing you images of what to do/eat, your Healer is more likely to give you strong physical urges like cravings for foods, herbs, or teas that you need for health, an impulse to run or dance or stretch, and a strongly favorable response to an aromatic oil that might stimulate a healthful response in your immune system.

Not only can getting to know this guide help keep your own health in check, but you can also tap into the healing potential that is inherent to the human energy structure. If you don't already work with your chakras, energy field, and intuitive healing, your Healer can show you how. Likewise, if you do work with a healing modality, your Healing Familiar can deepen your practice and help you reach your full potential.

While you may not see yourself as a "healer," per se, your body inherently has the potential to heal and nurture itself and others. The Witch has classically always known (and been trained) how to use the Arts to heal. Exploring this power will bring you more fully into the power of the Witch. Your Healer is here to help.

Exercise to connect with the Healer:

Healers love it when you treat your body to "feel good" exercises like yoga, dance, or a walk - something you enjoy that doesn't feel like strenuous work. To get better in touch with your Healer, arrange some time doing some light physical activity, and pay attention to the most prominent Spirit who shows up. What do you know about the spirit's location, appearance, personality, etc?

Joy Spirit

Some Familiars are focused entirely on our happiness. They bring us images of beauty, experiences of love, and the inspiration of hope. These Familiars, whether physical or spiritual, are Joy Guides.

We are all blessed by the presence of a non-corporeal Joy Spirit. Your favorite color, scent, song, flower, etc can all be linked to this guide. Often, Joy Guides appear to you simply as your favorite color or scent; or sometimes they are wearing or otherwise accompanied by these favorites.

Though we are mainly talking about Unseen Spirits, it's worth noting that many of us are also blessed by physical manifestations of joy in the forms of our pets. Most physical Familiars are going to be Protectors,

Healers, or Joy Familiars. The cat that nestles into your blankets for warmth and purrs contentedly, the rabbit that goes nose-to-nose with you for kisses, the bird that sings and repeats your family's funny phrases - these are all Joy Guides made manifest.

Their biggest concern is your happiness, just like that job title suggests. When you're happy, so are they. To this end, Joy Guides tend to be in excellent communication with our Healers. In fact, they often work together, as feelings of joy and pleasure are more accessible when our physical and mental health needs are met.

Exercise to contact your Joy Spirit:
Gather together as many of your favorite things as you can. Light a scented candle that you love, wear your favorite clothes, play a song that makes you giggle and wiggle, all while petting or playing with your puppy.

Invite your Joy Guide to walk with you, show herself, or send you impressions. Maybe you'll have a sudden flash of inspiration to do a favorite activity that you haven't made time for recently. If you get an impression of a physical manifestation including appearance, scent, or other sensation, note it in your journal.

Runner
This category of spirit Familiar can be very tied to the land where you live. If you move, your Runners usually change. They are spirits who know the energies and resources of your area, and they can acquire the things you need. (This isn't always the case, though. My Runner is an Angel associated with the day of my birth. I'll tell you a funny story about her in a minute.) Call on your Runners to help you get a convenient parking space, a hairstylist who understands you, or to track down an object you've misplaced.

Runners are the spirit guides with whom you'll probably have the least personal relationship, but that doesn't mean they won't share their names and personality traits with you. Ask them and see what information you receive.

If you're very adept at finding lost items, you probably have a natural affinity with your runners. Dowsing with rods or pendulums may be a skill you should explore.

If you are exceptionally talented at finding lost things or navigating your way around unfamiliar terrain, you may have a Runner Spirit who stays with you and is connected to the land in a larger capacity than a local land spirit. For example, I have always been exceptionally talented with pendulum spells to find lost objects, keeping my directional orientation even in unfamiliar surroundings, instinctively knowing where other people have lost things even when I wasn't present during the losing of the object, etc. My mother used to teach me, jokingly, to pray to the "parking fairy" for a good parking spot during the winter holiday shopping season. Years later, a friend told me that the name of the "parking goddess" was Mabel, so I started asking Mabel for a good parking spot. And I always said thank you. Just a few months after I started talking to Mabel specifically, I discovered that the angel associated with the time and day of my birth in the Hebrew system is known as Mebahel. The pronunciation is very very close to Mabel. I'm taking that as a sign that Mabel has been with me since birth, and has always been helping me find things. As an Army brat, I've lived all over the world. Mabel is clearly not connected with just one geographic location but has gone with me and is probably able to tap into energetic patterns in the land and the ley lines. (And my connection with Mabel/Mebahel has gotten VERY strong since the beginning of 2018!)

Exercise to connect with Runner Guides:

Visualize finding a dime on the ground and asking for the assistance of your Runner to help you find it. Keep working with this and see if you can find that dime today. Once you have the dime in your hand, SAY THANK YOU (out loud -- and mean it)!! Next, see if you can find a quarter. It really doesn't matter what the object is. If you drive a car, the next time you're driving, ask your Runner for a parking space very close to the door. Visualize it being open and waiting just for you. Be polite! Always say thanks!

I started with: "Mabel, Mabel, full of grace, help me find a parking space." (So cheesy. And so damn effective.) And everyone in the car says THANK YOU, MABEL, for whatever spot we get. =)

Protector

Protecting a Witch from malignant forces is one of the traditional roles of Familiars. These negative forces and unfortunate circumstances can show up on the physical plane, as well as the psychic.

The Protector will act as a guardian for you, both blocking the negative and sometimes battling against the source of attack or turmoil. Your Protector can teach you how to erect and strengthen your energy shield so that you are less vulnerable to attack. Protectors also give us valuable advice and guidance so as to avoid accident and injury. You can think of your Protector as your "guardian angel" -- although the Spirit may not be an *angel* at all. Your Protector could be an Ancestor, a Djinn, a Dragon, a Nature Spirit, or even a Daemon.

Spiritualists of the U.S. tend to report primarily Native American spirit guides fulfilling the role of Protector. Perhaps this role is most often filled by indigenous or ancient peoples in the area where a Witch lives or is born. I know my own Protector is Kiowa Indian, having lived in Texas about 100 years before I was born there. (I have recently found a picture of my Protector -- the exact man I have seen in vision, labeled with the name he gave me for himself. He has confirmed this is image is of himself, but he is generally pretty tight-lipped with me.)

Of course, there are no *rules* regarding the ethnicity of Spirits and their function in your life. Your Protector may be a Viking, a Celtic warlord, or Samurai. They may be either male or female -- or androgynous. They may not even look like a warrior. As with other roles, the Spirit filling this function in your life may not have been human, even. The way in which your Protector appears to you will probably make sense to you in some way, and it will undoubtedly instill a feeling of security and protection in you. The way that they have chosen to appear should project confidence and dependability as well as strength and an ability to defend you, even if their physical characteristics may be a bit perplexing at first.

As with the Healer, you may find that your Protector isn't much of a talker. Mine definitely has that whole "silent bodyguard" vibe going on. He's even more silent than my Healer, in fact. At least, that's my experience right now. These things evolve.

Exercise to connect with Protector Familiar:

Do martial activity, like shadow boxing or Tai Chi, and invite your Protector to make him/her-self known to you.

Gatekeeper:

The function of Gatekeeper is one that is usually filled by a spirit already in your Spirit Tribe. For instance, one of my Teachers is my Gatekeeper. Because she serves both of these functions, I work with her so much and rely on her as my Gatekeeper, which is such a vital role, that she has always been my primary Familiar.

The Gatekeeper's job is to help you establish and maintain orderly contact with other Spirits. You can think of her as a bouncer or a maitre d'. She keeps Spirits away whom you do not wish to contact, and she assigns a sort of speaking order when you are working with multiple Spirits at a time. My Gatekeeper also has a good sense of fun, and when I've led group seances and talking board sessions, we've been told by multiple Spirits that S has entertained the other Spirits while they are waiting. This is particularly true at Samhain, when we may have twenty or more Spirits waiting to speak with us via the talking board (Ouija board). My Gatekeeper lines up those Unseen Guests, maintains order, and pacifies the ones we are unable to get to in a particular evening.

In the case of a coven, one person's Gatekeeper will often act as Gatekeeper for the group. My former coven used the talking board about once a month, and my Gatekeeper usually acted as the "switchboard operator" for us. When mine wass too tired to perform this task, which can happen, another Familiar from within our group would take over.

If you work with your own Spirit Tribe, on a regular basis, your Gatekeeper will be the one who is of great assistance in hearing, seeing, or knowing what the Spirits have to say and how they prefer to communicate. Likewise, if you explore the art of necromancy (which is literally "Spirit Communication" or "communication with the Dead"), your Gatekeeper will be your closest ally in that work.

Your Gatekeeper figuratively holds the key to the kingdom when it comes to other spirits having access to you. My own Gatekeeper keeps a very strict control over this function, as I would hope that she would do. It's worth noting though, that even spirits can have prejudices, and there are certain types of Spirits that my own Gatekeeper does not like. In her particular case, she has a prejudice against a class of Spirits known as the Djinn, which are the types of spirits from which the modern word Genie is derived. One Djinni was trying to reach me for a matter of months, possibly years, and when she finally got through on a small level, I asked for my Gatekeeper to allow her to speak. My Gatekeeper relented against her own judgement, and the Djinni, proceeded to refer to my GateKeeper with the epithet "that overprotective nanny goat Gatekeeper bitch." This actually amuses both my Gatekeeper and myself, as her job is to be a bit overprotective, and as a historical spirit with a documented reputation, she is often seen traditionally in the form of a small horse, a donkey, or even a little goat. (Even spirits have senses of humor -- and tempers.)

Exercise to connect with your Gatekeeper:

In order to connect with the spirit in your Spirit Tribe who is already acting as your Gatekeeper, first use your intuition about who in your inner band might be filling this role. If you have the sense that a spirit you already know has taken on this task, you may very well be right in your assessment. Often it is an issue of more subtle intuition to determine which spirit is acting as a Gatekeeper since this is usually a role that develops within the ranks of the Tribe. In most cases, it will be either a Teacher or Protector. If you are a healer yourself, this role may be filled by your Healer Familiar. You can write the names or roles of your Spirit Tribe in a semi-circle on a piece of paper and use a pendulum to dowse for the answer, if your intuition is coming up blank (or it you doubt the answer currently in your mind).

The Spirit Lover

Would it shock you to know that some Witches maintain a romantic relationship with their Spirit Familiar? Maybe it shocks you to hear that you aren't the only one who has this sort of relationship with a spirit.

If you have never contemplated the possibility of a romantic relationship with a spiritual being, hearing that others are actively engaged in this type of intimacy in the Unseen Realms can be startling, disconcerting, and even off-putting. The truth is, though, that mythology and folklore from all over the world tell of people engaging in sexual encounters and long-term committed relationships with spirit lovers. The medieval witchcraft trial records are also full of stories of Familiars who are intimate with their keepers on a physical and emotional level. Often, the Spirit Lover was also the great teacher who initiated and trained the Witch in the Mysteries of Craft. I mentioned Dame Alice Kyteler and her familiar, Robin Artisson, last month. Robin's role in Alice's coven is recorded as that of teacher and lover. The German witch Walpurga Hausmannin and her spirit Federlin are another famous example.

Of course, the medieval woodcuts and trial records often paint a lurid picture of Witches having sex with spirits in degrading or scandalous ways. Images of the "osculum infame" leap to mind – the infamous "Kiss of Shame" that was said to be exchanged as a greeting between a Witch and the Devil (whom we know to be none other than the Horned God or the Witch Father). This greeting is depicted as the "Devil" presenting his backside to the Witch for the "kiss." Another common sexual motif in the woodcuts is the Sabbatic orgy, in which Witches are shown in various states of disrobement, engaging in sexual acts with each other, winged and horned spirits, and the "Devil" (or Magister).

Why is spirit-sex presented so scandalously? My theory is two-fold. One, Witches are transgressive, often openly embracing concepts, clothing, and customs that are seen as taboo by the majority. Second, the Church was actively engaged in a smear campaign against the "old religions" of Europe, and making the common person believe that the cunning folk were lewd and lascivious beasts engaged in freakish and aberrant acts when a long way in turning neighbor against neighbor.

Luckily, we are given examples of plenty of other types of Spirit Lovers that can shed more light on the spirit-mortal relationship. Some cultures have embraced the idea of the Spirit Lover in a respectful and almost revered way. That's not to say that the relationship was understood to be "normal" by the common culture, but it was known and not shunned for its strangeness. Spirit Spouses are known in every continent as one of the most widespread elements of shamanism. The spirit husband/wife is seen as the primary helping spirits of the shaman, who assists the shaman in their work, and help them gain power in the world of spirit. In some cultures, gaining a spirit spouse is a necessary and expected part of initiation into becoming a shaman. Many traditions of Witchcraft, of course, embody European expressions of shamanism, so it stands to reason that the romantic, sexual, or symbolic relationship between the Witch and the Familiar can serve a similar purpose as in other cultures.

Shamans and Witches engage with their spirit spouses through dreams, trance, and other ritual elements. Fantasy and visualization are often key elements in this engagement. So, if you have found yourself engaged in a torrid affair with your Spirit Familiar, know that you are not alone. The relationship with the Spirit Lover may be one of the great unspoken common experiences of the Craft.

Historical and Goetic Familiars

Do not be surprised if one or more of your Spirit Familiars belongs to a group of famous spirits – or if you come to discover that you have unwittingly named a Physical Familiar one of these well-known names. Some spirits have gained notoriety over the centuries, either because their living companions were tortured into revealing their Familiars' identities, or because certain magicians recorded the names in their grimoires.

On the other hand, don't feel left out if none of your spirit friends have made the "Who's Who of the Unseen Realms." Most of us aren't celebrities either, after all, but that doesn't diminish our contributions or our potential power.

Historical Familiars are those spirits who are known to have worked with other Witches and magicians. These Spirits, though, aren't necessarily so well-known or universally worked with that they are considered deity by the culture in which we see them. If you're well-read in Witch lore, you've probably come across names like Robin Artisson (Dame Alice Kyteler's familiar, not the contemporary Trad Craft author who borrowed the name) or Pyewacket and Greymalkin (brought into pop culture by William Shakespeare's famous Wyrd Sisters).

In most cases, these Spirits worked with other Witches and magicians before they worked with the one who made them famous. In some cases, the Witch created the perfect familiar for herself. (That's known as creating an egregore, and is more advanced that we can cover in this course. But it is very doable.) In either case, these Spirits didn't cease to exist when the famous Witch died. They've continued to come to magical practitioners to help them in the ways that each Spirit is talented. Sadly, the old trial records, filled with salacious misinformation, don't give us much useful information on these Spirits' areas of influence.

Goetic Familiars are those spirits whose names and attributes are catalogued in the Lesser Key of Solomon, a document which was first published in the Middle Ages but shares information about the 72 spirits who were said to aid King Solomon in building his great temple. The word "goetia" means sorcery or witchcraft, and it is related to another word that means wailing or howling.

These spirits prefer to be called "the Legion" instead of "the Goetia," as they were grouped into a variant of military structure when they were bound into service. They are inaccurately referred to as "demons" by most people, though only a few are "demonic" according to contemporary usage of that term. The Greek word "daemon" means spirit, without connotation of evil or malfeasance. Many of the Spirits of the Legion are spirits of the Dead, some are Djinn, and a couple are interdimensional stellar beings. A great many of the Legion are helpful and kind, with only a few bad apples presenting a (very real) threat.

So what does it mean if you do have a famous Familiar? It might mean that your Spirit is getting a boost of energy because more people are feeding into the magic simply by knowing, reading, and talking about them. But this is impossible to measure or account for. It's so deeply integrated into the Spirit that it is simply a part of how you have always known them (even if you only recently realized that anyone else knew about them).

The bigger benefit is that you can find more information about these Spirits. The Spirits of the Legion, in particular, have had many volumes of work written about them. My ex-wife and I have even contributed to the body of work available about these spirits. All of this information can add rich layers to your understanding of your Familiars. And while you may not need it, you can also get confirmation of your abilities by reading what others have written about a Spirit you know so well.

Spirit Keeping

The decision to have a Familiar is not a unilateral one. A Witch does not simply choose a Spirit from a list and then trap it within a seal, a bottle, or a figurine. A Familiar is not a spiritual slave or a prisoner.

The relationship between "master" (the traditional term for the Witch/Magician -- not one I chose/use lightly) and Familiar should be mutually beneficial. The Familiar assists in magic, according to his abilities; and the Witch returns energy in the forms of gratitude, gifts, ritual, or something specific to the Familiar. Spirits will often tell you specifically what they want if you just talk to them.

Look to traditional texts and lore for inspiration regarding what your Spirit may like, but don't rely solely on these sources. No one person who knows you is privy to all the things you may like or dislike. The same is true of Spirits. The traditional texts and lore can't encapsulate all there is to know about a Spirit.

Most Familiar spirits want some sort of housing. This is often a jar or bottle. The housing can also take the shape of a candle or a statue, a piece of jewelry, or some other item. Just ask and they will be very clear, often asking for something you already own. The purpose of the house is to give the Spirit a vessel to inhabit. There are benefits to having a physical form, after all. The house or vessel brings a certain level of pleasure to the Spirit.

They almost all like offerings, as well; though the nature of the offerings varies greatly from Spirit to Spirit. I know a coven Familiar who wants smoke, and she gave a specific incense recipe to be made and burnt for her. The Familiar of one of my students wanted ashes. She didn't care what was burned to create the ash, as long as it was burned with the intention of giving it to her. Some like honey, mint candies, liquor, or other comestibles. Others want energy in the form of dancing, laughing, or sex. Again, we recommend asking your Spirit directly what he wants and how often he wants it.

Spirit Magic and Communication

Finding a Spirit with whom you can work magic, communicate, and build a relationship isn't as tricky a task as it may sound. There are hundreds or even thousands of different "races" or types of Spirits (Mighty Dead, Nature Spirits, Wights, Angels, Demons, Djinn, Dragons, etc. Within each race, there are countless individuals. Someone on the other side of the veil is right for you.

There is literally no end to the work you can accomplish with the help of "your little daemon." Liberal sciences, necromancy, alchemy, art, foreign language, diplomacy, law, love – these Spirits know all of the things that you want to know. The can make learning significantly easier. They love what you love and will help you pursue, protect, and promote those passions.

This is sorcery, witchcraft. You don't have to make it complicated unless that placates your sense of the Arte Magical.

Each Spirit is an individual and will have his preferred method of working, as well. Some are chatty, others communicate with images. Some might like complicated ritual and arcane language, while many prefer simplicity. Some sing – All. The. Time. (Paimon.) They are as individual and quirky as the magicians who work with them.

However old the Spirits you work with may be, the traditional descriptions you may find of them online or in books may be equally old (and outdated). Everybody changes at least a little in 400 years, even Spirits.

Furthermore, some details weren't recorded accurately in the first place. (As an example, the Spirits of the Goetic Legion were all originally described as inherently masculine, regardless of how anciently that Spirit may have been worshipped as a Goddess. As an obvious example, just look at Astaroth.)

Communicate with your chosen spirit in whatever way makes the most sense. If he is verbal, use automatic writing or a talking board as you develop your clairaudient abilities. If she is visual, use a scrying mirror, cauldron, crystal ball, etc. Try trance, flying out, lucid dreaming, smoke/fire scrying, trance dance, or sexual energy; or simply try listening and looking for your Familiar.

The Unseen World is not a separate place, distinct and untouched by This World. Beings of Spirit and beings of flesh walk in both places. We ourselves are, ultimately, beings of Spirit who are also beings of flesh. Spirits know that we inhabit both spaces at once. Witches should know this, as well.

Affinity With a Spirit

Not every Spirit is a good fit for each Witch. Not only are some Spirits dangerous and should be avoided, but many are simply incompatible for a given individual. You have undoubtedly met people with whom you couldn't work or whose company you didn't enjoy. They aren't inherently bad people. You just don't like them. The same will be true of many Spirits. The goal with spirit keeping is to find those Spirits with whom you can build a working, fraternal, familial, or even romantic relationship.

A Witch will have a number of potential Spirits from whom she might choose. During the time that she is researching those Spirits, they might also be observing her.

When a particularly strong attraction presents itself to a Witch, this Spirit is a natural candidate to become a Familiar. Indeed, the Spirit may already be acting in that capacity for the Witch, and the Witch needs only to recognize the Spirit's presence.

Of course, more than one Spirit may be available to you from the hosts of individuals on the Other Side, but it is important that you pay close attention to how well these spirits work with each other before you take on multiple working partnerships with various Spirits. They don't all get along, after all, and to bring too many of them into your life (all at once) is to court madness. (You may end up having a great many Spirits in your tribe eventually, but start slowly. See who's there now, and don't be too eager to add everybody all at once. Remember, you have to keep up the agreements on your end. You have "care and feeding" to do.)

<u>Assignment</u>	Tell me about your Familiar(s) -- both corporeal and non-corporeal. What sort of relationship do you have with them? What are they like -- personality, background, quirks, peeves, talents? I want to know about any Familiar that is close enough to you to have a vital magical working relationship. This includes any Spirit that is in your Spirit Tribe, any Spirit that you have (or should) provide a Spirit Vessel, and any animal that you consider a physical Familiar. Include pictures of the Vessel (or the animal). =) Be sure to tell me how long you have been working with each Familiar, as well.

As a little extra touch, please note any new Spirits that you are starting to notice. Very often, doing work like this (taking on a course of study, especially spiritual study) will light a beacon for new Spirits to come into our lives. Have you noticed any new Spirits in your world since you started this course? |
| <u>Additional Resources</u> | Witches' Key to the Legion: a Guide to Solomonic Sorcery by Laurelei Black -- available in Kindle, PDF, and paperback formats -- http://asteriabooks.com/books/legion.html

AFW Article about Familiars by Natalie Long -- http://afwcraft.blogspot.com/2011/08/familiars-and-familiar-spirits.html

"Forgetting Human" guest blog posts on AFW by Robin Artisson -- http://afwcraft.blogspot.com/search?q=forgetting+human |
| <u>BoS Pages Included</u> | Conjuration Pack |

Godd-Friends

Prerequisite Lesson

10-01 Triple Soul, Evocation and Banishing, Communication
10-03 Familiars

Objectives

- To discuss the benefits of a Godd-friend relationship
- To open to the possibility of a Godd-friend relationship
- To establish a set of practices in the case of a Godd-friend relationship

Materials Needed

Journaling materials

Study Notes

I'm going to make a shocking statement that flies in the face of what I have read from most other authors and teachers: Having a personal relationship with a God or Goddess ("Godd" -- as a term inclusive of all gender expressions that Deity might take) isn't so very different from having a relationship with a Familiar. Yes, the Spirit in question is different in the sense of being much BIGGER (more well-known, more powerful), but the love and the reciprocity that can exist between you is often very similar.

In fact, if you think back to the lesson on Familiars (10-03), you'll recall that some Spirits are recognized as Godds in one culture and time period, but have been demonized by another culture in another time. Godds that aren't being worshipped are very often thought of as some other type of Spirit -- nature spirit, fey, demon, etc.

Of course, we're talking in this lesson about Deities that are still acknowledged as Godds, at least within the Pagan subculture. It's different now. They aren't worshipped by whole cultures, or even by large majorities. They aren't always worshipped in traditional ways, per se. Parts of their attributes and traditional worship have very likely been lost to time. But they are still with us, and they are still willing to share with us. In fact, they are hoping to share with us and to be shared by us. What is remembered lives -- and that includes the Godds.

What is a Godd-Friend?

There are a lot of different terms we could use for the relationship between a Deity and a human. I'm using the term Godd-friend which is based on the Icelandic word *fulltrua/fulltrui,* which has come to mean someone with a close, personal, on-going relationship with a Godd. It is understood within Norse

Heathenry that we are descended from the Godds, that we are kith and kin to them, so it isn't so far a stretch to believe that we might develop a deep and meaningful relationship with one or more of them.

This concept is popular in modern Paganism (usually under the auspices of the "personal God/dess" or "patron/matron Deity"), but shouldn't be dismissed as a "fluffy" conceit. Granted, there are some folks out there who are being adopted by a new Godd every week, and we might look at them a bit shrewdly.

The Godd-friend relationship isn't one to take on lightly. There are expectations involved, not all of which will be clear to you when you first enter the relationship. Just like falling in love with a mortal person, you can't always know how the relationship might unfold. The Godds don't let us out of our vows easily, though -- if at all. So, be aware of that before you give yourself enthusiastically to any Deity. You even have the right to politely decline the offer, if you don't feel like it's a good fit for you. I'd recommend declining carefully and only after great deliberation and divination, but I'd suggest the same for *accepting. Go into it (or walk away from it) with your eyes as open as possible.*

Some questions that you will want to ask: Will your relationship be that of parent & child (ancestor & descendant)? Or will it be romantic/sexual? Will it sometimes/rarely/often be that of employer & employee or mentor & protege? Are you (or will you be) a representative of this Deity in the world for other people? You'll likely think of other questions relevant to yourself or the Deity/proposed relationship, as it is presented.

Honoring Your Godd-Friend

You'll also want to know about specific rituals and offerings that your God/dess will want from you, but be aware that these things can change over time. The Godds are living, which means that they have evolved and grown with us as a culture, so their tastes have changed over time. They are open to some new ways of doing things because we do things differently. The Godds made us, and we make the Godds. So don't be too shocked if you ask Brighid (with whom you've always felt a connection) what She would like as an offering and hear back from Her that She wants you to give Her rum and hot peppers and that you should make these offerings at the gravesite of the oldest woman in your local cemetery. First off, yes, you're still talking to Brighid. You just tapped into a very New World face of her -- Maman Brigitte, who was brought to Haiti and the Dominican Republic by Celtic-descended indentured servants, where she was adopted into a nation of Spirits (loa) as the wife of Baron Samedhi. She's a protector of the Dead and cusses way more than the Brighid you were probably used to. But she's still essentially Brighid. If you're open to listening, and willing to put in the work, you will come to know Her as a face of the Witchmother, for She certainly has both White/Goda and Black/Kolyo aspects.

You have the techniques and know-how to communicate with Spirits of all sorts. Godds are no different. Ask them what they want, and be prepared to follow through on anything you have agreed to.

It's often wise to make room for your Godd-Friend within your sacred spaces. Give Them an altar of their own or make space for them within your current altar. You can include statuary, artwork, or other representations. One of the easiest and most frugal ways to create iconography is to find a picture you like from the internet, print it (at a local print shop, if needed), and affix it to a prayer candle (which can be found at most grocery and dollar stores).

Red (and Green), White, and Black (again)

You may have noticed that this Tradition doesn't ask you to adhere to a particular pantheon of Deities. In fact, throughout the course, there have been times when I've referenced Celtic, Norse, Greek, Sumerian, and even Voudon Godds (or Lwa, in the case of Voudon). *Strictly* traditional practice demands that you stick with the pantheon of not just a specific place, but also a specific time. It also demands that you work with a concept called hard polytheism in which you adamantly accept the Godds as being distinctly separate from both yourself and from each other. (In the view of hard polytheism, Brid of the Celts, St. Brighid of Kildare, and Maman Brigitte are NOT the same being.)

I struggle with this strict interpretation of Traditional Witchcraft. I've said right from the beginning of the course that I'm more a mythic poet than that. I see too many archetypal intersections. And while I'm not going to say that all White Goddesses are the same Goddess, I'm comfortable talking about Aphrodite's White Goddess-ness as well as Brighid's White Goddess-ness, etc. I'm willing to look at the Venn diagram of where their White Goddess-ness intersects. And I'm further willing to look at all the White Goddess attributes and know THAT is Goda, THE White Goddess.

The thing about looking at Deity this way is that every Deity conceived by humanity ostensibly fits into one of four major categories (by the Spiral Castle Trad way of thinking) -- Red or Green Gods, and Black or White Goddesses. (Yes, I hear you. We could make other categories, too. We could further subdivide. For that matter, we could, and do, combine these dualities back to One -- Witch Father and Mother. But notice how elegantly these divisions keep repeating themselves in our symbolism.)

Red Gods -- the light bringers, the rebels, the wanderers, the makers, the alchemists, the betrayers, the adversaries, the challengers, the opposers, the warriors, the horned Gods.

Green Gods -- the shepherds, the sacrifices, the harvest kings

Black Goddesses -- covered ones, veiled ones, Fates, weavers, spinners, crones, wise ones, grandmothers, owl Goddesses, night goddesses, devourers, silver ones, bloody ones, strategists

White Goddesses -- shining ones, golden ones, fiery ones, enchantresses, sirens, lovers, dawn Goddesses, water-bird Goddess

You'll note I mentioned Green Gods here, and I haven't mentioned Green before as a main color within the system. There's a reason for that. It's not to disparage the importance or value of the Green God, but the Path of Green (the message of the Dying and Resurrecting God) has been covered by enough Pagans and Christians alike. It has a place, even within our Mysteries, but our study and effort focuses on transformation from within (the Red Path), not salvation from without (Green Path). That is the way of Cunning Folk. That is what is transgressive about us and our Godds. We do not look to be saved. We seek our own liberation.

Magistellus

In a guest-blog post that he wrote on the American Folkloric Witchcraft blog back in 2011, Robin Artisson wrote a fascinating piece on the role and nature of the magistellus, or *little master*. I highly recommend you read his article, but I'll explain it in short here.

He basically says that it is pretty well agreed that Witches in the middle ages did indeed make covenant with the Witch Father, and all evidence seems to indicate that different covens enjoyed personal relationships with him in various ways. But there are enough discrepancies between accounts to make the case for a sort of ambassador, called a magistellus. Essentially, a Spirit comes to the local coven with all the hallmarks of the Master, including one of his names and a sigil. He comes with a significant portion of power -- enough that the coven would never know the difference. After all, could you tell the difference between one level of Spirit and the next higher level? He comes with the authority of the Master, and in his name. A lieutenant.

Robin goes on to say that he and his students have been working with and under the auspices of such a magistellus for several years. The name of this Spirit is one of the secrets of their tradition, as is the sigil.

When you meet a Deity, ask directly if they are the Deity in full, or if the Spirit you are encountering is a magistellus. It is no small feat to have attracted the attention of a magistellus. Indeed, I suspect that more people are dealing with magistelli than with Deities than they realize.

As you are encountering Deities (both those with a close personal tie to you and also those who come to you for a single ritual working or a brief period of time), they could be from any pantheon. I can think of none that are truly off-limits. Maybe you will meet the Black Goddess as Kolyo, or maybe she will come as Kali, the Cailleach, Hella, or Hekate -- or perhaps as a magistella of one of these. All of these are possible, right, and good.

Nor do you necessarily HAVE to have a specific Godd-Friend to be considered somehow authentic as a Witch. I believe that to be another misconception of neopaganism. Spirit work is a cornerstone of the Craft, certainly; but Deity patronage isn't, per se. Do not feel pressured one way or the other in this regard.

Assignment

If you are already claimed by a Godd-Friend, please write a short essay about that relationship. Describe how it began, what it has been like, and what you anticipate it being like in the future. What sort of offerings do you make? How do you communicate with this Deity? How close are you? Share a picture of your altar space for Him/Her.

If you do not already have a Godd-Friend but wish to have one at this time, lay the compass on a Dark Moon, choose one of the ways of making magic, and (if it is your Will to do so) invite a Deity to walk close with you for your mutual benefit. (You can put other parameters on your phrasing, of course. You can even offer yourself to a specific Deity, if you want to be so bold. Just understand that they could reject your offer, if you are too specific.) Perhaps something like: "I stand where the roads cross, waiting for that Devil or Dame who has always shielded my back on this Crooked Path to stand beside me, so I might know and honor my Benefactor." After you've done the ritual, write the essay with the information you have. Research as much as you can about this Deity, and share some of what you have discovered in your research. Share a picture of the beginnings of your altar space.

Additional Resources

Forgetting Human, Part 3 (blog post) by Robin Artisson -- the last section of this blog post is "The Master of Spirits and the Magistellus," but I recommend reading the entire series -- http://afwcraft.blogspot.com/2011/10/forgetting-human-pt-3-guest-post-by.html

For the Love of the Gods: The History and Modern Practice of Theurgy (book) by Brandy Williams -- https://amzn.to/36lL60H

Aphrodite's Priestess by Laurelei Black (book) -- This is a book I wrote to help others following a Godd-friend relationship with Aphrodite -- http://asteriabooks.com/books/aphrodites-priestess.html

BoS Pages Included

Gods, Goddesses, and Mighty Ones set

Red Thread Academy — Unit 11: History and Lore
Traditional Witchcraft — Lesson 1: Trad Craft Reading List 1
Year 1: Foundations

Traditional Witchcraft Reading List 1

Prerequisite Lesson — None specified

Objectives — To be knowledgeable in the lore, history, symbolism, and foundations of Traditional Witchcraft

Materials Needed — Complete copy of ONE of the texts below

Study Notes — These writings are central to Traditional Witchcraft and should be read by the Witch. They are sometimes difficult to penetrate, but they are well worth the effort. Indeed, these are works that the Witch is likely to come back to again and again. They are especially instructive and foundational to seekers within the Spiral Castle.

The Taper that Lights the Way: Robert Cochrane's Letters Revealed by Shani Oates -- https://amzn.to/2G6kEhc

The White Goddess by Robert Graves -- https://amzn.to/3jkGYSr

1734-witchcraft.org -- This website was originally maintained by Joe Wilson (now an archive, held in trust by a council of 1734 elders from different covens).

Assignment — Choose one of the titles above to read in its entirety. Write a book analysis in which you address the following:
- Relevance of this work to Traditional Witchcraft
- Accessibility of this work, given your current level of understanding of the Craft
- Three points made by the author which offered clarity or deeper understanding
- Four concepts presented by the author that you would like to explore on a deeper level in the future

Additional Resources — In truth, I recommend that the serious student of the Spiral Castle path make themselves familiar with all three of these foundational sets of writings. While we don't claim lineage to Cochrane or Wilson, our heritage is very much with them.

Red Thread Academy
Traditional Witchcraft
Year 1: Foundations

Unit 11: History and Lore
Lesson 2: Trad Craft Reading List 2

Traditional Witchcraft Reading List 2

Prerequisite Lesson — None specified

Objectives — To be knowledgeable in the lore, history, symbolism, and foundations of Traditional Witchcraft

---

Materials Needed — Complete copy of ONE of the texts below

Study Notes

This list of books is longer than Trad Craft List 1, but it is also very potent. I honestly recommend reading all of these texts as you study the Craft, but I ask that you read at least one as part of this course.

Unfortunately, the first several are published by Capall Bann and are now all out of print, making them quite hard to find and expensive -- exorbitantly so, in some cases. If you can find a used copy in your budget, snatch it up and covet it. If you can read it any other way (under the watchful eye of a Craft friend, for example), do it.

These titles are written by authors practicing some variation of Traditional Witchcraft:

Call of the Horned Piper by Nigel Jackson -- https://amzn.to/3cHCDGz

Masks of Misrule by Nigel Jackson -- https://amzn.to/2GcgQuK

Pillars of Tubal Cain by Nigel Jackson & Michael Howard -- https://amzn.to/3n7ehLd

Witchcraft: a Tradition Renewed by Doreen Valiente and Evan John Jones -- https://amzn.to/3n6tmfJ

The Forge of Tubal Cain by Ann Finnin -- https://amzn.to/3iithlM

Grimoire for Modern Cunning Folk by Peter Paddon -- https://amzn.to/36iAxLU

The Witching Way of Hollow Hill by Robin Artisson -- https://amzn.to/36kYT7K

Tubelo's Green Fire by Shani Oates -- https://amzn.to/2IzoEBR

Black Toad by Gemma Gary -- https://amzn.to/2S9ZBN5

Besom, Stang & Sword by Chris Orapello & Tara-Love Maguire -- https://amzn.to/3jgzH6h

1734-witchcraft.org -- This website was originally maintained by Joe Wilson (now an archive, held in trust by a council of 1734 elders from different covens).

Assignment

Choose one of the titles above (or find another well-respected title and author exploring traditional Craft) to read in its entirety. Write a book analysis in which you address the following:
- Accessibility of this work, given your current level of understanding of the Craft
- Three points made by the author which offered clarity or deeper understanding
- Four concepts presented by the author that you would like to explore on a deeper level in the future

---

Additional Resources

The Real Mother Goose by Blanche Wright -- Add this to your library and read with a Witchy lens! So many gems hidden in these rhymes.-- https://amzn.to/2Iw5IEf

---

BoS Pages Included

Red Thread Academy
Traditional Witchcraft
Year 1: Foundations

Unit 11: History and Lore
Lesson 3: General Craft Reading List

General Witchcraft Reading List

Prerequisite Lesson None specified

Objectives
- To be knowledgeable about general witchcraft practices
- To be able to compare and contrast other forms of witchcraft to RTA

Materials Needed Complete copy of one of the texts below

Study Notes

These titles present information about the practice of Witchcraft in more general and universal terms, but many still have a Traditional flavor:

Mastering Witchcraft: A Practical Guide for Witches, Warlocks & Covens by Paul Huson -- https://amzn.to/2G9xNWE

The Triumph of the Moon by Ronald Hutton -- https://amzn.to/3kWe23C

The Rebirth of Witchcraft by Doreen Valiente -- https://amzn.to/34dUWiR

Witchcraft for Tomorrow by Doreen Valiente -- https://amzn.to/3n0ljkJ

Natural Magic by Doreen Valiente -- https://amzn.to/2HzhO4q

Witches All by Elizabeth Pepper -- https://amzn.to/2GhXl3J

Aradia or the Gospel of the Witches of Italy by Charles G. Leland -- https://amzn.to/3inh6nT

The Golden Bough by James George Frazer -- https://amzn.to/3n6CYHI

Assignment

Choose one of the titles above (find another well-respected title and author that explores the Craft in either more general or something akin to academic terms) to read in its entirety. Write a book analysis in which you address the following:
- Accessibility of this work, given your current level of understanding of the Craft
- Relevance to Traditional Craft
- Three points made by the author which offered clarity or deeper understanding
- Two concepts presented by the author that you would like to explore on a deeper level in the future

Additional Resources

BoS Pages Included

Red Thread Academy
Traditional Witchcraft
Year 1: Foundations

Unit 11: History and Lore
Lesson 4: Other Craft Reading List

Other Magical Traditions Reading List

Prerequisite Lesson None specified

Objectives To be familiar with other forms of Craft, Paganism, and Magick

Materials Needed Complete copy of ONE of the texts below

Study Notes These titles present a solid understanding of other types of Witchcraft, Paganism, and Magic:

Witchcraft Today by Gerald Gardner - https://amzn.to/2S9Qpbl

Italian Witchcraft: The Old Religion of Southern Europe by Raven Grimassi - https://amzn.to/2SnH00d

Essential Asatru by Diana Paxson - https://amzn.to/3jeXKCD

The Druidry Handbook: Spiritual Practice Rooted in Living Earth by John Michael Greer and Phillip Carr-Gomm - https://amzn.to/36piAv8

Sticks, Stones, Roots, & Bones: Hoodoo, Mojo, and Conjuring with Herbs by Stephanie Rose Bird - https://amzn.to/33evUAQ

Assignment Choose one of the titles above to read in its entirety. Write a book analysis in which you address the following:
- Relevance of this work to Traditional Witchcraft
- Accessibility of this work, given your current level of understanding of the Craft
- Three points made by the author which offered clarity or deeper understanding
- Four concepts presented by the author that you would like to explore on a deeper level in the future

Additional Resources

Red Thread Academy
Traditional Witchcraft
Year 1: Foundations

Unit 12: Initiation
Lesson 1: Planning for the Future

Planning for the Future

Prerequisite Lesson All previous lessons should be completed to a level of proficiency or mastery

Objectives
- To reflect on the course work and any insights gained
- To pause before moving into whatever the next stage of study or growth might be
- To consider a further course of study within RTA/SCT
- To provide feedback to Laurelei/RTA for improving the course content
- To prepare for the final exam first degree initiation

Materials Needed

Study Notes

Congratulations! You have done a phenomenal amount of work during this course. As you take this lesson to pause and reflect, I am hoping that you are able to enjoy a sense of achievement and accomplishment. This was no minor task that you set yourself. Well done!

Did it take you longer than a year? Who cares! Let that go right now. I made this course intentionally rigorous. Yes, some weeks were easy. Some weeks were distinctly NOT. In fact, some of the lessons would have been spectacularly challenging to complete in a single week. So, if you completed this much of the course in 49 weeks, you are not only very dedicated to your Craft studies, you are also a time management genius.

The Final Exam (lesson 12-02) is the proving grounds for your growth as a Witch. Everyone who comes to this course, who joins this Academy, who takes the Red Thread through this Tradition starts on the Crooked Path from a different access point. We all know different things when we begin, and we've had different experiences. But think back over the course of this year (or more) and know that everyone who gets to THIS point, who faces this level of testing and initiation has done this same amount of work, has faced the same challenges, has overcome those challenges in their own ways, and become a stronger Witch because of it. Everyone standing here has made or found a Stang, made it theirs, and learned something about how to use it. You are proficient in three forms of divination, at least -- an accomplishment you might have thought impossible a year ago. You have written and performed a complete ritual, honored all the moons and all the festivals in the year. And these are just a few of the things!

The Initiation Ceremony seals the work. There are some Mysteries and further tests within the ritual that I can't reveal here. It isn't just a pretty graduation ceremony. I don't think that is fair or kind. You deserve more than a pat on the head, a shake of the hand.

Of course, the script/outline has been here in the course manual the whole time you've studied, and perhaps you've already peeked at that section. If not, you'll have "spoilers" when you do look at the ritual in order to gather materials and prepare for it, but I am trusting that the impact of the performance will be greater than the impact you feel when you read it. What nothing on the ritual script/outline can tell you is what you'll actually experience in the initiation. This is why it is a Mystery rite.

Assignment

For now, I would like you to think about some questions. Please explore them deeply, taking as much time as you need.
- What were your biggest challenges during your 1st Degree studies?
- What was an insight that you gained about yourself or this path during this course?
- Do you want to pursue 2nd Degree (which takes a Witch further into their studies along a more focused path -- like healer, clergy, diviner, guardian, summoner, bard, artisan)?
- What sort of worries or concerns do you have about the initiation?
- I'd like you to consider proposing ways in which I might make this class more useful or meaningful to students. I know you still have an exam and initiation to complete, so you might want to reserve critical feedback until those are done. But I am open to hearing suggestions.

Additional Resources

BoS Pages Included

Red Thread Academy
Traditional Witchcraft
Year 1: Foundations

Unit 12: Initiation
Lesson 2: Final Exam

Final Exam

Prerequisite Lesson — All previous lessons should be completed to a level of proficiency or mastery

Objectives — To synthesize and assess the year's study

Materials Needed — All of them. Whatever you feel like you need — though you can answer the questions with paper and pen (or in a DOC file).

Study Notes — This exam is obviously an "open book test." After all, we have access to resources, most of the time, and I feel that this test should be no different. However, I would challenge you to rely more on yourself than your study materials and previous work. The point of the test is to get at what *you know*, not what you can look up in your previous assignments. What have you taken to heart? What has made an impact? I'm hoping that I've designed the test (and that you'll approach it) in such a way that we'll be able to draw those things out together without you regurgitating things I wrote or previous work you did for an assignment.

Assignment — Answer the questions from the next page. Congratulations! You're almost ready for initiation.

Additional Resources

BoS Pages Included

Red Thread Academy
Traditional Witchcraft
Year 1: Foundations

Unit 12: Initiation
Lesson 2: Final Exam

Final Exam

Instructions: *Most of the questions are open-ended and will require a few sentences or maybe even a couple of paragraphs. Write as much as you need to say to fully answer the question.*

1. What does it mean to you to walk the path of the Witch?

2. Explain your current Ethics. How do you determine what is an ethical action to take and what actions are outside your ethical boundaries?

3. Describe some ways you might celebrate Lammas.

4. What are some significant associations of the colors Red, White, and Black? Have you had any personal connections to these colors in the last year (or more) of study that haven't been mentioned as part of the course-work? If so, please share.

5. What is your relationship with your Familiar like?

6. Describe the differences between the three knives that a Witch in this Tradition uses.

7. We draw three circles when we Lay the Compass in this Tradition. Describe how you know to draw those three circles based on what we've discussed this year.

8. What is a Stang and how do you use it?

9. What is your Fetch?

10. Describe your Spirit Court.

11. If you needed to rid yourself of a harmful person in your immediate sphere of influence, describe what magical steps you might employ and how you approach them.

12. How do you Align the 3 Souls?

13. If you needed to do a prosperity spell, how would you go about writing and performing it.

Red Thread Academy — Unit 12: Initiation
Traditional Witchcraft
Year 1: Foundations — Lesson 3: 1st Degree Self-Initiation Rite

1st Degree Self-Initiation Rite

Prerequisite Lesson — All previous lessons (including 12-2 Final Exam) should be completed to a level of proficiency or mastery

Objectives
- To raise Dedicate to the level of 1st Degree within the Spiral Castle Tradition
- To initiate pathways for the transmission of Tradition Mysteries
- To create Family bonds between the Initiate and the Tradition

Materials Needed

Stang, candles, lighter

Cauldron, water

Anvil, hammer, lancet

Three knives (red, black, white)

Red Cord, Black Cord, White Cord

Bread, lipped dish or bowl

Red wine, cup, mugwort, lemongrass, honey, teaball

Initiation incense, holder, charcoal

Bath sachet, dressed candle, anointing oil

Stone Bowl with stones, Dark Mirror

Initiation Gift (amber, jet & bone necklace)

Study Notes

Mindset

It is impossible and improper for me or anyone to tell you how you should feel as you prepare for this momentous rite of passage. Whether you're feeling excited, nervous, merely curious, or even a little detached (or something else altogether) -- it's all "within normal limits."

In fact, it's even within the acceptable limits of this stage of your journey to have doubts, fears, and uncertainties about proceeding to the next step. This is a perfect time, I think, to be asking hard questions of yourself about whether or not you wish and Will to go further. You are under no obligation, after all. All of this study, work, and ritual is for YOU, and if this path doesn't resonate with you, now is a great time to make a change.

Initiations in our tradition are not awards ceremonies that commemorate the work you have already done. That is not the traditional purpose of initiatory rites, at all. (Remember that to initiate means to start.)

This is a time of testing. You have already given yourself a portion of that test -- the intellectual portion via the final exam. There are other ways, though, in which you will test your own readiness to continue into the 2nd Degree work.

This is a time of Mysteries. You are enacting ritual steps that will open you to the Spiral Castle Tradition Mysteries. That is no small thing. In my own work, sharing coven and tradition Mysteries with others in my group has been incredibly meaningful, special, and enlightening. I hope you find the same to be true.

This is a time of bonding. I may not be with you in the flesh for this initiation, nor may any others of our tradition, but you are creating bonds with us nevertheless. We are joined by the same oaths, connected by the same Red Thread of blood and fire upon which those oaths have been made, and undergone the same initial training.

Under normal circumstances, you wouldn't fully know what to expect at your initiation. There is an air of secrecy around the rite, and I will endeavor to maintain that for the in-person variation of the 3rd Degree initiation. These self-initiations, though, are available to students the moment they purchase the book. The steps and actions of the initiation ritual, therefore, are not mysterious, at all. It is what might transpire within them where the Mysteries can be found.

For this reason, I hope that you will give yourself ample opportunity to experience them by approaching them with love, reverence, and preparation. (This is NOT one of those rituals where you can wipe the cheet-oh dust from your fingers onto your sweatpants and say, "Let's do this.")

Take some time to understand and administer the preparations below before performing the initiation.

Space/Time

This is not a short initiation ritual, and you will need privacy for it. The braiding of the cords is part of the ritual. Trust me, I know better than anyone in our tradition how long this takes. Give yourself time and space for all of it. (If you know from your braiding of seasonal cords that you are a super-slow braider, you might want to make some of the initial single braids ahead of time. Approach ALL of your time working with the cords in the same spirit -- giving yourself space and time to focus on the ideas presented in the ritual outline.)

Our home coven always takes time away from our normal routine for initiations. We rent a cabin in the forest together for two nights, performing the ritual the first night after the sun has set and taking as much time as we need for the initiate. (It's always a little different. Some take just one night. Others last into the following day.)

Somehow, give yourself some space and time apart from the people with whom you live. It is even better if you can get into a different (wilder) space -- like the woods, desert, seashore, etc. Getting away from your own domesticity and daily experience can heighten the experience and help you achieve the liminality of the rite much easier. Rent a cabin. Camp in your backyard. Claim space in a spare room or garage for the weekend.

My preference will always be for going to a cabin in the woods because I can get all the amenities I want and need (privacy for duration, bath, toilet, stove, fireplace, private or nearly private access to the forest, campfire outside, comfy beds, etc.). Ultimately, though, you want to make sure that you set-up the surroundings that will allow you to immerse yourself in the experience, feeling safe from outside threat or distraction.

Fasting & Meditation

Fasting and meditation are important acts of preparation leading up to any initiation ceremony. However, we do not have strict guidelines about what this fast should look like or what your meditation practice must entail. Don't let the flexibility here fool you into thinking this step is purely optional. It isn't.

Consciously changing your eating habits and sitting in contemplation of the step you are about to take will start to make the shifts of consciousness for you that will help open you up to the initiatory process. Visionary work is often aided by this sort of preparation, and you will be engaging in multiple layers of psychic work during this ritual.

Choose the type of fast that is most appropriate to your health circumstances. Please don't cause yourself a health crisis in pursuit of spiritual revelations. This is completely unnecessary. Altering your food choices a little and eating with mindfulness is truly enough to accomplish the psychic shifts needed, without bottoming out your blood sugar, triggering a migraine, or causing other health problems.

Give yourself a 3-day fast -- so that your initiation day is the 3rd day. So if you are performing the rite on Friday, start your fast and meditations on Wednesday morning. You will not be resuming your normal eating patterns until after the initiation, which will be completed sometime after midnight (or early morning) on Saturday morning.

Definitely cut out sugar, alcohol, and as much caffeine as you can without triggering rebound headaches. (If you are very caffeine-addicted, you may need to have one coffee/soda per day to stave off such a headache/migraine. Do what you gotta do. You won't be performing an initiation through a migraine, after all.)

As far as what you DO eat, the focus should be on "clean eating" in some capacity. There are a number of ways you could approach that. Whole foods. Vegetarian. Vegan. If your body can handle it, you can certainly do a liquid fast. Or maybe do a combo of these -- whole foods on Wednesday, vegetarian on Thursday, liquids only on Friday.

The fast that was required by my initiator was a "no-kill" fast. It was inherently vegetarian, but it also meant that we had to be mindful regarding the plant-based foods we consumed. Root veggies (carrots, beets, etc) were out because the entire plant had to die to harvest the root, and so were onions and garlic, which made using almost anything pre-packaged (like sauces) impossible. We really had to read labels, and I learned so much about how various plants grow. At 25 (my age at my 1st Degree initiation), you'd be shocked how clueless I was!

Potatoes, I learned to my surprise, were a viable option on a "no-kill" fast because you can dig up a single potato from the garden without killing the whole plant. Corn was also okay. Even though modern farmers harvest the whole plant, you can certainly pick a single ear from the stalk without killing the other ear. (Corn, like mammals, usually has two.)

This type of fast is still my favorite because it requires mindfulness at every stage -- from menu selection to meal preparation to dining. Well, I bring the mindfulness to the dining; but after 20 years of developing recipes that I eat almost exclusively during initiation-prep, when I sit down with these dishes, the sense memory is very strong. It helps link me to the initiations I have received, the ones I attended, and the ones I performed for others. Each meal becomes a little housle.

Ritual Cleansing

It goes without saying that both you and your garments should be clean when you come to the ritual space for ceremonies of this nature. For this rite, you will go a step further and perform a ritual cleansing in addition to your standard bath/shower.

I know that not everyone bathes/showers and engages in ritual purification before every magical working, and I see this as one of the differences between the strictures around "high magic" and the practicalities of "low magic." However, this is no spell, and it is no run-of-the-mill ritual. Initiations are the rarest of the rites witches engage in, and it is proper that we should fully prepare ourselves on all levels.

This step will be undertaken the evening of the ritual. In an ideal scenario, you will shower first to get your body clean, and then you'll fill the tub with water and allow the bath sachet and yourself to soak in it while burning a specially dressed candle.

There are two things you want to happen as part of this cleansing. You want the light of that candle to touch you while it burns. This is a fire cleansing. And you want to immerse yourself in the bath water three times.

If you don't have a tub, don't fit in the tub, or have mobility issues that would make this impossible or dangerous for you, get creative. Fill a bucket that you soak the sachet in, and pour this over yourself three whole times. Soak that sachet in the water each time, and get every bit of you wet. (Do this in your shower, obviously.) Or, if even this is genuinely not possible, pour the sachet-infused water over your head three times and use it to wash your hands and heart three times each.

Dressed Candle, Bath Sachet, Ritual Incense, Anointing Oil

I've included the recipes that Spiral Castle Tradition uses as our base recipes for the dressed bath candle, the bath sachet, the incense to be burned during the ritual, and the anointing oil.

I wanted to add this note about the recipes. They were formulated very specifically for use within our tradition to connect us to the forces that guide SCT. You may add a botanical element to represent yourself, but please don't eliminate anything from the blend if/when you make them for your own use. (If you do add something, remember that the blend is YOURS, and wouldn't be appropriate to use at the initiation of another SCT witch -- if a situation arose where that might come up for you. But you could certainly use it for your own 2nd or 3rd Degree, as long as it is still fresh enough. Certainly the incense should be.)

Don't have access to one or more ingredients? I can help. My Etsy shop doesn't make many apothecary items right now, but I would be delighted to blend these items for you. Just use the link below to contact me, and I'll set up a custom order, if you'd like.

First Degree Initiation Gift

It is customary to present a new Initiate with gifts, often ones that are emblematic of their new role. In my initiating tradition (Clan of the Laughing Dragon), we were given amber to wear at first dree and jet to carry at second, but both together to wear at third.

Coven Caer Sidhe (the first coven in SCT) gives amber, jet, and bone necklaces to newly Raised Witches. They have always been hand-knotted by me and have featured a silver triskele to represent the Spiral Castle -- although the style of the triskele varies from Witch to Witch.

The necklace is one of the traditional Witch jewels, a personal circle of power, and a ladder. I recommend purchasing or fashioning one for yourself as a gift for this momentous occasion. (This is another item that I no longer offer for public sale in my Etsy shop, but I would be delighted to arrange a custom order for RTA students. Just contact me through the link below if that's something you'd like to discuss.)

Sabbat Wine

You can make regular mugwort tea (infusion), if you prefer; but it's so bitter that I prefer our full herb-infused sweet red wine blend. Get the sweetest red wine you can find for this -- Oliver's soft red or Manischewitz or something similar. For one person, the ratio should be 1 teaspoon of dried herb to 1 cup of liquid. Heat up the wine in a saucepan over low heat. Put equal parts mugwort and lemongrass in a tea-ball. Steep the herbs in the hot wine for five minutes. (Don't let them over-steep. They get more bitter and much stronger.) If you need to do so, sweeten the brew even further with local, raw honey.

You'll be drinking this early in the ritual, so you could prepare it and bring it before the Compass is raised -- perhaps in a thermal cup.

Secrecy

As I mentioned earlier, initiatory rites are usually cloaked in secrecy. This one, in Spiral Castle style, has been published for the world to see, if they care to look. That has been our way, since we first started the American Folkloric Witchcraft blog.

There is no secret about the structure or nature of this ritual that I could ask you to keep. Even rituals that I don't intend to publish (private, personal rituals or the variation of the 3rd Degree ritual that I offer to witches in-person) aren't necessarily "secret" because the nature of the ritual isn't meant for public consumption.

In some cases, it is to preserve the element of surprise and allow ritual teams to both utilize and subvert expectations during the ritual itself. In most cases, though, the "secrets" are more about the personal experiences of the witches undergoing the rituals and the nature of the Mysteries they uncover. These things are ineffable and inviolate, and it is for these reasons that we speak of them only with those who were present -- and then only in love and trust.

As you undergo your self-initiation, you may experience things that you will never feel comfortable speaking to another living soul. Not because they are horrible or shameful, but because they were for you alone. Or you may find that you can only share them with others who have had similar initiatory experiences and share the Oaths.

Oaths

As someone who has been through two different initiatory lineages, I can say that access to oaths isn't always given before the oath is actually being administered. You have the benefit here of previewing the Oath and deciding whether or not you are prepared to make it.

You may add your own additional oaths to the words here, but this is the Oath of a Raised Witch in the Spiral Castle Tradition. This is the oath we all take. We share this in common. If you feel you cannot commit to this oath, then stop here. There is no need to test yourself further by undergoing the initiation.

Again, I repeat that you are under no obligation to proceed. If you have come this far, you have done great work, and you are certainly a proficient Witch. I hope I have gotten a chance to know you personally through our social media group, and there is no reason for friendships to end.

To make an oath is a serious commitment that will follow you, even if you decide to walk away. It is still there, lingering. The Spirits, Gods, and Ancestors who bore witness to it will remind you -- and often exact a price if you don't hold up your end. (Not us. We won't stalk you or guilt trip you, I swear.)

All that being said, I do not believe our Oath is particularly restrictive or terrifying. If you find that it IS too restrictive or scary for you, that is probably a good indication from your Soul or your Spirits that this Tradition is not truly where you'll find your spiritual family. If that is the case, I hope you are happy with the training you received (and maybe the connections you've made), and I wish you all the best in finding that fit.

Challenges

I have asked several times whether you are ready and whether this is indeed the right choice for you. Consider these my "challenges at the gate" before you proceed. It is right and proper that members of the Tradition and your initiator should ask you again and again if you are sure about this.

I'm not your initiator. You are, and the Godds are if they decide to show up and really put you through your paces. However, I am the co-founder of the Tradition and the vessel or instrument through which this initiation has come. That involves me to the extent that I feel it is important to pose these challenges, to be honest, and to offer my support for your decision to proceed or to walk away.

You can't un-ring a bell, as they say. Once you've taken your initiation, you've *started something*. Things change within you and around you. I say again that this ritual is not an award ceremony for having completed the year of study. Among its nested purposes is to initiate sorcerous and mystical changes in you for the work ahead, such that the Mysteries of this Spiral Castle are open to you, and to create a lasting bond with other members of this Tradition.

This is the last challenge I will give you: We can celebrate you for your accomplishment without you having to initiate. Are you sure about this?

RITUAL

Note: You should begin this ritual after your shower and ritual bath.

Try not to adapt this ritual. If changes must be made, make sure to note them in your debrief (and on your copy of the ritual itself.

Arrange the ritual supplies around the base/holder of the Stang.

Smolder the incense throughout the ritual, starting from the very beginning. Anoint yourself with the oil before beginning the ritual and again after you have taken the Oath.

It's time for you to administer challenges to yourself. Ask yourself again if you are ready to take this step.

Weigh your choices and possible consequences carefully before beginning the ritual.

Raise the Stang

Stand with the Stang in the center of your Compass space. The cauldron is placed behind the Stang, and the anvil (or Oath Stone) is placed in front of it, with the hammer on top. Take a moment to energetically connect with the energy of the Forge-fire at the center of the Earth, far below the iron foot of the Stang; and also connect with Star-fire in the heavens, high above but still between the horns of the Stang. Breathe deeply and say, "May the three souls be straight within me." Feel yourself centered.

Lay the Compass

Using your Stang, walk the perimeter of the space, moving in a circle. Mark a circle on the ground by either dragging the Stang or dragging one of your feet. Allow the "lame step" to remind you that you walk between worlds. The Seen and the Unseen are ever present. The Living and the Dead are both here. As one of the Cunning Folk, you lay this compass as a reminder that the hedge is this, and you straddle it.

Open the Gates

Begin by calling the West this time. (Note: I can't know which season it is, as you perform your initiation. If you have just passed Samhain, start by opening the Western Gate. Just passed Imbolc? Northern Gate. Etc. As always, you can change the wording of these calls, and it would be great to add language that mentions the initiation you are undertaking.)

Stand in the Center and face the West. Hold your arms out in front of you, hands cupped. Say, "I call to the Ocean beyond the West Gate. Open the door from the West, place of Water, Azazel-Qayin's domain. By the cup, the quench tank, and the helm, I call you to open wide the Gate and send forth your road to the center of this, my compass. So mote it be!"

Turn to the East. Hold one arm up, fist raised. Say, "I call to the Sunrise beyond the East Gate. Open the door from the East, place of Fire, Lucifer-Qayin's domain. By the steel, the anvil, and the sun, I call you to open wide the Gate and send forth your road to the center of this, my compass. So mote it be!"

Turn to the South. Hold both arms down by your sides, palms flat and facing the ground. Say, "I call to the Fields beyond the South Gate. Open the door from the South, place of Earth, Goda's domain. By the plate, the soil, and the shield, I call you to open wide the Gate and send forth your road to the center of this, my compass. So mote it be!"

Turn to the North. Hold both arms up, fingers spread wide. Say, "I call to the Winds beyond the North Gate. Open the door from the North, place of Air, Kolyo's domain. By the spear, the wing, and the smoke, I call you to open wide the Gate and send forth your road to the center of this, my compass. So mote it be!"

Challenges & Trials

- **Challenges** -- Within the ritual space, at the time and place of initiation, ask yourself and answer aloud: "In my *mind*, do I *know* that I am prepared and do I choose freely to submit to the trials of initiation? In my *heart*, do I *feel* that I am prepared and do I choose freely to submit to the trials of initiation? In my *spirit*, do I *believe* that I am prepared and do I choose freely to submit to the trials of initiation?"
- **Sabbat Wine** -- Drink the entire cup (8 oz) of Sabbat Wine or Mugwort Tea. Feel free to drink slowly, mindfully. Be conscious of the properties of mugwort, lemongrass, and wine -- all ingredients known to

help relax the borders between the Seen and the Unseen. They are not hallucinogenic, but they are certainly allies for trance work, vision, and divination.

- **Three Stones** -- Turn your attention to your Stone Bowl. Pull out the stones and lay the small piece of cloth in the bottom, as you will not be using the bowl for it's usual purpose. Close your eyes while holding the red, black, and white stones in your hands. Ask the stones which of our Deities is choosing to guide you in your future studies, work, and service within the Spiral Castle. Keeping your eyes closed, drop the stones into the bowl. Without opening your eyes, use one hand to reach into the bowl. The first stone you touch holds your answer (white-Goda, black-Kolyo, red-Qayin). Take a moment to notate this information. If you need a moment to journal your first thoughts and impressions, do so. Many of us have big surprises here. Don't resist the choice, however thrown you may feel. Roll with it and see where it takes you. (A few of us aren't surprised at all -- and there are Mysteries to uncover about that experience, as well.)

- **Black Mirror** -- Check in with yourself before starting this next phase. The wine should have loosened your connection to consensus reality just a little. You should be able to feel a shift. If not, ask yourself if you need a little more. Maybe you didn't have enough, or maybe you took an hour or more journaling about the Three Stones. Either way, a second cup of Sabbat Wine could be okay. (But that's all.) Give it about fifteen minutes to take effect and then turn your attention to the Black Mirror. Refresh the incense and adjust the candles in the room to accommodate your ideal scrying set-up. You will be scrying for these things: 1) your Craft names -- secret and known, and 2) your Mark. This may be a quick process for you, or it may be a long one. As you look, allow the Godd of our Tradition who has just stepped forward to guide you to reveal the significance of each of these things to you. One of the things I have come to know is that our Names and Marks within the Family are full of meaning and so often tied up with our Soul-Work -- at least in this lifetime and maybe beyond. Let Them show you something of what yours mean. When you are satisfied that you have seen all you can for now, journal what you learned. Record as much detail as possible.

- **Triple Cords** -- Braid the black cords, the white cords, and ultimately, the full set of Triple Cords together while contemplating Kolyo and her role as Weaver of Magic and Fate. You can rock and sway while you do this. You can definitely change positions, as needed. It is fine to contemplate Goda a bit while you work on the white cords, as well, or Qayin as bind the three together with his blood and fire; but this act of weaving is so intimately tied to Kolyo and her arts, that she deserves a hearty portion of acknowledgement. Consider also, the Triple Soul as you weave their respective cords. When you finish, tie the cords at your waist, and journal your revelations.

Vows, Oath & Presentation

- **Vows & Oath** -- Move to the Oath Stone and turn your attention to the Vows of the Raised Witch. Ask and answer aloud each question. If you are ready to make your Oath, prick your finger to raise blood, and then grasp the Oath Stone. You will be making your oaths using your full Craft name, which is the name you found in the Mirror, plus a sort of surname granted by the Deity who claimed you tonight. (They are Ta'Qayin, Ni'Goda, and De'Kolyo. The spellings of the prefixes are variable by person, but the ones I've used here give a good idea of pronunciation.) This is the custom of our Tradition. It is a name of power -- a Craft name, known only to Raised members of the Tradition.

- **Presentation** -- Stand up, anoint yourself with the initiation oil, and say, "So now do I proclaim myself a true Witch of the Spiral Castle. So shall I be recognized among my Folk and Family! I present myself to the Realms, Gates, Towers, Spirits, and Godds of the Spiral Castle. I am, [Complete Craft Name], a fully Raised Witch of the Spiral Castle! So Mote it Be!"

- **Gift** -- Give yourself the gift you have made or purchased for the occasion. Sain it using a bit of the mixture from your Red Meal, wiping it clean, and then putting it on.

Red Meal

Moving counterclockwise, bring the sacrificial meal to the Stang or center of the Compass, while singing the Housle Song, below. Make at least one full circle as you tread the mill. Three is better.

<u>The Housle Song</u>
(To the tune of <u>Greensleeves</u>)

To Housle now we walk the wheel
We kill tonight the blood red meal
A leftward tread of magic's mill
To feed the Gods and work our Will.

Red! Red is the wine we drink!
Red! Red are the cords we wear!
Red! Red is the blood of God!
And red is the shade of the Housle

Say, "For my Ancestors, my Gods, and Myself, I do this."

Bless the bread by saying: "Here is bread, flesh of the Earth, blessed to give us life and strength. I consecrate it in the name of the Old Ones."

Kill the bread by saying: "I take its life and give it to Them." Cut it with the red knife.

Bless the wine by saying: "Here is wine, blood of the Earth, blessed to give us joy and abundance. I consecrate it in the name of the Old Ones."

Kill the wine by saying: "I take its life and give it to Them." Slide the knife over the top of the cup to cut its throat.

Eat and drink of the Meal, making whatever personal offerings you like into the bowl.

The remainder of the wine is poured into the bread bowl. Dip your finger in and anoint yourself. This can also be used for blessing tools, etc.

The Meal is either given to the ground now (if outside) or later (if inside) with the following Declaration:

"By the Red, and Black and White,
Light in Darkness, Dark in Light --
What we take, we freely give.
We all must die. We all must live.
Above, below, and here are One.
All together -- ALL! (And none!)
Here is shown a Mystery. As I Will, so Mote it Be."

<u>Assignment</u>	Perform the ritual included here. Use your judgment, if you need to make minor modifications regarding supplies or peripheral details; but try to keep the major components of this initiation intact. There are deeply interwoven symbol sets at play.

As you have done with other rituals during your studies thus far, take time to write about your experience during and after the initiation. Your debrief should also include:
- any impressions you had or challenges you experienced during the set-up
- a notation of the date and general time you did the ritual
- impressions, insights, and sensations you had throughout the ritual (during the opening portions, the working, or the meal)
- any challenges you experienced while executive the ritual
- ideas that this ritual sparked for you (either for other rituals or for other creative/philosophical endeavors in your world)
- anything else that you feel should be noted. |
| <u>Additional Resources</u> | **Blade & Broom shop** -- www.bladeandbroom.etsy.com -- Convo me through Etsy to set up a custom order for a dressed chime candle, bath sachet, incense, or anointing oil using the SCT Initiation formulas , if you'd like the ones I make instead of crafting them for yourself. |
| <u>BoS Pages Included</u> | Laying the Compass
Opening the Gates
The Housle
Saining of Tools
No-Kill Fast Food List
No-Kill Fast Recipes
SCT Initiation Recipes
RTA First Degree Self-Initiation
SCT Raising Vows
SCT Raising Oath |

Book of Shadows

Gods, Goddesses, and Mighty Ones

Faces of the God

The God of the Witches is often viewed as the Horned God, Sun King, and Lord of the Greenwood. Within Wicca, he is seen as the consort or child of the Goddess, while Traditional Witchcraft views him as the Magister, the Dark and Wild God who brings initiation, liberation, and enlightenment. Like the Great Goddess, the God is often approached under the guise of one of his many archetypes, as evidenced by his many aspects throughout the world.

The Sun & Fire God
Apollo, Horus-Ra, Belanus, Helios, Sol, Kane, Freyr, Heimdall, Bielobog, Lucifer, Lugh

The Lord of the Greenwood
Cernunnos, Herne, Robin Goodfellow, Puck, Dionysos, Pan, the Greenman, Silvanus, Gran Bois, Krishna, Buccos, Basajaun

The Heroic Son
Herakles, Arthur, Cuchulain, Achilles, Hektor, Perseus, Jason, Theseus, Fionn MacCumhaill, Amergin, Gilgamesh

The King & Father God
Arthur, Zeus, Jehovah, Allah, Vishnu, Dagda, El, Damballah

The Warrior God
Ares, Thor, Ogun, Bran, Tyr, Nuada

The Craftsman God
Hephaestus, Ptah, Wayland the Smith, Tubal Cain, Goibhnu, Simbi, Lugh

The God of the Oceans
Poseidon, Manannan MacLyr, Agwe, Njord

The Sacrified God
Tammuz, Mithras, Adonis, Jesus Christ, Osiris, Baal, Lyr, Baldur, Attis, John Barleycorn

The Death Lord
Hades, Anubis, Ghene, Baron Samedi, Saturn, Gwyn ap Nudd, Holt

The Wisdom God/Sage
Oghma, Thoth, Legba, Odin, Hermes, Merlin, Shiva, Taliesin, Apollo, Math ap Mathonwy, Solomon, Baphomet

The Trickster/Anti-God
Loki, Seth, Raven, Coyote, Iblis, Lucifer, Prometheus, Chernobog, Melek Taws, Azazel

Copyright Astoria Books 2017

Faces of the Goddess

The Great Goddess of the Witches is a universal Goddess figure honored in such foundational Craft literature as "The Charge of the Goddess" and Robert Graves' *The White Goddess*. She is equal to the God, and in some aspects is considered more powerful.. This great, all-encompassing Goddess is frequently identified by a number of archetypes, which we see in the faces of specific Goddesses from various cultures.

The Maiden/Virgin
Kore, Flora, Hebe, Mary, Artemis, Idun

The Moon Goddess
Diana, Selene, Ixchel, Mawu, Chang-O

The Bright Lady/Sun, Fire & Light
Brighid, Arianrhod, Aine, Amaterasu, Uzume, Sarasvati, Holle, St. Lucia, the Muses

The Wisdom Goddess/Justice
Athena, Sophia, Aradia, Maat, Themis, Medusa, Cerridwen, Medea, Tara

The Queen of Heaven
Isis, Ishtar, Astarte, Arianrhod, Nuit, Kwan Yin, Hera, Aida-Wedo, Shekinah, Ariadne, Mary, Aphrodite

The Love/Fertility Goddess
Aphrodite, Venus, Hathor, Eostre, Erzulie Frieda, Freya, Oshun, Parvati, Goda, XochiQuetzal

The Goddess of Healing/Waters
Thetis, La Sirene, Lakshmi, Sulis, Melusine, Yemaya, Nimue, Sedna, Tiamat

The Battle Goddess/Destroyer
Badb, Cailleach, Scathach, Morrigan, Kali, Maeve, Sekhmet, Brunhild, Durga, Macha, Oya, the Valkyries, the Furies

The Crone/Wise Woman
Sheila na Gig, Baba Yaga, Cailleach, Nicnevin, Cerridwen, Annis, Badb, Grandmother Spider, XochiQuetzal

The Dark Lady/Night & Death
Persephone, Lilith, Kolyo, Ereshkigal, Blodeuwedd, Nephthys, Black Madonna, Maman Brigitte, Eris, Hel

The Magician
Ishar, Isis, Nephthy, Hekate, Circe, Herodias, Aradia, Oya, Cerridwen, Zorya, Freya, Ereshkigal

Copyright Asteria Books 2017

Witch Mother

The three sacred colors of red, white and black appear in many forms and iterations in American Folkloric Witchcraft, but one of the most direct and pervasive manifestations of these colors is in the three central Deities of the Trad: the Black Goddess, the White Goddess and the Red God.

The White Goddess rules in the South at Lammas, and the Black Goddess dominates the North at Imbolc. In truth, these are two faces of the SAME Goddess — the quintessential Witch's Goddess. She is both light and darkness. But just as the sun does not shine during the darkness of night, She does not fully reveal both sides of Her nature simultaneously.

Through the light half of the year, we mark the influence of the White Goddess whom we call upon as Goda. In the dark half of the year, we honor Kolyo, the Black Goddess.

However, as much as the Black and White Goddesses counterpoint each other on the Year Wheel and within the compass that we lay, we must acknowledge and understand that they work along a continuum. They are not truly separate from each other. One requires the other for full manifestation, and the dynamic balance maintained between the two is critical to the practice of the Craft as we know it.

Each holds within Herself the core of the other. Within the darkness of the night, the light of the moon and stars reaches us. During the brightness of the day, shadows lurk and provide respite.

Just as the white knife cuts in the physical realm, and the black in the astral; so, too, do the Goddesses relate respectively to the physical and astral. The two are, in fact, reflections of each other.

A rare few Goddesses are both Black and White — Hela, Hekate, Lilith. These, we know as the Witch Mother.

Copyright Asteria Books 2015

Witch Father

Traditional Witches often refer to the Angel or God who brought enlightenment, alchemy, and magic to mankind as the Witch Father. This being has been revered and respected by those few in each generation of man who were ready and open to receive gnosis — ready to understand and embrace their own divine nature. He has been despised and demonized by the masses who find terror and blasphemy in his message.

The Witch Father is usually depicted with horns between which a green fire burns. This is the Cunning Fire, the Witch Fire. It is this fire that is the symbol of enlightenment. A Red Thread of ancestry connects us to this Witch Father and reminds us that we carry the blood of the rebel, the blood of the heretic, the blood of the scapegoat, the blood of the wise.

He is called by many names, this Witch Father. He is Azazel. He is Qayin and Tubal Cain. He is Melek Taus. He is Lucifer. He is Shamash. It is the experience of witches in the American Folkloric Tradition that these are not different beings. Rather, the names are different titles, different cultural depictions of the same God.

"Melek Taus" means "Peacock Angel/King." The peacock angel is the central figure, the benevolent and creative demiurge, of the Yezidis. He is seen as repentant after the fall from God's grace, his tears quenching the fires of hell. The Yezidis equate Melek Taus with Azazel. Muslims consider Melek Taus to be a *shaitan* or adversary.

The Nephilim, the "Fallen Angels" or spirits who descended into the material realm to interact with and guide mankind, were first seen as the "Shining Ones" or Gods of Sumerian lore. Both Lucifer and Azazel are considered Fallen Angels, and the name Lucifer means "light-bringer."

Shamash is the Babylonian name for the Sun God of justice, law, and salvation. He is linked in a triad with the Nannar-Sin (the Mood God) and Ishtar (the fertility-Earth Goddess, who incidentally is represented by the planet Venus, the Morning and Evening Star). Ishtar and Shamash are divine twins.

Copyright Asteria Books 2015

Ancestors

The most important link that a witch makes is the one that links her to the ancestors of the tradition. This link is the Red Thread. Once made it cannot be severed except by the will of the witch alone. It is this link that creates a witch in our tradition. It is the link that creates us as family.

The ancestors are more than just names on our family tree. They are the guardians and guides that shape our practice from the other side. They are our allies in magic and our protectors in spirit.

Although none can truly claim full knowledge of what happens to our spirits after our bodies expire, we believe that the spirit and the eternal soul continue on. The eternal soul flies from us to the shining realm of the ancients, the land of fey, Elphame, the isle of apples, Ynys Avalon, where it takes its repose. This expression of the soul lives in our bones, and it is for that reason that we honor our ancestors through the symbolism of bones. The spirit, an expression of our ego and "self", may wander here for a time after death, creating the phenomenon we recognize as ghosts, or it may return to the source, the great cauldron, from which we are reborn anew.

Of special interest to us are the Mighty Dead. These are the dead that have returned to the cauldron and have retained themselves in whole (both spirit and eternal soul) through many lives. They are the great heroes and heroines of myth and history. Their influence shapes our world, and their guidance can teach us much.

We access the ancestors by honoring them in word and deed. The names we take are a litany of the generations before us. We make offerings to the dead throughout the year, and especially when the veil is thinnest at Samhain. We learn to tap the bone, to create communication with our guiding ancestors, through meditation and offerings.

The ancestors are honored at the center of the compass, by the skull placed at the foot of the stang.

Copyright Asteria Publishing 2012

Aradia's Gifts

According to an Italian legend, Aradia is the daughter of Diana and her brother Lucifer. Aradia was said to be an avatar of Diana sent to earth to teach people the ways of Witchcraft to free them from slavery and degradation.

The Gifts of Aradia

In the fourteenth century, Aradia was said to have taught that the traditional powers of a witch would belong to any who followed in the ways of the Old Religion. Aradia stressed that these gifts were the benefits of adhering to the Old Ways and not the reason for becoming a witch. These are the powers:

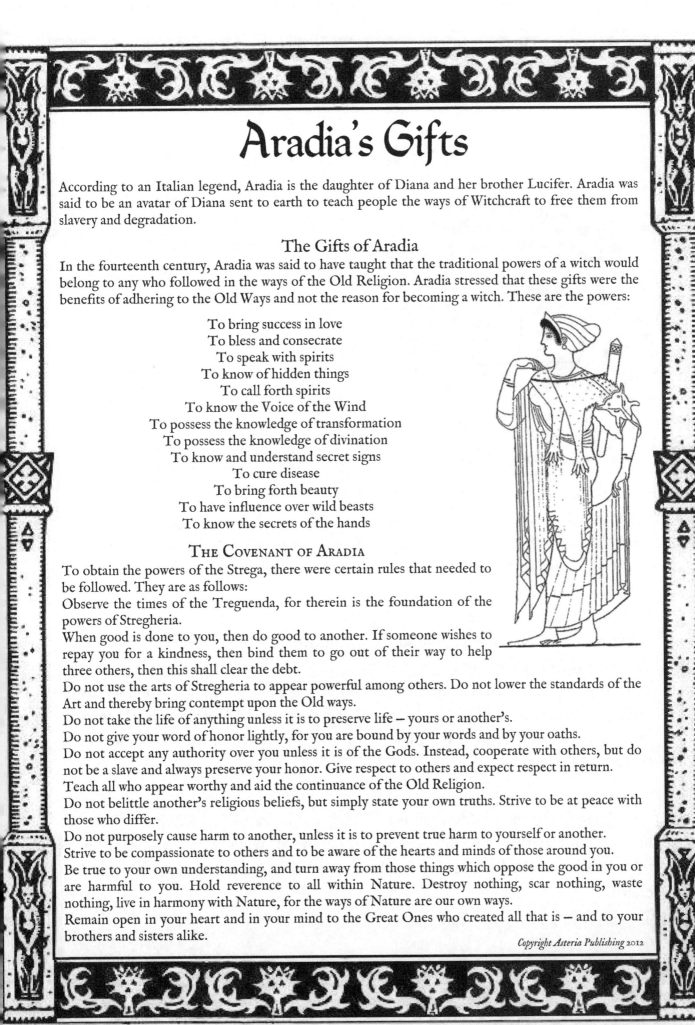

To bring success in love
To bless and consecrate
To speak with spirits
To know of hidden things
To call forth spirits
To know the Voice of the Wind
To possess the knowledge of transformation
To possess the knowledge of divination
To know and understand secret signs
To cure disease
To bring forth beauty
To have influence over wild beasts
To know the secrets of the hands

The Covenant of Aradia

To obtain the powers of the Strega, there were certain rules that needed to be followed. They are as follows:

Observe the times of the Treguenda, for therein is the foundation of the powers of Stregheria.

When good is done to you, then do good to another. If someone wishes to repay you for a kindness, then bind them to go out of their way to help three others, then this shall clear the debt.

Do not use the arts of Stregheria to appear powerful among others. Do not lower the standards of the Art and thereby bring contempt upon the Old ways.

Do not take the life of anything unless it is to preserve life – yours or another's.

Do not give your word of honor lightly, for you are bound by your words and by your oaths.

Do not accept any authority over you unless it is of the Gods. Instead, cooperate with others, but do not be a slave and always preserve your honor. Give respect to others and expect respect in return.

Teach all who appear worthy and aid the continuance of the Old Religion.

Do not belittle another's religious beliefs, but simply state your own truths. Strive to be at peace with those who differ.

Do not purposely cause harm to another, unless it is to prevent true harm to yourself or another.

Strive to be compassionate to others and to be aware of the hearts and minds of those around you.

Be true to your own understanding, and turn away from those things which oppose the good in you or are harmful to you. Hold reverence to all within Nature. Destroy nothing, scar nothing, waste nothing, live in harmony with Nature, for the ways of Nature are our own ways.

Remain open in your heart and in your mind to the Great Ones who created all that is – and to your brothers and sisters alike.

Copyright Asteria Publishing 2012

Arianrhod

Arianrhod is a Welsh Goddess whose name means "Silver Wheel." He story appears in the Fourth Branch of the *Mabinogi*. She is the daughter of Don, the niece of Math ap Mathonwy, King of Gwynedd. In her story as told in the *Mabinogi*, she gives birth to two sons through magical means. Her sons are Dylan ail Don and Llew Llaw Gyffes. According to the tales, Math would die unless a virgin held his feet when he was not at war. Circumstances forced Math to find a new footholder, and Arianrhod's brothers recommended her for the job. Math tested her virginity by having her step over an enchanted wand, and she gave birth to two sons. Dylan was a water spirit and departed immediately for the sea. The other boy, however, got the full brunt of his mother's humiliation and outrage. She placed a *geise* on him that he would not have a name, weapons, or a human wife. All of these were traditionally the mother's right to give, and they were all marks of masculinity and adulthood. Gwydion, Arianrhod's brother (and possibly the boy's father, according to much theory), took the boy in as his son or fosterling. Together, they tricked Arianrhod into giving the boy the name Llew Llaw Gyffes ("fair-haired, skillful-handed one") and weapons (in defense of her home — in an attack they arranged). With his use of magic, Gwydion made a bride for the boy out of flowers.

Caer Arianrhod is the Goddess's home. "Caer" means "castle." There is a rock formation called by this name off the coast of Gwynedd, Wales that is visible at low tide. This is also the Welsh name for the constellation *Corona Borealis*, the northern crown.

Copyright Asteria Books 2015

Azazel

Azazel was chief among the angels in the story of The Fall of the B'nai Elohim in the Book of Enoch. The B'nai Elohim is a term that refers to angels. These fallen angels, or Watchers, descended to the realm of matter (earth) where they took the descendants of Cain as human vessels. They took women as their wives and taught them witchcraft and other skills. Azazel took Tubal-Cain, the blacksmith, as his vessel and further improved the arts of smith craft and witchery.

Enoch reveals to us that Azazel shares with humanity "all the metals and the art of working them...and the use of antimony." As it turns out, antimony was critical to the alchemical process of creating the Philosopher's Stone. This same element was called *kuhl* (or kohl) by the ancient Arabs. (You might also recall references to women decorating their eyes with this substance, and that art also being taught by Azazel. This may, in fact, have been a veiled reference to the alchemical process and not to cosmetics at all.) Sir Roger Bacon tells us that when antimony is processed with vitriol, it is reduced to a "noble red oil" with all of the lesser sulfur having been purified out of it in the process. Red, then, is Azazel's color.

It is doubly his color when we consider that man is made from red clay, according to Middle Eastern tradition, and that Azazel is master of the material world from which man is made.

In American Folkloric Witchcraft, we honor Azazel as the sunset face, the Samhain face, the Saturnian face of the Witch Father.

Invocation

Come, Azazel-Qayin, come from the West!
Come, Witch Father, Wisdom's Father, and teach me your Truths, as you taught the Ancients!

Come, Azazel-Qayin, Gatekeeper of the Paths of the Dead.
From the Samhain-place, walk the Red Path, the line of Qayin to the midst of magic's crossroads.

So mote it be!

Copyright Asteria Books 2015

Belenus

Belenus is one of the most important, ancient, and far-reaching Gods of the Pan-Celtic pantheon. His influence was noted in Gaul, Iberia, Britain, and Italy. He is a God of the sun and also of horses. Like Apollo, he is said to draw the sun across the sky in his horse-drawn chariot. Other names for him include Bel, Beli, and Beli Mawr — as well as many variant spellings of Belenus. The root "Bel" means "Fair Shining One." Beltane was originated as a festival in honor of this deity, and the word Beltane means "bright fire." Etymologically and mythologically, Belenus and Apollo share much in common, including association with the sun, horses, the wheel, the ram, healing, the fire, mantic oracles, music, poetry, knowledge, wisdom, and more. Belenus is associated very much with the oak and the acorn, as symbols of both wisdom and masculine fertility and strength. He is also associated with the torch, a very phallic and fiery symbol that combines aspects of both the masculine generative forces and the shining light with which his name is synonymous. Appropriate offerings to Belenus include fruit and cake. Dancing, drumming, bonfires, the very phallic Maypole, and revelry are all traditional ways to celebrate his feast day — Beltane.

Copyright Asteria Books 2015

Blodeuwedd

Blodeuwedd is a Welsh Goddess whose story is told in the *Mabinogi* along with Arianrhod and Llew Llaw Gyffes. Arianrhod, in her anger and shame, had cursed her son not to be married to a human woman. Gwydion, the young man's uncle (and possibly his father) is a skilled magician, though, who conjures a girl from nine flowers — or just three (the oak, broom, and meadowsweet), depending on the version. The name Blodeuwedd means "flower face." The couple is happy for a year and a day, but then Blodeuwedd meets a man of her own choosing, Gronw. She falls in love and has an affair, and she starts to realize that she was created and has been used for another person's purposes. Despite that, she has a will of her own, and she decides to live and love on her own terms. Seeing no other way out, she and Gronw stage an elaborate plan to murder Llew, who leads a charmed life. Their plan fails, but Llew is changed into an eagle and flies away. When his uncle finds and rescues him, they put Gronw to death and punish Blodeuwedd by transforming her into an owl. She is sentenced to wander the night alone, hated and assaulted by other birds. "Blodeuwedd" is the Welsh word for "owl," and the owl is seen as a solitary and wise bird, if also lonely. In Blodeuwedd's story, we see the price we must sometimes pay to be true to ourselves, as well as the reminder that no other person must be compelled to serve our whim, however entitled we feel to the need.

Copyright Asteria Books 2015

Bran the Blessed

In Welsh mythology, Bran Fendigaidd (literally "Blessed Crow/Raven") is described as a giant and the High King of Britain. He is a mighty warrior, and he appears in several of the Welsh triads as well as the Second Branch of the *Mabinogi*. He is the brother of Branwen, Manawdan, Nisien, and Efnysien. He is a son of Lyr and Penarddun. The Irish high king comes to him, asking for his sister Branwen's hand in marriage, forging an alliance between the two islands. Efnysien, though, is insulted that he wasn't consulted, and mutilates the Irish horses. To placate the Irish, Bran gives the king a large cauldron with the power of regeneration. It will bring slain warriors back to life. The wedding proceeds, but when the new couple returns to Ireland, Branwen is terribly mistreated — beaten daily and forced to work in the kitchen. She tames a bird and sends word back to her brother, pleading for help. He comes with many warriors, but the cauldron makes it nearly impossible for the British to hold their ground. Efnysien slays Branwen's son, and Branwen dies of a broken heart. Efnysien hides himself among the Irish slain in order to be placed inside the cauldron. Once inside, he destroys the cauldron, sacrificing himself in the process. Only eight warriors survive, and Bran the Blessed is mortally wounded. He instructs his companions to cut off his head. Bran's head entertains and advises them for several years until they ultimately bury it on White Hill to act as a guardian for Britain. It is thought that White Hill is Tower Hill, the location of the Tower of London, which even today has ravens guarding the tower and the land. Bran the Blessed is associated with courage, wisdom, protection, and good advice.

Copyright Asteria Books 2015

Brigid

Brighid is a Pan-Celtic Goddess whose worship was so widespread in the British Isles and Europe that she was canonized by the Catholic Church. She is known by many variations of the same name:

Brighid (Modern Irish)
Bríd (Reformed Irish)
Bridget (Anglicanized)
Brìghde/Brìde (Scotland)
Brigantia (Great Britain)

The goddess Brigid presided over the hearth and the forge, over the inspiration and skill of sacred art and craft, and over the world of crops, livestock, and nature. The 10th-century Cormac's Glossary states that Brigid was the daughter of the Dagda, the "Great God" of the Tuatha de Danaan. It states Brigid to be a *"woman of wisdom... a goddess whom poets adored, because her protection was very great and very famous."*

The early Church could not very easily call the Great Goddess of Ireland a demon, so they opted to canonized her instead. She would become Saint Brigit, patroness of poetry and healing. The church's explanation to the Irish peasants was that Brigit was actually an early Christian missionary, and that the miracles she performed misled the common people into believing that she was a goddess. In some of the many legends about St. Brigit, there is a belief that she was the foster-mother of Jesus, having spent some part of his boyhood in Britain and Ireland, or that she was the mid-wife at his birth.

Maman Brigitte is the Haitian manifestation of this goddess brought to Haiti by indentured servants from Ireland and Scotland in the 1700's-1800's. She is the Queen of the Cemetery and consort of Baron Samedi, the gatekeeper of the graveyard. She is often depicted as a white woman with red hair, and she is believed to be a powerful witch. The grave of the first woman buried in a cemetery is consecrated to her and she is also believed to protect all the graves in the cemetery that are properly marked with a cross. In this guise, she is still shown to us as a healer and midwife – albeit of the next life and not this one.

Copyright Asteria Books 2015

Cailleach

The name Cailleach derives from a proto-Indo-European root that means "veiled one" and has come to mean "hag" in Irish and Scottish Gaelic. There are many Goddesses and mythic figures who are referred to by this moniker, but the primary figure we have come to think of as the Cailleach is known by the full name Cailleach Beira, which is a Scottish name related to her tales as the Winter Queen. As such, she rules the time from Samhain to Beltaine (with Brighid ruling from Beltaine to Samhain). She ushers in the winter by washing her great plaid in a gulf off the coast of Scotland — a process that takes three days. After the washing is complete, her woolen plaid is snow white and the snows settle on the land in earnest.

Spring windstorms are associated with old women called *Cailleachean*, or Storm Hags, and they are considered very dangerous.

She is credited with having shaped the mountains and hills (which some legends say she did purposefully, and others say she did haphazardly).

Cailleach is also very much an ancestral Goddess, since it is believed that the poem "The Old Woman of Beara" refers to her. She lived through seven periods of youth, taking husbands and bearing children. She lived so long as a young woman that each of her husbands, in turn, died of old age before she ever started aging. She is credited with being the foremother of tribes and races of men.

Copyright Asteria Books 2018

Horned God

According to most witchcraft traditions, the primary God of the Craft is a horned figure. The names given to that figure vary by tradition and include, Cernunnos, Herne, Holt, Tubal Qayin, and others.

Cernunnos in Celtic iconography is often portrayed with animals, in particular the stag, and also frequently associated with the ram-horned serpent, besides association with other beasts with less frequency, including bulls, dogs, and rats. Because of his frequent association with creatures, scholars often describe Cernunnos as the "Lord of the Animals" or the "Lord of Wild Things," and Miranda Green describes him as a "peaceful god of nature and fruitfulness."

Herne the Hunter is a specifically British figure, the ghost of the huntsman who was hanged upon a tree known as Her's Oak in Windsor Forest and who bears horns upon his head. Some scholars suggests that "Herne" as well as other Wild Huntsmen in European folklore all derive from the same ancient mytho-poetic source. The name "Herne" could be derived ultimately from the same Indo-European root, *ker-n-, meaning bone or horn from which "Cernunnos" derives.

In the Early Middle Ages, Windsor Forest came under the control of the pagan Angles who worshiped their own pantheon of gods, including Woden, who was sometimes depicted as horned, and whose Norse equivalent Odin rode across the night sky with his own Wild Hunt and hanged himself on the world tree Yggdrasil to learn the secret of the runic alphabet. It has been suggested that the name *Herne* is derived from the title *Herian*, a title used for Woden in his role as leader of fallen warriors.

Copyright Asteria Books 2015

Cerridwen

Cerridwen is a potent and prominent figure in many modern Craft traditions. She is associated with the cauldron, the most recognizable of all witchcraft tools; and her tale is one of deep transformation – the work of the witch!

Her name means "White Sow" and this great queen of Celtic legend is known for devouring her offspring, just a s a sow will sometimes do.

Her myth tells how she set the young servant boy Gwion to the task of stirring a cauldron of knowledge and wisdom. The brew within was intended for her son, but when three scalding drops landed on Gwion's hand, he instinctively sucked away the pain - and wisdom. Enraged, a pursuit ensues in which Gwion shapeshifts to escape Cerridwen's wrath, but she transforms to capture him. When he was a hare, she was a greyhound. Then he was a fish and she an otter. Next, he was a bird, and she was a hawk. Fourth, he changed into a grain of corn, and she transformed into a hen, pecking every grain until she had consumed him. Once she had him, she transformed again to the shape of a woman, and gave birth in nine months' time to the great bard Taliesin. This last is their fifth and final transformation.

Cerridwen is honored as a lady of wisdom, of familial protection, and of spiritual transformation.

Copyright Asteria Books 2015

Cuchulainn

Cuchulainn is an Irish God who appears in the Ulster cycles and also shows up in Scottish and Manx folklore. His name means "Culann's hound." He was born Setanta, son of Lugh, but after killing Culann's guard dog in an act of self-defense, the young man offers to take the dog's place until a suitable canine replacement can be reared and trained. Cuchulainn's life was foretold to be short but full of renown. He is a celebrated hero of the city of Ulster, which he defended single-handedly against invasion by Queen Medb and her army in the *Tain Bo Cualigne* ("Cattle Raid of Cooley"). Cuchulainn is trained in the art of battle by the famous warrior woman, Scathach, on the Isle of Skye in Scotland. It is Medb and her allies who eventually conspire to kill Cuchulainn. He has a geise (taboo) against eating dog meat, but there is a general geise in Ireland against refusing hospitality. When he is offered a meal of dog meat by an old woman, he feels compelled to partake, but it weakens him spiritually. One of his enemies has fashioned three spears that are prophesied to slay three kings. One strikes and kills Cuchulainn's horse, the King of Horses. The second strikes and kills Cuchulainn's friend, the King of Charioteers. The third mortally wounds Cuchulainn himself. Being near to death, he lashes himself to a standing stone so he may die on his feet while facing his enemies. It isn't until a raven lands on his shoulder that his enemies will believe he has died. When one approaches to take his head in victory, Cuchulainn's arm falls and cuts off the man's hand.

Copyright Asteria Books 2016

Dagda

The Dagda is an important God of Irish mythology. His name likely means "the Good God," and he was seen as a protector and benefactor of the people. His brothers include Ogma and Lir, although his parentage is debatable — probably because he is so often cast in the role of the Father God. His many epithets include "All-Father", "Creator", "Lord of Great Knowledge", and "Horned Man." He also has epithet that means either "Cauldron" or "Iron." He often depicted carrying a huge club, and he is associated with a cauldron of plenty. The Dagda was said to be immensely powerful, and his club could kill eight to nine men with a single blow. The handle, however, could return the slain to life. The Dagda's cauldron was called Undry was said to be bottomless. No man left it unsatisfied. He also possessed an oak harp that, when he played it, put the seasons in order and arranged the order of battle. Depictions of the Dagda as oafish and crude were likely insinuated by Christian detractors of the Old Religion in order to make the Celtic All-Father less potent to the people. However, he was seen by the Celts as beautiful and powerful, his name (like Lugh's) have Proto-Indo-European roots that indicate a "shining" vision of the Divine. Newgrange was said to be the Dagda's home, until his son Aengus tricked him out of it. It was, however, said to be the place of the God-King's death.

Copyright Asteria Books 2015

Diana

In Roman mythology, DIANA is the goddess of the hunt, the moon, and childbirth, being associated with wild animals and woodlands, and having the power to talk to and control animals. Oak groves were especially sacred to her. According to mythology, Diana was born with her twin brother Apollo, who is sometimes referred to by the name "Lucifer" (which means "light-bringer" in Latin).

In Italy, the old religion of Stregheria embraces the goddess Diana as Queen of the Witches; witches being the wise women healers of the time. Diana was said to have created the world of her own being, having in herself the seeds of all creation yet to come. It was said that out of herself she divided the darkness and the light, keeping for herself the darkness of creation and creating her brother Apollo, the light. Diana was believed to have loved and ruled with her brother Apollo, the god of the Sun.

In Charles Leland's *Aradia: Gospoel of the Witches*, Diana is not only the witches' goddess, but she is presented as the primordial creatrix. After giving birth to Apollo-Lucifer, Diana seduces him while in the form of a cat, eventually giving birth to Aradia, their daughter. Diana demonstrates the power of her witchcraft by creating "the heavens, the stars, and the rain." This book presents the original witches as slaves that escaped from their masters, beginning new lives as "thieves and evil folk." Diana sends her daughter Aradia to them to teach these former serfs witchcraft, the power of which they can use to "destroy the evil race (of oppressors)." Aradia's students thus became the first witches, who would then continue the worship of Diana. Leland was struck by this cosmogony: "In all other Scriptures of all races, it is the male... who creates the universe; in Witch Sorcery it is the female who is the primitive principle"

Hecate

Hecate or Hekate is an ancient goddess, most often shown holding two torches or a key and in later periods depicted in triple form. She is variously associated with crossroads, entrance-ways, fire, light, the Moon, magic, witchcraft, knowledge of herbs and poisonous plants, necromancy, and sorcery. She has rulership over earth, sea and sky, as well as a more universal role as Saviour (Soteira), Mother of Angels and the Cosmic World Soul.

Hecate is also one of the 'patron' goddesses of many witches, who in some traditions identify her with the Triple Goddess, for Hecate has three faces, or phases. Her role as a tripartite goddess, which many modern-day Wiccans associate with the concept of 'the Maiden, the Mother and the Crone', was made popular in modern times by writers such as Robert Graves in <u>The White Goddess</u>. Historical depictions and descriptions show her facing in three different directions, a clear reference to the tripartite nature of this ancient Goddess.

Hecate was associated with borders, city walls, doorways, crossroads and, by extension, with realms outside or beyond the world of the living. She appears to have been particularly associated with being 'between' and hence is frequently characterized as a "liminal" goddess. Hecate was also associated with plant lore and the concoction of medicines and poisons. In particular she was thought to give instruction in these closely related arts. Medea was said to be taught by Hecate.

Hecate has survived in folklore as a 'hag' figure associated with witchcraft. Scholars note that Hecate, conflated with the figure of Diana, appears in late antiquity and in the early medieval period as part of an "emerging legend complex" associated with gatherings of women, the moon, and witchcraft that eventually became established in the area of Northern Italy, southern Germany, and the western Balkans.

Epithets

Aedonaea (Lady of the underworld)
Anassa eneri (Queen of the dead)
Apotropaia (that turns away/protects)
Atalus (tender)
Brimo (the terrible one)
Chthonia (of the earth/underworld)
Enodia (on the way)
Kleidouchos (holding the keys)
Kourotrophos (nurse of children)
Liparocredemnus (bright-coiffed)
Nyctipolus (night-wandering)
Phosphoros (bringing or giving light)
Propolos (who serves/attends)
Propulaia/Propylaia (before the gate)
Scylacagetis (leader of dogs)
Soteira (savior)
Trimorphe (three-formed)
Triodia/Trioditis (who frequents crossroads)
Zerynthia (of Mt. Zerynthia in Samothrace)

Copyright Asteria Publishing 2012

Hulda

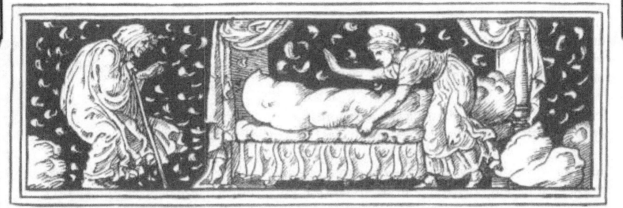

Hulda, or Frau Holle, is an ancient Germanic Goddess figure whose name is attested in Latin inscriptions as early 235 CE, though her worship undoubtedly well pre-dates these Roman records. She is known by a variety of names that are variations on Hulda (northern Germany) and Perchta (southern Germany). She is associated with Mother Goose and La Reine Pedauque, as well as being the forerunner for St. Lucia. She is also called Frau Goden and Frau Frekke, naming her Woden's wife (linking her with the Norse Frigga).

Holle is usually depicted in one of two ways: either as an old, bent grandmother with a crooked nose or as a young and lovely maiden whose white garments gleam like a fresh blanket of snow. She is often seen holding a lantern, and sometimes one of her feet is said to be a goose-foot.

Frau Holda is the matron of women's chores and domestic duty. She is particularly associated with spinning, a task almost entirely carried out by women and one of the few from which a woman could honorably receive payment in the Middle Ages. Spinning is intimately linked with magic, and it is Hulda who teaches both linen-making and magic.

She personifies the weather, particularly weather events that seem to transform the land, such as snow and fog. When it snows, the Folk would say that Frau Holle was shaking out her feather pillows. Fog, on the other hand, is said to be smoke from her fire. In the thunder, we hear Hulda reeling her flax.

The blustery winter weather helps to link Holda to the Wild Hunt, which she is said to lead alongside Woden. In this guise, she is linked to the harrowing visage of death, but it is said that Perchta, in particular, is surrounded by the souls of children who died before baptism, marking her is a protector of the young, even in death. She is also linked to Witch Flight, as it is said that she would ride the sky with Witches mounted on distaffs to the Sabbat.

Mother Holle is credited with nurturing an protecting children in several ways. She is known to rock the cradles of babes whose nurses have fallen asleep, and she is said to be the keeper of the pool through which the souls of newborn children enter the world. During the twelve days between Christmas and Epiphany (and especially at Twelfth Night), Perchta would roam the countryside to leave a silver coin in the shoes of children who were well-behaved and industrious.

Copyright Asteria Books 2017

Ishtar

Ishtar is the Babylonian goddess of love, war, fertility, and sexuality. She is often depicted riding a lion or flanked by two lions, and she is usually shown with a horned crown and wings. Her symbol is an eight-pointed star, and she is considered "the divine personification of the planet Venus."

Her worship seems to have involved sacred prostitution. Scholar have referred to her holy city Uruk as the "town of the sacred courtesans" and to her as the "courtesan of the gods."

Ishtar is also very deeply connected to both magic and sacrifice. In one account, she tricks her grandfather into giving her all of his magical gifts (the sacred laws of heaven and the knowledge of how to use them), promoting her to Queen of Heaven and Queen of Earth.

In one of the most famous myths about Ishtar describes her descent to the underworld, we spy her fiery rage:

> If thou openest not the gate to let me enter,
> I will break the door, I will wrench the lock,
> I will smash the door-posts, I will force the doors.
> I will bring up the dead to eat the living.
> And the dead will outnumber the living.

Other myths and poems show us the joyous lust and passion with which she is associated:

I bathed for the wild bull,
I bathed for the shepherd Dumuzi,
I perfumed my sides with ointment,
I coated my mouth with sweet-smelling amber,
I painted my eyes with kohl.
 He shaped my loins with fair hands,
The shepherd Dumuzi filled my lap with cream and milk,
He stroked my pubic hair,
He watered my womb.
He laid his hands on my holy vulva,
He smoothed my black boat with cream,
He quickened my narrow boat with milk,
He caressed me on the bed.
 Now I will caress my high priest on the bed,
I will caress the faithful shepherd Dumuzi,
I will caress his loins, the shepherdship of the land,
I will decree a sweet fate for him.

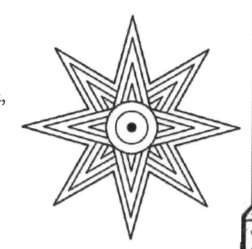

Isis

Isis is one of the most widely worshipped Goddesses of the ancient world. Her worship began in the period known as the late Old Kingdom in Egypt, and it was spread throughout the Classical world by the Romans and the Greeks. Much of her mythology was merged with that of the Virgin Mary by the early Church, as well, in the figure of the Virgin Mary. She continues to be widely worshipped and loved by modern Pagans.

The name "isis" means "throne," and one of her crowns is throne-shaped. She is a sovereignty goddess who acts as Divine Mother to the pharaoh.

Her associations are intimately linked to life and regeneration, and she is often shown holding an ankh, the symbol of life. She is also deeply connected to magic. Her magic restores her husband Osiris to life after he is torn apart by Set.

The following Awakening Prayer comes from the Book of the Dead:

Awake, awake, awake,
Awake in peace,
Lady of Peace.
Rise thou in peace,
Rise thou in beauty.
Goddess of Life,
Beautiful in heaven,
Heaven is in peace.
Earth is in peace.
O Goddess,
Daughter of Nut,
Daughter of Geb,
Beloved of Osiris,
Goddess rich in names!
All praise to You.
All praise to You.
I adore You. I adore You. Lady Isis!

John Barleycorn

One way to think about the Year Wheel is to look at the balladry figure of John Barleycorn. The stations of his life, as marked in the verses of the song below, are the Sabbats -- at least the ones dealing with planting and harvesting.

There were three men came out of the west,
Their fortunes for to try.
And these three men made a solemn vow:
John Barleycorn must die.

They've plowed, they've sown, they've harrowed him in,
Threw clods upon his head.
And these three men made a solemn vow:
John Barleycorn was dead.

They've let him lie for a very long time,
Till the rains from heav'n did fall.
And little Sir John sprung up his head,
And so amazed them all.

They've let him stand 'till midsummer's day,
Till he looked both pale and wan.
And little Sir John's grown a long, long beard,
And so become a man.

They've hired men with scythes so sharp,
To cut him off at the knee.
They've rolled him and tied him by the waist,
Serving him most barb'rously.

They've hired men with the sharp pitchforks,
Who pricked him to the heart.
And the loader, he has served him worse than that,
For he's bound him to the cart.

They've wheeled him 'round and around the field,
'Till they came unto a barn,
And there they've made a solemn oath,
On poor John Barleycorn.

They've hired men with the crabtree sticks,
To cut him skin from bone,
And the Miller, he has served him worse than that,
For he's ground him between two stones.

And little Sir John in the nut-brown bowl,
And the brandy in the glass.
And little Sir John in the nut-brown bowl,
Proved the strongest man at last.

The Huntsman, he can't hunt the fox,
Nor so loudly blow his horn,
And the Tinker, he can't mend kettle nor pot,
Without a little Barleycorn.

Copyright Asteria Publishing 2012

Lilith

Lilith is generally thought to be derived from a class of female demons called Lilitu in Mesopotamian texts. In Jewish folklore, Lilith becomes Adam's first wife, who was created at the same time and from the same earth as Adam. This contrasts with Eve, who was created from one of Adam's ribs.

Lilith's legend was greatly developed during the Middle Ages. In a 13th Century writing, Lilith left Adam after she refused to become subservient to him and then would not return to the Garden of Eden after she mated with archangel Samael. She was said to have spoken the secret Holy name of God and transformed herself into an owl to fly from Eden. In some medieval folklore, Lilith does return to Eden as a serpent. She then offers forth the fruit of the Tree of Knowledge to Eve, making her a kind of proto-Sophia or wisdom Goddess.

In some Traditional covens, Lilith is viewed as the embodiment of the Witches' Goddess, being both a White Goddess and a Black Goddess. She was said to have embodied herself in the form of Na'amah, the sister of Tubal Cain, and is therefore one of the original sources of Witchblood.

One of the old names for the moon is Lilith's Lantern, as it was said to be the light that Witches met by. Lilith is associated with the moon, owls, and serpents.

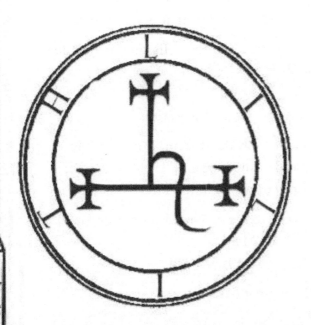

Enochian Invocation of Lilith by Dr. John Dee & Sir Edward Kelly

Black Moon, Lilith, mother darkest, Whose hands form the hellish mire, At my weakest, at my strongest, Molding my as clay from fire.

Black Moon, Lilith, Mare of Night, You cast your litter to the ground. Speak the Name and take to flight, Utter now the secret sound!

Copyright Asteria Books 2015

Lucifer

Lucifer is the "light-bearer" — the bringer of enlightenment to mankind. He is Qayin in the East, the Morning Star. He is the torch-bearer of wisdom, inspiration, the Divine Spark, the Cunning Fire. He is "Prometheus" (literally, "fore-sight"), who rebelled against God (the Gods) to give Fire (the Cunning Fire) to mankind and fell from Divine Grace.

Lucifer, more than any other name or title by which we can call our Gods, is a terrifying name for the non-witches of the world. This title is tantamount to calling him the Devil or Satan. While we don't see him as the great, evil, anti-God of the Christians, many traditional witches claim another measure of the transgressive power he represents by calling him "Devil" within their rites.

As the Red God of American Folkloric Witchcraft, Lucifer is simply another title for Qayin, the Witch Father. We see different aspects of Him at Beltaine and Samhain, but He is always the Red God. His is the red thread that offers us the foundational fiber for weaving magic and connecting with the Mighty Dead. He is the fiery red of sunrise, and His is the light that kindles the forge deep within the earth.

To the Romans, Lucifer was a Forge God of the Sun and brother to Diana, the Moon Goddess of wild places. Together, they conceived Aradia, the first of the Witches.

We honor Lucifer in the East, the place of sunrise and fire. His time is Beltaine, with its bel-fires and hints of gnosis through physicality.

Invocation

Hail to Lucifer-Qayin, Lord of Light
Lord of the Forge
Lord of the Cunning Fire!

Come to the crossroads, Morning Star
Golden Man
King of the Bel-Fires!

So mote it be!

Copyright Asteria Books 2015

Lugh

The Pan-Celtic God Lugus was known to the Irish as Lugh and the Welsh as Llew. The name means "Shining One" and is accompanied by many epithets, including "Long-Arm" (due to his skill with a spear), "Sword-Shouter" (due to his fierceness with a sword in battle), "Fierce-Striker", "Skillful-Handed", "Skilled in Many Arts" and "Strong-Handed." Lugh's tales portray him as a crafty, clever, and heroic king. Lugh, in Irish tradition, is the lone survivor of three triplets, and there are many other triplicities that recur in his myths, making him a Triple God, in many ways. He is often depicted as have three heads, not unlike Brighid, in Irish lore. As a young man Lugh travels to Tara to join the court of king Nuada of the Tuatha Dé Danann. The doorkeeper will not let him in unless he has a skill with which to serve the king. He offers his services as a wright, a smith, a champion, a swordsman, a harpist, a hero, a poet and historian, a sorcerer, and a craftsman, but each time is rejected as the Tuatha Dé Danann already have someone with that skill. But when Lugh asks if they have anyone with all those skills simultaneously, the doorkeeper has to admit defeat, and Lugh joins the court and is appointed Chief Ollam of Ireland. Lugh eventually takes his place as king, as well. He established a series of games called the Lughnasadh in honor of his foster-mother, Tailtiu, and even now the month of August bears the name *Lúnasa* in the Irish language. Lugh is the father of Cuchulainn.

Copyright Asteria Books 2015

Maiden

The Maiden is a Classical Goddess archetype that is honored within the world of witchcraft and contemporary Paganism, much as it was by the Ancients. The Maiden is associated with the waxing crescent moon and she is often depicted as a Hunter, Fire-Bearer, and Wild Woman. Like Athena, she may be associated with a Craft, like weaving. The Maiden is sometimes seen as part of the contemporary Wiccan vision of the Triple Goddess, though ancient Triple Goddess were as likely to include three Maidens as they were to include a Maiden, Mother, and Crone.

Some Maiden Goddesses include:

Artemis – associated with hunting, animals, the moon, and freedom

Athena – associated with wisdom, strategy, weaving, and technical skill

Hestia – associated with the hearth, home, and eternal flame

Hekate – associated with magic, the moon, divination, torches, and the Underworld

Flora – associated with flowers, springtime, fertility, and youth

Hebe – associated with youth, cup-bearing, and baths

Idunna – associated with apples youth

Blodeuwedd – associated with flowers, owls, and independence

Copyright Asteria Books 2017

Mother

In the archetype of the Triple Goddess as explored by Robert Graves, the Mother Goddess is represented by the radiant and shining full moon. She is the Lady of ripeness, of greatest fertility, of stability, fulfillment, and power.

She is most closely connected to the land, often being a representation of the land itself. In this role, she is frequently a sovereignty Goddess who grants to her consort the right of kingship. She is the Earth Mother whose body feeds and sustains all life. She is the Nurturing One, the Sustaining One, the Comforting One.

Some Mother Goddesses from various cultures include:

Gaia – associated with the Earth itself and with ecology

Demeter – associated with grain and with devotion to her daughter

Astarte – associated with sexuality and fertility in the land, the animals, and the people

Frigga – associated with weaving and women's magic

Danu – associated with fertility, protection, wisdom, and the wind

Pachamama – associated with fertile fields, mountains, trees, and holed stones

Copyright Asteria Books 2017

Crone

The final archetype in the Maiden-Mother-Crone vision of the Triple Goddess is the wise, venerable, and sometimes terrifying Crone Goddess. She is depicted as an old woman of great experience, often imparting wisdom to those who seek her via riddles, omens, or other tellings. She is very often depicted as cloaked and hooded, which is symbolic of the Mysteries she protects.

While she is often shown stooped with age and walking with a cane, it is unwise to assume the Crone is weak or fragile. She is often more than capable of defending herself with magic, with clever tricks, or even with martial prowess.

The Crone has passed through the phase of Maidenhood and understands its freedom. She has lived the industrious and creative times in her life, whether she bore children or not, and so she carries the memories of the Mother's power. Now, she dances with Death and prepares for the Mysteries that lie beyond.

Some examples of the Crone archetype include:

Hekate – associated with the Dark Moon, crossroads, and hounds

Annis – associated with wisdom, the Old Ways, and fear

Cailleach – associated with destruction, disease, death, seasonal rites, and weather magic

Copyright Asteria Books 2017

Morrígan

The Morrígan ("phantom queen") or Mórrígan ("great queen"), also known as Mor-rígu, is an Irish Goddess. She is primarily associated with fate, especially with foretelling doom and death in battle. In this role she appears as a crow, flying above the battlefield. The Morrígan has thus been likened to the Valkyries and Norns of Germanic mythology. She is also associated with sovereignty, and her connection with cows may also suggest an association with wealth and the land.

The Morrígan is often described as a trio of individuals, all sisters, called 'the three Morrígna'. Although membership of the triad varies, the most common combination in modern sources is Badb, Macha and Nemain. However the primary sources indicate a more likely triad of Badb, Macha, and Anand. Other accounts name Fea, Scathach, and others. The Morrígan is often considered a triple goddess, but this triple nature is ambiguous and inconsistent. These triple appearances are partially due to the Celtic significance of threeness. However, the numbers five and nine also play an important part in Irish magic, and the Morrígan often appears in these numerical combinations, as well as being depicted as a single individual.

The Morrígan is usually interpreted as a "war goddess." Her role often involves premonitions of a particular warrior's violent death, suggesting a link with the Banshee of later folklore. Her role was to not only be a symbol of imminent death, but to also influence the outcome of war. Most often she did this by appearing as a crow flying overhead and would either inspire fear or courage in the hearts of the warriors. In some cases, she is written to have appeared in visions to those who are destined to die in battle by washing their bloody armor or clothing.

Copyright Asteria Books 2015

Pan

In Greek religion and mythology, Pan is the god of the wild places, shepherds, and flocks, and rustic music, and a companion of the nymphs. Some scholars say his name originates within the Ancient Greek language, from the word *paein* (πάειν), meaning "to pasture," while others see in it the Greek word for "all."

He has the hindquarters, legs, and horns of a goat, in the same manner as a satyr. With his homeland in rustic Arcadia, he is also recognized as the god of fields, groves, and wooded glens; because of this, Pan is connected to fertility and the season of spring. The ancient Greeks also considered Pan to be the god of theatrical criticism — the word "satire" being connected to satyrs.

The goat-god was nurtured by Amalthea with the infant Zeus in Athens. Pan aided his foster-brother in the battle with the Titans by letting out a horrible screech and scattering them in terror.

One of the famous myths of Pan involves the origin of his pan flute, fashioned from lengths of hollow reed. Syrinx was a lovely water-nymph of Arcadia, daughter of Landon, the river-god. As she was returning from the hunt one day, Pan met her. To escape from his importunities, the fair nymph ran away and didn't stop to hear his compliments. He pursued her from Mount Lycaeum until she came to her sisters who immediately changed her into a reed. When the air blew through the reeds, it produced a plaintive melody. The god, still infatuated, took some of the reeds, because he could not identify which reed she became, and cut seven pieces (or according to some versions, nine), joined them side by side in gradually decreasing lengths, and formed the musical instrument bearing the name of his beloved Syrinx. Henceforth Pan was seldom seen without it.

Disturbed in his secluded afternoon naps, Pan's angry shout inspired panic (*panikon deima*) in lonely places.

Pan's greatest conquest was that of the moon goddess Selene. He accomplished this by wrapping himself in a sheepskin to hide his hairy black goat form, and drew her down from the sky into the forest where he seduced her.

Copyright Asteria Books 2015

Hymn to Pan

Aleister Crowley

Thrill with lissome lust of the light,
O man! My man!
Come careering out of the night
Of Pan! Io Pan!
Io Pan! Io Pan! Come over the sea
From Sicily and from Arcady!
Roaming as Bacchus, with fauns and pards
And nymphs and satyrs for thy guards,
On a milk-white ass, come over the sea
To me, to me,
Come with Apollo in bridal dress
(Shepherdess and pythoness)
Come with Artemis, silken shod,
And wash thy white thigh, beautiful God,
In the moon of the woods, on the marble mount,
The dimpled dawn of the amber fount!
Dip the purple of passionate prayer
In the crimson shrine, the scarlet snare,
The soul that startles in eyes of blue
To watch thy wantonness weeping through
The tangled grove, the gnarled bole
Of the living tree that is spirit and soul
And body and brain — come over the sea,
(Io Pan! Io Pan!)
Devil or god, to me, to me,
My man! my man!
Come with trumpets sounding shrill
Over the hill!
Come with drums low muttering
From the spring!
Come with flute and come with pipe!
Am I not ripe?
I, who wait and writhe and wrestle
With air that hath no boughs to nestle

My body, weary of empty clasp,
Strong as a lion and sharp as an asp —
Come, O come!
I am numb
With the lonely lust of devildom.
Thrust the sword through the galling fetter,
All-devourer, all-begetter;
Give me the sign of the Open Eye,
And the token erect of thorny thigh,
And the word of madness and mystery,
O Pan! Io Pan!
Io Pan! Io Pan Pan! Pan Pan! Pan,
I am a man:
Do as thou wilt, as a great god can,
O Pan! Io Pan!
Io Pan! Io Pan Pan! I am awake
In the grip of the snake.
The eagle slashes with beak and claw;
The gods withdraw:
The great beasts come, Io Pan! I am borne
To death on the horn
Of the Unicorn.
I am Pan! Io Pan! Io Pan Pan! Pan!
I am thy mate, I am thy man,
Goat of thy flock, I am gold, I am god,
Flesh to thy bone, flower to thy rod.
With hoofs of steel I race on the rocks
Through solstice stubborn to equinox.
And I rave; and I rape and I rip and I rend
Everlasting, world without end,
Mannikin, maiden, Maenad, man,
In the might of Pan.
Io Pan! Io Pan Pan! Pan! Io Pan!

Rhiannon

Rhiannon is a major literary figure of the earliest Welsh-British prose, the *Mabinogi*. Her tales appear in the First and Third Branch of the *Mabinogi*, and like a great many characters from British-Celtic lore, we are able to see the religious and mythological roots of this Great Queen Goddess. Rhiannon's name is synonymous with Rigantona and means "Great Queen." She is a sovereignty goddess of the Celts, meaning that the King ruled by right of being married to this Queen. She represented the Land and the People. Rhiannon is often associated with horses, and her stories are laden with horse imagery, which connected her to the Gaulish Epona. When Pwyll, the Prince of Dyfed, approached the fairy mound in search of wisdom and boon, Rhiannon appeared, riding a white mare. She gave chase, and his horsemen were unable to catch her for two days, until on the third day he rode after her himself and plead with her to stop. She did, but chastised him for not pursuing her on his own account from the start. Three years after they are married, Rhiannon bore a son to Pwyll, but the infant disappeared the night he is born. Her maids killed a puppy and smeared the sleeping queen's face and hands with blood, claiming that she killed and ate her son. Pwyll didn't believe this, but set a punishment for her at the insistence of the people. Each day, Rhiannon must sit at the city gate and tell her tale to those who enter and offer to act as their horse, carrying them or their goods throughout the city. This went on for several years until a golden-haired boy came to Dyfed with his foster-father. Every May Eve, his best mare would foal but the foal would vanish. Once, he kept vigil, hacking at the monstrous claw that snatched the foal. In the foal's place, it had left Rhiannon's infant son. The horse master reunited the boy with his mother, who named him Pryderi, which means both "delivered" and "loss."

Copyright Asteria Books 2015

Thoth

Thoth is an ancient Egyptian God whose associations include knowledge, the moon, measurement, wisdom, the alphabet, records, thought, intelligence, mediation, the mind, logic, reason, reading, hieroglyphics, magic, secrets, scribes, writing, arbitration, and judging the Dead.

Thoth was linked in Egyptian mythology to many types of mediation and judgment. He is the arbitrating power between Good and Evil, perpetually ensuring that neither establishes domination over the other.

He is a God who is mighty in magic, and his unparalleled power seems inexorably linked to words. He is associated with both spoken and written language, being credited as the creator of the written word. It is by virtue of "the Word" that creation happens — which is a theme that is carried forward in Greek philosophy and also in Biblical mythos. Thoth's words are the foundation for the creation of the celestial bodies and the ordering of their movements, which linked Thoth to the sciences. Ultimately, the Greeks eventually credited him with ALL areas of knowledge, both human and divine.

Ancient Prayer to Thoth

Come to me, Thoth, O noble Ibis,
O letter-writer of the gods,
O great scribe!
Come to me and give me counsel,
Make me skillful in your calling!
Better is your calling than all callings,
It makes men great.
He who masters it is found fit to hold office.
I have seen many whom you have helped,
Grant me your wisdom, O Thoth!

Tubal Cain

Tubal Cain, T'Cain, Qayin, Qābīl, Kain, Vulcan, Hephaestus, Wayland, Gobannus, Atho, Janus, Óss, Azazel, Azazil, Izrail, Melek Taus, Lucifer, Lugh, Shamesh, Shemyaza, Lumiel, Orion

TVBAL QAYIN

Of special interest to Witches is the concept of the Smithing God. Metalsmiths were among the first alchemists, and, by virtue of their powers of transmutation of ore into steel, they were once credited with magical powers. Blacksmiths were considered the mages par excellence of this group, and today we find iron horseshoes (iron ore transformed into the God's horns) prized as good luck symbols. The Smithing God is often associated with lameness, which is attributed to a folk practice of laming the village smith so that such an important member of society could not leave. The shambling step of the lamed God is echoed in the most basic Witch dances.

Tubal Cain appears to mean *he who spices the craft of Cain*. Gordon Wenham suggests that the name *Cain* means *smith*, or that he is called *Tubal Cain* in order to distinguish him from the other Tubal, the son of Japheth. Henry Morris suggests that etymologically, his name is the progenitor of the name of the Roman God Vulcan. Tubal Cain is sometimes thought to be the progenitor of the Celtic peoples. He is the "first ancestor" and the Witchfather.

Genesis 4:22 says that Tubal Cain was the *forger of all instruments of bronze and iron*. Although this may mean he was a metalsmith, a comparison with verses 20 and 21 suggests that he may have been the very first artificer in brass and iron. T. C. Mitchell suggests that he *discovered the possibilities of cold forging native copper and meteoric iron*. Tubal-cain has even been described as the first chemist.

According to the Book of Enoch, Azazel was among those in the Biblical story of the fall of the angels. Azazel is represented in the Book of Enoch as one of the leaders of the rebellious Watchers in the time preceding the flood; he taught men the art of warfare, of making swords, knives, shields, and coats of mail, and women the art of deception by ornamenting the body, dying the hair, and painting the face and the eyebrows, and also revealed to the people the secrets of witchcraft and corrupted their manners, leading them into wickedness and impurity.

According to Luciferian tradition, Azazel and Tubal Cain are the same entity. Azazel chose Tubal Cain as his earthly vessel when he lead the rebellion of the fallen angels. Tubal Cain is of the line of Cain, through his father Lamach, marking him with the holy blood of Lucifer. By teaching the daughters of man witchcraft, Azazel/Tubal Cain became the Witchfather.

Copyright Asteria Publishing 2012

Liber Qayin

Black Book of Lilith-Sophia

In the beginning there was only me.

I am the darkness.

From the wind in the night I came.

I am called Lilith.

The Elohim fashioned me from Wind and Blood and dark, rich Earth; for I am the womb of the world, and I am its tomb.

I was made equal to the first man, Adam, fashioned of Fire and Words and red Clay.

We lived together in the Garden of Eden, and the world was ours alone.

Adam and I lay together, and I conceived a daughter by him. She was Eve, the mother of all races.

Eve was my treasure, the Light I brought forth from my Darkness.

But she was also my rival. For I am the Darkness in the Light.

Ever have Gods and Men been drawn to her radiance, the promise of a jewel in the night.

And only those most truly called to be among the Wise might turn from that brightness toward my shades for succor.

I first used magic when Adam abandoned me to consort with our daughter. I transformed myself into an owl and flew away to the Land of Nod.

There, I howled against the wrongs of Adam. There, I raged against my torn and jealous heart that both loved and hated in an instant.

There, I inhabited the Tree of Wisdom and learned all its Mysteries.

And mine is the sad, cruel song of Knowledge that shrieks in the darkness.

I used the magic of conjuration to bring the spirit of Azazel into the world, and he came as a serpent to liberate my daughter.

At the serpent's urging, Eve ate the fruit of my deep knowing and was enlightened. She took the spirit of Azazel and the flesh of Adam within her womb and brought forth two sons.

Cain the Gardener bore the spirit of Azazel; and Abel the Shepherd bore the spirit of Adam.

Before there is peace, there must be strife. Knowledge brings pain, and Wisdom brings peace.

And so my grandson Cain was cast into Nod for slaying his brother Abel.

In Nod, I took Cain for a lover and taught him all magic. Through this magic Cain founded the first cities and built the first temple.

When I first passed from this world, the Elohim made me a spirit of many names.

I am the spirit of wisdom and peace. Sophia.

I am the great weaver and the giver of fate. Kolyo.

I am the darkness of chaos. Tiamat.

I am the dark road of death and am called Life-in-Death. Hekate.

I am the Wellspring of Holy Blood. Sang Real.

Copyright Asteria Books 2015

I am the owl of wisdom and strategy. Athene.
I am the source of all magic. Diana.
My seal is the white lily of peace. Lilith.
I returned to life as Na'amah, the sister of my beloved Tubal-Qayin, who was Azazel restored to flesh. Together we brought magic to the people of the earth.

Red Book of Azazel-Qayin

When all souls were One Soul, I was with God.

When all the worlds of Heaven were made manifest - creation upon creation - I was with God.

When all the people of this sphere were formed and given the Breath and Word of Life, I was with God who is All that is and was and shall be forevermore.

My eyes were on the All That Is, and my song was first in the Heavens.

And I saw the fashioning of all things and the Mysteries that lie within them. I saw the Fire that is Life and Wisdom and Magic, and this fire shown in each plant and person and creature. It shown from each stone and each drop of water. Each wind that blew carried the fiery Word of Life.

I watched All and gloried in the One that is both Creator and Created.

And I was with God, and I was God.

The Lilitu knew me as she looked upon the Tree that is both Life and Knowledge. And when she called to me, I came as the serpent that she might know transformation.

And when she called to me to free her child by means of Wisdom, I offered Eve all the sweet fruits of the One.

To me, Eve bore a son of wisdom and magic, and when I came into the world as a man I took his name and became Tubal-Qayin.

For Cain the Gardener was the first man of Fire, bearing the Mysteries within his Blood and upon his brow.

And Cain my son wandered in the wilderness, learning All That Is from Lilith and shaping civilization from the wild places.

And he was the scape-goat, the one driven out to bear the sacrifice that is required of magic.

And my name has been called Azazel, the scape-goat of God. For in the time of my Great Fall, I did turn my eyes away from that singular focus on All that I might teach those of mankind who would learn.

And I brought unto the people of Babel the green Fire of Life and Wisdom -

the Light of Heaven.

And so I am called Lucifer, the Light Bearer, for I bring transformation and freedom.

And this Light shines from the depths of All, and it is in the Blood of All.

For I am the Blood, the line and legacy of Cain - sprung from Lilith's fountain and carried in Eve's cup.

Mine is the forge - fire of change.

Mine is the anvil - rock of existence.

Mine is the water - tempering creation.

Mine is the bellows - breath of life.

Heaven and Earth are combined in my work, for the stars of the sky shed both iron and gold to be wrought among the elements of the world.

Heaven and Earth are combined in you, O Child of the Stars who is fashioned from clay.

And my forge is the Cunning Fire that fuels your Will.

And my anvil is your Heart, wherein all Mysteries are revealed.

And my water is the Witch Blood that links the line of Cain through the Ages.

And my bellows is the Word of Magic that creates the World.

Even as Heaven and Earth are joined in you, and as the angels of Heaven did join with the daughters of Earth, so too is all that is celestial met with all that is infernal in the crucible of alchemy.

And so shall it be that the equal-armed cross shall be a sign among those who bear my Blood and Fire.

And I shall meet my Witches at the crossroads, where light and dark, day and night, above and below, Life and Death are joined in the Mysteries.

And I will be the Devil to those who do not Know - tempter and guardian of Knowledge, both seductive and appalling.

For I am the Serpent in the Tree, the Stang on the Hill, the King of the Spiral Castle, and the Devil at the Crossroads.

White Book of Ishtar-Eve

Thus spake Ishtar-Eve, consort of Qayin:

I am the Bride, the Queen of Heaven, the joy upon the Earth.

My names have been many and beloved, as the stars of the heavens, for I am Asherah, Aphrodite, Babalon, the Magdalene, Aradia, Inanna, Astarte.

I am the Light in the Darkness, the star-fire of your soul, the hope and joy and pleasure of Gods and men. And I am also Death-in-Life, the little death found in the arms of love.

I am all possibility without limit.

You see in me the ocean or the vast starry heavens, opening into the fruition of your dreams. And so I am.

And if you have Wisdom, you tremble before me.

For I am untempered Life come rushing to meet you, unbounded Love poured upon you like the Sea.

Mine is the Garden of Paradise, the rosy bower, the fruitful place. For I was begotten in the Garden, and I am all that is fertile.

Know of my Love, and find the path to Understanding.

For first among all the creatures and beings of the world did I love my Mother, dark and secret and wise.

And from her root did my blossom spring.

And She was called Lilith, the Lily of Peace; and my name was called Eve, the Star of the Evening.

And ever has this been my sigil within the sky.

My Mother sent my liberation through Wisdom, the serpent's path through the Tree.

And I took for my own the Golden Apple of Understanding that I might know myself.

For I am called Gnosia, the golden lady of Knossos.

Deep is my love, and broad. For no woman is so unlovely, no man so unworthy, no child so unnoticed that I do not hold them deep in my heart.

Qayin is my mate, and I am his Queen. I am the Starry One, Astarte and Asteria, that is his Muse, the fodder for his forge.

His fire and my ocean combine in ageless alchemy.

I am the Great Whore with kohl black eyes and robes the color of the sky - the woman of Babel, of Babylon, of Ur, who civilizes the wild beasts of men with the magic of my sex.

I am the Mother of Giants, the Mother of Faeries, the Mother of all Mankind; for in my

Copyright Asteria Books 2015

first coming did I lie with my father-husband Adam and give birth to the race of Men.

And when I came to the desert as Ishtar, I did meet Azazel-Qayin at the ruins of Babel and unto him I bore the Nephilim.

And ever have I been the White Lady, Queen of Elphame.

Qayin is my love, and I am his consort. But I am made to love all the world, even his brother whom he reviles.

For Qayin is the Lord of the Witches, and the Adonai is Lord to all Mankind.

Adonis, Tammuz, Damuzi. Peaceful Prince and beautiful Shepherd. My undying, youthful love.

This lesson you must heed:

That Love and Life and Liberty come at the price of blood and tears that are like my ocean.

For in the earliest days of Men did I bear two sons.

One was called Abel, and the other was called Cain. And they were the joys of my world. Both were beloved of me, and I of them.

For Abel was like his father, and he was as a prince of our paradise; bright and beautiful.

And Cain was like my Mother, whom I adored, with a dark secret fire.

But Cain slew Abel, and I mourned for my great loss, for my beloveds; for truly they were both lost to me.

Yet ever in the tales of men is this sorrow and loss repeated in Love's white name.

The beautiful and bright Shepherd, Prince of Peace, is sacrificed on the altar of Love.

And ever does he return, young and whole and vibrant and willing, that he might once again show mankind the Way.

He is the Christos, anointed by my Holy Waters in the name of Love and Light, and he is my ever-green lover.

And I am his Magdalene.

The rose of my love is stained crimson with the blood of his sacrifice.

For it is unto me, the Lady of Love and Life and Liberty, that all blood sacrifice must be made and for whom all War must be waged. And so it is that I am She of Love and War, for both are bought with blood.

The first thrust of Love and the passage of Birth are marked with my crimson seal, the Rose of Blood, my red flower.

You may have neither Life nor Freedom nor Love without paying the price, for these are the deepest magics.

My mother Lilith-Sophia is the source, the Fountain, the Sang Real, the Holy Blood.

And I am Eve-Babalon, the vessel, the chalice, the San Graal, the Holy Grail.

And I am the first of the Witches.

Copyright Asteria Books 2015

For in the beginning did my mother Lilith-Sophia, who is the Wellspring of all Witch Blood, and the Serpent-Azazel whose Blood is the Fire of Magic bring me to the fruit of enlightenment, where I did taste Wisdom and find Understanding.

And when they fell and became flesh again, as Na'amah and Tubal-Qayin, I was the flame-haired woman at the Ziggurat of Babel.

And I knew them. And I loved them.

And together we were three - the fountain, the bloodline, and the vessel.

Ever have we remained so, and our names have been called Diana, Lucifer, and Aradia.

Ritual, Liturgy, and Spells

Orkney Charm for Becoming a Witch

While recording the rapidly disappearing folklore and traditions of Sanday in the 1880s, folklorist Walter Traill Dennison documented the ritual carried out by aspiring witches to gain their magical powers.

The witch had to first wait for a full moon. Then she would go to a solitary beach at midnight where she had to turn widdershins three times before lying prostrate on the ebb - the area between the limits of high and low tide. This was a liminal space, and we believe that this rite could also be held at a crossroads at midnight under a full moon.

She then had to stretch out her arms and legs, and place stones beside them. Further stones were also placed at her head, on her chest and over her heart. Once enclosed by the circle of seven stones, the witch spoke aloud:

Oh Master King of all that's ill,
Come fill me with the Witches' Skill
And I shall serve you with all my will.
Devil take me if I sin!
Devil take me if I fly!
Devil take me when I cannot!
Come take me now, and take me all,
Take eyes and liver, organs and feet
Take me, take me, now I say!
From the brow of the head, to the tip of the toe.
Take all that's out and in of me.
Take hair and hide and all to thee.
Take heart and brains, flesh, blood and bones
Take all between the seven stones!
In the name of the great black Witch Goddess!

The person must lie quiet for a little time after repeating the Incantation. Then opening his eyes he should turn on his left side, arise, and fling the stones used in the operation into the sea. Each stone must be flung singly; and with the throwing of each a certain malediction ("*Devil take these stones and witch's bones!*") was said.

Copyright Asteria Publishing 2012

Rite of Dedication

MATERIALS
- Candles, lighter
- Red knife, thumb pricker or lancet and alcohol swabs
- Black or White Robe or Hood
- Red Cord
- Offering of Whiskey or Dark Beer

You will need solitude and quiet for this ritual. Come to it freshly bathed and wearing only your ritual robe, hood up (or simple, clean dark clothes, with your shawl/scarf).

AT A LIMINAL PLACE (riverbank, lakeshore, crossroads, graveyard, etc), make the following Declaration: "I come to this liminal place, ready to begin my study and practice of the Craft. My name is _____, and I am a Witch."

TYING THE RED THREAD

Clean your finger with the alcohol swab and draw a large drop of blood using the lancet. Dab the blood onto your Red Cord.

Dedication Oath: "I make this Oath. I vow to dedicate myself to the study and practice of Witchcraft for at least a year and day. I honor the Witch Blood that is my inheritance from the Witchfather. I vow to act with honor within the Family and to hold sacred the teachings of the Craft. I seek the starfire at topmost spire of the Spiral Castle, as well as the forge-fire at its bottommost roots. Before the Witchfather and Witchmother, I make this vow. Before my Spirits, I made this vow. Before my Holy Self, I make this vow. So mote it be!"

Make your offering and spend some time in quiet meditation of the step you just took and the vows you have made. Contemplate your link to other Witches. Open yourself to messages from the Godds or Spirits.

When you are done, clap your hands three times and say, "The work is done."

Copyright Asteria Books 2020

Aligning the Three Souls

A helpful daily practice (and certainly one that is very effective for what many people would call "grounding and centering" prior to ritual) is that of bringing the Three Souls into alignment. This is simple and can be done with little fanfare, in a matter of a few short breaths. If your Sense of Arte favors more complicated ritual, there are certainly more elaborate accommodations that can be made.

Start by getting your feet planted or otherwise feeling your connection to the earth below you. Then state, "May the Three Souls be straight within me."

Continue by taking a deep breath out, sending your energy like a taproot into the earth. On the inhale, pull the earth's energy (and with it, the Forge Fire at the center of the earth) into your belly — the seat of the Black Soul (the fetch, the personal identity, the Soul most connected with this life and your sense of Self).

On the next breath, pull the energy higher, to your chest — the seat of the Red Soul (the Bone Soul, the ancestor connection through blood and fire).

On the third breath, pull the energy higher yet, to the skull, the crown of the head — the seat of White Soul (the higher self, the Holy Guardian Angel, the God-Self).

On the final breath, pull/push the energy all the way through yourself, connecting to the Star Fire above, releasing the breath with a sigh. You are connected to the Witch-Fire above and below, within and without. All three soul-parts are connected and in harmony.

Copyright Asteria Books 2020

Witches' Lesser Banishing Ritual

This ritual is an adaptation of the Lesser Banishing Ritual of the Pentagram. It uses forms of Witch Gods in place of the traditional Hebrew names of God. It also replaces the Archangel guardians with the four Watchtowers of Celtic lore. The purpose of the LBRP is to banish all undesirable forces from oneself and the local area and to create Sacred Space. It is often recommended as a daily magical exercise to discipline the mind and create peace.

Qabbalistic Cross

Imagine a ball of light above your head. Reach up with your right hand and grab the light. Now when you touch yourself with that hand part of the light will go into you. Touch your forehead as you say "Coronis." (Crown) Let it fill with the light. Touch your pelvis at the pubic bone and say "Serpentis". (Serpent) Let it fill with light. Touch your right shoulder and say "Clementia". (Mercy) Let it fill with light. Touch your left shoulder and say "Severitas". (Severity) Let it fill with light. Hold your hands in prayer over your heart and say "Fortunia". (Blessings) Let it fill with light. Feel your whole body fill with the cross of light.

The Pentagrams

Face East. Before you in the air draw a giant pentagram using your right index finger (or if you prefer use the whole hand) in the direction shown in the illustration. Now imagine that pentagram shining in front of you. Electric blue is a nice color to see it in. If you see it a different color that's fine. Take a step forward with your left foot. Just the left. Leave your right one where it is. The size of the step will be determined by your space. At the same time you step forward thrust your open hands, side by side, palms downwards, into the pentagram, as if you are diving in. This is called the Sign of the Enterer. As you enter the pentagram you will say one of the names of the Witch God or Goddess. Here, at the first pentagram you will shout "Lucifer."

Now, step back with your left foot so it is once again beside your right foot. Touch your right index finger to your lips like you are making the "Shhh, no talking" gesture. Point your right index finger to the center of the pentagram and make a quarter turn to your right. As you do so, draw an imaginary arc of white light around to the next direction. Now draw a pentagram in South. Enter the pentagram singing "Goda." Make the "shhh" gesture and turn to the right drawing an arc. Draw a pentagram in West. Enter the pentagram intoning "Azazel" in a low voice. Make the "shhh" gesture and turn to the right drawing an arc. Draw a pentagram in North. Enter the pentagram whispering "Kolyo." Make the "shhh" gesture and turn to the right drawing an arc.

The Watchtowers

You are now standing in the center of a circle of white light. At each quarter there is a giant electric blue pentagram. Now we post a guardian between each pentagram. Open up your arms. Stretch out like you are a cross: feet together, arms out at shoulder height. Call the watchtowers to their posts. Stand in the cross position and say: "Before me stands the Castle of Stone. Behind me stands the Castle of Glass. On my right stands the Castle Perilous. On my stands the Castle of Revelry."

Stand in pentagram position and say: "Around me flame the pentagrams. Above me shines a six-rayed star, and below me spins a three-armed triskle. I stand within the Spiral Castle. I am the World Tree."

Now repeat the Qabbalistic Cross as you began. "Coronis, Serpentis, Clementia, Severitas, Fortunia".

Copyright Asteria Publishing 2012

Ritual Participant Roles

Priest & Priestess - In some groups, the individuals holding these positions are called by other titles. "Magister" and "Maid" are titles more commonly used in Traditional Craft, for example. Most groups refer to the man or woman who "centers" the ritual by one of these titles. "Centering" a ritual refers to the weaving together of the group's energy and keeping the ritual cohesive and on-track. Traditionalists don't always bestow these titles on someone in a permanent sort of way (though some groups do, as a way to recognize clergy or other leadership positions within a coven). Your ritual may have one or two people acting in this role, individually or as a partnership.

Quarter Callers - Very often a different individual will be assigned to each Quarter. Sometimes, only one or two individuals will call all the Quarters (or other sacred spaces/entities).

Herald/Summoner - Sometimes a ritual will benefit from someone calling the celebrants to the door of the compass/circle. Sometimes the Summoner will go to a separate space to retrieve a person who has been isolated from the ritual and bring them to the ritual grounds. The Herald/Summoner serves that role, welcomes them, and will often also issue a challenge before allowing admission.

Smudger - This person will pass the smoke of incense over each participant as they enter. This is almost always accompanied by someone asperging participants with saltwater.

Guardian/(Wo)Man in Black - The nature of some rituals requires an extra level of protection. You may want an Outer Guardian if you are in an exposed public area, or you may need an Inner Guardian if you anticipate difficult psychic work. Choose this person very carefully. They should be very experienced in such work.

Copyright Asteria Books 2018

Ritual Preparation

Before leading a group ritual, it is wise for a person be able to do ALL of the following:

1. Grounding and Centering — This foundational skill is the mainstay of meditation and a key way of staying healthy. It simply involves taking a time-out to clear all the little nagging distractions of your mind and body and concentrating on what you're doing and how you're really feeling. You'll need to do this at the beginning and end of the ritual. A great way to ground excess energy at the end of a magical practice is through group discussion and food.

2. Laying the Compass — You should have a solid, if basic, working knowledge of the Realms, Gates, and Castles and what energies and powers reside in each. You can use words or gestures that help you, but it is far more important that you are able to call on the energies in an etheric sense. Practice calling them individually and meditate with each until you are comfortable with everything you or your group will be calling.

3. Summoning and Banishing — You must be able to call on and stir up energies, spirits, and other powers, and you must also know how to release and/or banish those same powers. Practice the Witches' LBRP or study other banishing techniques until you feel confident in your abilities.

4. Raising Energy — Clapping, dancing, stamping, chanting, praying, yelling, laughing, drumming...the trance-inducing activities most common to ritual are all means of raising energies, and anything that holds your attention and usually garners some enjoyment works well for energy raising.

5. Directing Energy — After you've raised energy, you need to be able to collect it and assign it where it's supposed to go. This takes a developed discipline in visualization and skill in describing what task precisely you wish that energy to perform. Energy ball games are excellent for developing this skill.

6. Visualizing — A skill for use in and out of ritual - it's not just imagining something with your mind's eye. It's about seeing, hearing, touching, smelling, or tasting something with such vividness that your visualization, while you know it is a visualization, actually looks real to you.

7. Shielding — This is a basic skill for practice of any form of magic, generally a visualization sometimes aided by spell components to turn off your psychic responsiveness.

Copyright Asteria Books 2015

Cleansing Chants

Each portion of the chant requires a Witch to walk the compass either once or thrice, wielding the appropriate cleansing tools.

With Incense:

*Smoke and fume, now as you burn,
cause all harm from us to turn;
let nothing harmful here be found,
as we tread the witch's round.*

With Flame:

*Fire that burns and light that glows,
send all harm away from us;
let nothing harmful here be found,
as we tread the witch's round.*

With Salt Water:

*Water and salt, brine of the sea,
wash this circle clean and free;
let nothing harmful here be found,
as we tread the witch's round.*

With Broom:

*Besom sweep and besom clean;
above, below and in between;
let nothing harmful here be found,
as we tread the witch's round.*

Laying the Compass

Red Thread circles are cast by setting the caim — defining the area of protection and power within which the Witch or coven will perform the work. We call Powers that lie opposite each other as a pair — both being called toward the center of the circle. Thus, they form a road or an energetic pathway, with the Stang as the center point.

CENTER AND FIRST CIRCLE — Raise the Stang, which serves as the world tree and connects Three Realms. At the base of the stang is the Oath Stone or anvil upon which we make our blood oaths to the tradition, as well as the cauldron. Also placed at the center of the compass are the personal fetishes of each member of our Clan. It is not uncommon to also keep a skull and bones (crossed or open) and other tools relevant to the working here. With the Raising of the Stang, the 1st Circle is cast.

SECOND CIRCLE — Lay the Compass by walking the perimeter of the space within which you will work while treading with the Lame Step. Use the Stang or Staff or Distaff. This is also known as Marking the Moat.

THIRD CIRCLE — Open the Gates by calling North and South, East and West toward the center of the compass. At the North gate are placed the staves of the coven, along with the spear, and the troy stone, or gate stone. Also at this gate are symbols of the Black Goddess. Any tools associated with Air are kept at this gate, such as the censer if one is used.

The South are symbols of the White Goddess, Earth, and the shields of the coven. The binding cords and the bread for the red meal are placed at this gate.

In the East are the tools of Fire. Here we place the blacksmith's hammer and tongs and keep a bonfire burning, if we are outdoors. The coven sword is here.

The West is the gate of Water, the quench tank of Tubal Cain. Representations of water are placed here. The weapon of this gate is the helm, and the masks of the Clan are kept here.

Thus is the compass laid. It may be as elaborate or as minimal as your tastes and needs dictate. Although the instructions above explain the placement of all of the gates, tools, and weapons, simply treading the mill once and acknowledging the four gates is enough to lay the compass.

Copyright Asteria Books 2018

Opening the Gates

North Gate

I call to the Winds beyond the North Gate. Open the door from the North, place of Air, Kolyo's domain. By the spear, the wing, and the smoke, I call you to open wide the Gate and send forth your road to the center of this, my compass. So mote it be!

South Gate

I call to the Fields beyond the South Gate. Open the door from the South, place of Earth, Goda's domain. By the plate, the soil, and the shield, I call you to open wide the Gate and send forth your road to the center of this, my compass. So mote it be!

East Gate

I call to the Sunrise beyond the East Gate. Open the door from the East, place of Fire, Lucifer-Qayin's domain. By the steel, the anvil, and the sun, I call you to open wide the Gate and send forth your road to the center of this, my compass. So mote it be!

West Gate

I call to the Ocean beyond the West Gate. Open the door from the West, place of Water, Azazel-Qayin's domain. By the cup, the quench tank, and the helm, I call you to open wide the Gate and send forth your road to the center of this, my compass. So mote it be!

Mill Songs

Treading the Mill is the act of walking 'round the circle while focusing energy on the center. This is sometimes done while chanting to raise power.

The Mill of Magic

Fire flame and fire burn, make the Mill of Magic turn.
Work the Will for which we tread by the Black and White and Red.
Earth without and earth within, make the Mill of Magic spin.
Work the Will for which we tread by the Black and White and Red.
Water bubble, water boil, make the Mill of Magic toil.
Work the Will for which we tread by the Black and White and Red.
Air breathe and air blow, make the Mill of Magic go.
Work the Will for which we tread by the Black and White and Red.

Power of the Elements

Power of Sky and power of Wind and power of Air the North doth send,
We tread the Mill to work our spell, both by your Breath and by out Will.
Power of Spark and power of Fire, power of all our hearts' desire,
We tread the Mill to work our spell, both by your Flame and by out Will.
Power of Ice and Water free and power that hides in depth of Sea,
We tread the Mill to work our spell, both by your Wave and by out Will.
Power of Stone and power of Land and power of rich Soil in our hands,
We tread the Mill to work our spell, both by your Earth and by out Will.

Copyright Asteria Publishing 2012

The Housle

As with many faiths, we partake of a small meal with a spirited drink after our rites. In many witchcraft traditions this is called "Cakes and Wine." We call it the Housle, or Red Meal, and base it in part on a ritual created by fellow walker of the crooked path, Robin Artisson.

The Housle Song
To the tune of Greensleeves

To Housle now we walk the wheel
We kill tonight the blood red meal
A leftward tread of magic's mill
To feed the Gods and work our Will.
Red, red is the wine we drink!
Red, red are the cords we wear!
Red, red is the Blood of God!
And red is the shade of the Housle.

When the compass is laid, place in the southwest corner: Dark bread in a bowl (or lipped dish) and Red Wine in Silver Quaich or Chalice. In the center, near the stang will be placed the Red Knife.

1. The sacrificial meal is brought from Castle Perilous to the Spiral Castle by an Initiate.
2. Tread the Mill widdershins three times while singing the Housle Song.
3. At the place of sacrifice say: "For our Ancestors, our Gods, and Ourselves, we do this."
4. Bless the bread with the right hand: "Here is bread, flesh of the earth, the source of strength and life. In the name of the Old Ones, I consecrate it."
5. Cut the bread with the left hand, using the Red Blade: "I take its life and give it to Them."
6. Bless the wine with the right hand: "Here is wine, blood of the Gods, the source of joy and Mystery. In the name of the Old Ones, I consecrate it."
7. Slice across the cup with the left hand, using the Red Blade: "I take its life and give it to Them."
8. Each person eats and drinks of the Meal, making whatever personal offerings they like — taking their portion of the Meal with their left hand, saying "With my left hand I take it."
9. The remainder of the wine is poured into the bread bowl, and each person dips their finger in and anoints themselves. This can also be used for blessing tools, etc.
10. The Meal is either given to the ground now, if outside, or later, if inside, saying the following:

> "By the Red, the Black and White,
> Light in Darkness, Dark in Light —
> What we take, we freely give.
> We all must die. We all must live.
> Above, below, and here are One.
> All together — All! (And none!)
> Here is shown a Mystery. As we Will, so Mote it Be!"

Sabbats

Samhain

Samhain is the point in the Wheel that is directly opposite to Beltaine, and the intents behind the holiday and the season are, subsequently, directly opposite to those of the fertility and mirth of Beltaine. Furthermore, Samhain is the beginning of the New Year in Celtic lands. The Celtic calendar had 13 months. Samhain was the last night of the 13th month.

For the ancient Celts, a new day began in the dark of night, and a new year began in the dark half. Samhain (the midpoint between the Fall Equinox and Winter Solstice) was seen as the beginning of the dark half of the year. It was a time when the veil between the worlds of the living and the dead was the thinnest, and communication and passage between the worlds was easiest. It was a time to commune with deceased ancestors and loved ones. Though the ancients honored and revered their ancestors throughout the year, this was the perfect time of year to set aside sacred time to honor those who had passed.

Of course, since the veil was so thin, it was also expected that some rather nasty spirits might enter through the veil at that time, which would cause folks to be wary. Guardians of various types would be placed at doors and windows and hearth (all the entry ways into the home) to keep unwanted and unwelcome spirits out. Gourds, turnips, and apples are commonly carved and offered as vessels for these Guardian spirits. The custom of dressing in costume comes from the idea of disguising oneself so as not to be recognized by unfriendly spirits.

Furthermore, it was a time of remembrance. The ancients had a deep respect for their ancestors, and this was a time to remember the deeds of forefathers and foremothers. They would recall the names of the people in their lineage and honor them with feasts (often in silence because the Dead don't speak aloud) and gifts. The ancestors would have a special place in the home during this time, usually in the form of an ancestor altar.

Since this was the last festival of the harvest, it was imperative that farmers have all of their crops harvested before sundown on Samhain night. If not, tradition held that whatever was left in the fields belonged to the *sidhe*.

Some Craft traditions hold that their male God(s) go away at this time – either to die and be reborn, or for a period of rest. These Gods are most often reborn with the Solstice sun at Yule.

In American Folkloric Craft, Azazel-Qayin is honored as the keeper of the gates to the Dead at this time of year, and his guidance may be sought via oracle for the year to come.

This is a time of beginnings and endings. As such, it is a time of introspection, reflection, communication with the Otherworld and Underworld. It is a time of profound spiritual growth. It can be quite intense.

Copyright Asteria Books 2019

Samhain Ritual

MATERIALS
- Stang, candle, lighter
- Cauldron, water, lancet
- Anvil, hammer
- Three knives (red, black, white)
- Red Cord
- Bread, lipped dish or bowl
- Dark beer
- Red wine, cup
- Incense, holder, charcoal
- Carved gourd/pumpkin, tealight candle
- Skull (real human OR human-shaped ceramic, glass, crystal, paper-mache, wood, etc)
- Lineage chant

RAISE THE STANG

LAY THE COMPASS

OPEN THE GATES (beginning in the West)

WORKING

- LIGHTING JACK ~ Hold your carved pumpkin or gourd (or turnip) in your hands and send energy into it to "wake it up." Call on a specific guardian Spirit, or ask that a guardian from your tribe of spirits comes forward to inhabit the vessel and keep watch over you and your home during Samhain-tide. Light the candle inside the jack-o'-lantern, and set it as a Ward at the edge of the Compass.
- RECITATION OF LINEAGE ~ Pick up the skull. With pride and love, declare, "I am, (name), child of (name), child of (name), child of (name), child of (name)." Go back as many generations as you know. If you want to focus on the matrilineal or patrilineal line, you may. It is equally acceptable to recite the lineage of adoptive and foster families if that is your circumstance and preference.
- ENLIVENING OF SKULL ~ Still holding the skull, send a thread of energy to the skull, feeling it come alive with the energy of your blood, your breath, your flesh. Say something like, "I invite my ancestors, those names and those un-

named, to be with me, speak with me, eat with me, dance with me, laugh with me during these dark days at the the turn of the year. I offer you this vessel, now and always, as a seat in my home." Place the skull at the base of the Stang. In future rituals, always place the skull here. Outside of ritual, place the skull upon your altar or ancestor shrine.

- Dark Beer for Qayin ~ At the anvil or Oath Stone, pick up the hammer. Strike the anvil and call out, "Tubal Qayin!" Strike again and call out, "Tubal Qayin!" Strike a third (final) time and call out, "Witch Father!" Pour the dark beer over the anvil/stone or into the cauldron. (If you're inside pour all of it into the cauldron. If you're outside, reserve at least part of it for the cauldron.) Acknowledge with whatever words or gestures come to you that this offering us to Tubelo. It is not inappropriate to share a drink, so take a swig from the bottle to share with the Red God, if you feel so moved.

- Scrying ~ Sit down in front of the cauldron. Get comfortable. Refresh the incense, if needed. Pour some water into the cauldron if more liquid is needed. Clean the top of a finger with an alcohol swab and prick with a lancet. This works best on the outside edge of a fingertip, where you are not calloused. Keeping your hand below your heart, raise a drop or two of blood. Drop them into the liquid if there cauldron. Gaze at the cauldron, relax your focus, and allow images and impressions to come to you. Don't try to force a conversation with the spirits. They will speak in their own way. You may experience images, sounds, ideas, temperature shifts, sensations, smells. Any of these may seem to generate spontaneously within your own mind, like a stay thought. Let them come. Allow the session to continue as for a little while. You'll probably have a good sense of when you're finished and nothing else is coming through. If needed, you can end the session early and beginning to ground by moving into the Red Meal.

Housle

Sabbat - Samhain Incense

About This Blend

This blend was designed to honor and celebrate Samhain, the final harvest of the Autumn and the beginning of the Celtic New Year.

As with all loose incense blends, this formula can be burned on a hot, self-igniting charcoal tablet (like those used for hookahs) or it can be thrown onto the glowing embers of a fire.

Incense Recipe

1/4 cup Apple wood

1/4 cup Rose petals

1/4 cup Dittany of Crete

1 tablespoon Oakmoss

1 tablespoon Sage

1 tablespoon Benzoin resin

2 teaspoons Corn kernels, ground

1 teaspoon Pumpkin seeds

9 drops Wormwood oil

Special Notes

This unusual blend helps set Samhain aside as a liminal time, a time of reaping, and a time of Ancestor worship.

Copyright Asteria Books 2017

Yule

Yule is celebrated on the Winter , which is the shortest day of the year. Solstice celebrations are universal, being celebrated in nearly every culture the world over.

Groups as different as Iranians are to the Swedes, Chumash Indians to the Germans, and Spain to peoples of Tibet have very old traditions for the same solar event. The impetus for the holiday, nearly the world over, is the fear that the failing light of the sun may not return and therefore needs some help. According to many traditions, there are evil spirits that thrive in the darkness and require light and warmth to drive them out. This accounts, in part, for the extensive use of candles and lanterns to drive away the darkness. Of course, the flame of a candle is also similar (though a much smaller representative) to the light of the Sun itself.

Structures have been built, as far back as the dim memory of mankind and beyond, that mark and honor the Winter Solstice. Stonehenge (which marks both Solstices), Newgrange in Ireland, and Maeshowe in the Orkney Islands off the coast of Scotland are some of the most well known of these ancient pieces of architecture. However, there are also similar structures throughout Europe, Asia, the Middle East, Indonesia and the Americas. One has even been found recently in Africa.

The Romans celebrated Saturnalia, which was a combination of the traditions already in use by the Egyptians and Persians. Saturnalia was a 12-day celebration that involved decorating with greenery and burning candles to chase away evil spirits. Naturally, it became a party in the pure Roman style with the passage of time.

Yule was the Norse and Celtic celebration of the Solstice. "Yule" means "feast" or, possibly, "wheel." As with the other cultures, the Celtic and Norse traditions tend to revolve around the return of light, warmth, and fertility brought by the Sun. Of course, the peoples to the North had a much rougher time in winter than their neighbors to the South, so their need for the return of light (and heat) may have helped imbue this holiday with special significance.

Boughs of holly were used in decoration because their verdant color was a strong reminder of life in the midst of the white, snow-covered world they lived in. White, interestingly, was a color of death and mourning to the Northern people, and winter was the time of the Earth's death in preparation for rebirth. Holly was also hung in windows because of its prickly leaves and poisonous berries, which make it excellent for guardianship.

The Holly King rules at this holiday, but loses his battle to the Oak King, who will then rule until Summer Solstice. All solar deities are honored, and this day is accounted as the birth of many of them.

Copyright Asteria Books 2019

Yule Ritual

MATERIALS
- Stang, candle, lighter
- Three knives (red, black, white)
- Red Cord
- Bread, lipped dish or bowl
- Red wine, cup
- Incense, holder, charcoal
- Skull
- Yule candle, log, and/or firewood
- Wassail, bowl
- Lemon, ribbon, orris powder, cinnamon, ginger, whole cloves, toothpick

RAISE THE STANG

LAY THE COMPASS

OPEN THE GATES (beginning in the West)

WORKING
- VIGIL FIRE ~ Keep a fire burning all night. Stay with it, tending to it as needed. This isn't always an easy task. The night is long. It invariably becomes a time for self-reflection, much as the winter itself is. But it can also be a time for mirth, family, friends, and craft.
- WASSAIL THE TREES ~ Take the wassail bowl outside, if you aren't already outside. Salute the trees that surround your home. Wish them health and long life and offer them a drink. Sing the song "Here We Come A-Wassailing" as you go, if you choose. As with other offerings, it is appropriate for you to share the drink, as well, if you are so moved.
- PROSPERITY POMANDER ~ These clove-studded, dried citruses take some time to be fully made, but they are well worth it. Place in a dish on your altar while it dries.

HOUSLE

Copyright Asteria Books 2018

Sabbat - Yule Incense

About This Blend

This blend is designed to honor the Winter Solstice. It is suitable as a temple incense for Yule rituals and Midwinter feasts.

As with all loose incense blends, this formula can be burned on a hot, self-igniting charcoal tablet (like those used for hookahs) or it can be thrown onto the glowing embers of a fire.

Incense Recipe

1/2 cup tablespoons Rosemary

1/2 cup Lemongrass

1/4 cup Fennel

1 teaspoon Ginger

1 teaspoon Cinnamon

1 teaspoon Cloves

10 drops Ylang Ylang oil

Special Notes

This spicy and sweet blend is reminiscent of clove-studded pomanders and pumpkin pie.

Copyright Asteria Books 2017

Pomander

No. 1. No. 2.

The name "pomander" means "apple of amber" (or rather, ambergris — the perfume component) and comes to use from the French *pomme d'ambre*. Pomanders are first mentioned in literature in the mid-13th century, and they were in popular use for about 400 as a means of warding off disease and negative spells, while promoting a sense of ease and peace.

Some traditional pomanders are made by rendering resins and other botanical ingredients until a ball (apple) of paste is formed, which is then hardened and carried inside a bag or piece of jewelry which allows the fragrance to circulate. In these cases, the encasement is also sometimes called a pomander.

The simplest pomanders are citrus fruits whose skins have been pierced, exposed to fragrant resins and herbs, and then studded with cloves. This is the type of pomander we often still see in contemporary Yule decorations. These are associated with solar magic, including wealth, health, and courage.

To make your own:

1. Choose an orange with a thick skin.
2. Pierce the skin liberally with a toothpick or burin.
3. Roll the orange in a mixture of powdered orris root, ginger, cinnamon, and other money-drawing spices.
4. Poke whole cloves into the holes on the skin.
5. Tie a gold, green, or red ribbon, if you wish to hang it.

Copyright Asteria Books 2021

Here We Come A-Wassailing

Here we come a-wassailing
Among the leaves so green,
Here we come a-wand'ring
So fair to be seen.
[REFRAIN]
Love and joy come to you,
And to you your wassail, too,
And God bless you, and send you
A Happy New Year,
And God send you a Happy New Year.

We are not daily beggars
That beg from door to door,
But we are neighbors' children
Whom you have seen before
[REPEAT REFRAIN]

Good master and good mistress,
As you sit beside the fire,
Pray think of us poor children
Who wander in the mire.
[REPEAT REFRAIN]

We have a little purse
Made of ratching leather skin;
We want some of your small change
To line it well within.
[REPEAT REFRAIN]

Bring us out a table
And spread it with a cloth;
Bring us out a cheese,
And of your Christmas loaf.
[REPEAT REFRAIN]

God bless the master of this house,
Likewise the mistress too;
And all the little children
That round the table go.
[REPEAT REFRAIN]

Copyright Asteria Books 2018

Wassail Recipe

1 gallon Apple Cider
1 can (6 oz) Frozen Orange Juice
1 can (6 oz) Lemonade
4 cups Water

Put the above ingredients in a 30 cup coffee percolator.

In the basket, put:

6 Cinnamon Sticks
1 & 1/2 tsp whole Allspice
1/2 tsp whole Cloves
1 cup Brown Sugar

This wassail recipe can be adapted to taste, and it serves a crowd. It is my family's favorite! You can also add some extra holiday cheer to it, if you like. It combines well with both wine and liquor, depending on your preference.

Imbolc

Imbolc is the mid-point between Winter Solstice and Spring Equinox. It is the time of the year when one begins to notice that the sunlight is waxing once again. In colder climes, like the ones many of our European pagan forebears lived in, this would have been the coldest part of the year. They would know that Spring was on its way, but there was very little physical evidence in the land that gave obvious witness to this fact. In fact, the returning light was about the only thing that really heralded the return of warmth and growth. Because this was the time of year that the ewes would come into their milk (for the lambs they were about to bear), the holiday was named "Oimelc" in some places. For human women, too, this could be a season of birth. (A woman who gets pregnant at Beltaine, and carries the baby to term, will be in labor near the beginning of February.)

Brighid is associated with this holiday due, in part, to her association with birthing and midwifery. She was one of the highly loved and honored pan-Celtic Goddesses, and this was an ideal holiday for celebrating her role as midwife and mother. Because of this, some traditions refer to this holiday as "Brighid" or "The Feast of Brighid" or even "Bride's Day" in honor of her.

Some traditional witches work within the Celtic framework of the John Barley-Corn cycle. At this time of year, John Barley-Corn would be in the womb, waiting to be born. As a part of the John Barley-Corn celebrations, the last mug of beer and the last loaf of bread would be drunk and eaten to help revitalize John Barley-Corn.

Many traditions send the Gods to their rest around the time of Samhain. Among those that do, there is a portion who would be calling the Gods back to life and fertility at this time of year, leaving them to rest during the darkest part of the cycle.

Candlemas, a festival that the Christians picked up on some centuries ago, is also associated with this time of year. Many covens use this time of returning light to make and/or bless their candles. This is not surprising, as Imbolc was one of the four great fire festivals of the Celts.

Fire and Ice are common themes (very often in conjunction) for this festival, as the hope of spring stirs beneath the frozen land.

In American Folkloric Craft, Kolyo (the Black Goddess) is honored at this time.

Copyright Asteria Books 2019

Imbolc Ritual

MATERIALS
- Stang, candle, lighter
- Three knives (red, black, white)
- Red Cord
- Bread, lipped dish or bowl
- Red wine, cup
- Incense, holder, charcoal
- Skull
- Novena candle, Kolyo label, packing tape
- Florida Water or other perfume

RAISE THE STANG

LAY THE COMPASS

OPEN THE GATES (beginning in the North)

WORKING
- Kolyo Candle ~ Affix a Kolyo candle label onto a novena jar candle. Or draw Kolyo sigils onto a glass jar. Hold the jar between both hands and send energy into it while you seethe (next). Once ready, keep this candle on your altar all year long. If needed, you can transfer the flame and every into a new novena.
- Seething ~ Rock back and forth, side to side, in a circle or however the energy encourages you. Whisper or intone the name Kolyo while you do this. Enliven the candle with the Kolyo energy you are raising.
- Uneasy Seat ~ When you feel compelled to stop, allow yourself to sit still for a moment, sensing the energies around you. Focus on Kolyo and listen for Her voice in your mind and in your heart. Allow your spirit to sense Her and be in communication. See Her, hear Her, feel Her, smell Her, taste Her. Be in close contact with Her. Understand the messages She has for you. Let this continue until you are ready to stop, or She is. Dab Florida Water or another perfume onto your hands, feet, and the back of your neck to fully end the session and come back to yourself (and only yourself).

HOUSLE

Copyright Asteria Books 2018

Sabbat-Imbolc Incense

About This Blend

This incense was designed to accompany your Imbolc celebrations and rituals.

As with all loose incense blends, this formula can be burned on a hot, self-igniting charcoal tablet (like those used for hookahs) or it can be thrown onto the glowing embers of a fire.

Incense Recipe

1/4 cup Blackberry leaves

1/4 cup White Willow bark

1/4 cup Lavender

1/8 cup Barley

1 tablespoon Pine resin

2 teaspoons Cinnamon

7 drops Myrrh oil

A few drops Red Wine

Special Notes

This incense blend offers a special nod to Brighid, the pan-Celtic Goddess most frequently associated with this holiday. It also contains elements that connect to the Black Goddess, who is honored at this season within American Folkloric Witchcraft.

Copyright Asteria Books 2017

Spring Equinox

It seems that the most popular and common name for this holiday (and many of the traditions surrounding it) has sprung from the not-so-common (in her own time) Teutonic Goddess Eostre (or Ostara). She was a fertility Goddess whose symbols were bunnies and eggs and the like. The idea of fertility is linked closely with this time of the year, and even the early Church couldn't get rid of the symbols. It is them, in fact, that we have to thank for popularizing the name and spreading the love of sweet Eostre's bunnies far and wide.

Within traditions that focus on the cycles of the sun, this is one of the four major events in the year. The vernal equinox is the solar event that marks the point of balance between day and night, while moving into longer and longer days. It is viewed as a time of balance with the understanding that we are moving into a time of increased light, action, and fertility.

Within the Greek cycle of the Eleusian Mysteries, this is the time when Persephone returns from her stay with her husband, Hades, in the Underworld. She is welcomed home by her rejoicing mother, Demeter, who is a Goddess of the fields. During Persephone's long absence, the fields gave no food and the land was dark and cold. With her return, flowers spring to life at her feet and the land is blessed with fertility. This is the joy of the reunion between mother and daughter.

This is also one of the two times of year attributed to Aphrodite's ritual cleansing and sacred bath. As such, some groups use this as a time of cleansing and renewal. Indeed, "spring cleaning" after a long winter is in order for most homes, and spiritual spring cleaning is a wise course of action, as well.

The Great Rite, in symbol or truth, can be done at this time in keeping with the fertility running so rampant in the land.

For groups who work with a John Barley-Corn myth cycle, little John is born (planted) at this holiday.

Copyright Asteria Books 2019

Spring Equinox Ritual

Materials
- Stang, candle, lighter
- Three knives (red, black, white)
- Red Cord
- Bread, lipped dish or bowl
- Red wine, cup
- Incense, holder, charcoal
- Skull
- Broom (ritual besom or practical broom)
- Shell, water, salt, evergreen sprig
- Candle, oil lamp, or lantern

Raise the Stang

Lay the Compass

Open the Gates (beginning in the North)

Working
- Cleansing the Space ~ Using the Cleansing Chants and accompanying tools (broom, saltwater in a shell with evergreen sprig, smoking incense, and lantern or lamp) energetically clean and cleanse the sacred space in which you work. You can, of course, go a step further and cleanse the whole house and/or property. Visualize all the staleness of winter, all the remnants of last year's harvest, all being swept and washed away.
- Cleansing the Self ~ Using the same tools, energetically cleanse yourself. You probably already bathed before ritual, but you can use these same tools to cleanse yourself and your energy. The broom is the only one that may feel awkward, due to size and shape. Use the evergreen sprig instead.
- Standing the Broom ~ Center yourself in your newly cleansed space. Feel the balance within you. Work on finding that external point of balance, via the broom. Try to get it to stand on its own long enough and steady enough that you can walk away from it. Once you've found the "sweet spot," it's often easy to do again and again -- any day of the year.

Housle

Copyright Asteria Books 2018

Sabbat -Spring Equinox Incense

About This Blend

This incense is designed to complement your Spring Equinox rituals and celebrations.

As with all loose incense blends, this formula can be burned on a hot, self-igniting charcoal tablet (like those used for hookahs) or it can be thrown onto the glowing embers of a fire.

Incense Recipe

1/4 cup Hibiscus flowers

1/4 cup Calendula

1/4 cup Sage

1/8 cup Birch bark

1/8 cup Dandelion root

1/8 cup Hops flowers

1 tablespoon Myrrh resin

7 drops Jasmine essential oil

Special Notes

This light, fresh incense includes several flowers and herbs that are traditional Spring Equinox fare.

Copyright Asteria Books 2017

Beltaine

Beltaine is one of four Celtic fire festivals that are associated with the agricultural turns of the seasons. It is, therefore, one of the Greater Sabbats, and it marks the opposite end of the Wheel from Samhain. Traditional Beltaine activities include blowing horns (a symbol of the male reproductive power) and gathering flowers, making garlands, and hanging greenery (flowers being the symbols of female fertility). Hawthorn was especially sacred to this holiday. In fact, old traditions dictate that the date of Beltaine is set by the flowering of the local Hawthorn tree, and the Hawthorn was usually the tree of choice for the Maypole. The Maypole itself would be symbol of male and female fertility conjoined once the dance was complete and the ribbons had been snugly wrapped about the pole. (While frolicsome and youthful, this is certainly not a dance for children, as it has become in modern culture.)

Beltaine is linked to the Sacred Marriage (hieros gamos) and fertility almost universally. Many Wiccan trads see this as the wedding day of the May Queen and May King. Mothers and fertility are especially honored, and the contemporary secular holiday of Mother's Day (which occurs within about a week of Beltaine) may have Pagan roots associated with this festival.

Communing with fairies has frequently been associated with this holiday, and a lot of lore surrounds ways to contact and work with fairy energy during this time for those who feel inclined to contact the Good Neighbors.

Sacred bonfires were used in many ways in May Day celebrations. Many people would jump balefires for fertility or pass cattle and other livestock between bonfires for protection, fertility, purification.

Walpurgisnacht is a May Eve celebration that originated in Southern Germany (Bavaria). Its purpose is to scare away all the evil spirits that lurk in the shadows before the bright day of Beltaine. Interestingly, Walpurgis is the name of both a well-known nun and a famous witch, but it doesn't seem to have been a Goddess name.

Within American Folkloric Craft, Lucifer-Qayin is honored as the May-King and the Lord of the East, the direction associated with Beltaine on the Year Wheel.

Copyright Asteria Books 2019

Beltaine Ritual

MATERIALS
- Stang, candle, lighter
- Three knives (red, black, white)
- Red Cord
- Bread, lipped dish or bowl
- Red wine, cup
- Mugwort, lemongrass (1/2 tsp each)
- Honey
- Incense, holder, charcoal
- Skull

RAISE THE STANG

LAY THE COMPASS

OPEN THE GATES (beginning in the East)

WORKING

- SABBAT WINE ~ Prepare Sabbat Wine for yourself by steeping a tablespoon of mugwort (or a blend of mugwort and lemongrass) in a cup of warm red wine for 10 minutes. Remove the herbs (easiest done when using a tea ball), and add raw honey to sweeten. I like to use a local sweet red wine and local honey, as well as local herbs (when I can get them). Drink the wine without gulping or chugging. Give it time to work with you to open your psychic senses.

- GUIDED MEDITATION ~ Journey through the Walpurgisnacht Flight guided meditation either by reading it aloud while recording (prior to ritual) and then playing it back for yourself during the ritual, or by reading through the meditation prior to ritual so that you are familiar enough with the steps, and then doing your best to follow those steps without guidance. You can also read through the meditation after you feel the soft focus from the wine wash over you, doing what you can to walk between the worlds of reading and meditating. (Or you can listen to the recorded version on the RTA YouTube channel.)

HOUSLE

Copyright Asteria Books 2018

Sabbat -Beltane Incense

About This Blend

This incense is designed to accompany your Beltane festivities and rituals.

As with all loose incense blends, this formula can be burned on a hot, self-igniting charcoal tablet (like those used for hookahs) or it can be thrown onto the glowing embers of a fire.

Incense Recipe

1/4 cup Cowslip

1/4 cup Saffron or Safflower

1/4 cup Angelica root

1/4 cup Cinquefoil

1/8 cup Hawthorne berries

1 tablespoon Frankincense resin

9 drops Honeysuckle oil

A little honey

Special Notes

Beltane is also known as May Day or Bel's Fire. It is a fire festival that welcomes in the summer season and the light half of the year. This incense has both spicy and sweet notes that pay homage to the Lord of Light and the May Queen who reign at this time.

Copyright Asteria Books 2017

Walpurgisnacht Flight

Close your eyes and and follow your breath. Take long, slow inhalations, followed by long, slow exhalations. As you breathe, you notice a white mist settling around your body. It quickly becomes a thick fog obscuring sight and sound. The fog is cool and numbing, and you find yourself a little tingling and disoriented. A strange heaviness pervades your body as you continue to breathe deeply, in and out. After a moment, the fog begins to lift, and you also feel lighter. You stand, gripping your Stang and use it as a walking stick. You move a few paces off, and the fog clings a little less, though you still can't see where you are. You take another step and are able to recognize your surroundings, though they look altered in ways that are difficult to describe fully. You notice yourself and your surroundings for a moment, seeing both this familiar place and your own self with the eyes of Spirit. You move out of this familiar space and into unknown territory. You're surprised how rapidly the landscape shifts into unfamiliar scenery. You may have thought you knew this place well, but only a few yards from familiar ground, you find yourself confronted with a hedgerow unlike any that could have been there before. It is thick, dense, made of several kinds of hedge trees, and it is quite a lot taller than most hedges. Far on the other side of this hedge, the Dancing Place of the Witches awaits you. You can hear the distant call of the pipes and drums and bells. The sounds are so distant, you are sure it isn't your ears that hear them. You smell the wood smoke and feast meats. You can taste the promise of mead and kisses and laughter beyond this hedge. You look down the row to the left and the right and don't see a gate. There may be one if you talk a walk, of course. A rabbit pops up from a burrow about six feet away from you. Yes, *under is an option. You lean on your Stang to think and it leans back. Ah! Over it is.* You straddle the Stang and lift into air. You notice a star shining from the candle flame between the horns of the Stang and are reminded of the iron foot at the base. Be aware of the sensations you experience as you mount the Stang. From above the hedge, you notice a wild landscape. A patchwork of ancient forests, fertile countryside, villages, hills, and a mountain range looming in the distance. It is here where the Witches dance. The peak you seek is the Brocken. The highest. Your soul knows the way. You land at the Hexentanzenplatz (Witches' Dancing Place) to find the Sabbat in full revelry. More Witches than you'd ever dreamed are gathered here. Witches of every color, from every place, who have made covenant with the Witchfather are here to celebrate the great Beltaine Sabbat. And not just Witches are here. As you take a moment to observe the stunning spectacle, you see many Familiars, too. This Dance is a revel for all the senses and offers any delights you care to indulge. Food, sex, music, drink, wisdom, mysticism, laughter, scent, beauty, inspiration. You stay as long as you choose, taking your fill, before eventually returning the way you came (across the sky, over the hedge, and back into the fog).

Copyright Asteria Books 2018

Midsummer

The Summer Solstice is considered one of the Lesser Sabbats to most Neo-Pagans, since it is one of the solar holidays. It is the longest day of the year, and the shortest night. Many Wiccan groups refer to this holiday as Litha.

The Oak King and Holly King story is once again enacted, and this time the Holly King takes power and the light of the sun begins to diminish. The Holly King is the ruler of the dark half of the year, and his reign signals the beginning of the sun's wane in energy.

In a spiritual sense, many groups typically view this holiday in terms of its influence on their own power and ability. This is the height of the active force in nature, and the ultimate display of our own potential and ability to put our plans into action. The sun on this day reminds us of our own potential for greatness. It also reminds us that this potential does have an upward limit, but we can strive to reach that potential by calling on all our resources.

Traditionally, this holiday has a strong historical association with fairies. In fact, it is only eclipsed by Samhain in terms of fairy lore. Unlike Samhain, however, those wishing to experience a positive interaction with the Good Neighbors are more likely to do so at this Sabbat. Be cautious and do your research, though. Fairies are tricky, even when the sun is shining!

Since this is the shortest night of the year, it is a traditional bonfire vigil (and revel) night. Fireworks, lanterns, fire-dancing, and more all common practices today that stem from traditional Celtic roots. Unlike Yule vigils, which often test endurance after the merriment of the feast has faded, Midsummer revels are frolicsome and fast.

Solar and fire Deities are often called at this time, as are those who represent action, potential, and drive.

Within American Folkloric Tradition, we associate the Oak King with Cernunnos and Herne, the Lords of the forest and the hunt.

Copyright Asteria Books 2019

Midsummer Ritual

MATERIALS
- Stang, candle, lighter
- Three knives (red, black, white)
- Red Cord
- Bread, lipped dish or bowl
- Red wine, cup
- Incense, holder, charcoal
- Skull
- Fire pit, fire wood, kindling OR
- Cauldron, Epsom salt, rubbing alcohol
- Recorded music or musical instruments, drums, etc.

RAISE THE STANG

LAY THE COMPASS

OPEN THE GATES (beginning in the East)

WORKING

>BONFIRE OR CAULDRON FIRE ~ This is best done outside, for obvious reasons, but it is possible to build a very, very small sacred fire indoors in a cauldron with Epsom salt and rubbing alcohol. Another alternative is to place a candle in your cauldron. Of course, the preference here is to build a fire outside, if at all possible. It doesn't have to be large. Midsummer fires are wonderful for revelry, music, dancing, and the high spirits that come with the joys of summer. Play music, make music. Dance. The type of music and style of dance don't matter. Get your blood up, your energy up. Have fun! Keep it going as long into the night as you like. This is a celebration of life, io the ability to DO, and of the ripeness of the world.

HOUSLE

Copyright Asteria Books 2018

Sabbat - Midsummer Incense

About This Blend

This incense was designed to accompany Summer Solstice rituals and celebrations.

As with all loose incense blends, this formula can be burned on a hot, self-igniting charcoal tablet (like those used for hookahs) or it can be thrown onto the glowing embers of a fire.

Incense Recipe

1/4 cup St. John's Wort

1/4 cup Chamomile

1/4 cup Oakmoss

1/4 cup Patchouly

1/4 cup Cedarwood chips

1 tablespoon ground Acorn

1 tablespoon Pine resin

5 drops Lemon oil

3 drops Bergamot oil

Special Notes

In the American Folkloric Withcraft tradition, Midsummer is the sacred time of Cernunnos. This blend is reminiscent of sunshine in the forest.

Copyright Asteria Books 2017

Lughnasadh

Lughnasadh is another of the Greater Sabbats, one of the High Holy Days - a Celtic fire festival based on the agricultural wheel. It is named after the Pan-Celtic God Lugh whose name comes from "lugio" meaning "oath" - marriages and other contracts were made at this time. Both the Welsh stories of Lleu and the Irish ones of Lugh are very much tied up with oaths, promises, and bonds.

Another name for this holiday is Lammas, which means "loaf mass." Because this is the first of the harvest festivals, grain and the first fruits were often blessed and honored at this holiday. The loaf mass was a Catholic adaptation of the blessing of the grain that clearly had Pagan roots. This holiday gave rise to country fairs that still happen (and are particularly popular in the Midwestern United States) at this time of year. The country craft fairs also give unknown honor to Lugh in another way (since he is the master of all crafts).

Lughnasadh is named after Lugh because he instituted funeral games in honor of Tailtiu, his foster-mother, who died after clearing a forest for cultivation.

Traditional activities include picking bilberries (as representative of all of Earth's bounty), playing games, having contests of wit and strength, and making a corn dolly. The corn dolly represents the harvest itself and is ploughed or burned in the spring to prepare for the next sowing and harvest cycle.

Obviously, Lugh is the most obvious Deity for this holiday, as it is his festival. However, other commonly honored at this time of year include the Dagda (and other regional harvest Deities) and Tailtiu.

Within American Folkloric Witchcraft, this holiday is sacred to Goda, the White Goddess of the land.

Copyright Asteria Books 2019

Lughnasadh Ritual

MATERIALS
- Stang, candle, lighter
- Three knives (red, black, white)
- Red Cord
- Bread, lipped dish or bowl
- Red wine, cup
- Incense, holder, charcoal
- Skull
- Green corn husks (removed from corn), twine/cord
- Bread, corn, tomatoes, melons, local seasonal produce

RAISE THE STANG

LAY THE COMPASS

OPEN THE GATES (beginning in the South)

WORKING
- CORN DOLLY ~ Fashion a human-shaped figure from the corn husks, using the string to tie the head, body, arms, and legs. Place on your altar and allow to dry. Name your doll.
- FIRST FRUITS FEAST ~ Offer a blessing of the seasonal fruits, vegetables, and grains. Place some of each in the sacrificial bowl before consuming them for yourself. Give thanks to Goda for the bounty. Eat and enjoy!
- OATH TAKING ~ Consider an area of your life that needs a commitment from you. Make an oath to improve or address that area. Be specific. Write down the oath in your journal. Hold yourself accountable for it.

HOUSLE

Copyright Asteria Books 2018

Sabbat - Lughnasadh Incense

About This Blend

This Sabbat blend is specifically designed for Lughnasadhe and is suitable as a temple incense during that time.

As with all loose incense blends, this formula can be burned on a hot, self-igniting charcoal tablet (like those used for hookahs) or it can be thrown onto the glowing embers of a fire.

Incense Recipe

1/4 cup Lavender

1/4 cup Apple fiber

1 tablespoon Frankincense

1/4 cup Blackberry leaves

6 drops Amber oil

3 drops Dragon's Blood oil

Special Notes

This incense can be used for either the celebration of Lughnasadh or Lammas. Although they are attributed to the same day, Lughnasadh was a funerary-game festival honoring the Celtic God Lugh's foster-mother, while Lammas is very specifically a first-harvest festival. This incense combines both intentions and is a great way to honor the potent fruitfulness at the end of summer

Fall Equinox

The Autumn Equinox is one of the four solar holidays of the year – one of the two in which the day and night are balanced, but the emphasis this time is on moving into the darkness. This is the second of the harvest festivals, and the beginning of the hunting season.

The name Mabon (which is often associated with this Sabbat) refers to the great hunter of the Welsh Gods, Mabon, who was taken from his mother at birth. Both Mabon and Modron grieved for this separation. The boy was imprisoned for thirty years until a hunting party lead by Cyllwch came to find him. Mabon was the only hunter skilled and talented enough to claim the comb of a specific (and very wild) boar. The story told in *The Mabinogian* relates a sacred journey in which the five sacred animals of the Celts (the Lapwing, the Stag, the Eagle, the Owl and the Salmon) are consulted in finding the hero-hunter.

As a harvest holiday, this is traditionally the grain harvest. Thinking in agricultural terms, this is the time of year when the farmers begin clearing the fields in earnest. The grain harvests empty the fields, and country crafts festivals pop up in their place with candy apples, fried meats and sweets, handicrafts, etc.

Common ritual themes at this Sabbat include the Hunt for Mabon, the brewing and drinking of the mixture of Cerridwen's Cauldron, and also Harvest Homecoming (or Pagan Thanksgiving). This is a time of preparation for the winter to come, and a continued reaping of the spring's planting.

Mabon, Modron, Cerridwen, and all harvest Deities as well as all hunters are appropriate to honor during this holiday.

It is interesting to note that there is little evidence to suggest that our forebears marked this time with a feast or celebration. It would have been a busy time of bringing in the harvest and preparing for winter, and only the relative luxury of our modern lives affords us the opportunity to celebrate this second harvest and give our Year Wheel the balance of eight tidy holidays.

Copyright Asteria Books 2019

Fall Equinox Ritual

MATERIALS
- Stang, candle, lighter
- Three knives (red, black, white)
- Red Cord
- Bread, lipped dish or bowl
- Red wine, cup
- Incense, holder, charcoal
- Skull
- "Hunter" mask of your own design and creation
- Animal print-outs (placed around Compass as indicated)
- Mirror (placed at base of Stang)
- Colored pencils, crayons, pen (in a basket or bag that can move with you)

RAISE THE STANG

LAY THE COMPASS

OPEN THE GATES (beginning in the South)

WORKING

- MASKING ~ Create a mask as a representation of the Hunter. Before you don your mask, name it and bless it. Know, as you put it on, that you become one of the hunting party in search for Mabon.
- PURPOSE OF THE HUNT ~ The Harvest is underway and the Dark Days of Winter are approaching. The tribe, the clan, the Family needs the assurance of sustenance during the lean times to come. This is a time to be grateful for the bounty of the Harvest, which is still being brought in, but it is also a time to take action to prepare for the hard times, the lean seasons. The Great Hunter acts a guide to help you, as do the animals who point the way to him.
- HUNT FOR MABON ~ In your reenacted search for the Great Hunter, you will move from one quarter to the next, spending time with each of the Sacred Animals. Begin in the East, with the Lapwing. As you move to each animal, understand that you are seeking their wisdom and guidance. Read the words on the page, then spend some time in reflection, listening for any direct message that animal may have for you. Fully tread the mill between each animal.

HOUSLE

Copyright Asteria Books 2018

Sabbat - Fall Equinox Incense

About This Blend

This blend is designed to accompany your Fall Equinox celebrations and rituals.

As with all loose incense blends, this formula can be burned on a hot, self-igniting charcoal tablet (like those used for hookahs) or it can be thrown onto the glowing embers of a fire.

Incense Recipe

1/4 cup Comfrey

1/4 cup Bladderwrack

1/4 cup Vervain

1 tablespoon ground Walnut hull

1 tablespoon Dragon's Blood resin

1 tablespoon Juniper berries

9 drops Wormwood oil

Pinch of Sea Salt

A few drops Red Wine

Special Notes

Whether you celebrate Fall Equinox as Mabon, Harvest Home, or some other name, this incense is intended to help you honor this harvest holiday.

The American Folkloric Tradition honors Cerridwen as the Lady of the Cauldron at this time of year, and this incense blend also pays homage to her.

Copyright Asteria Books 2017

Spiral Castle Tradition Spirit Allies

Spirit Allies Quick Reference

January
Wolf - guardianship, ritual, loyalty
Blackthorn - blasting, guardians
Blackbird - territoriality, omens,

February
Cat - mystery, magic, independence
Willow - divination, lunar magic, healing
Owl - wisdom, magic, night, change

March
Hare - lunar magic, fertility, swiftness
Birch - new beginnings, healing, cleansing
Goose - feminine power, questing

April
Serpent - rebirth, initiation, wisdom
Ash - connections between concepts
Moth - transformation, illumination

May
Cow - fertility, prosperity, nourishment
Hawthorn - fertility, cleansing, protection
Bee - fertility, community, celebration

June
Stag - nobility, pride, grace
Oak - security, steadfastness, vigor
Robin - growth, territoriality, fire

July
Hound - loyalty, protection, guidance
Elm - elves, light, purification, wisdom
Eagle - light, renewal, intelligence, courage

August
Horse - travel, power, freedom, civilization
Apple - beauty, choices, love, inspiration
Swan - shape-shifting, love, grace, beauty

September
Boar - hunt, search, putting up a fight
Vine - prophesy, prediction and omens
Hawk - visions, guardianship, messenger

October
Salmon - wisdom, knowledge, inspiration
Hazel - wisdom, intuition, creativity
Lapwing - resourcefulness, distraction

Samhain
Toad - transformation, inner visions, death
Elder - death and rebirth, change
Crane - remembrance, past lives, mystery

November
Fox - trickster, invisibility, shape-shifting
Rowan - protection, psychic power
Raven - shape-shifting, trickster, initiation

December
Goat - surefooted, achievement, sacrifice
Holly - protection, balance, unity, defense,
Wren - resourcefulness, boldness, sacrifice

Copyright Asteria Books 2015

January Spirit Allies

Wolf *(Faol)* - guardianship, ritual, loyalty, free spirit, intuition, shadow
Blackthorn *(Straif)* - blasting magic, guardians, boundaries, no choice
Blackbird *(Dru Dhubh)* - territoriality, omens, enchantment, gateways

Wolf allows you to go beyond "normal" barriers to learn and grow. Wolf reminds us of the inner power and strength that come when we are alone, and it teaches us to know our deepest selves. Sadly, the Wolf is highly misunderstood and has often been shown as an adversary to humans in movies and stories. This animal embodies many qualities of the hound, but with a wildness not to be found in the domesticated dog. It is valued for its affinities with humans. Wolves are highly social, friendly and intelligent.

The Blackthorn is a tree of winter. The fruits of the tree, known as sloes, ripen and sweeten only after the first frost. The blackthorn has vicious thorns that can cause painful infections and forms dense thickets when left to spread on its own. Blackthorn's Gaelic name "straif" has connections with the English word strife. This, combined with its use in cudgel-making, accounts for its associations with cursing and blasting magic.

The Blackbird notoriously sings at twilight and dawn -- the liminal times -- making it a guardian of the gateways and between-places. This makes it an ideal totem of January, the time when one year ends and another begins. The blackbird, or ousel, is the first animal Culhwch asks regarding the whereabouts of Mabon, as it was the oldest animal that Culhwch knew of. Again, the blackbird stands as the gateway to the animals that remain in the quest: stag, owl, eagle, and salmon.

Copyright Asteria Books 2015

February Spirit Allies

CAT - (*Cath*) mystery, magic, secrecy, independence, sensuality
WILLOW - (*Saille*) divination, lunar magic, healing, night
OWL - (*Comhachag*) wisdom, magic, night, inner visions, change

The Cat is an animal of mystery and magic, largely because she is more active and communicative at night. She is capable of observing multiple worlds (physical and non-physical) at one time without making decision or passing judgment. She is very independent, accepting affection on her own terms and warning of caution and respect. The Cat is also a symbol of guardianship, attachment and sensuality.

The Willow has very feminine overtones. It is strongly lunar in its energy pattern. Willows are found at the edges of streams and lakes, giving them the elemental powers of both earth and water. The Willow is a water-loving tree and responds to the lunar cycle. Willow is thought to have healing properties over diseases of a damp nature. The Anglo-Saxon *welig* (willow) means pliancy, and willow is certainly flexible.

In the western tradition, Owl is inextricably associated with the quality of wisdom. This is due in part to its ancient associations with the Goddess Athena and also with its large forward-facing eyes. In folklore, the Owl is associated with death, night, and silence. The Owl is much noted for its unique feather and wing structure which allows it to fly silently. Owl is associated with betrayal of a spouse in the pursuit of being true to oneself, as we see in the stories of both Blodewudd and Lilith.

Copyright Asteria Books 2015

March Spirit Allies

Hare (*Gearr*) - lunar magic, fertility, sensitivity, swiftness, intuition
Birch (*Beithe*) - new beginnings, healing, cleansing
Goose (*Geadh*) - feminine power, springtime, questing, vigilance

Rabbits are notorious breeders, and are a symbol of the fertility of spring. The expression "mad as a March hare" comes from the rabbit's habit of fighting, courting, and mating during the early spring. The tradition of the "Easter bunny", or Eostre rabbit, reflects this springtime symbolism. Rabbits have always been associated with witchcraft. They are sacred to Hecate and have the peculiar habit of gathering in a circle, the "hare's parliament". Witches are often thought to be able to transform into a rabbit.

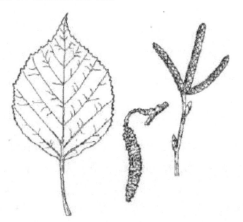

Birch Trees represent the Otherworld. This tree is the first to bud and is considered a sign that spring is just around the corner. It is a symbol of new beginnings, the start of new plans and taking significant steps in a forward direction. The Birch is considered a protective wood for women, as it is associated with safe childbirth and protection from the Underworld. It is the wood most commonly used to kindle the magical fire.

The goose is the companion of that ancient and powerful goddess, Hulda, as Mother Goose. The goose is a fierce defender of its family and territory, and many ancient gates and warrior's graves have been adorned with the motif of the goose. We often speak of "a wild goose chase" as geese are notoriously difficult to capture or kill. The goose is a symbol of early springtime, as it denotes both snow and returning light. The goose who lays the golden egg is laying the growing sun of spring.

Copyright Asteria Books 2015

April Spirit Allies

SERPENT (*Nathair*) - resurrection, rebirth, initiation, wisdom, transformation
ASH (*Nuin*) - connections of past to present, spirit to earth, high and low
MOTH (*Lèomann*) - transformation, seeking illumination, initiation

The Snake has a very paradoxical and mythical reputation. It is essentially associated with transformation, healing, and life energy. The Snake can glide through crevices into the Underworld. It represents our ability to die and be reborn, thereby symbolizing rebirth, resurrection, initiation and wisdom. The Snake can journey through life gracefully and magically, shedding old life easily when time comes. The snake is also associated with sexual energy, allowing us to be born.

Ash is the traditional Celtic and Norse World Tree. Odin hung from the great Ash tree Yggdrasil and endured an initiatory that revealed the runes. Ygddrasil's branches were in the heavens, roots were in Hell, and Earth was around its center. The Ash symbolizes connections - past & present, spiritual & earthly, lowest & highest, self & cosmos. It also represents divination, healing, inner and initiation.

The moth and the butterfly represent transformation, due to their metamorphosis from caterpillar to winged creature. The word for moth in old Lancashire dialect means "soul" (just as psyche means both "soul" and "butterfly" in Greek). The spirit of a witch is sometimes said to travel forth from the body in the form of a moth or butterfly. Just as the moth seeks the flame, so do we seek enlightenment and illumination.

Copyright Asteria Books 2015

May Spirit Allies

Cow (*Tarbh/Bò*) - fertility, prosperity, protection, nourishment
Hawthorn (*Huathe*) - fertility, cleansing, protection, joy
Bee (*Beach*) - fertility, community, sweetness, celebration, organization

The Bull (*Tarbh*) is associated with health, potency, beneficence, fertility, abundance, prosperity, and power. The number of cattle owned were an indicator of wealth. The Cow (*Bo*) represents nourishment, motherhood and the Goddess. In Celtic lands, Cows have long been considered sacred. In Britain there were sacred herds of white cattle. Ireland was gifted with cattle when three Cows emerged from the sea - one red, one white, and one black.

Hawthorns are often used in hedges (some linguistic studies shows that its name may actually mean "hedge thorn"). The Hawthorn has very sharp thorns that are sometimes used for ritual tattoos. Its white flowers are often woven into garlands for doors and Maypoles at Beltane. Indeed, long ago Beltane was reckoned by the first flowering of the Hawthorn tree. Its wood is the traditional material for the Maypole itself.

No animal is a better example of the power of community than the bee. Each bee in a hive has a specific function which she will perform even if it means giving her life for the hive. Because they are the agent that carries the reproductive pollen from one plant to fertilize another, bees are strongly associated with fertility and abundance. Honey was anciently the only source for a sweetener. Thus, the bee has come to symbolize the sweetness of life.

Copyright Asteria Books 2015

June Spirit Allies

Stag (*Damh*) - nobility, culling the herd, call to adventure, pride, grace
Oak (*Duir*) - security, steadfastness, primeval vigor, doorway, strength
Robin (*Spideog*) - growth, territoriality, fire

The Stag is the male aspect of the deer. As such, some discussion of the qualities of deer in general is helpful to understand Stag. Deer are associated with gentleness, innocence and a luring to new adventure. Many legends exist in which deer lure hunters and/or kings into the forest for adventures. The Stag is a symbol of pride and independence. He is an example of grace, majesty, integrity, poise and dignity. The Stag is a symbol of fertility and rampant sexuality, which is also related to the Lord of the Hunt and the Horned Gods.

Ancient Celts observed the oak's massive growth and impressive expanse. They took this as a clear sign that the oak was to be honored for its endurance, and noble presence. Wearing oak leaves was a sign of special status among many ancient European peoples. There are accounts that trace the name "druid" to *duir*, the Celtic term for the oak. The oak is a tree of protection and strength.

Robins are very territorial, and their red breasts signal other males to leave their space. Even their bright and cheery song is a used as a method of battling with other males for dominance over territory. The Robin's bright blue egg is distinctive in color. Both male and female Robins share in the feeding of the young. The Norse associated the bird with Thor and considered it to be a creature of the storm.

Copyright Asteria Books 2015

July Spirit Allies

Hound (*Cu*) - loyalty, protection, guidance
Elm (*Lemh*) - elves, light, purification, wisdom
Eagle (*Iolair*) - light, renewal, loyalty, intelligence, courage

The Dog is animal of faithfulness, protection, guidance, loyalty and warning. It is an excellent companion and work-mate. Dogs have been used for herding, hunting, and sporting for thousands of years. In India, Dog is a symbol of all caste systems, indicating the small becoming great. In Greece, Dog is seen as a companion and a guardian to the places of the dead. The term Cu (Dog) was given to many chiefs, warriors, heroes and champions in Celtic lore.

Elm's folk name is "Elven" (because of its long-standing association with elves, both the Seelie and Unseelie Courts of the Fey). It attracts love when carried and protects against lightning strikes. Associated with death, the grave and rebirth in legend and myth, Elm was also used for coffin wood later in English tradition, linking it to the death mythos and to the elven lore that connects the elves with burial mounds.

In America, the two primary species of Eagle are the Golden Eagle and the Bald Eagle. It is a symbol of freedom for Americans, and it was likewise a royal and potent bird among Romans, Egyptian pharaohs, Greek Thebans, and the Celts of Ireland and Scotland. The Eagle has a long association with sky Gods, such as Zeus and Ashur, which strengthens the bird's connections to the sun, storms, lightning and fire. Eagle is often associated with war and bravery, as well.

Copyright Asteria Books 2015

August Spirit Allies

Horse *(Each)* - travel, power, freedom, civilization
Apple *(Quert)* - beauty, choices, love, inspiration
Swan *(Eala)* - shape-shifting, love, grace, beauty

The Horse is associated with the female Divine, the land, and travel both on the inner and outer planes. It is connected to the Sun and is a symbol of sexual desires. Furthermore, it is associated with power and freedom, divination, the spread of civilization, birth. Wind and sea foam often signify the power of the Horse. The Horse is often a phantom creature or provoker of nightmares, who get their name from her, as Mare is an Irish Goddess. Sovereignty is another aspect of the Horse.

Apple represents the choice between similar and equally attractive things. It is one of the "Seven Chieftain Trees" of the Celts. It's fruit and bark are used in tanning. It is related to the rose family, along with Hawthorn, and so it develops thorns from spurs on its branches. The Apple is associated with love spells, likely due to its associations with Aphrodite. Avalon, a sacred Celtic land, is named the "Isle of Apples."

The Swan is often depicted with a silver or gold chain around the neck in Celtic legends -- possibly a carry-over from the Aphrodite tradition of the golden sash. The Swan is very prominent in love stories in Celtic lands, including the tale of Oenghus and Yewberry (who is a Swan Maiden). Swan is associated with Otherworldly travel and migration of the Soul. This bird's skin and feathers were used to make the bard's ceremonial cloak. Swans are also intimately linked with shape-shifting.

Copyright Asteria Books 2015

September Spirit Allies

SWINE (*Torc/Muc*) - hunt, search, nourishment, putting up a fight
VINE (*Muin*) - prophesy, prediction and omens
CHICKEN (*Cearc*) - fertility, battle, sexuality, watchfulness

The Boar (*Torc*) is as symbol of the Warrior spirit, leadership, and direction. It is wild and powerful. There are ritual boar paths in Wales, Cornwall, Ireland and Scotland. These paths exist in the Inner Realms, too. The Boar's tusks and comb are significant and are frequently mentioned in lore. The Sow (*Muc*) is a symbol of nourishment, as swine are a particularly potent food source. Just as the sow gives life as food, so does she take life away. Any pig farmer can attest to the practice of sows eating their own piglets after birth.

While not actually a "tree," the Vine stands firmly amongst the grove of totemic trees. The fermented juice of the grape is wine, which appears in almost every Indo-European mythos at some point. The vine stands for the release of prophecy, predictions and omens. Grapevines are used to make baskets, wreaths and magical tools.

Fowl have been domesticated for over 8000 years as a provider of meat and eggs. Chickens are diurnal, being most active in the day. In fact, they are so associated with the coming of the day that the crowing of a rooster is seen as synonymous with daybreak. Chickens are highly social and quite polygamous. Pair bonding is unheard of. Yet despite this abundant promiscuity, there is tremendous territoriality and rivalry between two roosters as to who gets to mate with whom.

Copyright Asteria Books 2015

October Spirit Allies

SALMON (*Bradan*) - oldest animal; wisdom, knowledge, inspiration
HAZEL (*Coll*) - wisdom, intuition, creativity, divination, the source
LAPWING (*Curracag*) - resourcefulness, distraction, wisdom, divination

The Salmon is the "Oldest Animal" in Welsh mythology and is critical in the search for Mabon. Salmon is a symbol of wisdom, inspiration and rejuvenation. The Salmon will return to place of its own birth to mate (often with great difficulty) and is, therefore, a reminder that we need to journey back to our own beginnings to find wisdom. It swims in the well of wisdom (Connla's Well) at the source of all life, a sacred pool that has 9 Hazel trees growing around it.

Hazel is one of the "Seven Chieftain Trees" of the Celts, and the unnecessary felling of Hazel trees brought the death penalty in Ireland. Hazel's magical associations include fertility, wisdom, marriage, divination, healing, protection, intuition, dowsing wands, individuality, finding the hidden, luck and wishes. The Hazel is considered to be the Tree of knowledge for the Celts. Its nuts are ultimate receptacles of wisdom.

The Lapwing guards the Mysteries of the Wise by "disguising the Truth." She does this by feigning injury to make herself appear helpless to predators who have come to close to her nest. Because Lapwing's nest rests on the ground in the spring, hares have been known to sit in them, looking like they are hatching eggs (which is where the combined association of bunnies and eggs come from for spring fertility celebrations).

Copyright Astoria Books 2015

Samhain Spirit Allies

Toad (*Buaf*) - transformation, inner visions, death and rebirth, hidden power and beauty
Elder (*Ruis*) - death and rebirth, change and transition
Crane (*Corr*) - longevity, remembrance, past lives, secret knowledge, patience

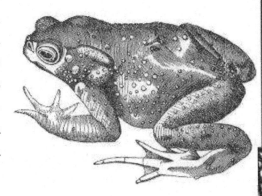

The Toad is a powerful symbol of transformation, as it grows from tadpole to Toad. It has associations with fertility, magic, fairies, and Witchcraft. Toads secrete a thick white poison through their skin. This "Toad's Milk" or *bufotenine* is sometimes hallucinogenic, and is said to be an ingredient in some ancient flying ointments. Witches' marks are sometimes referred to as a "Toad's foot," and a birthmark shaped like a Toad is a sure sign of witch blood.

The Elder tree is associated with death and rebirth. The 13th month is a time of endings and balances, and the Elder is a tree of balance. This is a tree of the Faery. If one cuts down this tree without seeking the will of the Tree Spirits and of the Faery, a blight or curse will fall on that person. Her wood is never burned as it is considered bad luck to do so. Elder berries are a potent and delicious medicinal and are used to make wine.

Crane represents longevity and creation through focus. In Celtic lore, Cranes are often associated with the Underworld and are thought to be heralds of war and death. They are also associated with perseverance due to the fact that they will stand for hours looking into the water and waiting for the right time to strike at fish. The Crane symbolizes "secret knowledge" which is represented by the Ogham script of the Celts, which is said to be based on the shapes of the Crane's legs as they fly.

Copyright Asteria Books 2015

November Spirit Allies

Fox - (*Sionnach*) trickster, invisibility, shape-shifting, diplomacy, wildness

Rowan - (*Luis*) protection against enchantment, psychic power, self-control

Raven - (*Bran*) underworld messenger, shape-shifting, trickster, initiation, protection

Fox is credited with being a "cunning one" who is "strong in council." In nature, the Fox is stealthy and clever. He knows when to stay hidden and when to come out into the open. Fox can teach you the discernment to know when to speak your mind and when to keep silent. Similarly, Fox teaches invisibility. Fox is very intelligent, diplomatic, and charming. These qualities can be seen as sly and deceitful, though, when used dishonestly. Fox is often regarded as a trickster, for this reason. He is "quick on his feet" and can teach you to make quick decisions and put them into action right away.

The Rowan is sometimes referred to as the "Tree of Life" or the "Lady of the Mountain" and is thought to protect against enchantment. The wood of the Rowan was often used for rune staves (sticks which are engraved with the Ogham or runs and used as a divinatory tool) and as a divining rod for metal. The Rowan berry has a pentagram in its center and is red in color.

Raven is a bird of magic and mysticism, shapeshifting, creation, birth and death, healing, initiation, protection and prophecy. Raven is great at vocalizations and can even be taught to speak. Raven can use tools, is not intimidated by others, is fast and wary, and does not make easy prey for other animals. Raven is strongly associated with Odin, Bran the Blessed, and the Morrigan. In all of these cases, Raven is linked to messages, battle, and death.

Copyright Asteria Books 2015

December Spirit Allies

Goat (*Gabhar*) - surefooted, achievement, sensuality, sacrifice
Holly (*Tinne*) - protection, balance, unity, defense, battle
Wren (*Drui-En*) - resourcefulness, boldness, sacrifice

The Goat's horns indicate an ability to perceive future and are also associated with weapons and defense. Its thick coat enables it to survive hostile conditions. The Goat was depicted in the zodiac through Capricorn - a time of year for culminating new moves or initiating them. Originally denoting the Goat that was slaughtered, "Yule Goat" now typically refers to a goat-figure made of straw. It is also associated with the custom of wassailing, sometimes referred to as "going Yule Goat" in Scandinavia.

The Holly is the strongest protective herb, offering protection against evil spirits, poisons, short-tempered or angry elementals, thunder and lighting, and uninvited spirits. As an evergreen, it represents immortality and is said to bring luck and prosperity. Holly is also associated with dream magic, clear wisdom and courage. Its flower's petals form an equal-armed "cross" which resembles a star. The berries are poisonous to all but birds.

The Wren was said to be crowned the king of the birds, after riding an eagle to the highest point in the sky, above all other birds, and then soaring above even the eagle! The Wren is noted for its cunning for this stunt, and for the trick of building many false nests to lead away hunters. Breton Druids claimed that it was the wren who first brought down fire from heaven, forever singeing its tail feathers, causing the wren to have its distinctive blunt tail.

Copyright Asteria Books 2015

Sun, Moon, and Star Lore

Wheel of the Year

THE WITCH'S COMPASS AND THE YEAR WHEEL

The Year Wheel doesn't have be a simple calendar of the holy days of the Witch's year. While many modern Craft traditions share the "eight spokes on the wheel" that is the typical Neopagan festival calendar, some Craft traditions (like the American Folkloric Tradition) recognize that the Year Wheel is in fact a reflection of the entire macrocosm of the Craft — encompassing within its frame both a map of the Mill Grounds and several Craft Mysteries.

Copyright Asteria Books 2019

Planetary Influences

☉ **Solar Influences:** General success and recognition; spiritual illumination; decisiveness, vitality; activities requiring courage or a mood of self-certainty - making big decisions, scheduling meetings for reaching decisions, giving speeches, launching new projects; seeking favors from father, husband, boss, authorities.

☽ **Lunar Influences:** Health; home (buying home, moving); journeys / vacationing (time of leaving home or takeoff); activities remote in time or space - meditation, making reservations, finding lost objects or people; planting food crops; hiring employees; seeking favors from mother, wife, employees.

♂ **Mars Influences:** Courage, adventure; enforcing your will; success with drastic action (lawsuits, conflicts, going to war, surgery); sports, exercises; risk-taking; making complaints; firing employees; seeking favors of husband or boyfriend.

☿ **Mercury Influences:** Success in studies / communications; children; making a good impression; routine activities and activities needing clear communications; teaching / learning; important business letters / phone calls; meetings to develop or communicate ideas; buying / selling; routine shopping, errands, travel; job applications / interviews; seeking favors from neighbors, co-workers.

♃ **Jupiter Influences:** Wisdom, optimism; money (borrowing / lending / investing / earning / winning); activities necessitating enthusiasm; buying lottery tickets; seeking advice / consultation; settling disputes; seeking favors from grandparents, aunts and uncles, advisers (doctors, lawyers, accountants, astrologers).

♀ **Venus Influences:** Love; friendship; artistic and social success; enjoyable, sociable and aesthetic activities such as parties, social gatherings, recitals / exhibitions, weddings, visits, dating and seeking romance; planting ornamentals; buying gifts, clothing, luxuries; beauty treatments; seeking favors from women.

♄ **Saturn Influences:** Discipline and patience; giving up bad habits; overcoming obstacles; success with difficult tasks or difficult people; projects of long duration - breaking ground, laying foundations; planting perennials; treating chronic illness; making repairs; seeking favors from older people (not relatives) or difficult people.

For example, a person should ask a woman for a favor while Venus is influencing the situation (but ask a man for a favor during a Mars influence); one should ask one's boss for a favor during a solar influence; money should be invested during a Jupiter influence; medical treatments should commence under a lunar influence (except surgery should commence under a Mars influence); and so on. Each zodiac sign and day of the week is ruled by a planet which lends its influence.

Copyright Asteria Publishing 2019

Planetary Correspondences

The seven classical planets are the basis of most systems of magical correspondence, and they can form a very important part of a Witch's understanding of sympathetic magickal operations. Of particular use in designing your spell or ritual may be your consideration of the planetary influence in the timing of your working. Each of the days of the week and signs of the zodiac are ruled by a planet. Even the 24 hours in each day are divided between these planets, if you want to be precise and powerful in your timing. (You'll have to use an ephemeris or an app to help determine planetary hours.)

☉ SUN: Sunday; Leo

☽ MOON: Monday & Cancer

♂ MARS: Tuesday; Aries & Scorpio

☿ MERCURY: Wednesday; Gemini & Virgo

♃ JUPITER: Thursday; Sagittarius & Pisces

♀ VENUS: Friday; Taurus & Libra

♄ SATURN: Saturday; Capricorn & Aquarius

Copyright Asteria Publishing 2019

Lunar Magic

More than any other celestial body or natural force, the Moon and its magick have been linked to the Witch and her Craft across cultures and millennia. Its monthly cycles were observably connected to the tidal movements of the world's waters and menstrual flows, linking women inherently with the Moon's mysterious influence.

Ancient Greek and Roman Witches were especially noted for their ability to "draw down the Moon," a ritual procedure which Horace notes in reference to the Witch Canidia. She says "… *I, who can move waxen images and draw down the moon from the sky by my spells, who can raise the vaporous dead, and mix a draught of love …*"

Werewolves famously shape-shift during the full moon, and the cult of the werewolf has ties to the ancient witch-cult. However, Witches are famously known to "fly out" in numerous animal shapes, not just that of wolves -- including the form of hares, goats, cats, toads. The full moon is an excellent time to use the moon's power to enhance shamanic shape-shifting work.

In Charles Leland's <u>Aradia, The Gospel of the Witches</u>, Aradia, the holy daughter of Diana, left these instructions to her followers in a speech that later became the basis of the Charge of the Goddess: "*Whenever you have need of anything, once in the month when the Moon is full, then shall you come together at some deserted place, or where there are woods, and give worship to She who is Queen of all Witches. Come all together inside a circle, and secrets that are as yet unknown shall be revealed.*"

The word "esbat" is a derivation from the Old French term of the same spelling meaning amusement or diversion. It is not necessarily a Full Moon celebration or magical working, as Janet and Stewart Farrar and Doreen Valiente have noted in their own works. It is simply NOT a Sabbat. Esbats are times when Witches gather or set aside personal time to work with the Moon's energy. The Full Moons of the year are generally considered the most important and potent magickal points, and Traditional Witches tend to honor and observe the Full Moons more ardently than any other cyclical celebrations.

Copyright Asteria Publishing 2019

Drawing Down the Moon

Ancient Greek and Roman Witches were said to perform a ritual to draw down the moon -- a ritual tradition that survives into current times. It is depicted on a Greek vase from the second century B.C.E., illustrated below. Of this ritual, Thessalian Witches were reputed to have said, *"If I command the moon, it will come down; and if I wish to withhold the day, night will linger over my head; and again, if I wish to embark on the sea, I need no ship, and if I wish to fly through the air, I am free from my weight."*

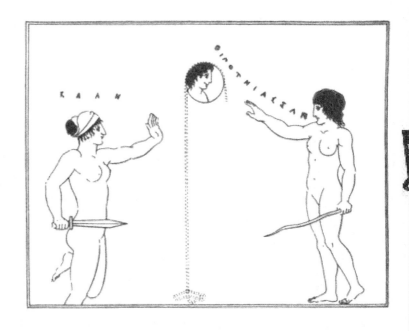

This ritual produces a trance-like state for the Witch, who is filled with lunar energy. Traditionally, this has been a High Priestess who has been aided in achieving the lunar trance by the coven's High Priest. Once she is imbued with the divine lunar energy, she speaks the words of the Charge of the Goddess. However, this ritual can be performed by a person of any gender, with or without assistance.

After conducting your ritual preparations, including the preparation of your sacred space, hold your arms aloft to the Moon, drinking in its beams. Feel it filling your mind, body, and spirit as you chant:

I invoke thee and call upon thee, Mighty Mother of us all, bringer of all fruitfulness by seed and root, by bud and stem, by leaf and flower and fruit,
By life and love do I invoke thee to descend upon the body of this, thy servant and priest(ess).

Spend time in reflection or performing magic while in this invoked state. When finished, administer unto yourself the fivefold blessing by anointing your body with oil:

Blessed be my feet, that have brought me in these ways.
Blessed be my knees, that shall kneel at the sacred altar.
Blessed be my sex, without which we would not be.
Blessed be my heart, formed in beauty.
Blessed be my lips, that shall utter the Sacred Names.

Copyright Asteria Publishing 2019

Moon Phases

The Full Moon rises at sunset and sets at sunrise. Astrologically, the sun and moon are in opposition (i.e., opposite each other in the sky and in opposite signs of the zodiac). She is visible all night long, from moonrise to moonset. Etheric energy peaks during Full Moons, and they are considered to be most favorable for all magic. The moon will remain full for two or three days. The full moon has a special connection to shapeshifting magic and invocation. Complete your work prior to the fading of the moon's fullness for best effect. The 13th Moon, or "Blue" Moon can occur at any time during the year. A Moon is called Blue only when it is the second full Moon to take place that month (moon-th). Blue Moons are considered to be stronger than regular Full Moons.

The waning period of the Moon's cycle is the time after the Full Moon when the light lessens as she progresses toward her Dark phase. It is the best time to do work that likewise focuses on ideas of lessening, removing, decreasing, minimizing, etc. It is also a good time to seek answers and inner wisdom, as outside distractions are decreased. During the waning moon, do spells to banish evil influences, lessen or remove obstacles and illness, neutralize enemies, scry, divine, and to remove harm. These influences become stronger as the moon darkens. The half-face of the last quarter moon is suited to work of balance and justice, but in a darker and more final sense than would be performed during the first quarter. The days of the Balsamic Moon (or Waning Crescent, or even Hekate's Sickle) are well-suited to harvesting, trance-work, and deep intuition.

The Dark Moon (also called the "New Moon") is the time between the last sliver of the Balsamic Moon (or Waning Crescent) and the first sliver of the Waxing Crescent. Astronomically, it is the time when the Moon is positioned between the Earth and the Sun, making her essentially backlit and ostensibly invisible. She rises and sets at roughly the same times as the sun, as well, leaving the night sky without any lunar influence. The Dark Moon is the most auspicious time for divination, banishing, and neutralizing spells. It is the peak of darkness, the time for blasting and battle magic. The second Dark Moon in a month is known as a Black Moon and is considered stronger than a regular Dark Moon.

The waxing period of the Moon's cycle is the time after the Dark Moon when the light increases as she progresses toward her Full phase. The days of and around the waxing crescent moon are the most powerful time to work spells for new growth and beginnings, which should manifest at the Full Moon. This moon is the silvery bow of Artemis and offers a fresh start to all workings. The waxing moon, in general, is the best time to do spells for growth, beginning new projects, initiation, and enhancement. It is the time to focus on increase, gain, forward movement, and all types of abundance. The clean half-face of the first quarter moon is also well-suited to work of balance and justice, especially with a focus on hope and positive restoration. The days of and around the gibbous moon are the most powerful time for spells of fruition and completion.

Copyright Asteria Books 2019

13 Moons of the Year

MONTH—MOON NAME—LUNAR POWERS

January—Wolf Moon—*Powers of Blasting and Binding*

February—Ice Moon—*Powers of Stillness and Warning*

March—Wind Moon—*Powers of Quickening and Inspiration*

April—Budding Moon—*Powers of New Growth and Vitality*

May—Mother's Moon—*Powers of Joy and Celebration*

June—Mead Moon—*Powers of Fertility and Passion*

July—Herb Moon—*Powers of Healing and Strength*

August—Grain Moon—*Powers of Abundance and Love*

September—Wine Moon—*Powers of Ecstasy and Dreaming*

October—Blood Moon—*Powers of Sacrifice and Necromancy*

November—Mourning Moon—*Powers of Endings and Offerings*

December—Cold Moon—*Powers of the Wild Hunt and the Fool*

2nd Full Moon in a Month—Blue Moon—*Powers of Blasting and Binding*

Copyright Asteria Books 2018

Cosmology and Magical Theory

Ethical Witchcraft

The Ardanes (Witch Laws) and the Wiccan Rede are relative newcomers to the practice of the Craft of the Wise. They were both devised in the middle of the last century to make Witchcraft more palatable and acceptable to our largely Abrahamic society. The Craft (in its truest sense) does not offer a moral guidepost. It is a system of magic, a way of reaching out to the Unseen World and being more closely a part of it. The Black Goddess, White Goddess, Tubal Qayin – do not look to them for your moral compass, for they are Nature's Compass, Magic's Compass. They are Powers, neither "male-" nor "bene-" (bad, good).

You are responsible and accountable to yourself, your Clan, your Cuveen, your community, your country, and your world. How you keep yourself on your path is up to you.

That being said, as a piece of Craft Lore (and even as a starting place in thinking about your own ethics), it is interesting to look at the Ardanes and the Rede. Bear in mind that these pieces are modern constructs with occasional bits of arcana thrown into the mix. Some of the advice contained within them is worth a look. Other pieces seem very out of keeping with the Craft as we know it.

The Ardanes or Ordains first appeared in Craft documentation in 1957, when Gerald Gardner presented them to his coven after a disagreement about his own interactions with the media while insisting on secrecy within the coven. No known record of them in any older documentation exists prior to that date. These Laws have had several iterations, and they vary amongst covens/Traditions who hold to them. Some are anachronistic, misogynistic, or oddly Christo-centric.

Many, if not most, Witchcraft traditions use the Wiccan Rede as the foundation of their code of ethics. The first published form of the Wiccan Rede is a couplet that appeared in 1964 by Doreen Valiente: "Eight words the Wiccan Rede fulfill, An it harm none, Do what ye will." Rede is a Middle English word meaning "advice or council," while, in this case, an is an archaic conjunction meaning "if." Other versions, have been written since then, but this is the basic tenant of Wiccan ethics.

Ultimately, each Witch must pursue a line of *independent* thought regarding ethics and a Code. In other words: know what YOU believe to be ethical behavior and hold to it. Remember that ethics and morals are not really about being held accountable to a power higher than yourself. If you believe an action is wrong, and you proceed in doing it, you will pay a price for doing it.

Copyright Asteria Books 2015

Laws of Magic

The Laws of Magic are not rules that your Maid, Magister, or another Witch will hold you accountable for. In simple truth, they are more like scientific principles that apply to the practice of magic. Different authors have suggested some different groupings of "laws" based on the way they noticed magic working. However, since magic works based on the (sometimes subconscious) restrictions imposed upon it by the operator, you will need to explore your own relationship with magic to fully understand how magic works for you.

The following "Laws of Magic" are interpretations of guidelines attributed to Isaac Bonewits and Hermes Trismegistos, two of history's most notable magicians, indeed. (These are not at exhausted list. You can find more "laws" to explore.)

Law of Knowledge - The more you know about a given person, object or situation the more effective and complete your magic will be concerning that object, person, or situation. Research and study are very important skills within the Craft. Shun ignorance, and never go into a spell blindly.

Law of Cause and Effect - If exactly the same actions are done under exactly the same conditions, the same effects will be produced, usually. Similar strings of events usually produce similar outcomes. We say "usually" because you can't completely control the conditions. Chaos will find her way in.

Law of Contagion - Objects or beings that are in physical or psychic contact with each other continue to react after separation.

Law of Positive Attraction - Like attracts like. To create a particular reality you must put out energy of a similar sort.

Law of Names - If you know the complete and true name of a person, object, or process you can have control over it.

Law of Personification - Any energy can be considered to be alive and to have a personality and be dealt with accordingly.

Laws of Invocation and Evocation - You can communicate with entities from either inside or outside yourself.

Law of Identification - It is possible, through extreme association between oneself and another being, to be able to share power and knowledge. This often begins with a process of imitation, then identification, and

Copyright Asteria Books 2019

ultimately possession until the knowledge and power is shared.

Law of Personal Universes - Every sentient being is the center of his or her own universe. You are the center of your world. You experience your own reality, and it may or may not be exactly the same as the reality anyone else has. In fact, it can't be. We've all agreed to certain terms and arrangements, which we call "consensus reality." On some level, though, your universe is different than all others, and you are the one ultimately in control of your world.

Law of Pragmatism - If you believe it, if it works for you, no matter on what level of reality it works, then it is true and real.

Law of True Falsehoods (Law of Paradox) - It is possible to be wrong and still be correct.

Law of Unity - Everything is connected. Ultimately, each object that you think of as solid is nothing more than a collection of atoms - energy. Trees, buildings, gasses, people, tectonic plates, and paper plates - we're all energy, and we're all connected to each other. Given all the other laws, this means that we have an effect, both magical and mundane, on absolutely everything.

Law of Mentalism - The Classical Greeks referred to the Supreme Being as the All. Sometimes the All was also called the "logos," which means "word," but it also means everything having to do with a person's words or speech, including their thoughts and reasoning. The Law of Mentalism reminds us that the All is mind itself, and the All encompasses everything in the universe. Magic is an act of thinking.

Law of Correspondence - All things are related. The physical, spiritual, and mental realms are connected, with one flowing out the other. The separations that we perceive between them are illusions.

Law of Vibration - Everything vibrates. Nothing rests. Modern science has confirmed that everything vibrates, just at different frequencies. Our eyes perceive light frequencies at different wavelengths as various colors in the spectrum. The same principal applies to auditory perception. New breakthroughs and understandings are happening all the time in the realm of quantum physics to confirm what magicians and Witches have practiced for millennia.

Law of Polarity - Everything has its opposite. According to Hermetics, opposites are actually the same in their core nature, but they differ in their degree or rank. As examples, you can think about heat and cold, peace and war, love and hate.

Law of Rhythm - There is a constant flow of energy. The tide always turns. The cycle always continues. When the pendulum swings to the right, it will eventually swing equally to the left. This is the reason why there is always some price to be paid for magic.

Copyright Asteria Books 2019

The Three Realms

In many cultures where shamanism is practiced spiritual movement takes place in three planes, worlds, or realms. The three realms are the world above (the sky, heaven, land of the gods), the world around (the land, middle-earth, place of the elemental gates, land of the nature spirits), and the world below (the sea, the underworld, land of the dead). In Celtic lore these realms are named *Ceugent* (ky-jent), *Gwyned*, and *Abred*.

Sky, land, and sea,
Three-in-one, one-in-three.
-Celtic prayer

Shamans use certain techniques of trance to access these realms. In many cultures a tree or pole is visualized as standing at the center of all things, reaching up into the sky and down into the underworld. Shamans use this pole to climb or descend to other realms. In our tradition we use the image of the Spiral Castle, Caer Sidhe, spinning around to open its gate to the different points of the wheel of the year. Its spire reaches up to the stars, and its caverns are home to the great forge and the cauldron. The pole is symbolized literally in our circles by the raising of the stang. By its virtue we can "ride" the stang to any place in the realms, though we may also use our own personal riding-pole, or gandreigh, to do so.

First Realm	Second Realm	Third Realm
Ceugent	Gwyned	Abred
Upperworld, Upper Realm, Realm of Sky, Wind	Earth world, Center world, Realm of Land, Middle Earth	Underworld, Realm of the Sea
Otherworld	Consensus reality	Underworld
Birth, beginnings	Middles	Death, endings
The mind	Living bones and flesh	Emotion
Breath	Physicality	Inner self
Metacognition	Consciousness	Subliminal, Unconscious, Subconcious
Perspective	Limits and limitations	Deep mystery
Movement, setting in motion (beginning)	Progress, action, doing	Rest
Struggle and enlightenment	Going through something	Truth beyond substance or thought
Preservation: the undying realm, absence of decay	Day-to-day struggles and concerns	Healing the soul
Expansion/expansiveness	Manipulation of perception/glamory	Empathy
First arm of the Triskle	Second arm of the Triskle	Third arm of the Triskle
Spire of the Spiral Castle	Place of the Doorway of the Spiral Castle	Initiation chamber beneath the the Castle
Entry through flight or climbing	No entry needed (already in this realm)	Entry through caves, wells, barrows, etc.
Black Knife/Athame	White Knife/Kerfane	Red Knife/Shelg

The Airts

The Airts of Traditional Craft correspond to different elemental quarters than those found in Wiccan and Ceremonial traditions. The Airts are based on old "Celtic" lore.

The North - Air
Values: Intellect, Thoughts, Inspiration, Communication, Flight, Divination
Colors: White, sky blue, black, silver
Symbols: Circle, bird, bell, flute, chimes, clouds, Sylphs, the Angel
Tools: Keek stone, flail, knives
Weapons: Staff/Spear
Musical Instruments: Reed instruments
Times: Imbolc, Midnight, Winter, Old Age
Places: Sky, mountaintop, treetop, bluffs, summit of a mound
Zodiac: Aquarius, Gemini, Libra
Sense: Scent
Power: To Know
Process: Chanting, Visualization, Reading, Speaking, Praying, Singing, Fragrance, Charms

The East - Fire
Values: Passion, Power, Will, Energy, Courage, Strength, Light
Colors: Red, orange, amber
Symbols: Triangle, lightning, flame, candle, Salamanders, the Lion
Tools: The lamp, wand, staff
Weapons: Sword
Musical Instruments: String Instruments
Times: Beltane, Dawn, Spring, Youth
Places: Volcanoes, ovens, hearths, bonfires, deserts
Zodiac: Aries, Leo, Sagittarius
Sense: Sight
Power: To Will
Process: Dancing, Burning, Candle-magic, Solar magic, Mirrors

The South - Earth
Values: Growth, Experience, Authority, Money, Physicality, Security, Nourishment
Colors: Black, brown, russet, green
Symbols: Square, cornucopia, scythe, salt, stone, Gnomes, the Bull
Tools: The casting bowl, pentacles, horns
Weapons: Shield
Musical Instruments: Drums
Times: Lammas, Noon, Summer, Coming of Age
Places: Caves, forests, fields, gardens, canyons
Zodiac: Capricorn, Taurus, Virgo
Sense: Touch
Power: To Keep Silent
Process: Burying, Grounding, Binding, Eating, Totemic magic, Wortcunning, Clay figures, Dirts

The West - Water
Values: Emotions, Intuition, Cleansing, Mystery, Sacrifice
Colors: Grey, turquoise, blue, indigo
Symbols: Crescent, shell, boat, anchor, cup, Undines, the Eagle
Tools: The chalice or quaiche, cauldron
Weapons: Helm
Musical Instruments: Chimes
Times: Samhain, Twilight, Autumn, Adulthood
Places: Oceans, rivers, lakes, waterfalls, wells, beaches, baths
Zodiac: Cancer, Scorpio, Pisces
Sense: Taste
Power: To Dare
Process: Bathing, Healing, Drinking, Baptism, Charged Waters, Blood magic

Copyright Asteria Publishing 2012

Elemental Air

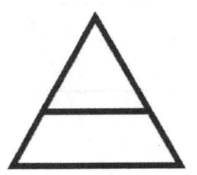

Within Traditional Craft, the element of Air is associated with the North, the sky above one's head; however, in Ceremonial Magick and Wicca, the East is the Quarter associated with this element.

The power of Air is "To Know," and it is associated with the intellect, thoughts, inspiration, communication, darkness, flight, and divination. It is also linked to movement, freshness, the initiation of change, and the sense of smell. The processes best used to tap into Elemental Air include, chanting, singing, speaking, reading, writing, praying, casting a charm, and visualization. You can also play wind instruments, ring a bell or chime, burn incense, or apply a perfume.

Air's tools and symbols include the keek stone (seeing stone), flails, wands, the circle, birds, bells, flutes, reed instruments, chimes, and clouds. The colors are white, sky blue, black, silver, and yellow.

The weapon of Air is a staff. On a smaller scale, the staff is the wand. Tipped with a point, it is either the spear or the arrow, depending on size.

The time of day associated with Air is midnight, the dark time. Likewise, the Sabbat Imbolc, which comes in the bleakest part of the Winter, as well as Old Age, are linked to the knowledge, reflection, and wisdom of Air. Zodiacally, Libra, Gemini, and Aquarius are considered "Air signs."

Places of air include the sky, mountaintop, treetop, bluffs, and the summit of a mound.

Copyright Asteria Books 2017

Elemental Earth

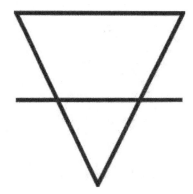

Within Traditional Craft, the element of Earth is associated with the South, the ground below one's feet; however, in Ceremonial Magick and Wicca, the North is the Quarter associated with this element.

The power of Earth is "To Keep Silent," and it is associated with growth, experience, authority, money, physicality, security, and nourishment. It is also linked to fertility, abundance, and the sense of touch. The processes best used to tap into Elemental Earth include burying, grounding, binding, eating, totemic magic, and wortcunning or herbalism. You can also play drums or touch coarse, firm, or dense textures.

Earth's tools and symbols include the casting bowl, pentacles, horns, the square, cornucopias, scythes, salt, stone, clay figures, and dirts. Gnomes the Bull are considered the creatures of Earth. The colors are black, brown, russet, green.

The weapon of Earth is a shield. On a smaller scale, the shield is a plate or paten, and it can be viewed as the altar itself.

The time of day associated with Earth is noon, the productive time. Likewise, the Sabbat Lammas, which comes at the height of Summer, as well as Coming of Age, are linked to the virility, productivity, and abundance of Earth. Zodiacally, Capricorn, Virgo, and Taurus are considered "Earth signs."

Places of Earth include the caves, forests, fields, gardens, canyons.

Copyright Asteria Books 2017

Elemental Fire

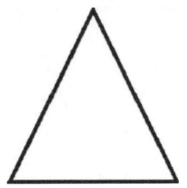

Within Traditional Craft, the element of Fire is associated with the East and the rising sun; however, in Ceremonial Magick and Wicca, the South is the Quarter associated with this element.

The power of Fire is "To Will," and it is associated with passion, power, will, energy, courage, strength, and light. It is also linked to sexuality, transformation, and the sense of sight. The processes best used to tap into Elemental Fire include dancing, burning, candle magic, solar magic, and mirror magic. You can also play string instruments or engage in an activity that makes you sweat.

Fire's tools and symbols include the lamp, wand, sword, triangle, lightning, flame, and candle. Salamanders and the Lion are considered the creatures of Fire. The colors are red, orange, amber .

The weapon of Fire is a sword, having been formed and strengthened within the flames. On a smaller scale, the knife is a versatile blade possessing the same qualities and honed for a more specific purpose.

The time of day associated with Fire is dawn, the fiery beginning of each day. Likewise, the Sabbat Beltaine, which comes at the height of Spring, as well as Youth, are linked to the passion, activity, and inception of Fire. Zodiacally, Leo, Sagittarius, and Aries are considered "Fire signs."

Places of Fire include Volcanoes, ovens, hearths, bonfires, deserts .

Copyright Asteria Books 2017

Elemental Water

▽

Within both Traditional Craft and the Ceremonial and Wiccan systems, the element of Water is associated with the West, the place of the setting sun.

The power of Water is "To Dare," and it is associated with emotions, intuition, cleansing, Mystery, and sacrifice. It is also linked to death, the ancestors, healing, and the sense of taste. The processes best used to tap into Elemental Water include bathing, drinking, baptism, and blood magic. You can also play chimes or charge waters for use in magic.

Water's tools and symbols include the chalice or quaiche, cauldron, crescent, shell, boat, and anchor. Undines and the Dolphin are considered the creatures of Water. The colors are grey, turquoise, blue, and indigo.

The weapon of Water is the helmet, being an armored bowl.

The time of day associated with Water is twilight, the end of each day. Likewise, the Sabbat Samhain, which comes at the end of the Autumn harvest, as well as Adulthood, are linked to the transition, submersion, and healing of Water. Zodiacally, Pisces, Cancer, and Scorpio are considered "Water signs."

Places of Water include oceans, rivers, lakes, waterfalls, wells, beaches, and baths.

Copyright Asteria Books 2017

The Humours

Around 450 BCE, Aristotle advocated for the theory of a Four Element system as the basis for which all things in the Universe (including the human body and psychological temperament) are comprised. Elemental philosophy took shape in Hippocratic medicine in the form of "humors" — a system of fluids related to the elements of Earth, Air, Fire, and Water. Imbalances in the humors, which are most often attributed to the positions of the stars at the time of an individual's birth, can cause constitutional and psychological weaknesses or overbalances. The job of the physician (or, in some later cases, the alchemist) was to create medicines or apply procedures to rebalance the humors. These philosophies dominated medical practice through the mid 1500's — and still held influence until the 1800's.

PHLEGMATIC - Water; the Moon; Cancer, Scorpio, Pisces; Mucus; White; calm, quiet, easygoing, meditative, organized, dependable, conservative, caring, following, contemplative, diplomatic, peaceful, feminine, unmotivated, lazy, selfish, stingy, stub-

SANGUINE - Air; Venus; Gemini, Libra, Aquarius; Blood; Red; outgoing, charismatic, warm, friendly, responsive, lively, amorous, optimist, lively, carefree, compassionate, entertaining, generous, restless, loud, obnoxious, egocentric, insecure, exaggerative,

MELANCHOLIC - Earth; Saturn; Taurus, Virgo, Capricorn; Black Bile; Black; gifted, perfectionist, conscientious, loyal, aesthetic, idealistic, sensitive, analytical, creative, spiritual, moody, poetic, artistic, pessimistic, critical, touchy, vengeful, martyrish, judgmental, pompous, manic, flippant, unsociable

CHOLERIC - Fire; Mars; Aries, Leo, Sagittarius; Yellow Bile; Brown; determined, independent, productive, decisive, practical, athletic, optimistic, confident, quick, leading, energetic, passionate, masculine, insensitive, hostile, sarcastic, domineering, proud, impatient, obstinate, hot-tempered, sadistic

Copyright Asteria Books 2019

Powers of the Sphinx

There are said to be four primary things essential to magic. These four principles are the Powers of the Sphinx: To Know, To Will, To Dare, and To Keep Silent.

Eliphas Lévi indicates where to start in our endeavor to use the Powers of the Sphinx: "When one does not know, one should will to learn. To the extent that one does not know, it is foolhardy to dare, but it is always well to keep silent."

Thus the Four Powers are employed much like steps in a process; we must know before we can will, and so on. This idea is reinforced in Lévi's *Transcendental Magick*: "To learn how to will is to learn how to exercise dominion. But to be able to exert will power you must first know; for will power applied to folly is madness, death, and hell." Also: "In order to Dare we must Know; in order to Will, we must Dare; we must Will to possess empire and to reign we must Be Silent."

These four principle powers relate to the four fixed signs of the Zodiac, and the four magical elements. Together these faces of the fixed signs of the Zodiac create the four creatures composing the Sphinx.

Latin	Power	Sphinx	Zodiac	Element
Scire	To know	Human	♒ Aquarius	△ Air
Velle	To will	Lion	♌ Leo	△ Fire
Audere	To dare	Eagle	♏ Scorpio	▽ Water
Tacere	To keep silent	Bull	♉ Taurus	▽ Earth

For our purposes, there is no substitute for any of these powers. Firstly, it is imperative to Know one's Craft ins far as one can at the level that they currently are. Secondly, one must have proper force of Will in order to raise and direct power for a purpose. Thirdly, a magician or Witch must have great Daring to walk the Crooked Path, to travel to other realms and stand in sacred space. Finally -- and this is the most sacred and most challenging Power, as it is the Power of Earth, which is lowest of matter and closest to beginning over at Spirit -- is the Power to Keep Silent. In Silence is Wisdom, and there are many Mysteries that cannot be spoken of but must only be felt with the soul.

Copyright Asteria Publishing 2012

The Triple Soul

Many world shamanic traditions, recognize either a tripartite soul or three souls in one body. These three souls, for us, correspond to the triple colors of witchcraft - red, black, and white.

The first soul is the Black Soul, or "spirit." This is our astral body, and it is capable of traveling beyond this world into other realms while we live. The spirit is what we identify as our Self, our ego. It is our identity in this lifetime, and it is an exact copy of "us" in the astral realms, although it can take any form you wish for it as the Fetch. Upon death, the spirit (Black Soul) may wander as a ghost or revenant, it may stay to act as a guide or guardian to others, or it may travel back to the cosmic cauldron where its energy will dissolve to create new spirits.

The second soul is the Red Soul, or "eternal soul." We often call this the Bone Soul, as it lives in the bones of each of us and cannot be destroyed. It is the divine spark of the Witchfather's blood within every true Witch's heart. The Bone Soul, after death, is awarded a period of rest in Ynys Avalon (Elphame, the Summerlands, as you prefer), after which it is reborn. The eternal soul holds our past life memories and our connection to our ancestors.

The third soul is the White Soul, or "higher self." It is also known as the Holy Guardian Angel. The higher self exists just above our bodies, like a crown or halo. Inspiration, enlightenment, and divine wisdom all come to us through the higher self. It is one of the main goals of a witch to gain knowledge of this higher self and to commune with it regularly. The eternal soul (Red/Bone Soul) is alchemically married to the higher self (White Soul), and so true lasting communion is reveled to us upon death - and possibly even within our lifetimes.

Copyright Asteria Books 2018

The Black Soul

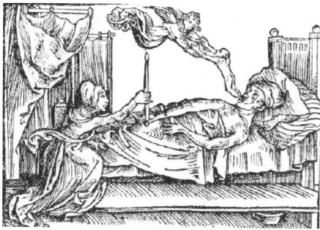

The Black Soul is that part of the spirit that retains memories and the personality connected to a particular life. It is very individual, and it is separate from the Higher Self (White Soul) and the Eternal Soul (Red Soul). It is the part of the energy structure that may become a ghost, haunting a particular location; but more often, it is the Black Soul who acts as a guiding Ancestor for future generations.

If you've talked to the Mighty Dead via a medium, talking board, your own clairvoyance, or other tool, this is the Black Soul of that Ancestor. The White and Red Souls have remained together and gone on to do other work, probably as another incarnate being. The Black Soul has remained here to act as a guide.

While still living and working with the White and Red Souls as part of the YOU that you are right now, your Black Soul is able to leave your body through witch flight and Fetch work. Some spiritual traditions call this astral travel. What they are calling the astral body, we are calling the Black Soul.

When Isobel Gowdie famously said, "I shall go into a hare," she was talking about sending her Black Soul out to roam in flight. The hare was a favorite choice of Fetch among Witches for its associations with the moon, shapeshifting, graveyards, and fertility.

Copyright Asteria Books 2018

White Soul

The White Soul is generally called the "Higher Self." In some traditions, it is called the "Holy Guardian Angel" (or HGA). Other names for this Soul from other religious systems include Augoeides (Neo-Platonism), Daemon (Platonism), Atman (Hinduism), God Self, etc.

Those who are able to see and interpret the aura often describe the White Soul as a crown or halo. In individuals with a very well-developed White Soul, this corona is often more visible and sometimes manifests as a visible star or bird above the head (especially when viewed in shamanic or highly receptive trance states).

Those on a path of enlightenment are said to be seeking "knowledge" of and "conversation" with the White Soul, and practices related to meditation, reflection, and invocation will all help the true seeker clarify their Soul's purpose and gain a better understanding of itself. Natural by-products of this "knowledge and conversation" are inspiration and wisdom.

The White Soul is the truest and purest Self, the Soul that is God-like in the sense that it is a Deity unto itself. It knows its Divinity and calls you to know it of yourself, as well. In rare glimpses throughout your mortal life, you will have true alignment of all Three Souls (as well as all Three Realms) and see yourself fully for the immortal and Divine Being you are.

Copyright Asteria Books 2018

Red Soul

The Red Soul (or Bone Soul) is eternal and linked in a sort of alchemical marriage to the White Soul. Whereas the Black Soul is only with you for a single lifetime, your Red and White Souls are bound together throughout all your lives, deaths, and periods of rest and reflection that come in between.

We call the Red Soul the "Bone Soul" as a nod to both the blood-producing marrow that reminds us of our connection to Tubal Qayin and also because of this Soul's ability to connect us with those in our bloodline, both physically and spiritually. Here, we see the old maxim, "Blood calls to blood," play out again and again as we reincarnate into the same family lines in multiple lives or are connected to the same soul-mates in several incarnations. In this sense, the marrow is the Red Thread that connects the line of Witches back to Qayin. The Red Soul also acts as the thread that links the Black and White Souls, thereby connecting us to our Selves.

Where the Black Soul is responsible for our sense of self and identity in this life, and the White Soul is responsible for our sense of purpose and learning throughout all our lives, the Red Soul is the agent of our deepest connection to our world, our work, and our loved ones.

Copyright Asteria Books 2018

Witch Blood & Witch Marks

Witch Marks

During the Medieval European witch trials, there was a belief that during a witch's initiation the Witchfather (whom the world called "Devil") would place his mark somewhere upon the body of the witch. Many of these same marks have been associated with *spiritual gifts* in cultures who were not so consumed with "witch frenzy." European witch hunters and Inquisitors would search the bodies of women and men accused of cunning craft looking for extra teeth, supernumerary nipples, red hair, unusual birthmarks, double-crowned skulls, etc. Historically (and contemporarily) many witches have taken a special tattoo at the time of initiation to mark themselves as a member of the People. These tattoos vary in shape and location by Clan.

Witch Blood

It is said that the blood of the Witchfather is passed via the bloodline – which is rooted in lore from the book of Enoch. This is part of the reason why the Craft at large is referred to as "the Family" and groupings of covens who operate under similar practices are called Clans. This heritage is often marked in terms of "lineage" and phrases like "daughter coven" are used to denote ancestry. While many who are newly drawn to the Craft many be unable to verify their Craft lineage (not having been taught by a blood relative), there is a common understanding that "blood calls to blood" and that those called to the crooked path are heeding the call of T'Qayin himself, whose blood sings in their veins. By forging the blood bond with him directly, you are igniting the Red Thread of the Craft – a link that no other can deny or break asunder.

The Kuthun

A kuthun is a magical inheritance that allows a witch to pass her power in this life to her spiritual descendant. It is a physical object that is tied to her work as a cunning person and acts as an incentive to teach her Arte to another.

Copyright Asteria Books 2019

Energy and Using Power

Eight Ways of Making Magick

You can combine many of these ways to produce more Power.

1. MEDITATION OR CONCENTRATION ~ Focused concentration on a subject is the most basic form of raising and sending energy. Meditation is a deeper form of concentration, and can be enhanced through specific postures and gestures.
2. CHANTS, SPELLS, INVOCATIONS ~ We speak the Universe into being. Chanting brings "enchantment." Spells were once written or "spelled" documents detailing the results desired. Invocations and evocations are vocal magic calling on Spirits and Gods for aid in our desires.
3. PROJECTION OF THE ASTRAL BODY, OR TRANCE ~ In truth, all of the ways of making magic seek to bring the magician into a form of trance, even if it is very light. Through trance we perceive other realms and can manipulate the energy links that connect all things as one.
4. INCENSE, DRUGS, WINE, ETC. ~ Entheogens (substances which enable us to embody the Gods) have a long and storied history in the Craft. They have been used in flying ointments, transformation elixirs, herbal incenses, smokes, anointing oils, washes, and any herbal mixture you can think of. Wine, of course, is central to the Red Meal, and also serves as a gentle way to let slip our egos and find ourselves outside of consensus reality when used in moderation. All can be dangerous, some are illegal. A few are lethal, even in small amounts. This Path of Power should not be attempted by the untrained Witch.
5. DANCING ~ Dancing may be the oldest form of celebration and communication. It is central to the raising of power through the treading of the mill.
6. USE OF THE CORDS ~ Warricking cords are often used to restrict blood flow to produce the desired trance state, frequently in combination with body postures also intended to restrict circulation. Ladders are used in knot magic.
7. THE SCOURGE ~ Light, rhythmic application of the scourge at the base of the spine can produce trance just as would a steady drumbeat, or the use of the lamed step. Some covens use a scourge as part of initiatory or other gateway rituals, where the strike of the flails can either be mild, moderate, or even more severe. In these cases, the symbolism of the scourge varies widely from coven to coven, but the effect is almost always to alter consciousness in some way.
8. THE GREAT RITE ~ The Great Rite "in truth" is the act of sexual congress between two individuals who have each invoked a God or Goddess. The Great Rite "in symbol" is routinely performed in the Wiccan version of the eucharistic sacrament, in which a cup and a blade represent the creative forces of the universe that bless the cakes and wine. Sex magick is a great source of power, but it should be approached cautiously and consentingly by all parties.

Copyright Asteria Books 2019

Grounding & Centering

Your energy can be "off" in lots of ways that would benefit from grounding and centering techniques. You may need to realign your energy if you are feeling spacy, disoriented, clumsy, confused, overwhelmed, anxious, agitated, hyper, drained, etc. You might have too much energy coursing through your system, not enough energy, someone else's energy, or just too many conflicting energetic desires of your own.

"To ground one's energy" means to root oneself, to draw energy from the earth, and to allow one's excess energy to flow into the earth. If you are familiar at all with the electrical trade, it is much like grounding an electrical current. This allows for better flow and steadier, more focused control of the energy current running through your system (your physical, spiritual, emotional, and energetic bodies).

There are many ways to accomplish energetic grounding. The simplest is to make yourself aware of your energetic connection to the earth and allow your energy to balance out with it. You're standing right on it, all the time. Even if you're inside a building, only thin layers of concrete (rock) separate you from (and yet connect you to) the Earth. Visualize that connection and tap in. Or, if you need to get hands on, go outside and get your hands and feet in some dirt, on some stones. Stomp, dance, walk. Move your energy in rhythm with the ground, and this alone will ground you.

"To center one's energy" refers to the practice of bringing one's energetic awareness into a core energy center in the body. Centering is about focus and clearing the mind of distractions. It helps us to be present in the moment. Bring your focus to the energy center in your belly or your heart, for best results.

One can center using a number of techniques and tools. If you have just grounded, you now have an open channel to the ground below you. Do the same for the sky above. It is exactly the same, except you are reaching up and drawing on celestial energy (starfire), which you gently draw into your energetic body. Your head, heart, and belly are the cauldrons, wheels, *receptacles* of those energies, which swirl and mingle within you. Let them expand and fill you with the energy you need, and then let them recede back to a comfortable space where you can move about your day. Know that you can always reach up or reach down and touch into those primal and eternal energies to draw on them. And you can always rebalance, if needed.

Copyright Asteria Books 2019

Seething

Seething is a linguistic derivative of Seiðr (Seithr), which is a type of sorcery that was practiced in Norse society during the Late Scandinavian Iron Age. Modern witches use seething as a way to shamanically get outside of themselves, into an altered state, and to raise the Power for charging a spell, tool, or talisman or to come into contact with Spirits. Whether the seething practice that has come down to us is a well-distilled form of the sorcery practiced by Norse women (for it was primarily a women's magic) or a corruption of it, that is hard to say. Based on the resources we have (the Eddas, etc), it seems that what we practice now is very much linked to what they did then.

"To seethe" has also come to mean "to be turbulent, to boil." The word had this definition by the Middle Ages, which tells us that the trance state achieved by this technique is not one of calm and peace. Much like the name suggests, you will be "working yourself up" when you seethe.

There are two basic modern interpretations of the practice of seething. The first method is very much like the practice of Treading the Mill. The witch bears a gandreigh (riding pole), such as a staff, broom, or stang. He treads a wide circle while focusing power on a central point, such as a central stang, altar, or lead witch. Alternately, the witch may choose to use their own gandreigh as the focal point and circle around it while holding it as the axis point.

The second method of seething is a seated variation in which the witch raises a great deal of great emotion and force of Will through the act of rocking back and forth (or side to side, or in a circle). Breath control, muscle flutters, and chanting are adjunct techniques used to deepen this practice. While it sounds complex, even simple rhythmic control of the physical body frees the mind to wander as it will. Here, the gandriegh can still be employed to tap out rhythms for the witch to "ride" into trance.

Copyright Asteria Books 2019

Energy Centers of the Body

There are many ways to view the energy centers, or "wheels," within the body. The current, most codified and widespread view arising from Eastern tantric practice proposes seven wheels, but others suggest radically different numbers and positions. The energy wheels illustrated here align with a traditional northern European shamanic (and Craft) view of the energetic body. The wheel in the belly is linked to the Black Soul, the lunar tides, and the digestive and reproductive systems. The heart wheel is connected to the Red Soul, the heart fire, Witchblood, respiration, circulation, and self-expression. The head wheel is connected to the White Soul, star-fire, the HGA, universal consciousness, intuition, and intellect.

Copyright Asteria Books 2019

The Lame Step

The lame step is one of the old and identifying markers of Witches and of their God. And their Goddess. Nursery rhymes show us the evidence of the lame step in magic, the Forge God -- the first and mightiest God of Witchcraft -- is more often lamed than not, and the Witches' Goddess hobbled on a goose's foot.

The Forge God and the Lame Step

The lame step could be said to originate, as it relates to magic, with the God of the Forge. Nearly all Forge Gods were depicted with a lame step or a misshapen leg in antiquity. The mundane reason for this was very likely due to the residual heavy metal poisoning suffered by actual smiths -- or the fact that otherwise strong men who had suffered some crippling childhood disease or injury could still be trained to blacksmith work. Whatever the case, the image of the smith is intimately linked with that of a hobbled or ham-strung, yet powerful, man. A man who understands something related to the alchemical process, and therefore magic. In the case of T'Qayin and Azazel, this image is that of a goat-footed God. The goat-foot is one variation of the lame step, and it is very intimately linked to the forge. Heavy metal poisoning bunched the muscles of the leg in a way that it pulled the smith's legs and foot up into a position like he was walking on a stiletto heel.

The Goose-Footed Goddess

The lame step appears again in the Witches' Goddess in at least one instance. In France, there is a notable story of La Reine Pedauque, the goose-footed queen. She is the original Mother Goose. Mother Goose, is so closely related to the Teutonic Hulda that they are reflections of one another. Frau Hulda, Holda, Holle, Hel rides a goose through the night sky and is a spinner. She is the Dark Grandmother and the White Lady. With her goose-foot, she shows us another aspect of the lame step.

Use of the Lame Step

The lame step is a marker for those who walk between the worlds. Symbolically, it represents having one foot in consensus reality and one foot in the realms beyond the veil. The lame step is a way of showing that you are between the worlds. It is the most basic step in Witch dances and is used when Treading the Mill.

Copyright Asteria Publishing 2012

Widdershins & Deosil

The terms deosil and widdershins come to common Craft usage from older German and Gaelic terms that refer generally to clockwise and counter-clockwise movements, respectively.

Deosil is a more modern spelling of the Irish and Scots Gaelic terms meaning "right" or "sunwise" -- as in "turning in the direction of the sun." It was considered propitious to turn to the right and to favor right-handed movements, a propensity that carried over into ritual practice and was handed down into superstition to the point that some people even believed that drinking or performing other actions with the left hand could prove to be fatal.

Widdershins, on the other hand, comes from an old Germ word *widersinnig ("against" + "sense")*. This form of "sense" is actually most closely related to words like "practicality" and "aptness." So, to move widdershins is to move against the norm. This bears out when we look at the way the word was cited in the Oxford English Dictionary's entry in an early attestation from 1513, where it was found in the phrase "widdersyns start my hair", i.e. my hair stood on end.

Some traditions have strict rules about only moving deosil or only moving widdershins within the caim. Many Traditional Witches use both types of movement during ritual, though we use them very deliberately. We acknowledge that every step within the compass is an act of treading the mill. Be cognizant with each step you take of whether or not you are building on the magick of the work you are aiming to do, or if you are unwinding it by moving contrary-wise.

You can use the mill to lead you either up and out or down and within. When treading sunwise, the energy rises upward, spiraling us into the first realm. Treading widdershins brings the energy down into the land where we can access the third realm. Neither of these movements is more desirable than the other, they are both as necessary and as benign as the positive and negative poles of a magnet.

Copyright Asteria Books 2018

Practical Craft

How to Write a Spell

DEFINE THE NEED. What do you need to happen? Will it happen through the natural course of events? Is this need in everyone's best interest? Will something be harmed if you get what you need through magic? Are you okay with that harm? If not, what needs to change?

DETERMINE THE INTENT. This is the final outcome or purpose of the spell. What do you plan to accomplish by doing this spell? What do you want to change? What result do you want? Make sure you understand and describe for yourself how you feel, what you will see/hear/etc when the outcome has been obtained. You want to be able to feel it as a reality when the spell is concluded -- and feel gratitude for it.

PLAN THE BODY OF THE SPELL. What tools do you need? What sacred space do you require? What Deities, Elements, trees, animals, herbs, energies, mythical creatures, etc. do you plan to use to empower the work? What oils, candles, incenses, symbols or other objects can you use? Will you chant? How will you raise and focus energy? Will you make an amulet or a talisman? When should your spell be done for maximum effect? Is the time of day, lunar phase or astrological sign important? All of these things will have some effect on your spell. Is your need strong enough to overcome possible astrological conflicts? Where should you do your spell for greatest effect?

DOCUMENT YOUR SPELL CRAFT. Write down everything you have decided to do. Write down the words of the spell, since variations in wording can change the outcome of the spell.

REFLECT AGAIN ON WHAT YOU HAVE DECIDED TO DO. Look at the whole thing. Are there any troublesome areas? Are your intentions clear? Is this spell in keeping with your personal ethics? Will it achieve the desired outcome? What are all the possible ramifications of this magic? Have you done divinations? What have they told you? What is the price of the magic?

PERFORM THE SPELL. Document any last-minute changes as well as the impressions that you got while performing it. Make note of the outcome in your records and reflect on the overall effectiveness as well as the minutia.

Copyright Asteria Books 2018

Spell Record

Specific purpose:

Moon Phase & Sign: Sun Sign: Planetary Hour:

Elementals:

Totemic Animals or Plants:

Deities:

Other Spirits:

Type of Sacrifice:

Materials:

Pre-spell set-up (if needed):

Specific location (if needed):

Steps:

1.

2.

3.

4.

5.

Results
Did the spell work?
How long did it take to manifest?
Is there a time limit on the spell?
Does it need to be repeated?
Describe the specific results and how they manifested:

Amulets & Talismans

"Amulet" and "talisman" are often used as interchangeable terms by those who don't practice magick. Even those within the Craft can sometimes confuse the meanings of the two words. However, careful study and consideration of historical talismans and amulets will reveal their differences. While both are magical objects purported to bestow protection or certain forms of good fortune upon their bearer, they are different in their creation.

More specifically:

An AMULET is a naturally occurring object whose physical properties give it inherently protective or magical energies. For example, a stone with a natural hole (a "hag stone," as pictured above), the fur or feathers of your totem animal, and the parts of sacred tree are all amulets. An amulet doesn't necessarily need to be embellished or empowered — just claimed, recognized, and honored (and used). It can be cleansed and empowered, if desired, but this isn't always necessary.

A TALISMAN is a man-made object designed and produced for a specific magical purpose. It may incorporate natural materials or it may not. It can be inscribed or drawn on a piece of paper or other surface or be an object that includes braiding and knotting, color associations, beads, magical alphabets, sigils, numbers, sacred geometry, metal- or woodworking, textiles, angelic/demonic names, Gods, etc. The possibilities are almost endless in terms of both construction and application. It must be prepared and charged by a Witch or Magician to have power. All aspects of the talisman's design should work together to achieve its goal. (The talisman to the right is a Solomonic device called the 4th pentacle of Venus.)

Amulets and talismans are usually (but not always) small enough objects to be portable, and they are very frequently worn or carried in a pocket or pouch to convey their properties to their target.

Copyright Asteria Books 2018

Witch Symbols

- △ Fire
- ▽ Water
- ⍙ Air
- ⍌ Earth
- 🜍 Alchemical Sulfur
- ⊖ Alchemical Salt, Castle Peri-
- ☆ Pentagram
- ⊛ Pentacle
- ✡ Hexagram
- ⬡ Unicursal Hexagram
- ✷ Septagram, Fairy Star
- ☯ Triskele, Spiral Castle
- ☘ Triquetra

- ♈ Aries
- ♉ Taurus
- ♊ Gemini
- ♋ Cancer
- ♌ Leo
- ♍ Virgo
- ♎ Libra
- ♏ Scorpio
- ♐ Sagittarius
- ♑ Capricorn
- ♒ Aquarius
- ♓ Pisces
- ☉ Sun, Sunday, Castle of Revelry
- ☽ Moon, Monday
- ♂ Mars, Tuesday
- ☿ Mercury, Wednesday

- ♃ Jupiter, Thursday
- ♀ Venus, Friday
- ♄ Saturn, Saturday
- ⊕ Planetary Earth, Stone Castle
- ⬬ Yoni, Vesica Piscis, Man-Stang, Witch Fire
- ⸫ Blessings, Witch Blood, Sacrifice
- ☸ Year Wheel
- ✹ Chaos Star
- ✵ Eight Ways of Making Magick
- ☽○☾ Triple Goddess
- ⛤ Horned God

Copyright Asteria Books 2019

Florida Water

Florida Water Lore

Florida Water is actually a brand name of inexpensive perfume that was developed by Murray (who formed the company Murray & Lanman) in 1808. It is a simulation of Eau de Cologne. It has been utilized by the Hoodoo community for generations for cleansing the body and home and for banishing negative forces. It is also a component of many protective spells and recipes. It is a staple of American Folk Magick. The recipe shared here is great for those of us who like to make our own blends.

Florida Water Recipe

Vodka — half of a 1.75L bottle

6 ounces Rose Water

8 drops Musk oil

7 drops Bergamot essential oil

6 drops Neroli essential oil

3 drops Lavender essential oil

3 drops Lemon essential oil

3 drops Cinnamon essential oil

3 drops Jasmine essential oil

5 whole Cloves

* Shake well before each use to redistribute the oils

Florida Water Uses

Add some Florida Water to your bath, making sure to fully immerse yourself three times before coming out of the tub and drying off.

Put some Florida Water in your floor wash to clean up the muck that you, your family members, guests, and others have tracked into your home.

Make three crosses (or x's) on each window, doorway, and hearthstone of your home to cleanse and protect these entry points.

Copyright Asteria Books 2017

Non-Toxic Flying Ointment

Flying Ointment Lore

Flying ointment is one of the traditional potions of witchcraft. It is the salve used by Witches to induce hallucinations and astral journeying (their method of "flying" to Sabbat). Unfortunately, the recipes for flying ointment in the old grimoires are full of extremely poisonous herbal ingredients. In order to achieve anything but the mildest of psychic "nudges" from those plants, you must literally risk death. This (mostly) non-toxic flying ointment is a witch salve with KICK. It is not a subtle brew! Infused with eight herbs, each of which is known for its psychic/journeying properties, this ointment will "knock you into next Tuesday."

Formula Recipe

4 ounces Olive Oil

1 ounce Beeswax, grated

1 ounce Honey, raw

2 tablespoons Mugwort

2 tablespoons Cinquefoil

2 tablespoons Lemongrass

1 tablespoon Rue

1 tablespoon Dittany of Crete

1 tablespoon Balm of Gilead

1 tablespoon Wormwood

1 tablespoon Calamus root

2 drops Clary Sage essential oil (add after the mixture has been strained)

Formula Uses

Follow the instructions for ointment preparation in the Herbal Crafting section. Pour the salve into airtight containers and store in a cool, dark place. To use, take a three-finger scoop and rub it on until the skin is warm. Apply it to pulse points such as the neck, the wrists, the underarms, the inner thighs & the feet. The scent is intoxicating and smells different on the skin than in the jar. Give it about 15 minutes and begin focusing on 'flying out." It works well just before bedtime to produce lucid dreams, and (as it was designed) it's ideal for an aid to astral travel, especially visions of flying out on a riding pole. Guided meditations benefit favorably from the use of a smaller dose. It combines well with other entheogens also. We've used it with excellent results with Sabbat wine.

Copyright Asteria Books 2017

Khernips

Formula Lore

Khernips is the sacred cleansing water of Ancient Greek ritual. It is sometimes called "lustral water" as it is used in lustration — the act of cleansing before entering the sanctuary. To enter the sacred space in an unclean state, according to Greek culture, can taint the people and objects inside and is also considered offensive to the Gods. Flowing "living" water is the simplest form of khernips, but it can also be created by combining the elements of Earth, Air, Fire, and Water.

Formula Recipe

Mix a little salt (Earth) into a bowl of water. Light a stick of wood to create a Flame. I prefer palo santo, cedar, or white willow. Blow out the fire and allow the wood to smoke momentarily (Air). While smoking, plunge the glowing end into the saltwater.

Formula Uses

Pour khernips over the hands of the ritual participants prior to entering the sacred space. You can also use it to sprinkle the entire space prior to ritual.

Sabbat Wine

"Entheogen" is a Greek-derived word that means "generating the divine within." An entheogen, therefore, is a psychoactive substance that is used in a religious, spiritual or shamanic context. Traditional Witches have used entheogens of several types for centuries, as recorded in the lore of mythology, in the records of the trials and persecutions, and in the regional indigenous shamanic practices that have been assimilated into the Craft in various locales. Among the most commonly used and widely known entheogens in European and American Witchcraft practice are Sabbat Wine and Flying Ointment.

Sabbat Wine

Wine, just as it is, constitutes a powerful entheogen. The Dying and Resurrected God is embodied in the wine in the form of Dionysos -- and in Jesus, for that matter, whose symbolism and mythology associates him with the wine. Dionysos, though, is the "Twice Born" God of the Vine, and his cup is the offering of ecstasy and madness. "I am the vine," he says, and he offers insight into death and rebirth, despair and joy.

Many Witches drink wine -- either a little or a lot -- as a part of their Sabbat rites no matter what. In American Folkloric Witchcraft, we include Sabbat Wine for two separate and distinct purposes -- and the wine is different depending on that purpose.

If we are celebrating the Housle as we usually do within the regular course of ritual, we will sacrifice a cup of red wine. It is the shed blood of the Red Meal that is the Housle. In this instance, we don't add anything to the wine because we don't need any additional entheogenic effect.

If, however, we are doing trance work, flying out, seething, or otherwise seeking an altered state of consciousness, we might prepare our special Sabbat Wine (vinum sabbati). We also prepare this Sabbat Wine for initiations. The vinum sabbati is a sweet red wine in which mugwort and lemongrass have been mulled. After straining the herbs, we add honey to sweeten the mix and cut the bitterness of the mugwort. Both mugwort and lemongrass have gentle psychoactive properties.

It's interesting to note that the term "vinum sabbati" has actually been associated with flying ointment, or the witches' salve, which is the other major entheogen of witchcraft. In fact, Nigel Jackson said flying ointment was "the black wine of owls."

Copyright Asteria Publishing 2012

Sabbat Wine

Sabbat Wine Lore

Sabbat Wine is the name of a group of entheogens used by Witches to induce an ecstatic or altered state during rituals. Flying Ointment is sometimes called Sabbat Wine, although many modern Witches make a mulled wine that is sometimes drunk in addition to applying Flying Ointment. This Sabbat Wine blend is suitable for occasional use, such as initiations or special oracle rituals. For more frequent consumption, consider replacing the mugwort with another herb, as it can build up in your liver if drunk too often.

Formula Recipe

2 parts Mugwort

1 part Lemongrass

Steep 1 tsp of the above mixture in 1 cup of warmed sweet red wine. Add raw, local honey to taste.

Formula Uses

The mugwort and lemongrass blend is a very effective, albeit bitter, tea. Blade & Broom Botanica has sold this mix as "Sabbat Night Tea." The bitterness of the herbs works well with a particularly sweet red wine and a little local honey.

Drink a cup or two of the Sabbat Wine before flying out, performing possessory rituals, or holding initiations.

Copyright Asteria Books 2017

Balefire

A balefire, by strictest definition, is a large, open-air bonfire. Historically, it has often been used as a signal fire. The term may refer to Bel or Belenos, a Celtic fire God for whom bonfires were a central part of his celebrations. It may also refer to a funeral pyre (bael) or to the dance (bail) that happens around bonfires at Beltane and Midsummer.

The name of the Sabbat Beltane is likewise related to Belenos and the balefire.

According to Craft practice, a balefire is a magical fire that is kindled when need is great in order to achieve a goal. To this end, it is sometimes called a "needfire." It is kindled without the use of metals, usually by utilizing a bow.

Traditionally, the balefire includes nine woods, though the woods vary by Trad practice and locale. The two most well-known variants are as follows:

Druidic Balefire	Wiccan Balefire
Apple	Birch
Cedar	Grapevine
Dogwood	Willow
Elder	Hawthorn
Holly	Hazel
Juniper	Apple
Oak	Oak
Poplar	Fir
Rowan	Rowan

Copyright Asteria Books 2017

Witches' Ladders

String/cord and knot magick have been used for both spell-working and meditation within traditional forms of Witchcraft all over Europe. The tools made from this method are known in various locales as Witches' Ladders, Garlands, or Girdles or simply as "rope and feathers" due to the predominant use of the those particular materials in the ladders' construction.

In Robert Cochrane's article "On Cords," he describes the use of both devotional and magickal ladders:

"When worked up properly they should contain many different parts --herbs, feathers and impedimenta of the particular charm. They are generally referred to in the trade as "ladders," or in some cases as "garlands," and have much the same meaning as the three crosses. That is they can contain three blessings, three curses, or three wishes. A witch also possesses a devotional ladder, by which she may climb to meditational heights, knotted to similar pattern as the Catholic rosary."

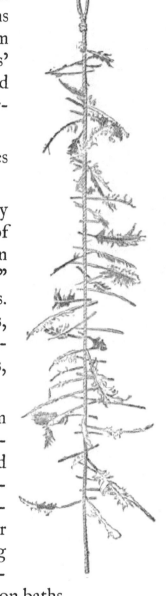

Historically, the oldest sets of preserved ladders seem to have been used for cursing and included either gander feathers or black hen feathers. The cord contained usually three, nine, or thirteen knots; but more contemporary versions base the number of knots on a variety of factors, including alignment with a particular magickal intention or system. Ladders used for cursing could only be thwarted by finding the rope and untying the knots, sometimes followed by special purification baths.

Contemporary ladders are just as frequently (maybe even more frequently) made for meditational purposes like a rosary or for beneficent spellwork. The "rope and feathers" of traditional ladders are more commonly replaced by braided or knotted string or cord and beads, charms, and other trinkets. Initiation cords, for covens who use them, are a variation of witches' ladders.

Copyright Asteria Books 2018

Seasonal Protection Cords

Protection cords are a specific kind of Witch's Ladder that our Tradition crafts seasonally (four times a year) at each of the solar Sabbats. The cords are made from three braided strands of natural fiber in colors that are symbolic to the season. They are finished with seven knots.

The Goddess knots are the first knots in the cords. They are created with a loop in one end for the White Goddess, Goda, and a "flail" in the opposite end for the Black Goddess, Kolyo. In the center of the cord is the knot for the Witchfather, Tubal Cain.

The four intermediate knots are for the three realms – above, below, and between – the four cardinal directional and elemental gates – north/air, south/earth, east/fire, and west/water – the four Watchtowers or castles, and the totems of the season.

The cords are worn on the body of the each family member of the coven for the duration of the season until new cords are made. The old cords are then cut, collected and burnt. You may also wish to make cords for your familiars.

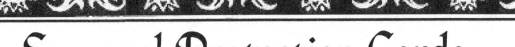

Divination

Palmistry

Palmistry is the divinatory art of telling a person's fortune by examining the lines, shape, and coloring of the hand. It is also known as *chiromancy* after a palm reader who made the art famous. Below is a reproduction of a 17th century palmistry chart.

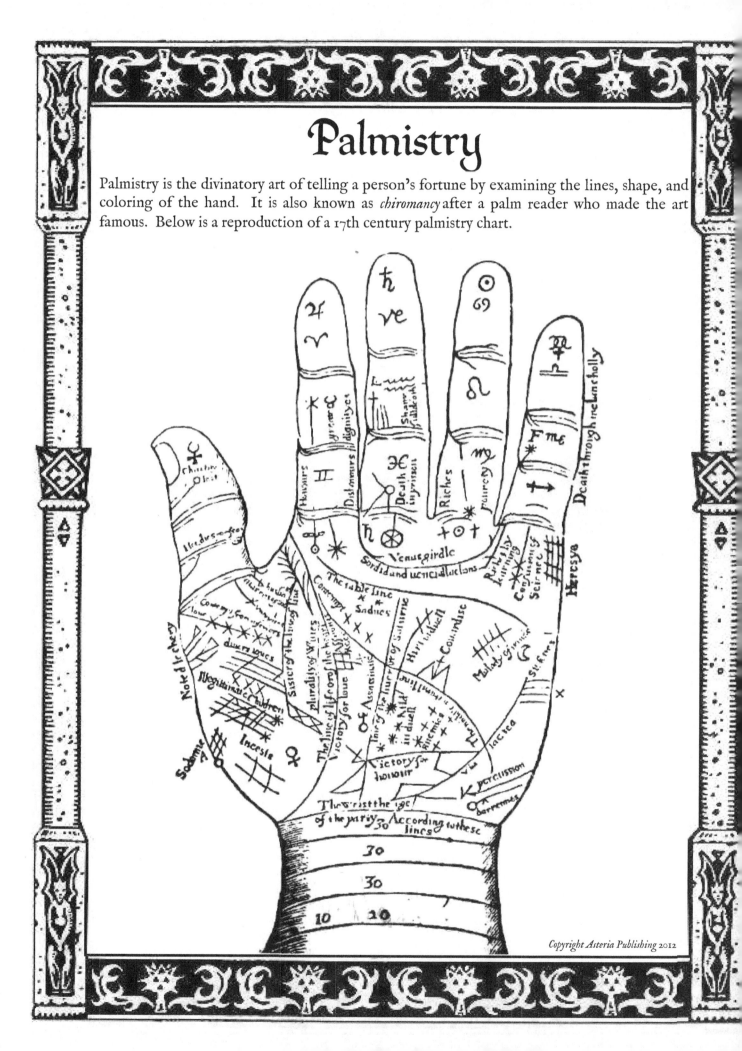

Runic Divination

The Norse alphabet varied a bit from place to place and changed somewhat over time, but one of the more commonly used versions today consists of 24 letters that are divided into three sets called *aettr*, which were ruled by specific Gods. Runes were often considered *alive* and therefore needed to be fed, usually with ritual oils, powders, and (at least in their initial blessing) a bit of the Runester's own blood. To divine with the Runes, you can draw a single Rune from a pouch (or three, for a more well-rounded view), or you can cast the entire set onto a circular field, reading only those runes that are face up within the circle. The Runes are also very helpful as symbols for magic and can be combined to create powerful bindrune sigils.

Freya's Aett

Fehu (F) Increase of wealth and possessions, protection of valuables. Used to send energy on its way, fire in its uncontrolled, primal state.

Uruz (U,V) Used to create change, healing, vitality, strength, to boost energy of magickal work.

Thurisaz (Th) Beginning new projects, luck- the hand of fate helping you, protection, the hammer of Thor, opening gateways.

Ansuz (A) Communications, wisdom and clarity, to attract others to your cause, increase magickal energy.

Raido (R) Safe travel, movement, obtaining justice in an issue, used to keep a situation from stagnating.

Kenaz (K) The hearth fire, artistic pursuits, healing, love and passion, creativity, strength.

Gebo (G) Gifts, partnerships on all realms, sex magick, brilliance, integration of energies.

Wunjo (W, V) Joy, happiness, love, fulfillment in career and home life, the icing on the cake.

Heimdall's Eight

Hagalaz (H) Slow, steady pace, no disruptions, asking for a hand from fate within a situation you do not control.

Nauthiz (N) Need, desire, fulfilling those needs, love and sex magick, motivation created by distress.

Isa (I) Cessation of energy, freezing an issue where it stands, cooling relationships, separation, division.

Jera (Y) Harvesting tangible results from efforts already sown, fertility, culmination of events, abundance.

Eihwaz (EI) Banishing magick, removal of obstacles and delays, invoking foresight, clearing up hidden issues and situations.

Perdhro (P) Unexpected gains, hidden secrets coming to light, discovering that which has been lost, spiritual evolution.

Algiz (Z) Protection, fortunate influences, fate on your side, victory and success, good luck and personal strength.

Sowulo (S, Z) Victory, power, strength, health, the rune of the sun, vitality, drive to work and produce.

Tir's Eight

Teiwaz (T) Victory, leadership, success over other competitors, increase in finances, virility and passion (especially for men).

Berkana (B) Growth, abundance, fertility, Mother Earth, protection, the zenith of an idea or situation.

Ehwaz (E) Abrupt changes, moving into new home and environment, travel, swift change in situation.

Mannaz (M) Cooperation, teamwork, collaboration, help and aid from others, beginning new projects, especially with others.

Laguz (L) Intuition, imagination, success in studies, creativity, vitality and passion (especially for women).

Inguz (NG) Fertility, successful conclusion to issue or situation, ending one cycle and beginning another.

Dagaz (D) Increase and expansion, prosperity, growth, major turning points in life, turning in new directions.

Othila (O) Material possessions and protection of those possessions, inheritance (can be genetic traits inherited from elders).

Copyright Asteria Books 2018

Numerology

Embedded within the study of numerology is the belief that certain basic numbers reflect universal Truths which are observable in the natural world and have been reflected in art, poetry, and myth in cultures all over the globe. Studying the way the numbers that are important in our own lives can give us greater clarity into the primal patterns at play in shaping our reality — and our perceptions of that reality.

A person's "Life Path" number is determined by adding together all the digits of their birthday (and adding the resulting digits, until a single digit number (or the number 11) is reached. The Life Path number indicates a soul's purpose in this life. It can also shed insight on the challenges you've experienced in this life. The "Expression" number is determined by assigning a numerical value to each letter in the full name given to you at birth and then adding those numbers together until you have a single digit (or 11), as above. Suffixes like Jr, II, etc. should be omitted. The Expression number is a reflection of the soul's purpose and reflects gifts, talents, abilities, and motivations.

1	2	3	4	5	6	7	8	9
A	B	C	D	E	F	G	H	I
J	K	L	M	N	O	P	Q	R
S	T	U	V	W	X	Y	Z	

Sept. 25, 1975 —> 9/25/1975 —> 9+2+5+1+9+7+5=38 —> 3+8= 11

Laurelei Black —> 3+1+3+9+5+3+5+9+2+3+1+3+2 = 47 —> 4+7 = 11

1 ~ Sun, unity, ambition, courage, the male principle, Divine spark
2 ~ Moon, duality, emotions, harmony, differentiation, the female principle, balance
3 ~ Jupiter, creativity, joy, the triangle, the divine child
4 ~ Earth, will, discipline, equality, the cross, the square, order
5 ~ Mercury, communication, freedom, magic, humanity, the star
6 ~ Venus, love, beauty, wisdom, union, perfect pairing
7 ~ Cosmos, mysticism, spirituality, contemplation
8 ~ Saturn, law, authority, eternity, infinity, As Above/So Below
9 ~ Mars, action, proficiency, completion, the mystic rose
11 ~ Manifestation, Master Number, Justice

Copyright Asteria Books 2019

Pendulum

The pendulum is perhaps one of the simplest divination tools to create, carry, and use. It is also, arguably, the least offensive or frightening tool to those unfamiliar with occult studies. In fact, one simple method of pendulum divination common among Christians for determining the sex of an unborn child involves dangling one's crucifix over the belly of a pregnant woman. Straight-line swings indicate a male baby, while circles indicate a female baby.

A pendulum can be created by suspending any type of weight (or "plumb") from a string. Many pendulums are made from semi-precious stones, shells, woods, and metals that were chosen due to their alignments with particular energies. However, you can use any combination of materials that resonates with you. Indeed, a necklace with a pendant or heavy charm that you wear daily may serve as your truest pendulum, as it is already attuned to your energy.

When you wish to use your pendulum for divination, start by holding it in your dominant hand. It helps to put your elbow on a table or hold it close to your side to minimize your movement. Still your mind with a few breaths and then ask the pendulum to show you YES, then show you NO. Make note of the types of swings. For some people, these will always be the same, every time you ask. It is important to begin with this simple exercise, however, because the energy of other individuals (including Spirits) can occasionally change the direction of your pendulum's movements – which would change everything about the reading you conduct. From here, you can conduct a "reading" by asking Yes/No questions.

A pendulum reading can also be conducted using a semi-circular "board" drawn on paper, wood, leather, or cloth onto which you have inscribed letters, numbers, names, or other information you wish the pendulum to indicate. This can be very elaborate and can extend the usefulness of your pendulum into many different areas beyond Yes/No questions.

Pendulums are also very helpful in "dowsing," which is an energetic or intuitive method for finding things. To do this, you can either draw a map and allow the pendulum swings to guide you to the area where the thing you seek is located, or you can write the place names in a semi-circle, as in the "board" method above.

Copyright Asteria Books 2019

Scrying

Scrying is the divinatory practice of seeking visual messages through the use of a tool or medium. Though you can scry with any of the elements, water scrying might be the oldest version of divination known to humans. It reveals much in connection with our emotions, psyches, past-lives, ancestors - all of the things we associate with the western gate of elemental water and the Underworld. Learning to navigate these waters will help you understand the patterns and issues involved in your life.

TOOLS USED FOR SCRYING
Water in a black bowl, cup, or cauldron
Crystal bowl, polished stones, scrying jewelry
Black Mirror
Incense smoke
Flames

The technique for scrying in any element is going to be more or less the same. In short, you will enter a meditative state, relax your gaze while looking in the direction of your scrying tool or element, and then simply allow the messages or images to come to you.

TIPS AND TECHNIQUES FOR SCRYING SUCCESS

Some people like to add oils or herbs to the water (or choose visionary herbs for the smoke blend, if you are scrying in incense smoke or flames). Some add a silver coin or gemstone to bowl, cauldron, or cup. It is helpful to do this work in a darkened room to limit other visual stimuli. If you are gazing into water, glass, or crystal, light a single candle whose light is shining on the surface of the water or glass, but isn't directly in your line of vision.

Copyright Asteria Books 2019

Making a Dark Mirror

The dark mirror (or "black mirror") is the magical descendant of an obsidian mirror — a disc of polished black volcanic stone used as a scrying glass. While a highly polished piece of naturally occurring stone (such as a black variety of obsidian, tourmaline, onyx, agate, or hematite) can be an amazing scrying surface, it can also be cost prohibitive and might not afford a Witch the opportunity to take part in *crafting* an important personal tool. What follows are basic guidelines crafting one's dark mirror.

Materials Needed:
Glass surface (concave or flat)
Black enamel paint
Paint brush
Black fabric (felt, silk, velvet, wool)
Frame, stand, box (optional)
Adornments (optional)

Essentially, this tool is made by painting the backside of a piece of glass with black enamel (probably 2-3 coats to account for streaks). Enamel works best because it is both durable and glossy.

If you are using a concave piece of glass like a clock glass or an old-fashioned "bubbled" picture frame, you want to paint the outer bowl of the glass so that you will be looking into a clear, glossy black well or pool with the paint on the other side.

While the paint is still tacky, apply your black fabric to the entire backing. This will adhere to the enamel, adding an impenetrable layer of obscurity. No light will come through while you gaze into your mirror, and it will be protected from scratches.

You can encase the mirror in a frame or a wooden box (with a hinged lid, if you like), place it on a stand, or hang it on a wall.

Try to make the whole assembly of a size in which you'll be able to see your whole face at no further than arm's length away.

Embellish your dark mirror with runes, sigils, shells, stones, talismans, or other fetiches to enhance its power and lend you protection while you seek wisdom and guidance.

Copyright Asteria Books 2019

Witch's Runic Oracle

The Witch's Runes consist of 26 symbols divided into thirteen sets of two. They are based on ancient symbols for magic. Many cultures considered the runes to be alive, and it is recommended that you "feed" your runes oils and magical powders regularly. It is also traditional to mark each rune with a bit of your blood. To bless something is to blood it, and ancient runic carvings were often reddened to bring them life and power. To divine with the runes, you may draw one from a pouch or cast a handful of runes into a circle in order to interpret them. The runes are also useful as symbols for spell craft.

Womb: Life, Fertility, Beginnings

Blood: Sacrifice, Tears

Vulva: Woman, Feminine

Eye: Opening, Seeing, Visions

Lightning: Blasting, Disaster, Destruction

Moon: Night, Goddess

Land: Middles, Reality, Growth, Earth, Grounding

Flame: Source, Creation, Fire, Passion, Will

Hearth: Home, Family

Separation: Dissolution, Division

Scourge: Severity, Strength

Spiral: Rebirth, Inward, Fate

Accord: Peace

Bane: Death, Change, Endings

Stang: Increase, Joy

Phallus: Man, Masculine

Hand: Protection, Warding

Star: Blessing, Wishes, Gifts

Sun: Day, God

Sky: Upper Realm, Dreams, Goals, Air, Thoughts, Knowledge

Sea: Lower Realm, Intuition, Water, Emotions

Flight: Travel, Adventure

Union: Love, Relationships, Marriage

Salute: Mercy, Softness

Crossroads: Expansion, Outward, Choice

Strife: Chaos

Copyright Asteria Publishing 2012

Magical Tools

Saining of Tools

It is customary when a Witch acquires new tools to cleanse and consecrate them to their own use. This true whether the tools are purchased, homemade, or received as a gift, and also whether they are for personal or coven use.

The term "sain" is an archaic word that means to make the sign of the cross over something in order to banish evil or unwanted forces from it, or viewed another way, to bless it so that evil cannot touch it. The symbol of the cross as sign of blessing far pre-dates Christianity. Indeed, the equal-armed cross (often depicted with a circle encompassing it) is such a prehistoric and universal symbol of which every land and culture had some version. It is a symbol that is related to concepts of perfection and the totality of known existence.

You will need:
the tool to be sained
dark bread in a bowl (or lipped dish)
red wine in a cup
the Red Knife
a lancet (optional)
a portion of purification or blessing incense
a thurible with a lit charcoal

1.) Cast the Caim as usual.

2.) Place some of the incense on the lit charcoal and run the tool through the resulting smoke making the shape of a cross, visualizing all past energies of the tool being carried away and dissolved with the smoke.

3.) Say: "I cleanse this '*tool*' in the name of the Mighty Ones, that it may serve me well in my Craft."

4.) Raise power by seething. Rock back and forth, hum, chant, wail, and draw power up from the third realm and down from the first realm into yourself and into your tool.

5.) Perform the rite of the Housle.

6.) Anoint the tool with a cross of the sacrificial fluid, giving it a name at this time if you so wish. The Housle is the blood of the Mighty Ones.

Copyright Asteria Books 2018

7.) Finally, raise a drop of your own blood for the third and final cross in the Saining.

On Altars

In the ancient world, altars were places of offering and sacrifice. Devotees would petition a Deity by bringing an animal to be cooked (and often eaten communally), incense to be burned, or votive figurines to be placed in honor of the God or Goddess aligned with the petitioners' need. The altar was a consecrated place that was usually elevated, although on very rare occasions some specific types of altars (usually to Underworld Deities) were dug into the ground or incorporated into burial mounds.

Contemporary Neopagan and Witchcraft altars tend to be of two general types: the shrine and the working altar.

A shrine is an altar space that is consecrated and dedicated to prayer, service, or meditation related to a particular Deity, Spirit, energy, or idea. A Witch might erect an elemental shrine for Water in their bathroom, an ancestor shrine on their mantelpiece, or an Aphrodite shrine on a bedside table. These shrines might have collections of statuary, candles, flowers, offerings, photographs, jewelry, etc. However, they wouldn't necessarily have a full complement of tools for performing spells and rituals.

A working altar is the space where a Witch actually performs her spells and rituals, and it may also be where she stores a certain set of her symbolic or functional tools when not in use. It is her workshop table, in many ways. This is where candles are inscribed, poppets are sewn, and talismans are fashioned. It is also where trancework and other inner work is undertaken.

Most Witches have at least one altar space that is a blend of the shrine and the working altar. This is especially true for practitioners who can only create one altar due to space or privacy limitations.

Care should be taken to keep the altar both physically clean and energetically cleansed.

Copyright Asteria Publishing 2019

Witches' Stones

Hag Stone

Oath Stone

Mazey Stone

Casting Stones are used for divination. In their simplest version, they can include a yes-stone, a no-stone, and an indicator stone.

Hag Stones are stones with a naturally occurring hole (and are therefore sometimes called holey stones) that are enormously protective and luck-giving.

Keek Stones are stones with a clear, shiny surface that can be used for scrying. They can be light- or dark-colored. Also called Seer Stones.

Mazey Stones are stones with spiral carved onto their surfaces. The most common of these are made of slate and feature a labyrinth design that the Witch traces with a finger to induce a trance state. They are also called Troy Stones or Gate Stones.

Oath Stones are often featured in weddings and coronations, but within the Craft, they are the keepers of the vows and blood bonds made by the Family. The Red Thread that is the blood lineage of the Craft is passed through the Oath Stone, which is sometimes represented by an anvil. This stone is kept at the foot of the Stang.

Stroking Stones can be of almost type, though they should be smooth, about palm-sized, and of a pleasing nature to the healer, who is the one stroking or rubbing the stone.

Touch Stones were originally used to test the purity of soft precious metals like gold and silver. With its slight magnetic charge, a basalt touch stone is excellent as the core of the Broom, hidden at the crook of the Stang that forms its core.

Whetstones can be found on the altars of Cunning Folk, where a pentacle almost never would be. It is used to sharpen the knives, and it is sometimes skillfully carved with a man's head or face.

Copyright Asteria Books 2018

The Oath Stone

THE ANVIL

There are several types of stones that are important to Cunning Folk. With a Witchfather linked to the forge and alchemy, it is no surprise that the Oath Stone upon which we take our vows and form our sacred blood bonds is his anvil.

To do this, simply draw a small amount of blood using your Shelg (red-handled knife or thumb-pricker) or a sterile lancet and speak your oath while holding your blood to the anvil. If you are making vows of Initiation, all of the members of the coven should also have drawn their blood and touched the Oath Stone, as well. This forms the bond of Family.

In addition to being used for taking vows, the anvil can also be used as a way to call upon Tubal Cain as the Forge Master. Strike the hammer to the anvil three times, each time pausing to call his name. It is powerful. It still gives me chills when I call to him this way. Through iron. Through our blood. Through Tubal Cain's blood. Through the heartbeat that is pounded out in the rhythm of the hammer strokes. And heartbeats.

The symbolism of the forge is powerful, alchemical, mystical. The anvil is the foundation of Stone. The forge is the transformational Flame. The bellows are the Breath. The quench is the Sea (both womb and tomb).

Ours is a path of the Mysteries of Life and Death and all that lies Between. It is Creation and Destruction. Destroying in order to Create. Mixing Fire and Water to temper the steel and make it stronger. Knowing how and when to do that in the right proportion.

And the anvil is the rock, the hard place on which this great work happens. It is the altar on which we are pounded and shaped (at our own request!) into something useful, something beautiful, something dangerous.

The earliest anvils were actual stones, of course, and a great many cultures have had ceremonies involving oathing and coronation stones. The Lia Fail (Stone of Destiny) and Jacob's Pillow are two well-known coronation stones upon which dynasties of monarchs took vows to serve God and country. Furthermore, the custom has long-existed in Celtic countries for couples to make their wedding vows upon an oathing stone.

Within this Tradition, the Anvil as the Oath Stone sits at the base of the Stang when the Compass is drawn, along with the Cauldron.

Copyright Asteria Books 2018

The Stang

A stang, in its most basic form is simply a forked stick set with its long end into the ground. It acts as an axis on which magic can turn, and as a pole that can be "ridden" by the shaman or witch into different realms. Its forks represent the horns of the Witch Lord. The stang entered modern Craft by the hand of Robert Cochrane, who called it as "sacred to the People as the Crucifix is to the Christians."

A witch and her demonic familiar fly on a stang.

A masked family flies out on their stang.

The stang is sometimes represented by a iron-tined pitchfork or a pole with the skull of a horned beast on it. Often in these configurations there will be a candle or torch lit between the two horns or tines, in the style of the icon of Baphomet. Although not as popular as motif as, say, riding a broomstick, there are many examples of witches using the stang to fly in early woodcuts. The stang has antecedents in the Yggdrasill of Norse lore, the Poteau Mitan of Haitian Voudon, and the ascending-pole birch tree of the Yakut shamans. It is both a world-pillar on which the cosmos turns, and a gandreigh. Any wood is suitable for use as a stang, although ash, with its connections to Yggdrasill, the tree on which Odin was hung shaman-like for nine days, is a popular choice. The stang is hung with two arrows, one black and one white. These arrow point upwards during the light half of the year and downwards during the dark half of the year. Some covens don't always hang two arrows on the stang. Sometimes, it is a single arrow, with a linen shirt hung from it. The shirt can be either white or black, depending on the ritual or time of year. The stang is the hayfork that represents the Horned God, but it is also the spinner's distaff. The linen shirt on a single arrow is an allusion to the flax wrapped around the distaff.

Copyright Asteria Publishing 2012

The Three Knives

The Athame, the Kerfane, and the Shelg are the three knives, Black, White, and Red.

There are three knives associated with traditional Craft. These knives each represent the three realms, and the White Goddess, the Black Goddess, and the Red God. Each knife is used in a very specific and exclusive way.

The first of the knives is the black-handled blade, the Athame. It is the tool of the first realm and relates to the Black Goddess. The Athame is used for cutting and describing numen. It is used primarily to cut and direct energy links and sometimes to delineate sacred space. Gate portals are cut with the Athame, and it is the Witch's primary weapon when in liminal space.

The second knife is the white-handled blade, the Kerfane. It is the tool of the second realm and relates to the White Goddess. The Kerfane is used for cutting and carving in the physical realm. It may be used to fashion a wand, carve into a candle, cut cords, or harvest herbs. If the Kerfane is sickle-shaped and used for harvesting plant materials it is referred to as a boline. If the Kerfane is shaped like a pin and is used for inscribing materials it is referred to as a burin.

The third knife is the red blade, the Shelg. It is the tool of the third realm and relates to the Red God of the Forge, Tubal Qayin. The Shelg is used for blood magic and sacrifice. It may be used to open a small wound in the flesh in order to produce blood for oath-taking or binding links. It is also used during the Housle to activate the Red Meal as a true sacrifice. Although sterile lancets are often used in place of the Shelg for safe bloodletting in small amounts, the Shelg is still symbolically passed over the wound to seal the link to Qayin.

Copyright Asteria Publishing 2012

Athame

The black-handled blade, traditionally called the Athame, is usually a double-edged blade. It is the tool of the first realm and relates to the Black Goddess, Kolyo. The Athame is used for inscribing and cutting energy. It is used to cut energy links. It is the Witch's primary weapon when in liminal space, especially when dealing with baneful spirits.

The black-handled blade is almost never used to cut physical objects, though Traditional Witches are nothing if not pragmatists. Some will have only one knife and will use it equally for cutting energy, slicing through a magical threat, inscribing a spell candle, drawing blood for an initiatory oath, and slicing a roast for feast. It is for the individual Witch to determine the what is sanctified use of their own tool, and it is for that Witch to maintain those boundaries.

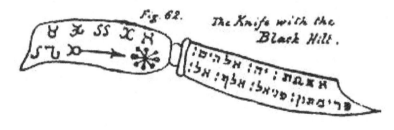

The black-handled knife as a magical tool dates back to the Key of Solomon, a medieval grimoire rumored to have been authored by the Biblical King. This knife was called by a slightly different name in that text, and it's appearance was a little different. However, its function was very similar. In that text, magicians are instruction in the forging of the knife using specific quenching liquids (hemlock juice and a coded herbal blend infusion) and sigils. It was recommended to make the knife on a Saturday in the planetary hour of Saturn.

Learn the meanings of these symbols — or choose/design several of your own to inscribe on the hilt of your blade. Begin at the hilt working toward the guard.

Copyright Asteria Books 2018

Kerfane & Boline

The white-handled knife is a tool of the second realm, the physical plane of existence. It is therefore used to cut physical objects and perform very practical, hands-on Crafting tasks. As such, it is related to Goda, the White Goddess whose domain is the abundant fields of the Lammas harvest and the rich soil of the Southern quarter in the American Folkloric Tradition.

Wiccan Tradition advocates for a crescent-bladed white-handled knife, the *Boline* — a name dating back to Solomonic texts (though the shape differed). The crescent has delicious lunar references and is often made of either silver or copper, for these magical blades.

The name *Kerfane* for a straight, single-edged blade seems to have Germanic origins and refers to a carving knife. Less lore and a great deal more every day practicality seems to surround this style of blade.

The white knife was described in the Key of Solomon, with directions to include mulberry sap and pimpernel extract in its quenching and to wrap in it a silk cloth for storage. The image below shows suggested inscriptions for both handle and blade.

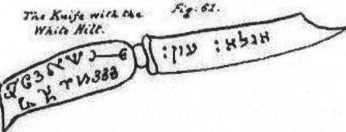

Shelg

The red-handled knife is the most secretive of blades within Craft practices. There are veiled references within both Solomonic lore and the writings of Joe Wilson (founder of the 1734 Tradition in the US) to a third knife, though its use is never specified. However, blood magic and blood bonds within the Craft and within traditional magical systems are both very well known.

There are at least styles of tool that can easily be used for this blade, depending on the preference of the Witch. The first is a hunting knife, which is the source of the name for *Shelg* (a Manx term that means to hunt or chase). The other is an awl or ice-pick, which hearkens back to the ancient practice of bloodletting through use of a lancet as a medical practice. Whichever style is chosen, great care should be taken to keep the blade razor sharp and sheathed when not in use.

The red-handled knife is dedicated in service to the Red God, Tubal Qayin, and should be sterilized, wiped clean, dried, and oiled with a thin layer of vegetable oil after each use.

Use this blade to "stab" the bread and "spill the blood" of the wine in your ritual sacrifice for the Red Meal or to make a small cut or puncture in the skin when doing blood magic or taking blood oaths. Remember that only a single drop of blood is needed to form a link. The code of your life is present in that single drop.

Copyright Asteria Books 2018

Care & Feeding of Steel

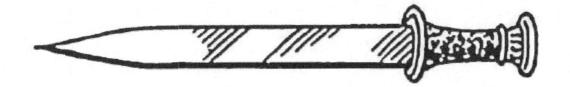

Witches use many types of blades within their Craft, and while blades can be fashioned from bone, wood, and other materials, it is most common for them to be forged from steel. It is wise, then, to know how to care for your steel blades to show respect for your tools and keep them in good repair.

To clean a blade, you'll first need to note whether it is Damascus or steel. If it is Damascus, use steel wool only, because it is delicate. If it is steel, you have the whole gambit of options — beginning with MetalGlo (or similar) cream and a clean, soft natural cloth. (Wash rags from auto supply stores work well.)

From there, you can try rottenstone (rust eraser). It works well on all sorts of metals.

After that, if you still have pitting from rust, you can move up to steel wool or sandpaper. Remember that the higher the number on the sandpaper, the finer the grit and softer it will be on the steel. For steel wool, look at the O rating. The more O's, the softer it is.

Always start with the softest abrasives available and work your way up when trying to clean up a problem. If you jump right into the harshest abrasive, you may forever ruin the finish or polish on your blade.

Once your blade is clean and rust free, put a light coat of oil on the steel. Use blade oil if it is a blade you do not use with food and drink (or to pierce your skin). Use vegetable oil if it is a blade you use for those purposes. Use a soft, clean cloth to apply the oil.

After each use, wipe the blade clean, and apply another thin layer of oil before securing the blade in its sheath.

Copyright Asteria Books 2018

The Cauldron

The cauldron is an ancient vessel of cooking and brewing that is associated in myth and legend with deep wisdom and transformation. This association stems, in part, to the story of Cerridwen and Gwion, in which Cerridwen sets her young farmhand the task of stirring a brew that is meant to bestow vast wisdom upon the one who drinks it. When three drops bubble onto Gwion's thumb, and he sucks the scalding burn, he is granted all the wisdom in the brew, and a perilous and transformative chase ensues. Eventually, Cerridwen consumes Gwion, when she is a hen and he is a grain, later giving birth to him as the renowned bard, Taliesin.

Another famous Celtic cauldron was that of the Dagda. His was called the Un-Dry Cauldron, for it was said to be bottomless. No man ever walked away from it unsatisfied. The cauldron had a ladle so large that two grown men could fit inside it.

Bran the Blessed had a cauldron called the Pair Dadeni ("Cauldron of Rebirth"), as recounted in the Mabinogian, a Welsh cycle of stories, that could restore the dead to life.

Robert Cochrane writes on the "two words that do not fit in the cauldron" as a mystery of the Craft. The answer to this riddle (which he provides in one of his letters) is "Be Still," for within the cauldron lies all motion, all potential, and all things. It cannot hold stillness, but this too is a mystery. The cauldron is used not just for the brewing of potions, but also as a vessel for scrying in liquid or flame. To accomplish this we must find stillness within the cauldron, by quieting our own minds.

The cauldron is also very similar to the Holy Grail of legend. We must ever seek it and its mysteries, for in it lies true communion with the Gods, and deep healing of our souls. "Who does the Grail serve?" is the riddle traditionally associated with this quest. The Grail serves all who seek it with honest intent, for it is only in not questing for the mystery that it serves no one.

"In fate and the overcoming of fate, lies the true Grail." - Robert Cochrane

Copyright Asteria Books 2018

Seasoning a Cast Iron Cauldron

If you only intend to use your cauldron as a symbolic ritual decoration, you don't need to take any special precautions for its physical care. However, it IS a functional piece of cookware that most Witches use in traditional ways to hold various liquids, make brews, and even light small fires. For these purposes, you will need to season it. A properly seasoned cast iron pot can last a lifetime, if cared for.

New Cauldrons
1. Heat the oven to 250°–300°F
2. Coat the cauldron with lard or bacon grease. Do not use vegetable oil, as it will leave a sticky surface, and the cauldron will not be properly seasoned.
3. Put the cauldron in the over for 15 minutes. Remove it and pour out any excess grease, wiping down the interior and exterior surfaces.
4. Return the cauldron to the oven to continue seasoning for another 2 hours.
5. Repeat this process several times, as it will create a stronger "seasoning bond."

Cauldrons Needing to be Re-Seasoned
If the cauldron was not seasoned properly, or if a portion of the season has worn off and there is now rust, the cauldron will need be cleaned and re-seasoned.
1. Remove residue or rust by cleaning thoroughly with hot water and a scouring pad. Heating the cauldron to a safely touchable temperature is also recommended to help with this process.
2. Dry the cauldron immediately with dish towel or paper towel.
3. Season the cauldron as outlined above.

Caring for Your Cast Iron Cauldron
When you first purchase your cast iron cook-pot, it will be medium grey in color and will darken with seasoning and use. This is normal. Store with the lid off (if it is a Dutch oven style) to prevent condensation, which leads to rust. Wipe clean and dry thoroughly after each use. If a liquid other than water was in the cauldron, use hot water to remove any sticky residue.

Copyright Asteria Books 2018

Conjuration

Banishing

In the event that you have summoned a spirit who won't leave on his own, you must know how to effectively banish. Banishing is a basic technique of psychic hygiene. To BANISH something is to make it leave. It is important to know how to banish before you ever call a spirit or energy to you. You wouldn't let someone in your house without knowing you can get them to leave. Some guests, like some spirits, will leave on their own at the end of a visit. Others need to be told politely that the time is up. And some folks have to be told (forcibly) to GO.

Anything from a good, strong impromptu dismissal to a full Star Ruby or Lesser Banishing Ritual of the Pentagram will work great. You can also write your own banishing incantations, if you like. If you write your own, be polite, specific, brief, and firm.

You can banish the entity by proclaiming "Get out" while focusing on the intruder. Or ... you can say/chant the following Greek words:

Hekas, o hekas, este bebeloi.

It translates to "Afar, afar, o ye Profane." So, really, it is saying "Get out, bad spirit." But in Greek.

Whatever you say, say it with meaning and conviction. And picture the spirit/energy being forced away.

You can also use physical items to banish. Florida Water or some other very floral perfumed water can be sprinkled around you, your working space, and your home. You can cleanse yourself with salt-water – including swishing some in your mouth. You can smudge with sage or cedar bundles – or burn an incense stick that has a clearing effect.

Gestures can also add potency to your banishing technique. Holding your hand up in the "stop" gesture or pointing vigorously toward a door are every bit as potent as drawing banishing pentagrams in the air with your hand or wand. Use what feels right to you.

All of these techniques should work wonders. You may have to "banish, rinse, repeat." Banishing is like sweeping the floors. Dust and schmutz can come back, and you have to sweep again.

Egregore Creation

Egregores and Servitors are thought-forms that have been created to serve a particular purpose. You can create a spirit to accomplish the goals you desire. Magicians do it all the time, and it is a traditional part of sorcery.

It can actually be quite difficult to tell the difference between a new creation or an older, existing being. That's because ALL spirits start somewhere, and many of them begin as servitors/egregores. Now, for a great many of the ones whose names we have recorded in old grimoires and such, they were created centuries or even millennia ago. Some were deities of conquered people whose Gods were demonized and brought low by the conquerors. Following this line of thinking brings a philosophical person back to the old question — did the Gods/God create us, or do we create them/him?

Generally, though, a newly created servitor isn't going to have the oomph behind it that an older being has. Not enough people have put their faith into that being, communicated with that being, etc. It hasn't done enough work to be as strong or as solid or as "weighty" as a spirit that has been around longer.

I would also suggest being open to working with newly "created" spirits. If they're getting the job done, and you enjoy them, then they can be every bit as effective and wonderful a companion as an older being. Thought creates reality, after all, which means that these beings are very "real."

When creating a new spirit, you can borrow the following symbols for creating the spirit's sigil, as well.

- Three dots means a very old spirit
- Little circles show realms of influence
- Crosses show good communication
- Moons show vision power and wisdom
- Triangles indicate crowns or high honors

Copyright Asteria Books 2016

Evoking Spirits

In regards to evocation of spirits, we advocate complete dismissal of traditional texts in which threats, binding, and torture by fire are called up in order to induce the spirits to appear before the mage and do his bidding. If you and the spirit don't have great enough affinity for each other, or if the spirit is too mischievous or angry for you to summon without the use of force, you're obviously better off leaving that spirit alone.

That isn't to say that every spirit will respond to softly-worded requests. Many of the Goetic Legion, as well as other types of spirits, require a firm hand and a strong Will in a Master. You must be strong, but not abusive.

The relationship you are seeking is an old-fashioned one. A great many (but not all) of the spirits covered in these pages refer to magicians as "Masters," but they are not our slaves. They are more like servants or employees; and if we are very lucky, they might become friends. We tend to make contractual agreements with them, whether we realize it or not, for either short or long periods of time. A simple magical working is relatively short, whereas having a spirit become your familiar is quite a long relationship. In either case, you do the spirit a disservice if you treat it like a slave. It is older than you, often by millennia, and it is probably willing and happy to help you if you treat it decently.

You may use the following summoning incantation until you have developed your own. Substitute the specific name, characteristics, and type appropriate to the spirit you are trying to call.

Orobas! Orobas! Orobas! Thrice, I call.

Wise and helpful, Orobas, come now to the Pyramid of Art

As my guest and counselor.

Appear to me now, friend Orobas!

Copyright Asteria Books 2016

The Fetch

The Fetch is an energetic form that the Witch creates and projects her Black Soul (astral body) into during flight. Some Witches do this so seamlessly and naturally that they are unaware of the projection and believe this is the natural form of the their Black Soul. In truth, this Fetch is an energetic shell that acts as a protective barrier and can even be sent independently of the Black Soul by an adept Witch.

The Fetch can be built to look like an exact copy of the Witch's physical body, or it might be constructed to look like a natural or mythological Animal Form. It can also be a combination of these forms. Whatever the nature of the Fetch, it should be one that the Witch resonates with on a deep level. Indeed, the Fetch should suggest its shape to the Witch (in a manner of speaking), more than the Witch defining the shape consciously.

Interestingly, this Fetch is not sentient in its own right. It is a shell that awaits the Black Soul to inhabit and enliven it. When it is en-souled (or programmed with enough directed energy) it can move among the Realms and even be seen in physical, consensus reality by some.

It is a good idea to create a physical vessel or "home" for the Fetch to inhabit when you aren't using it. The vessel (called a Fetch) can be practically anything, and since the Fetch is not a being of Will the way a Familiar is, it won't have its own opinion about what sort of vessel it prefers. You can make something that strikes your fancy and fits your needs. You might consider a large stone, a wood carving, a leather engraving, a painting, a sculpture, a statue, a spirit bottle, a doll, a talisman.

The more you work with a particular Fetch, the more powerful it becomes. You are feeding it energy each time you enter it and send it forth. You can also feed it energy when it is in residence it its house. Furthermore, you can create more than one Fetch and Fetch (house), though this is admittedly a division of your energetic resources. You may, however, find that you have reasons for doing this. You may also discover that you wish to deconstruct or destroy a Fetch, which you can do by destroying the Fetich and reabsorbing the energy. This should be avoided, if possible, though. In fact, you'll probably find that you have psychological or emotional resistance to such destruction. This is because the Fetch is a sort of egregore or Spirit. And while it may not have Will or sentience of its own, it does have a sort of Life. Still, that Life is an extension of yourself -- of your Black Soul, specifically. If the vessel is no longer able to serve, it must be cleared and rebuilt.

Copyright Asteria Books 2016

The Witch's Familiar

When a Witch talks about a "spirit known unto her" -- a familiar spirit -- that isn't a historical implication of the household cat. In fact, cats weren't even the most likely animals to be a witch's corporeal familiar in the Middle Ages, as the cat wasn't a common household compatriot at that time. The term "pussycat" most likely referred to the rabbit (Latin "lepus"), an animal that was much more associated with witchcraft, lunar magic, necromancy, and shapeshifting. Isobel Gowdie's famous confession is said to include the following chant for shapeshifting into a rabbit:

Corporeal Familiar

A corporeal familiar is a living animal with whom you have a working, magical relationship. This animal shows an interest and adeptness for some types of magic you perform. Some familiars love ritual, and they present themselves promptly at the start of every circle and spell. Some are magnificent energy workers, and they'll help you direct healing energy. Most animals like energy, and many animals are willing to help with the healing process in some capacity. As for willingness or talent to be a familiar in magic, you really need to pay attention to the proclivities of the specific animal. They aren't all interested or able, no matter how much you love each other.

Incorporeal Familiar

Witches didn't just have animals who helped them manifest their magic. Folklore, nursery rhymes, and trial records are filled with accounts of witches and other adepts calling upon familiar spirits to do their bidding and assist them with both mundane and spiritual struggles.

Nature spirits, angels, demons, magistelli, Deities, the Mighty Dead, the Good People —there are a host of unseen forces with myriad names. Witches have certainly worked with all of these. The Unseen World enfolds us, and we Witches walk within it, while maintaining a connection to consensus reality. Our familiar spirits help us navigate and understand the Unseen, for they are a part of that world.

Copyright Asteria Books 2019

Sphere and Pyramid

The truest working space of the Conjurer or Witch is not a flat space marked on the ground with words and symbols. Mark the circle and triangle with the names of Gods and Angels if it improves your focus, but understand that you live and work in three physical dimensions (and more which aren't of a physical nature). The Mage needs a sphere, not a circle, to stand within. She calls spirits into a pyramid, not a triangle. Enclose yourself and the entity on all sides for sure protection.

Most Witches already work within this paradigm, marking their circle in flat space while visualizing and energizing it in space. However, the concept bears repeating, in the event that readers haven't been exposed to this idea previously.

As far as the words and gestures used to create the sacred space, you can be very simple or very elaborate.

Another point to consider is that not every spirit needs to be called into a Pyramid. Many of the spirits you'll encounter are helpful and benevolent. Most Witches would call such entities into the Circle (Sphere) with themselves, not outside of it in a spirit trap. If you truly honor and respect the spirit whom you are calling, it makes sense to call it into your sphere.

Copyright Asteria Books 2015

Spirit Keeping

The decision to have a familiar is not a unilateral one. A Witch does not simply choose a spirit from a list and then trap it within a seal, a bottle, or a figurine. A familiar is not a spiritual slave or a prisoner.

The relationship between master and familiar should be mutually beneficial. The familiar assists in magic, according to his abilities; and the Witch returns energy in the forms of gratitude, gifts, ritual, or something specific to the familiar. Spirits will often tell you specifically what they want if you just talk to them.

Look to traditional texts and lore for inspiration regarding what your spirit may like, but don't rely solely on these sources. No one person who knows you is privy to all the things you may like or dislike. The same is true of spirits. The traditional texts and lore can't encapsulate all there is to know about a spirit.

Most familiar spirits want some sort of housing. This is often a jar or bottle. The housing can also take the shape of a candle or a statue, a piece of jewelry, or some other item. Just ask and they will be very clear, often asking for something you already own. The purpose of the house is to give the spirit a vessel to inhabit. There are benefits to having a physical form, after all. The house or vessel brings a certain level of pleasure to the spirit.

They almost all like offerings, as well; though the nature of the offerings varies greatly from spirit to spirit. Our coven familiar wants smoke, and she gave us a specific incense recipe that we were to make and burn for her. The familiar of one of our students wanted ashes. She didn't care what was burned to create the ash, as long as it was burned with the intention of giving it to her. Some like honey, mint candies, liquor, or other comestibles. Others want energy in the form of dancing, laughing, or sex. Again, we recommend asking your spirit directly what he wants and how often he wants it.

Copyright Asteria Books 2016

Witches and the Goetia

It has been the role of the Witch to summon and stir spirits as allies in magic since Witches first started practicing their Craft. We see evidence of that in folklore, trial records, and art. Spirit conjuration (what can rightly be called "demonic conjuration") is a long-standing practice in the sort of sorcerous witchcraft that is practiced by people like us. Lore and witch trial records (not ALL of which can be complete fabrications) are filled with accounts of witches calling upon familiar spirits to do their bidding.

The word "angel" comes from the Greek ἄγγελος pronounced "angelos", which means messenger. "Demon" also comes from the Greek – δαίμων pronounced daímōn, meaning nothing more or less than "spirit." Neither was inherently benevolent, nor was the other malevolent.

We humans are spiritual beings having a human experience. We are spirits enfleshed, and we walk within a world of ethereal spirits who act as guides, guardians, and aides to us, often whether we are aware of them or not. People find comfort in knowing that they are not alone, even if they cannot see their circle of friends because they dwell in Spirit. More than that, Witches find companions in magic among the spirits familiar to them (spirit familiars).

Like most beings, angels and demons are primarily looking out for themselves, but they're willing to make a deal with you. Actually, I think that can be said of ALL non-corporeal spirits. Some are naturally more amiable and inclined to work with you. Some, not so much. A few can be down-right nasty, but don't let their "racial" category be the deciding factor. There are more fey that I would recommend avoiding than there are Goetic demons, frankly.

In fact, Paul Huson, in his book *Mastering Witchcraft* suggests getting in touch with a particular Goetic demon pretty early in your Craft practice. "Goetia" may actually be one of the ancient Greek words for witchcraft.

γοητεία <u>goēteia</u> – charm, jugglery
γόης <u>goes</u> – charmer, enchanter, sorcerer

Don't approach any demon or other spirit lightly or unprepared, by any means. But having a good working relationship with a couple of these spirits is a good thing for a witch.

Copyright Astoria Books 2015

Spirit Magic and Communication

Finding a spirit with whom you can work magic, communicate, and build a relationship isn't as tricky a task as it may sound. There are hundreds or even thousands of different "races" of spirits. Within each race, there are countless individuals. Someone on the other side of the veil is right for you.

There is literally no end to the work you can accomplish with the help of "your little daemon." Liberal sciences, necromancy, alchemy, art, foreign language, diplomacy, law, love - these spirits know all of the things that you want to know. The can make learning significantly easier. They love what you love and will help you pursue, protect, and promote those passions.

This is sorcery, witchcraft. You don't have to make it complicated unless that placates your sense of the Arte Magical.

Each spirit is an individual and will have his preferred method of working, as well. Some are chatty, others communicate with images. Some might like complicated ritual and arcane language, while many prefer simplicity. Some sing - all the time. They are as individual and quirky as the magicians who work with them.

However old the spirits you work with may be, the traditional descriptions you may find of them online or in books may be equally old (and outdated). Everybody changes at least a little in 400 years, even spirits. Furthermore, some details weren't recorded accurately in the first place. (As an example, the spirits of the Goetic Legion were all originally described as inherently masculine, regardless of how anciently that spirit may have been worshipped as a Goddess.)

Communicate with your chosen spirit in whatever way makes the most sense. If he is verbal, use automatic writing or a talking board as you develop your clairaudient abilities. If she is visual, use a scrying mirror, cauldron, crystal ball, etc. Try trance, flying out, lucid dreaming, smoke/fire scrying, trance dance, or sexual energy; or simply try listening and looking for your spirit.

The Unseen World is not a separate place, distinct and untouched by This World. Beings of spirit and beings of flesh walk in both places. We ourselves are, ultimately, beings of spirit who are also beings of flesh. Spirits know that we inhabit both spaces at once. Mages and Witches should know this, as well.

Copyright Asteria Books 2016

Affinity With a Spirit

Not every spirit is a good fit for each Witch or Mage. Not only are some spirits dangerous and should be avoided, but many are simply incompatible for a given individual. You have undoubtedly met people with whom you couldn't work or whose company you didn't enjoy. They aren't inherently bad people. You just don't like them. The same will be true of many spirits. The goal with spirit keeping is to find those spirits with whom you can build a working, fraternal, familial, or even romantic relationship with.

A Witch will have a number of potential spirits from whom she might choose. During the time that she is researching those spirits, they might also be observing her.

When a particularly strong attraction presents itself to a Master, this spirit is a natural candidate to become a familiar. Indeed, the spirit may already be acting in that capacity for the Witch, and the Witch needs only to recognize the spirit's presence.

Of course, more than one spirit may be available to you from the hosts of individuals on the Other Side, but it is important that you pay close attention to how well these spirits work with each other before you take on multiple working partnerships with various spirits. They don't all get along, after all, and to bring too many of them into your life is to court madness.

Copyright Asteria Books 2016

Initiation

No-Kill Food List

Fruits & Berries
- Apples
- Apricots
- Bananas
- Blackberries
- Blueberries
- Cantaloupe
- Cherries
- Coconuts
- Cranberries
- Dates
- Figs
- Grapes
- Grapefruit
- Honeydew Melons
- Kiwi
- Lemons
- Limes
- Mangoes
- Nectarines
- Olives
- Oranges
- Pomegranates
- Pears
- Plums
- Raisins
- Raspberries
- Strawberries
- Watermelon

Many Vegetables
- Artichokes
- Asparagus
- Bell Peppers
- Greens (spinach, chard, collard, kale)
- Tomatoes
- Avocadoes
- Broccoli
- Squash (all varieties)
- Pumpkin
- Zucchini
- Brussels Sprouts
- Cauliflower
- Cucumber

Beans & Some Legumes
- Green Beans
- Peas
- Peanuts
- Black Beans
- Kidney Beans
- Navy Beans
- Pinto Beans
- White Beans
- Soy Beans, Edamame

Many Herbs, Spices & Seasonings
- Salt
- Pepper
- Cinnamon
- Cardamom
- Cocoa (unsweetened)
- Allspice
- Nutmeg
- Curry
- Chives
- Cilantro
- Dill
- Oregano
- Rosemary
- Mint
- Basil
- Parsley
- Sage
- Thyme
- (All the leafy herbs)
- Oil
- Vinegar

Most Seeds & Nuts
- Cashews
- Sunflower Seeds
- Pepitas
- Almonds
- Walnuts
- Pecans
- Pistachios

Grains & Starches
- Corn, Hominy, Grits, Polenta
- Oats, Oatmeal
- Quinoa
- Barley
- Buckwheat
- Bulgar wheat
- Couscous
- Potatoes
- Sweet Potatoes
- Rice

Dairy
- Butter
- Sour Cream
- Milk
- Cheese
- Yogurt
- Heavy Cream

Unrefined Sweeteners
- Agave
- Raw Honey
- Monk Fruit Sweetener

Copyright Asteria Books 2020

No-Kill No-No List

No-No Vegetables
Beets
Cabbage
Carrots
Celery
Garlic
Leeks
Mushrooms
Onions
Parsnips
Radishes
Turnips

No-No Legumes
Chickpeas
Lentils

No-No Herbs, Spices & Seasonings
Turmeric
Ginger
Most prepared condiments (will have onion, garlic, or turmeric -- or sugar)

No-No Grains & Starches
Pasta (prepared with egg)
Bread (prepared with egg & yeast)

No-No Sweeteners
White sugar
Brown sugar
Corn syrup
Light syrup

No-No Proteins
Animal meat (including fish)
Eggs

As with any type of fast, the No-Kill Fast is intentionally restrictive. However, it's purpose isn't to deprive your body of essential nutrients or create a state of lack or general privation. The purpose is to bring mindfulness, clarity, and purification.

You are free to choose other types of fasts, if you prefer. The Spiral Castle Tradition has always favored this one, however, because it draws such a sharp point of focus while allowing great room for personal choice without leaving any food groups out. With forethought, you should be able to eat balanced meals and snacks during your time of fasting.

Tips: Watch out for pre-packed foods. So many of them have onion or garlic powder or sugar! Read the labels carefully. When in doubt, research "home harvesting" or "is X a perennial" for the ingredient to see if the parent plant would likely be killed in your garden for you to eat this food.

Copyright Asteria Books 2020

A Few No-Kill Fast Recipes

Breakfasts
- Quick (or Steel Cut) Oats with honey, cinnamon, cream
- Grits with honey and butter
- Greek yogurt with berries and toasted oats

Snacks
- Cottage cheese with fruit (orange slices, pineapple chunks, or strawberries) and sesame seeds
- Parmesan crisps and homemade hummus or guacamole (leaving the garlic out of either dip, of course)
- Apple slices with sugar-free peanut butter
- Banana with a handful of almonds

Nachos
Corn chips
Freshly chopped tomatoes
Black beans
Shredded cheese (2-3 varieties)
Avocado slices
Sour cream

Three Sisters Bowl

2 cups cubed and peeled squash of choice
1 Tbsp balsamic vinegar
1 Tbsp olive oil
1 pinch salt
Toss these together and roast in the oven for 20-30 minutes (until fork tender).
Meanwhile, sauté the following in a Dutch oven:
2 ears corn
1 1/2 cups pre-cooked or canned beans
1-2 tablespoons olive oil
1 red pepper, diced
2 tablespoons chopped parsley
1 tablespoon chopped sage
1 teaspoon minced rosemary leaves
1 teaspoon thyme leaves
salt and pepper, to taste
Combine. Serve warm as is or over wild rice, quinoa — or even cold with kale/greens as a salad.

Creamy Vegetable Soup

I start with the most basic potato soup ever — peeled cubed white potatoes, water, butter, a little salt, and heavy cream. To this I add <u>barley</u> and whatever chopped vegetables I like and can find from our list, preferring ones that are in season. Favorites include okra and squash. I really don't measure anything, as you really can't "mess it up."

Copyright Asteria Books 2020

Initiation Recipes

Incense

2 tbsp Red rose petals (Kolyo)
2 tbps Jasmine blossoms (Koda)
1/2 tsp Forge scale for Tubal Cain
1 tsp Dittany of Crete
1 tsp White copal resin
1 tsp Rowan berries
1 tsp Sandalwood
10 drops Amber oil

Anointing Oil

1 oz Base oil (Jojoba, Grapeseed)
10 drops Rose oil
10 drops Jasmine oil
5 drops Amber oil
3 drops Clary Sage oil

Dressed Candle

Dress a white chime candle using a small amount of your anointing oil and incense. This is the candle you will burn during your preparatory bath.

Bath Sachet

Place the following in a muslin drawstring bag or cotton/linen hankie tied with a string:
2 tbsp Crushed rose petals
2 tbsp Crushed jasmine blossoms
1 tbsp Mugwort
Pinch of Sandalwood
Pinch of Sea Salt

Add 1/4 cup Apple Cider Vinegar directly to water

Sabbat Wine

Warm 1-2 cups of a VERY sweet red wine (like Oliver soft red or Manischewitz Concord grape) in a saucepan.

For every cup of wine, steep the following herbal mix in equal parts (using a teaball):

Mugwort
Lemon Balm

Steep for 5 minutes, then remove the teaball. Add raw honey to sweeten.

Copyright Asteria Books 2020

Rite of Raising - Self-Initiation 1

Materials
- Stang, candles, lighter
- Cauldron, water
- Anvil, hammer, lancet
- Three knives (red, black, white)
- Red Cord, Black Cord, White Cord
- Bread, lipped dish or bowl
- Red wine, cup, mugwort, lemongrass, honey, teaball
- Initiation incense, holder, charcoal
- Bath sachet, dressed candle, anointing oil
- Stone Bowl with stones, Dark Mirror
- Initiation Gift (amber, jet & bone necklace)

Raise the Stang
Lay the Compass
Open the Gates
Challenges & Trials

- **Challenges** -- Within the ritual space, challenge and query yourself by Mind, Heart, and Spirit.
- **Sabbat Wine** -- Drink the Sabbat Wine or Mugwort Tea.
- **Three Stones** -- Ask the stones which of our Deities is choosing to guide you in your future studies, work, and service within the Spiral Castle. The first stone you touch holds your answer (white-Goda, black-Kolyo, red-Qayin).
- **Black Mirror** -- Scry for these things: 1) your Craft names -- secret and known, and 2) your Mark.
- **Triple Cords** -- Braid the black cords, the white cords, and ultimately, the full set of Triple Cords together while contemplating Kolyo and her role as Weaver of Magic and Fate.

Vows, Oath & Presentation

- **Vows & Oath** -- Before the Oath Stone, ask and answer aloud each Vow. Then make your Oath in blood upon the Stone, using your full known Craft name.
- **Presentation** -- Anoint yourself with the oil, and say, "So now do I proclaim myself a true Witch of the Spiral Castle. So shall I be recognized among my Folk and Family! I present myself to the Realms, Gates, Towers, Spirits, and Godds of the Spiral Castle. I am, [Complete Craft Name], a fully Raised Witch of the Spiral Castle! So Mote it Be!"
- **Gift** -- Give yourself the Witch's Necklace (or other gift)

Housle

Copyright Asteria Books 2020

Oath of Raising

Turn to the Oath Stone.

Kneel and grasp the Stone with your blooded hand, both to give and receive the Oath of Initiation.

From this day forward, _____ will be my name in the Initiate circles of the Spiral Castle Tradition. As I will it, so mote it be! So mote it be! So mote it be!

I, _____, do take this solemn Oath of Initiation. I will be an Initiate member of this Family and Tradition from this day forward. I vow to honor Tubal Qayin, Kolyo, and Goda who have made this Path their own. I will hold secret all the Mysteries of this Family and the personal accounts of my Siblings. I will respect my fellow Initiates, and I will consider members of my Covenant as blood kin. By taking these vows, I freely twine my spirit with the Raised Witches of the Spiral Castle. I give you my trust and my honor. I give Tubal Qayin, Kolyo, and Goda my heart. I promise to speak honestly and behave with integrity. I will serve the Spiral Castle to the very best of my ability. [Additional vows may be added here.] So swear I, _____. As I will it, so mote it be. So mote it be! So mote it be!

So now am I proclaimed a true Witch of the Spiral Castle!

Copyright Asteria Books 2020

Vows of Raising

We do not sever the Red Cords of Adoption. A child of the Spiral Castle will always be Family ~ connected to the Craft, the Castle, its Caretakers, and this Kindred by Blood and Word. Having passed the Trials of Initiation - tests of mind, heart, and spirit -- I move forward. I have found my True Name (both spoken and silent), found and made my Mark, and seen the Vision Quest. I have proven myself worthy of the name Witch, but I am not bound to take it. I am free in all things. Furthermore, a Raised Witch is a full member of the family and can never be cast out of the tradition, even if the cords are burned, the Mark is cut from the flesh, and the blood withdrawn from the stone. The bond of the Secret Name exists between the Initiate and the Mighty Ones and can be broken by no one.

Do I choose with my own free will to take initiation in the Spiral Castle?

I have passed an examination of my knowledge of the Craft. Am I ready to fulfill my intellectual responsibilities as a Raised Witch?

I have sought and found answers from the Unseen. Am I willing to seek beyond the veil for the Truth, for both myself and my siblings?

Am I prepared to weave my spirit with the Witches in this Tradition by becoming an Initiate?

I have sought and found a vision for myself. Am I willing to share that vision and make it a reality as I grow?

I have been chosen by our Witch Father/Queen as a child of the Craft. Am I willing to explore the Mysteries of this relationship as I grow?

I say plain: I would be sworn a Witch.
I say again: I would be worn a Witch.
By Thrice-three I lay my claim: I will be sworn an Initiate Witch in the Spiral Castle Tradition.

So mote it be!

Copyright Asteria Books 2020

Red Thread Academy
Traditional Witchcraft

Personal Mentoring with Laurelei

Some students need to form a more in-depth relationship with their teacher during their studies. Others need more personal guidance to make sense of the lessons. Yet others want to deepen their understanding and really dig into the work.

Whatever your goals, I am offering my RTA students an incredibly special opportunity to connect with my coaching services at a reduced amount. You are eligible to receive monthly 1-hour coaching sessions with me (via Zoom, Google Chat, Messenger, etc) — available through patreon.com/laureleiblack.

These sessions are a great way to tackle areas of challenge in both your personal life and magical practice. They will help you dive deeper into the material and have a great depth and breadth of understanding. This coaching experience is entirely customized to your needs, goals, concerns, and achievements.

<u>What makes you a good Magical Life Coach, Laurelei?</u>

- I am a teacher. -- Bachelor degree in Secondary Education with several years of classroom experience

- I am a Witch. -- 1st degree, August 2000, Clan of the Laughing Dragon tradition

- I am an ordained Priestess. -- 2nd degree, January 2002, Clan of the Laughing Dragon tradition

- I am a Queen. -- 3rd degree, January 2005, Clan of the Laughing Dragon tradition; co-founder of the Spiral Castle (American Folkloric Witchcraft) tradition, January 2009

- I am a public speaker. -- Presenting classes, rituals, and temple experiences at Babalon Rising Pan-Thelemic Festival, Chrysalis Moon Festival, Starwood, ConVocation, and most events at Camp Midian (from 2013 - 2021)

- I am a psychic intuitive. -- Offering professional readings online, in shops, and at festivals since 2010

- I am a Pagan community leader. -- Co-founder of Midian Festivals and Events in 2014, lead event organizer until 2022; former area coordinator for Indianapolis Pagan Pride Day, 2005-2011; co-founder of Indy CUUPS, 2005; organizer and co-director of Babalon Rising Pan-Thelemic Festival since 2009; director of the Women's Goddess Retreat since 2009

These are my credentials, but they aren't necessarily what makes me good at what I do. If anything, they are evidence that I am dedicated to serving my community and my Gods through teaching, advising, and practicing Witchcraft.

What makes me good at this is the fact that I love it and that I have a natural skill-set that I have honed through years of study and service.

I am called to teach. That is my work in this lifetime; maybe in all my lifetimes.

My greatest desire is to lead an authentic, meaningful, and passionate life and to help others do the same. I believe that the principles of Witchcraft are inherently tied to these goals, for me and for my students.

<u>What are the goals of the coaching relationship?</u>
That depends entirely on you. The goals are YOURS, not mine. What do you want and need to deepen your practice, broaden your understanding, or live a more magic-filled life?

Our monthly sessions can be focused on goals related to your Witchcraft studies:
- Get in-person, in-depth feedback on your assignments

- Practice your divination skills with me

- Explore Craft concepts in a personalized way

- Seek advice regarding specialties within the Craft

- Discuss personal experiences in ritual, meditation, and magic

- Get assistance with problematic projects or concepts

Or, our sessions can be focused on goals related to other areas of your life:
- Find your life's purpose (your Great Work)

- Untangle and decode the symbols in your own personal myth

- Create wealth and abundance

- Find your soul's mate(s)

- Implement new magical techniques and information

- Create healing for your mind, body, and spirit

I can help you achieve the goals that are important to you, whatever they are. Your sessions will include traditional coaching techniques, blended with divination, magic, meditation, and symbol exploration.

<u>What You Need to Know</u>

* As part of our coaching sessions, you will receive a 60-minute video-call each month, a personalized plan for reaching the goals you have set for yourself, the possibility of additional "homework" assignments and activities to help you achieve those goals, psychic reading services included within your call to support your efforts, and email communications throughout the month to check-in with your progress.

* Because of the deep discount on my coaching services for this special student offer, payment is required before each session, and refunds are not an option.

* A coach (even a psychic, witchy one) is not a counselor, but more of an advisor. My role in your life is different than a therapist or a doctor; and I am telling you unequivocally that I am neither of those things. I am here to help you reach your goals, and I will do that in a no-nonsense, plain-speak sort of way. I will be gently honest with you at every step of the way.

* I can't do the work for you. You have to take responsibility for your progress.

If you want to get started with your personalized coaching sessions, email me at laurelei@asteriabooks.com.

Red Thread Academy
Traditional Witchcraft

SCT Retreats

Coming Soon!

I love organizing and hosting weekend-long getaways with like-minded folks. It's one of my favorite things.

Starting in 2022 (maybe, if I'm super-diligent) or 2023 (if I want to give myself plenty of time and space), I plan to start hosting an annual Spiral Castle retreat close to my home in the Midwestern United States.

Here is a little of what we can expect from such a retreat:
- A recurring event happening each summer
- Open to all "corded" members of the Tradition
- Multiple group rituals
- Opportunity to witness and practice ritual and magickal techniques
- Engaging group discussions for SCT-ers at every level of study
- Special sessions for Initiates
- Bewitching bonfires for dancing, drumming, magick, and more

Please make sure that you download the Thread up so you can stay up-to-date with Spiral Castle Tradition news and events.

Red Thread Academy
Traditional Witchcraft

In-Person Initiation (3rd Degree)

Some students have asked for an in-person initiatory experience, and I am so ecstatic to be able to offer this amazing weekend-long retreat as a capstone for the full 3 years of study to those who are interested.

<u>Why do an in-person initiation?</u>
The benefits of an initiatory experience under the leadership of an experienced initiator (or initiatory team) include:

- Preservation of the Mysteries of Initiation. This initiation ritual is, by necessity, different from the one offered as a self-initiation at the end of the independent study course. As with all true initiatory experiences, you won't know the exact format or symbols included in the initiation until you undergo the ritual, which preserves the anticipation and heightened awareness that usually accompanies the initiation.

- Symbolically-Rich Ceremony. The language, actions, altar dressings, etc all work together to add many layers of meaning, which provides excellent fodder for reflection and gnosis.

- Safety. Not only am I an experienced ritualist and initiator, I am also CPR certified through the American Red Cross, and I have received training for crisis management and intervention.

- Passing of Craft Lineage. We will have worked together (albeit, at a distance) for three years or more. This in-person initiation allows me the opportunity to formally create the bond of mentor and initiator with you. That is an energetic reality that has some potent magical benefits, as attested by magical traditions worldwide.

- Confidence in Your Skills. All initiation has some level of ordeal or trial built into it. You must prove yourself worthy to move into the next stage of spiritual development, to join the group or society. It's difficult to fully and fairly test oneself. In our initiation ritual, though, it is me who is testing you (and the Godds through me). When you have passed those tests, you will never doubt that you really did pass.

- Bonding Within the Tradition. Because there is ordeal (uncertainty, testing, stress) within an initiation, you feel much more connected to your initiator and to any others involved in the process. You are truly part of the Family, and you will know at least a few siblings with whom you have a deep bond.

<u>What is the process?</u>
Our Initiation Weekend will be scheduled in advance. You should start the dialogue with me about 2 months before you would like to take advantage of this opportunity. I'll need to verify your assignments have been satisfactorily completed, and then we'll choose a weekend that is convenient for us both. I'll reserve the cabin and make arrangements for meals, as well as coordinate with the other members of the initiation team.

I'll provide you with a list of things you need to bring with you. Getting yourself and these few items to the initiation location will be your own responsibility. (I can pick you up from the airport or bus/train station, if you travel from afar. Or I'll give you the address of the cabin, if you are driving.)

We will either be renting a cabin in Southern Indiana or Central Kentucky, depending on availability and your preference. The address and phone number will be provided to you once the arrangements are made.

The experience is a retreat, so we suggest limited phone and social media usage, but the only time we will be incommunicado will be during the prep, ritual, and debrief. No photos or video of the initial ritual will be permitted, of course.

I'll also be getting information from you regarding medications, medical concerns, allergies, etc., as well as providing you with instructions for the preparatory actions you will need to take as we approach the initiation date.

We will be together for 3 days and 2 nights -- Friday afternoon to Sunday afternoon. The team will consist of me and at least one other person. If you wish, you may bring someone with you, but we will need to make arrangements for their meals (at an additional cost), and they will need to vacate the premises for the duration of the initiation ritual (several hours during the night and early morning), unless they are also a Spiral Castle Tradition initiate of at least the same degree.

What is included in the cost?
The following are included in the fee:
- Fasting-compliant meals on Friday (lunch and dinner) and Saturday (breakfast and lunch)

- Celebratory feast on Saturday night

- Non-fasting meals on Sunday (breakfast and lunch)

- Vacation-style cabin accommodations -- 2 bedrooms (bedding provided), at least 1 bathroom (linens provided), full kitchen (basic cookware provided), and possibly a hot-tub

- Private (and possibly group) coaching sessions -- at least one each day

- Psychic readings -- at least 2 (one before, one after initiation)

- Initiation cords, regalia, and other items

- Lineage binder

- Framed, signed certificate of initiatory degree

To schedule your initiation weekend and get a quote for current pricing, email me at laurelei@asteriabooks.com.

Asteria Books

Also by Laurelei Black

Aphrodite's Priestess
Cult of Aphrodite: Rites and Festivals of the Golden One
Temple of Love (fiction)
Crown of Violets: Words and Images Inspired by Aphrodite
Wisdom of Love: Cowrie Divination System

Red Thread Academy — Year 1: Foundations (Course Manual)
Red Thread Academy — Year 2: Practicum (Course Manual)
Red Thread Academy — Year 3: Mastery (Course Manual)
The Witches' Key to the Legion: A Guide to Solomonic Sorcery
Asteria Books' Complete Herbal Grimoire

Writing as Delilah Temple

To Call Ye Forth (Witches' Rune series, Book 1)

Coming Soon

Darksome Night and Shining Moon (Witches' Rune series, Book 2) — Delilah Temple
The Witches' Key to the Unseen World: A Comprehensive Guide to Spirit Work — Laurelei Black
Asteria Events' Guide to Pagan Festival Planning — Laurelei Black
Asteria Mystery School's Digital Lesson Library — Laurelei Black
The Hierodule Handbook (College of the Doves course manual) — Laurelei Black

Thank you for purchasing this book and taking part in the RTA Courses!

Your feedback matters.

Reviews on Etsy, Amazon, and even on your own social media accounts help others know if courses like this are the right fit for them.

Please take a moment to let folks know what you have valued about the Red Thread Academy.

Made in the USA
Las Vegas, NV
16 February 2023

67668820R00275